Cloth As Metaphor
(Re)-reading the Adinkra Cloth Symbols of the Akan of Ghana.

G. F. Kojo Arthur

DEDICATED TO:

Abenaa Otuwaa

Abenaa Abassawa

Esi Boamaa

Efua Debiwa

Efua Seguwa

Ama Otuwaa Hammah

Naana Yaa Debra

Kwabena Boama Arthur

Keep the touch aglow.

Table of Contents

ACKNOWLEDGMENT

There are several people to whom I owe a debt of gratitude for the support and assistance they gave to me in the preparation and completion of this book. I would like to thank ford Foundation and Marshall University for their generous financial support for the field research and the publication. A very special acknowledgement goes to Dr. Betty J. Cleckley, Vice President for Multicultural and International Programs through whose office the financial assistance from the University was granted. Her steadfast commitment to the infusion of diversity in Marshall University's curriculum made it possible for me to receive research grants that enabled me to visit Ghana, England and a number of cities in the United States to gather data. I would like to express my gratitude to the African Studies Program at the Indiana University, Bloomington for offering me the Ford Foundation Research Fellowship in the summer of 1996 to do further library and museum research in Bloomington and Indianapolis in order to revise the manuscript.

I am also grateful to Ford Foundation for awarding me a grant that made it possible for setting up the Centre for Indigenous Knowledge Systems in Ghana. This grant also partially supported the printing of this book.

I would like to express my appreciation to all those whose stories, proverbs and anecdotes taught me Akan mpaninsɛm (that is, the wisdom and knowledge of the past acquired through the elders). At the risk of offending some people and I hope they will forgive me-I have to acknowledge particular debts of gratitude to my father-in-law Rev. Joseph Yedu Bannerman, a retired minister of the Methodist Church of Ghana, and his wife and his extended family members; Nana Antwi Buasiako, Asantehene's Kyeame for allowing me to photograph his extensive collection of adinkra cloths; Rev. Peter Sarpong, Catholic Bishop of Kumasi; and Mr. Owusu-Ansah, UST, Kumasi.

My gratitude is extended also to Professor Robert Bickel of Marshall University who read various drafts of the entire book with great care and made elaborate comments from which I benefited a great deal. My thanks go also to Professor Joseph Adjaye of Pittsburgh University; Dr. Al Bavon, University of North Texas; Professor Robert Osei-wusuh; Dr. Ed Piou of University of South Florida, Tampa; Professor Kwesi Yankah and Professor Kwame Karikari both of the University of Ghana, Legon, Ghana; and Dr. William Kojo Darley of University of Toledo, Ohio for their useful comments and suggestions. This work, however, is entirely mine, and I am solely responsible for its shortcomings.

CHAPTER 1

Kyemfere se ɔdaa hɔ akyɛ, na onipa ɔnwenee no nso nyɛ dɛn?
The potsherd claims it is old, what about the potter who molded it?

SIGNS AND SYMBOLS FROM GHANA: A WRITING SYSTEM?

INTRODUCTION

Pre-colonial African societies are believed to have depended entirely on oral communication because it has been generally assumed they had not developed a recognizable form of writing (Goody, 1977, 1986). Even after phonetically-based and other writing systems were introduced through contact with outsiders, many African societies are believed to have continued to rely mainly on oral communication. Such critics of pre-colonial Africa tend to assume writing takes only one form—the phonetically-based form of writing, an example of which is the alphabetic system, and that all writing is linear. Non-linear and non-phonetically-based writing systems have come to be seen as inferior attempts at the real thing and thus, have been marginalized. Only recently has it been recognized that many writing systems in West Africa, the best known being those of the Vai in Liberia (Scribner and Cole, 1981; Pilaszewicz, 1985) and Mende (Bledsoe and Robey, 1986), for example, were developed outside of the Western context.

Writing is a system of conventional signs which can be used to transmit a specific content. These conventional signs function as containers for storing information over a period of time. Fraenkel (1965, p. 7) defines writing as "an acquired arbitrary system of visual marks with which people who know the represented language can communicate." Hunter and Whitten (1976, p. 409) also view writing as "communication by means of a system of conventional graphic symbols which may be carved, incised, impressed, painted, drawn, or printed in a wide variety of media." Both written English and written Russian rely on alphabets: Latin (Roman) for English and Cyrillic for Russian. Other writing systems, such as Japanese, use visual marks that correspond to different speech segments, at about the level of syllables; others, like Chinese, encode meaning units, or morphemes (Fromkin and Rodman, 1978; Liberman and Liberman, 1992).

On the other hand, the *quipu* system of the Incas and the *aroko* system of the Yoruba of Ijebu (Nigeria) used knots and ties in non-linear form to communicate. Dalby (1986), for instance, provides examples from the *aroko* writing system of the Yoruba of Ijebu. In this writing system cowrie shells and other objects were tied on the basis of the rebus principle for communication. One example that Dalby gives from eight symbolic messages recorded and translated in the 1880s is a message sent by an Ijebu general to a prince far away. It shows six cowries arranged two by two, face to face with a long cord. The implied message is: "Although the road between us both may be very long, yet I draw you to myself, and set my face towards you (that we may meet face to face)," Dalby (1986, p. 5).

Writing is essentially the coding of speech into more or less permanent, visual forms. Kroeber (1948), p. 510) speaks of three stages which may be distinguished in the development of writing:

ABCD -
#700

Abɔdeɛ
santaan - #1

Nyame dua
- #56

Owuo bɛgya
hwan - #99

Gye Nyame
- #2

Dɛnkyɛm
- #218

Wodu
nkwanta
a - #682

Ahahan -
#701

ONIPA BE
WUNASIKA
TE ASE

Onipa bɛwu
na sika te
ase - #112

Nsa korɔ
- #364

Adwa - #163

Nyame yɛ
Ɔhene - #11

Nsatea
korɔ -#10

The first is the use of pictures of things and actions, and, derived from these, pictorial symbols for qualities and abstractions. This is the pictographic and then the picto-ideographic method. In the second stage the presentation of sounds begins, but is made through pictures or abbreviations of pictures; and pictures or ideographs as such continue to be used alongside the pictures whose value is phonetic. This may be called the mixed or transitional or rebus stage. Third is the phonetic phase. In this, the symbols used, whatever their origin may have been, no longer denote objects or ideas but are merely signs for sounds and words, syllables, or elemental letter sounds.

Hunter and Whitten (1976) also indicate that writing systems may be grouped as those that are based on pictographs (pictorial signs or pictograms), ideographs (or ideograms), and phonographs (or phonograms). It needs to be pointed out that pictographic, ideographic, and phonographic systems of writing do not represent inevitable stages in the development of writing as no direct evolutionalry line can be drawn from the pictographic to the phonographic writing system (Fraenkel, 1965).

Pictographic writings are recognizable pictorial representations. Although they may be highly stylized, there is a clear representational link between the symbol and the meaning. Pictographs represent things, not linguistic forms. Pictographs have a semantic rather than a phonetic value. If the conventions are understood, they can be read in any language (Hunter and Whitten, 1976, p. 409). In that respect, pictographs can be used conveniently to communicate information to a multilingual public or in environments where reliance on alphabetic-based writing is impractical (see Table 1).

_____

Insert Table 1 here

_____

Ideographs or ideograms represent things or ideas, though not necessarily pictorially. Ideographic signs may be pictographic in origin, but they usually have broader ranges of meaning. Ideograms involve a closer relationship with language than pictograms in that the extensions of meaning assigned to the symbols follow the semantic domains of a language (Hunter and Whitten, 1976). Since their association with meaning is not mediated by the representation of sounds, they can be pronounced in any language. The numeral 5, for example, stands directly for an idea—a number, but does not have a phonetic value. It can be represented by a tally—///// or by V or the fingers (digits) on a hand. It can be pronounced *cinque* or *cinq* or *anum* as well as five. The word five is a phonetic symbol, while the numeral 5 has a semantic value. The musical notes, mathematical symbols such as infinity (4) and identical with (≡), some aspects of Egyptian hieroglyphic and cuneiform are often given as examples of writing systems that make use of pictographs and ideographs. Rock art and cave paintings and stained glass paintings are also well known examples of pictographic and ideographic writing systems. M. Màle (1919) is said to have viewed the medieval cathedral with its stained glass paintings, "as a book of stone in which were recorded for the ignorant all teachings of the Church in natural science, philosophy, morals, and history…" (Cited in Read, 1973, p. 24).

Phonologically-based script follows not ideas but the spoken linguistic forms (sounds of speech) for them. Phonological script has an intimate relationship with a language. It is focused on the minimal units of representation, that is the graphemes of the system and the speech sound units, phonemes, which they encode. Rebus writing, syllabic systems (e.g., logographs), and alphabetic writing systems are examples of phonologically-based scripts (Hunter and Whitten, 1976).

In an alphabetic system of writing, for example, one symbol or one letter is used to represent each significant sound (phoneme) in a language. The relationship between the visual and auditory codes in the alphabetic system of writing is arbitrary. The letter does not have any inherent meaning on its own; it only represents a sound in a

Yesu
asɛnnua
- #102

Aponkyerɛne
wu a -
#545

Osohor
- #716

**EKAA
NSEE
NKOA**

Ɛkaa nsee
nko a - #492

TV - #612

Asaawa -
#624

Ani hunu
yaa - #528

**ONIPA BE
HUNA SIKA
TE ASE**

Nipa bewu
na sika te
ase - #112

particular language.

Most alphabetic systems of writing do not actually achieve the one sound to one symbol principle but do represent most of the sound system of the language with a combination of letters from a very small set of symbols. The English language, for example, has 26 letters that are used in combination to produce 45 phonemes. The symbol "C", for instance, is used to represent the following distinct sounds: [s] as in cent, center or census; [k] as in calm, college or cost; and [tʃ] as in church, chin or chapel. The combination of letters of the alphabet is best understood when it is in a linear form to be read from left to right (or vice versa) and up and down. But even that does not explain the logic behind spelling in the alphabetic system of the English language. As Diamond (1994) illustrates, what is the logic for spelling the word "seed" as we do instead of "cede," "ceed," or "sied?" Or why the sound "sh" cannot be written as "ce" (as in ocean), "ti" (as in nation) or as "ss" (as in issue)?

Literacy on a mass scale is much enhanced in a writing system that uses very few symbols. It is in this sense that one may say the alphabetically-based system of writing facilitates mass literacy. On the other hand, in Mandarin Chinese, the logographic system of writing, that utilizes syllables requires the use of over 1500 basic characters. Literacy based on the logographic system of writing was, therefore, in the past limited to the elites of the society. While the alphabetic system for writing may be the most widespread form in the modern world, other systems—for example, the *kanji* and the *kana* syllabic systems used by Japanese for telegrams and the logograms of the Chinese—persist today.

As Coulmas (1996, p. 334) points out:

> The principal function of all writing is to convey linguistic meaning, but writing systems vary greatly in how they encode meaning. In purely phonetic transcription, access to meaning is mediated through sound representation, while a purely ideographic notation bypasses representation of sounds, encoding concepts instead. Actual writing systems belong to neither of these 'pure' categories, but are located somewhere along a continuum which ranges from sound-centered to meaning-entered.

Most writing systems utilize some combination of the principles involved in each of the forms of writing. For example, in writing the English language with Roman alphabets, use is made of symbols such as ? ; : ! and , for punctuation. These symbols do no represent sounds in the lnguage. Also, in order to facilitate international travel through airports, phonologically-based writing is often combined with pictographs to indicate telephones, access for handicapped people, and to direct people to toilet facilities on the basis of gender. Road signs often incorporate all three systems of writing. While pictographic and ideographic writing systems tend to be non-inear, phonographic writing systems tend to be linear.

Recent research into art forms and other material culture of various African societies has revealed that some societies such as the Akan did indeed develop and maintain certain forms of writing prior to contact with Europe (Hau, 1959, 1961, & 1964; McLeod, 1976; McGuire, 1980). Hau, in a series of articles that appeared in the French journal, *Bulletin d'IFAN*, uses the ivory carvings and other art work to make the claim that writing pre-dated Islam and the Europeans in certain parts of West Africa. McLeod (1976, p. 94) notes "that images in use" in Asante and "elsewhere in Africa also have a verbal component… many of the figurines used among the Bwami are used to call to mind certain aphorisms and, most importantly, the form of these images can vary within wide limits while still having the same aphorism as their basic referent." McGuire (1980, p. 54), to cite another example, describes how the Woyo people of Cabinda used pot lids to create "a pictographic language to convey their feelings about specific situations."

Niangoran-Bouah (1984) and Asante (1992, p. 73) distinguish three writing

Aya - #511

W'ano pɛ
asɛm - #524

Dadeɛ bi twa
dadeɛ bi
mu - #565

Kyınııɛ
- #170

Adwa - #151

Adinkrahene
ntoaso - #186

Esono
anantamu
- #222

Nyame
dua - #59

systems in Africa: (1) pictographs or pictograms, used in such areas as Zaire, Gabon, Cameroon, and the Central African Republic; (2) ideograms or ideographs such as the adinkra and *abramoɔ* (or *djayobwe*) systems in Ghana and La Côte d'Ivoire (the Ivory Coast), the *nsibidi* system of east-central Nigeria, and the *sona* and *lusona* systems in Angola and Zambia; and (3) phonologically or phonetically-based scripts (phonograms or phonographs) used in places such as Ethiopia (the Ge'ez system), Liberia (the Vai syllabic system), Guinea, Sierra Leone, and Cameroon. Dalby (1986) provides extensive examples of various writing systems that have been developed in Africa from the ancient pictograms and ideograms, which form the root of all writing, through to the contemporary indigenous and international efforts to represent the sound system of African languages syllabically and alphabetically.[5]

AKAN SYMBOLS

The Akan of Ghana and La Côte d'Ivoire incorporated the ideographic and pictographic writing systems in their arts in such media as textiles, metal casting, woodcarving, and architecture. The Akan's use of pictographs and ideograms reached its most elaborate forms in the king's court. As Kyerematen (1964, p. 1), has written:

> the regalia of Ghanaian chiefs have been of special significance in that they have not been merely symbols of the kingly office but have served as the chronicles of early history and the evidence of traditional religion, cosmology and social organization … [and] it has been customary for the regalia to be paraded whenever the chief appears in state at a national festival or durbar, so that all who see them may read, mark and inwardly digest what they stand for.

Among the Akan of Ghana the regalia of the kingly office included wood-carvings (e.g., stool—*adwa*, umbrella tops—*kyiniiɛ ntuatire*, and staffs—*akyeamepoma*), swords (*akofena*), and clothing (e.g., *kente*, *akunintam* and *adinkra*). These items in the king's regalia made use of pictograms and ideograms. The sets of pictograms, ideograms and signs encoded in the Akan cloths (kente, akunintam and adinkra), gold weights (*abramoɔ*, singular, *mmramoɔ*, plural), wood carvings (e.g. stools and staffs), pottery, and architectural designs are clearly understood, as they have meanings commonly shared by the masses of the population. These art forms carry proverbs, anecdotes, stories, and historical events through visual form.

In this book a neglected area in the study of Akan cloths—their function as a writing medium (Tsien, 1962; Mason, 1928) and thus, a communicative device—is discussed. The book takes the view that mutually interpretable significant symbols need not be limited to spoken and written alphabets and syllables which eventually are strung together in sentences and paragraphs. Instead, communication can be accomplished through the use of discrete graphical representation of commonly held ideas and views. In this way, ostensibly, "non-literate" societies may produce, through the use of their symbols and signs, a literature which pervades their environment by being emblazoned on their clothes, tools, and other common material artifacts.

The arts of a people offer an illuminating view of its culture, and hence of its thought processes, attitudes, beliefs, and values. The art of a particular culture can reveal ever-changing human images and attitudes, so awareness of a people's indigenous art, visual and cultural symbols can become an important medium for cross-cultural understanding. "Just as written documents [that utilize phonographs] materialize history in literate communities," as pointed out by Fraser and Cole (1972, p. 313), "so in traditional societies, art forms make the intangible past more real." Some of these art forms like the adinkra cloth of the Akan utilize pictograms and ideograms (see Figure 1), and are pregnant with text that symbolizes ideas on several levels of discourse. The focus of this study is to utilize the pictograms and ideograms encoded in the adinkra cloth to decode some aspects of the history, beliefs, social

Owuo
atwedeɛ - #91

Kra pa - #69

Nyame nwu
na mawu
- #48

Hye anhye
- #44

Sunsum - #36

Awia - #31

Nsuo - #40

Ananse
ntontan - #34

organizations, social relations, and other ideas of the Akan of Ghana.

Insert Figure 1 here

SYMBOLS: A FRAMEWORK FOR ANALYSIS

Communication in the form of writing is based on the use of arbitrary symbols. Every society—be it pre-literate, literate, or post-literate—uses symbols and signs as a complement to spoken language. When you draw a house, what you have is a symbol for a house. The picture is a symbol, just as the word used to indicate it (house) is a symbol. The meaning of the word (or the picture) depends upon social convention. Some symbols have evolved to the point of universal acceptance in such areas as music, mathematics, computers, travel, and many branches of science. It now appears that in some important areas there is an increasing need for an adjunct to sophisticated speech, and the use of new (and in some cases, the revamping of old) symbols and icons to ease communication and facilitate international understanding.

Symbols provide the means whereby human beings can interact meaningfully with their natural and social environment. Symbols are socially constructed, and they refer not to the intrinsic nature of objects and events but to the ways in which human beings perceive them. Ott (1989, p. 21) says the following about symbols:

> Symbols are signs that connote meanings greater than themselves and express much more than their intrinsic content. They are invested with specific subjective meanings. Symbols embody and represent wider patterns of meaning and cause people to associate conscious or unconscious ideas that in turn endow them with their deeper, fuller, and often emotion-evoking meaning.

Symbols are important as they create, change, maintain, and transmit socially constructed realities. Charon (1985) and Ritzer (1992) identify several functions of symbols. 1) Symbols allow people to deal with the material and social world by allowing them to name, categorize, and remember the objects that they encounter. 2) Symbols also improve a people's ability to perceive the environment. They improve a people's ability to think. 3) The use of symbols greatly increases human beings' ability to solve problems. Human beings can think through symbolically a variety of alternative actions before actually taking one. 4) The use of symbols allows people to transcend time, space, and even their own person; that is, symbols allow people to imagine alternative realities (Charon, 1985; Ritzer, 1992). These functions of symbols imply that symbols can be manipulated (symbolism) and, thereby, can be used to create or impede social change.

In politics, for example, a number of scholars have written about how political symbols are utilized to maintain established power, status, and resource differentials (Edelman, 1964, 1971, 1988; Evans-Pritchard and Fortes, 1967; Elder and Cobb, 1983; and Hayward and Dumbuya, 1984). It is not so much the symbols themselves that are significant in politics, but the meanings that people attribute to them. A national or party flag is more than a piece of cloth, it is used to evoke feelings of great loyalty, hostility, support or resentment.

Social life can proceed only if the meanings of symbols are largely shared by members of society. If this were not the case, meaningful communication would be impossible. The survival of human life is facilitated by communication. The means of communication and its constant improvement and development have been a major factor in the growth of human civilization. Communication among individual members of a social group enhances mutual understanding as individuals convey ideas, mental pictures, and concepts among themselves by verbal and non-verbal means. Language, the most complex form of the use of symbols, has become the primary medium through which a society's concepts, elements, values, and beliefs are communicated.

Onyankopↄn
dↄ wo - #81

Kristoni
papa - #87

Asↄre dan
- #89

Som
Onyame
- #71

Biribi wↄ
soro - #128

Nyame dua -
#56

Kera pa -
#63

Gye Nyame
- #9

Even though communication within and among social groups comprises verbal and non-verbal means, over time human communication has increasingly concentrated on verbal means. With the development and increased use of alphabetized writing, verbal expression has become fixed as visual marks that represent sounds and meanings, and has come to be seen as a rationalized method of communication. This visible form of communication, that is, writing, used to be the preserve of the privileged few in many societies—for example, the clerical elite in many societies and the literati of the ancient Chinese civilization. With the development of printing and mass production of texts using the alphabetic system of writing, the visible form of communication has been democratized. The development and expansion of formal schooling has further stressed the importance of phonetically-based forms of writing as the hallmark of literacy. Despite the popularity of phonetically-based forms of writing, "signs and pictograms are still under development and will in future become an absolute necessity for the fixing and transmission of a world-wide fund of knowledge" (Frutiger, 1989, p. 342) for their utility lies in their independence from language.

AKAN CLOTH SYMBOLS

In the days before printing and formal schooling as we know them now, the Akan society in Ghana was believed to have utilized only oral methods of communication for the transmission of knowledge and ideas. The Akan must have placed emphasis on the ability to influence by verbal skills and through the art of public speaking. This does not mean that they did not appreciate and did not utilize some visual markers as forms of writing. The Asantehene, for example retained the services of Arabic scribes (ↄhene krakye), yet honored the orator (e.g., the ↄkyeame) more than the scribe.

In this study an attempt is made to show how the Akan of Ghana used their textiles as one of the media in a highly complex system of fixing and transmitting that which was thought or spoken with pictures, symbols, signs, and signals. Not only are the symbols and patterns in the Akan textiles regarded as aesthetically and idiomatically traditional; more importantly, the symbols and patterns in the textiles constitute a code that evokes meanings: they carry, preserve, and present aspects of the beliefs, history, social values, cultural norms, social and political organization, and philosophy of the Akan. As Patton (1984, p. 72) notes: "The verbal element of these cloths makes them visual metaphors. The application of a phrase or word to an object it does not literally denote, to suggest comparison with another concept, is a recurring aspect of traditional Asante art. During important public occasions such as durbar, this visual metaphor reinforces traditional leadership roles." Metaphor, in this context, is much more than a figure of speech. As Hermine Feistein describes it

> Metaphor … is now considered to be an essential process and product of thought. The power of metaphor lies in its potential to further our understanding of the meaning of experience, which in turn defines reality. In art and language, metaphor urges us to look beyond the literal, to generate associations and tap new, different, or deeper levels of meaning. The metaphoric process reorganizes and vivifies; it paradoxically condenses and expands; it synthesizes often disparate meanings. In this process, attributes of one entity are transferred to another by comparison, by substitution, or as a consequence of interaction (Feinstein, 1982, p. 45).

In viewing the adinkra cloth as metaphor, it enables us to make sense of how the Akan use the adinkra cloth and its symbols as visual markers to express their world view, beliefs, attitudes and thoughts. This perspective makes it possible for us to see how the Akan link words and images or how the Akan construct meaning by metaphorically transforming words into visual images and vice versa.

The seminal work by Rattray (1927—see pp. 220-268), based in part on an earlier

12

Nsoromma - #117

Kera pa - #67

Yɛda Nyame ase - #86

Akyemfra - #137

Abɔde santaan - #1

Hye anhye - #42

Momma yɛmmɔ mpaeɛ -#70

Biribi wɔ soro - #128

work by Bowdich (1819), identified names and the symbolic meanings of several of the symbols and patterns in the adinkra and kente cloths. Rattray, however, failed to recognize that these cloths served as a powerful expressive medium for communication. McLeod (1981, p. 143), on the other hand, recognized that each of the cloths "and the way in which each was worn, served to communicate a distinctive message, and the subtleties of its significance were widely understood." However, he failed to elaborate on the communicative functions of the adinkra and kente cloths.

Other people who have written about adinkra cloth and its symbols continue to provide an elaborate catalogue of hundreds of adinkra symbols yet fail to address the ideas, events, and beliefs of the Akan that these symbols encode. Mato (1986), for example, provides an extensive number of symbols in the adinkra cloth and the proverbs and meanings associated with these symbols. He points out that

> As an art of public display adinkra images carried aphorisms, proverbs, symbols and metaphors expressed through visual form. As carriers of abstract or tangible information adinkra images were firmly rooted in the proverbial literature of the Akan. As a communicative system adinkra images carried Akan traditional wisdom regarding observations upon God and man, the human condition, upon things spiritual as well as the common-place and upon the unavoidability of death. Adinkra stamps [symbols] are therefore an example of the penchant and skill of the Akan to set proverb or verbal statement into visual form (Mato, 1986, pp. 228-229).

Mato notes that the adinkra cloth is an important form of funerary clothing, as well as clothing for other festive occasions. In connection with funerary rituals, he discusses some aspects of Akan cosmology. Mato, however, fails to elaborate on what he refers to as "symbolic literacy" (p. 223) as he does not go beyond the limited discussion of Akan cosmology to address other concepts and beliefs of the Akan (e.g., political beliefs, attitudes about money, social values) and the Akan social organization that the adinkra cloth and its symbols, as "symbolic literacy," write about.

On the other hand, the 1997 exhibition at the Smithsonian National Museum of African Art made the attempt to use one adinkra cloth believed to belong to Prempeh I to demonstrate how the Asante express complex cultural, spiritual, and philosophical concepts through their art (National Museum of African Art, 1997). This exhibition goes beyond Mato's (1986) discussion of Akan cosmology to recognize that the multilayered and complex meanings of the adinkra symbols express clear messages of the power and authority of the Asantehene (p. 13). Because the exhibition was based on only one cloth which was designed with a limited number of symbols— twenty-two symbols to be exact—other aspects of Akan beliefs, attitudes, and relationships encoded in scores of adinkra symbols were not discussed in the exhibition's accompanying catalogue.

Willis (1998, p. 28) recognizes that "the symbols on the constitute a language that is multi-layered." He also affirms the view that "the adinkra symbols reflect cultural mores, communal values, philosophical concepts, or the codes of conduct and the social standards of the Akan people" (ibid.). Willis further claims that

> Adinkra symbols have a historical "core" or group of original symbols. Over the years, new symbols have been periodically introduced, while "core" symbols have been stylized and fused. Others have been created with words being introduced into the designs, and others depicting man-made objects, for example, a Coke bottle and a Mercedes-Benz logo. Today there are over five hundred documented and identfiable symbols, but the total number of all adinkra symbols has not been accurately documented to date (Willis, 1998, p. 28).

Willis makes a significant contribution in recognizing that the symbols in the

Nya gyidie
- #135

Ananse
antɔn
ḳasa - #715

Kwadu hono
-#711

Akofena
- #166

Abusua dɔ
funu - #457

UAC nkanea
- #621

Nsa korɔ -
#365

Ɔdɔ aniwa -
#370

cloth constitute a language that is multi-layered. By providing us with a visual primer, he is recognizing that the symbols constitute a set of visual marks —a writing system. He, however, makes the mistake by assertingthat there is a historical "core" or group of original symbols. He does not provide the historical evidence to support this assertion. Apparently, he, as well as other writers, takes Rattray's 53 symbols as the "core" symbols. It must be noted that Rattray failed to include several symbols that were in use at the time of his stay in Asante. For example, Rattray did not mention some of the symbols to be found in the sample cloth that Bowdich collected in 1817. If "the total number of all adinkra symbols has not been accurately documented to date," as Willis claims, how does he know what constitutes the "core" symbols? He indicates the symbols are to be found in media other than cloth, for example, architecture and woodcarvings. Architectural designs and woodcarvings are media that make use of three-dimensional representation of symbols. The adinkra cloth makes possible a two-dimensional representation of the symbols. There are, therefore, symbols to be found in woodcarvings and architectural designs that cannot be found in the adinkra cloth. Similarly, there are some symbols to be found in the cloth and not in woodcarvings or achitectural designs. That the adinkra symbols include contemporary symbols such as the Mercedes-Benz logo (#606-607) reflects the dynamic nature of the language of the Akan as well as the creativity of the cloth designers in adapting symbols to express the new ideas and concepts that have become part of the Akan experience. A dynamic language is not limited to few concepts and ideas that are depicted by some core words or symbols. It is, therefore, puzzling for Willis to make the assertion that there is a historical "core" or group of symbols.

The present study views adinkra symbols that are found in several adinkra cloths, that have been used by both the royal and non-royal, as a system of visual marks—a system of writing—with which the Akan communicate. These visual marks serve to evoke, record, and communicate certain things about the Akan. The study elaborates on the communicative aspects of Akan textiles by interpreting the encoded meanings of the adinkra symbols and signs thematically with respect to concepts such as Akan philosophy, relationships, and social organization. It also argues that the set of pictograms and ideograms of the Akan, as a way of writing, has been in daily use as an aid to thought, a means of comprehension, and a method of bearing witness or authentication. Adinkra symbols draw extensively upon traditional expressive genres that include folk songs, riddles and quizzes (abrɔme ne ɛbisaa), poetry (awensɛm), stories (anansesɛm), drum poetry, libation and prayer (apaeyie), oral history (abak]sɛm or mpaninsɛm), funeral dirges (nsubaa or sudwom), and proverbs (mme or mmɛbusɛm). The adinkra symbols are utilized in this study as a multi-vocal metaphor to interpret the contextual meanings and functional uses of the symbols and signs developed by the Akan in their textile production and other visual media. This study links the verbal genres associated with the symbols in order to discuss some aspects of Akan viewpoints on a variety of issues such as the universe, self and spirituality; political beliefs and governmental organization; and social values.

The names and the interpretations of these symbols may also be useful for framing hypotheses for sustained research which looks at Akan cosmology, myths, histories, rituals, early public taxation and accounting systems, religion, folktale, political organizations, the role of the military in society, and daily customs. For the Akan in particular, as Cole and Ross (1977, p. 9) have noted, the relationship between the visual and the verbal is one of the cornerstones of their aesthetics. The identification of symbols and patterns embodied in Akan textiles in this study is just a first step in understanding the complexities of symbolism in Akan visual arts. As Ross (1977, p. 25) further points out, the highly conventionalized verbal component in Akan iconography demands a greater exploration of language, patterns of nomenclature, etymology, and the use of euphemisms, similes, and metaphors to fully appreciate nuances of meaning.

Nkuruma
kɛse - #199

Dwantire -
#281

Gyawu
atikɔ - #248

Nyame dua -
#58

Aban - #140

Dua afe -
#384

Akokɔ nan -
#424

Blɔk dan -
#438

Analysis of the textile symbols and patterns of the adinkra cloth provided in this study will facilitate the understanding of how the Akan use this expressive medium and writing system to record their beliefs, history, knowledge, and accomplishments. Such an understanding may help explain some of the changes and continuities in, for example, the bureaucratization of chieftaincy and new sources of wealth that have occurred and continue to occur in the Akan society. This study contributes to the view that a language includes the full spectrum of color, symbol, and word; that textile art and language are inextricably bound together; and that drawing, printing or weaving a symbol in cloth can make a legitimate and exciting involvement with literature and indigenous knowledge systems. Understanding such indigenous knowledge systems may help adult literacy program planners, for example, to utilize a people's symbols and signs to facilitate reading and writing among adults. The study of adinkra cloth symbols can also illuminate and help in the analysis of social and political organization of the Akan as well as of the greater Ghanaian society. Such an analysis may have value more generally for anyone involved in symbolic analyses within particular societies or cross-culturally.

Qualitative research methods have been employed in this study. Data collection included (1) inquiries to museums, galleries and private collections of Ghanaian textiles, particularly the adinkra, and observations and interviews of adinkra manufacturers and distributors and other crafts people in Accra and in the Kumasi areas, (2) correspondence with and interviews of persons knowledgeable about African textiles in general and adinkra cloth in particular, (3) interviews and discussions with elders and other people knowledgeable about Akan folklore and *mpaninsɛm*, (4) library research, and (5) procurement, classification and photographing of a collection of samples of adinkra stamps and cloths from Ntonso, Tewobabi and Asokwa in the Kumasi area, the main centers of adinkra cloth production in Ghana.

I have benefitted from the works of Rattray (1927), Antubam (1963), Kyerematen (1964), Sarpong (1971; 1972; 1974; & 1990), Menzel (1972), and Mato (1986) in identifying many adinkra symbols and the everyday expressions, proverbs, and aphorisms that have been associated with these symbols. Charts and monographs by Glover (1971), Quarcoo (1972, 1994), Kayper-Mensah (1976), Ofori Ansah (1978, 1993), and Owusu-Ansah (1992), and museum collections, catalogues and photographs have also been very helpful. I also benefitted tremendously from the discussions about the meanings of various proverbs and stories that I had with Nana Atwi Buasiako, Asantehene Kyeame, Kumasi; and Rev. J. Y. Bannerman and his group of folklorists and storytellers at Ampia Ajumako and Winneba.

In the foregoing discussion I have attempted to provide a framework for viewing the adinkra textile symbols as a writing system. The rest of the chapters in this book is developed as follows. Chapter 2 discusses the adinkra cloth history and adinkra production processes, origins of the adinkra symbols, and Akan color symbolism. Chapter 3 illustrates some aspects of the pictographic, ideographic and phonographic writing systems incorporated in the adinkra cloth symbols. The chapter also discusses stylization and how the adinkra symbols were (are) derived.

In Chapters 4 through 10 the adinkra symbols and the narratives associated with them are grouped into thematic areas in order to discuss some of the various ideas, events, and beliefs of the Akan that the symbols encode. These discussions draw extensively on Akan written and oral literature that include proverbs, aphorisms, stories, funeral dirges, riddles and quizzes, as well as songs and everyday expressions and interpretations that I derived from various discussions I had with my informants.

In Chapter 4, Akan beliefs and views about the universe, God, self, and spirituality encoded in some of the adinkra symbols are discussed. Chapters 5 and 6 discuss Akan governmental organization and political beliefs. Chapter 7 discusses some aspects of Akan views about beauty, love, marriage and family relations. Chapter 8 groups several adinkra symbols to discuss some aspects of Akan social and ethical values.

15

Gyawu
atikɔ - #251

Adepa bɛba -
#125

Anikom nnim
- #110

Hann ne
sum - #18

Biribi wɔ
soro - #128

Nnomaa ne
dua - #622

Donno -
#406

Wo nsa akyi -
#552

Chapter 9 decodes several adinkra symbols in order to address some aspects of the social and economic arrangements that the symbols encode while Chapter 10 focuses on symbols that relate to knowledge and education.

My arguments in the chapters of the book are multiple and overlapping rather than unitary and monolithic because the subject matter which the adinkra symbols write about is multi-dimensional and multi-disciplinary. Chapter 11 provides a summary of my contention that the adinkra symbols constitute a writing system, discusses the implications of such a contention, and makes suggestions for further research on Akan art from similar perspective, particularly with regards to the symbols of the goldweights, wood carvings, and other textiles (kente, akunintam and asafo flags). I provide an extensive bibliography to serve as resource for further research on the material culture of the Akan. I also provide a catalogue of all the symbols discussed in this book to serve as basis for further research on the cultural symbols of the Akan and possible cross-cultural studies in which the Akan symbols may be compared with symbols from other cultures, particularly those of African descendants in the New World.

Even though the discussions in the various chapters center on the bigger Akan society in general, specific examples are drawn from the Asante. The proverbs, aphorisms, and everyday expressions associated with these symbols are provided in italics in the Akan (Asante Twi) language with their meanings in English.

NOTES

1. The Portuguese are believed to be the first people to introduce the alphabetic (Roman) writing system to the Akan in the fifteenth century. The importance of Twi in West Africa forced missionaries and later, the colonial administration to set about standardizing and providing an alphabet for the language.

2. ∞ is the ancient Roman symbol for 100 million.

3. According to Male (1919, p. 456–457 as cited in Read, 1973), "by means of statues and windows in a church, clergy in the Middle Ages tried to teach their flock the greatest possible number of truths, They fully realized the power of art on souls still innocent and vague. For the immense body of illiterates, for the crowd which had neither psalter nor missal, and who only grasped in Christianity what they actually saw there, it was necessary to materialize the idea, to clothe it in a perceptible form."

4. The arbitrary nature of the relationship between the auditory and visual codes in alphabetic writing systems may be illustrated with the letter "b" in the Roman alphabetic writing system and the Cyrillic alphabetic writing system. The sound, in English, which typically goes with the visible arrangement of marks making up the (Roman) alphabetic character "b" involves closure of the vocal chords, or "voicing" (Ladefoged, 1975). This sound is broadly invariant across different spelling contexts—bat, table, combine, comb,

16

OWUOSEEFIE

#114

#679

#710

EKAA
OBI✳
NKOA

#489

perturb. The sound a reader of Russian would make in response to the same visual arrangement "b" occurring that (Cyrillic) alphabet is quite different, involving the tongue and the roof of the mouth, something like the way these are used when saying the italicized part of the English word "onion." And whereas, in the Roman alphabet the visible arrangement of "b" and "B" are lower and upper case versions of the same character (hence p[ronounced identically), the visual shape of "B" in Russian represents a different character to "b" and is pronounced like "v" in English (Folomkin and Weiser, 1963).

5.   The computer technology has made widespread the use of various font software to facilitate the alphabetic writing of various African languages.

6.   Cloth as medium for writing is believed to have been invented by the Chinese who wrote on fabric made of silk (Tsien, 1962). In the United States, one of the most noted and successful attempts at using pictograms and ideograms in cloth to write is the famous Penn Treaty wampum belt now in the possession of the Pennsylvania Historical Society in Philadelphia. This belt was given by the American Indians to William Penn as their record of the signing of the famous teaty at Schackamaxon on the Delaware in 1682 (Mason, 1928, p. 98).

7.   See Appendix - for the fifty-three symbols that Rattray identified from the adinkra cloth. It must be pointed out that Rattray failed to include some symbols that could be found in the samples of adinkra cloth that Bowdich had collected in 1817. Apparently, Rattray did not get to study samples of adinkra and kente cloths that the British took away as war booty from Kumasi the 1874 and the 1896–1900 Asante-British wars.

8.   Cloth designers, stamp carvers and cloth distributors and some of the knowledgeable people interviewed included the following:

a) Auntie Afia, former wife of Nana Baffour Gyimah who owns the cloth production and distribution company, Baffour Gyimah Enterprise, at Tewobabi near Kumasi and several of the employees of the company, particularly Agya Yaw Yamaa (cloth designer), Kwaku (cloth designer), and Wofa Yaw (stamp carver and cloth designer). Interviewed on May 23–24, 1993 and May 23–26, 1994.
b) "Teacher" John Kofi Nsiah (stamp carver and cloth designer, Ntonso, near Kumasi. Interviewed on May 23–24, 1993; May 23–26, 1994; May 29, 1996; June 2–3, 1998; and April 28-30, 2000. "Teacher" Kofi passed away in May 2000. It was indeed a privilege for me to have had the opportunity to learn so much *mpaninsɛm* from this gifted and eloquent teacher.
c) Stephen Appiah (stamp carver and cloth designer), Asokwa, Kumasi. Interviewed May 24–25, 1994; May 29-30, 1996; and June2, 1998.
d) Nana Antwi Buasiako, Asantehene Kyeame. Interviewed at Ayigya, Kumasi. May 23-25, 1994; May 29-30, 1996.
e) Kusi Boadum, cloth designer and member of the Kumasi Metropolitan Assembly. Interviewed at Asokwa, May 24-25, 1994.
f) Nana J. V. Owusuh-Ansah, Research Fellow and artist, University

of Science and Technology, Kumasi. Interviewed May 26, 1994.

9.   Other visual media that utilize some of the proverbs, aphorisms and stories encoded in the adinkra symbols include the gold weights (see Appiah, 1979), wood carvings (e.g., stools—see Sarpong, 1971; combs—see Antiri, 1978; and linguist's staff—see Yankah, 1995), and state swords (*akofena*—see Ross, 1977).

CHAPTER 2

Tete ka aso mu no, na ɛfiri kakyerɛ .
Nimpa a wonnim wɔn abakɔsɛm te sɛ dua a oni ntini.
Preservation of a people's culture has its roots in oral tradition.
People without knowledge of their history are like a tree without roots.

INTRODUCTION

Cloth use is almost a universal experience. Historically, cloth has been venerated by people of the most varied cultural backgrounds, and it has furthered the organization of social and political life. Davis (1992, p. 4) claims "that through clothing people communicate some things about their persons, and at the collective level this results typically in locating them symbolically in some structured universe of status claims and life-style attachments." Cloth, writes Borgatti (1983, p. 10), "can bridge both secular and sacred realms." And, Schneider and Weiner (1989, p. 1) write:

> Malleable and soft, cloth can take many shapes, especially if pieces are cut for architectural assembly. Cloth also lends itself to an extraordinary range of decorative variation, whether through the embroidery, staining, painting, or dyeing of the whole. These broad possibilities of construction, color, and patterning give cloth an almost limitless potential for communication. Worn or displayed in an emblematic way, cloth can denote variations in age, sex, rank, status, and group affiliation…. Cloth can also communicate the wearer's or user's ideological values and claims. Complex moral and ethical issues of dominance and autonomy, opulence and poverty, continence and sexuality, find ready expression through cloth.

The Akan have used cloth not only for personal adornment but also as a powerful expressive medium of communication. The communicative aspects of cloth among the Akan have been discussed in a limited way as "proverb cloths" by Aronson (1992) and Domowitz (1992) and as "textile rhetoric" by Yankah (1995), and, in the case of *adinkra*, as a funerary item by Mato (1986). Domowitz (p. 85), for example, notes that "proverb cloths offer an accessible public voice to those who are constrained to silence." Yankah (1995, p. 81), on the other hand, notes that the cloth design, along with the mode of wearing it may be used "not just to praise political heroes, to commemorate historical events, and to assert social identities, but also as a form of rhetoric—a channel for the silent projection of argument."

Davis (1992, p. 5) suggests, "clothing styles and the fashions that influence them over time constitute something approximating a code. It is a code, however, dissimilar from those used in cryptography; neither can it be more generally equated with the language rules that govern speech and writing." The code contained in cloths is heavily context-dependent, has considerable variability in how its constituent symbols are understood by different social strata and taste groupings; and it is much more given to "undercoding" than to precision and explicitness (Davis, 1992, p. 7). Undercoding occurs when in the absence of reliable interpretative rules, persons presume or infer, often unwittingly, on the basis of such hard-to-specify areas as gesture, inflection, pace, facial expression, context, and setting, certain molar meanings in a text, score, performance, or other communication (p. 11). At the same time it would be a mistake to assume that the undercoding of clothing and fashion is necessarily inadvertent or the product of an

A man wearing a sample of the Kwasiada adinkra

Sankofa - #636

Nyame dua - # 60

These messages [encoded in the adinkra cloth symbols] may be expressed philosophically, satirically or allegorically to depict religious, social or political concerns as well as reflections on issues pertaining to beauty, morality or other higher values. Almost every adinkra symbol is a literary and non-verbal illustration of a proverb, a parable or a maxim with profound interpretations (Kojo Fosu).

19

Nyansa pɔ
- # 649

Ɛkyɛm -
#269

Nsaa - #657

Obi nka obi -
#273

VW - #605

Sankɔfa -
#636

Nyame dua -
#60

Kata wo deɛ
so - #486

inherent incapacity of the unit elements constituting the code (fabric, color, cut, texture) to signify clearly as do words or icons (p. 11).

The *adinkra* cloth is one important art object that constitutes a code in which the Akan have deposited some aspects of the sum of their knowledge, fundamental beliefs, aspects of their history, attitudes and behaviors towards the sacred, and how their society has been organized. Adinkra cloth has played a significant part in furthering the organization of social and political life in the Akan society.

Mato (1986) has described the *adinkra* cloth as one of the significant items used in Akan funerary rites. The *adinkra* is more than an item for funerary rites. *Adinkra* cloth is an important item utilized in various rituals of the Akan. Besides funerary rites, it is utilized in some of the political rituals associated with the investiture of the king. For example, *adinkra* cloth features prominently in the oath swearing ceremony (ɔhene nsuae) for the king and queenmother. On May 30, 1996 at the Manhyia Palace in Kumasi, I witnessed the oath swearing ceremony for four chiefs who had been elevated by the Asantehene from sub-chief status to that of *manhene* (paramount chief). These four chiefs swore the oath of allegiance to the Asantehene. The Asantehene, the other paramount chiefs, and the four newly elevated paramount chiefs as well as their courtiers all wore *adinkra tuntum* (e.g., *kuntunkuni*) for the ceremony. Nana Antwi Buasiako, one of the twelve Asantehene *akyeamefoɔ*,[1] explained to me that the *hene nsuae* ceremony is a sacred and solemn occasion and that is why the *adinkra tuntum* is worn.[2] The *adinkra* cloth also features prominently in the sacred rituals associated with the blackening of the king's stool.

Another significant function of the *adinkra* cloth is evident from an analysis of the color background as well as the constituent symbols that are incorporated in the design of the cloth. The colors and the constituent symbols of the *adinkra* cloth evoke complex concepts that relate to social and political organization, beliefs and attitudes, moral and ethical issues about the self and one's responsibilities, and knowledge and education. The *adinkra* cloth symbols are but one example of a textile tradition that demonstrates how the Akan express complex cultural, spiritual, and philosophical concepts through their art.

The catalogue that accompanied the 1997 exhibition, *Adinkra: The cloth that speaks*, that was held at the National Museum of African Art indicates that "the multi-layered, ideogrammatic language of the symbols on this cloth reveals culturally specific yet universal concepts of leadership, diplomacy, philosophy, and government." The exhibition was about the cloth the Asantehene, Prempeh I was believed to have worn during his capture by the British in 1896. The catalogue, therefore, only explains this one cloth as "a unique historical document that reveals some of the complexity of the late nineteenth-century Asante political climate" (National Museum of African Art, 1997, p. 1).

When one studies symbols from several samples of the *adinkra* cloth one realiazes that the *adinkra* cloth is pregnant with text. For the Akan the *adinkra* text encodes some of the people's significant historical events and describes their institutions and their fundamental beliefs that have been preserved in the collective memory of the people. The text encoded in the *adinkra* cloth forms the subject of discussion in the rest of the book from Chapter 3 thereon. The color symbolism of the Akan is discussed later on in this chapter. To provide context for these discussions, we first examine the history of the *adinkra* cloth and the origins of the *adinkra* symbols.

HISTORY OF ADINKRA CLOTH

The country known today as Ghana has been inhabited almost continuously since the early Stone Age, some 500,000 years ago, with succeeding populations leaving traces of their respective cultures in the form of various tools, artifacts, and sites. The Iron Age came to Ghana about 5000 BC, and most of the ethnic groups now inhabiting the country had developed their modern civilization by 1200 AD (Boahen, 1977).[3] The first direct European contact with Ghana from the coast dates back to the mid-15th century (Dickson,

Adwa - #160

VW - #605

Nyansa pɔ - #649

Nsaa - #657

Obi nka obi - #272

Mmra krado - #288

Biribi wɔ soro - #126

Ɔhene aniwa - #191

1971). Prior to that, the Akan[4] states and empires had engaged in the trans-Saharan international trade and trade on the coast of the Gulf of Guinea (Boahen, 1966; Posnansky, 1987).

The Akan

The term Akan has been used to cover a wide variety of ethnic groups who occupy a greater part of southern Ghana and the south-eastern Ivory Coast. The groups constituting the culturally and linguistically homogenous Akan ethnicity include the Asante, Fantse, Akwamu, Akuapem, Akyem, Okwawu, Bono, Wassa, Agona, Assin, Denkyira, Adansi, Nzima, Ahanta, Aowin, Sefwi, and Baoule. Together, these groups constitute over 40 percent of the country's population (Dolphyne and Kropp-Dakubu, 1988; Bodomo, 1996); and they dominate about two-thirds of the country's land area (see Map). What is believed to have been the first modern day Akan empire, Bono, was established in the western area of present day Brong-Ahafo Region of Ghana before 1300 AD (Boahen, 1966; 1977). Other Akan and proto-Akan states thrived at one time or the other prior to direct contact with the Europeans.

The Akan have unique cultural traits and institutions that set them apart from the other ethnic groups in the country in particular and Africa in general. The most significant traits and institutions include, as Adu Boahen (1966; 1977) points out, a common 40-day calendar (*adaduanan*), common religious beliefs, marriage institutions, naming ceremonies, matrilineal system of inheritance, and an identical exogamous matrilineal clan system.

The Akan have, over the years, developed very complex and highly symbolic forms of weaving and printing textiles.[5] Archaeological findings from Begho in Brong-Ahafo Region provides "evidence inside the town of the manufacture of textiles, beads, and ivory ornaments in addition to brassware and, presumably, the crafts in perishable substances such as wood, basketry, and leather" that dates to around the middle of the second millennium A. D. (Posnansky, 1987, p. 17). The Asante, for example, not only developed the art of weaving (*nwentoma*) of which the *kente* is a special and well known one, they also developed the art of printing the adinkra cloth. With regards to weaving, the similarity between spindle whorls and loom forms found at Begho and that of the Mande of Jenne in the Timbuktu area "reinforces the idea of the transfer of technology south with traders," (Posnansky, 1987, p. 18). The Asante, as well as other Akans, also developed the *kyɛnkyɛn* cloth from the bark of a tree (Antiaris africana); cloth from raffia palm material (*doso*);[6] and *okunitam* (appliqued cloth).

Trade in Cloth

Before the arrival of Europeans on the coast,[7] the Asante traded with people outside the forest belt to the north, particularly Mande and Hausa merchants who acted as middlemen between the forests and coastal people on one side, and the caravans from across the Sahara Desert and the Mediterranean coasts on the other (Boahen, 1977). The trans-Saharan trade led to the development of the zongos of which Arhin (1987, p. 53) writes:

> The zongos must be regarded as a major savanna resource. Confined, before the colonial period, for both political considerations and environmental constraints, to the forest-savanna fringes and the savanna areas, they were the land equivalents of seaports and the gateway to the famed cornucopias that apparently lay beyond the savanna areas of Asante commercial travels. They were the locations of novel technical skills, such as those of smiths, potters, and weavers. The goods in the markets presented inspiring models to the Brong (northern Akan) and, through them, to the Asante and other southern Akan craftsmen. The zongos were the temporary or permanent lodges of itinerant and sedentary craftsmen from the Mande, Hausa, and Mossi countries whose work certainly contributed to the technological revolution which, Rattray asserted,

Owuo see fie
- #115

Ɔsrane -
#509

Adinkrahene
- #179

Abɛntia -
#173

Nsaa - #657

Mercedes
Benz - #607

Kramo bɔne
- #662

Nkotimsefoɔ
pua - #233

accompanied the emergence of the new Asante political order.

In addition to the trans-Saharan trade, there existed an extensive trade along the coast among the peoples of what later came to be known as the Gold, Ivory, and Slave Coasts in the Gulf of Guinea. The main articles of trade on the coast before the arrival of the Europeans were cloths and beads (Boahen, 1977). Astley (1745, p. 231) points out that the Ivory Coast cloth, known as *quaqua* cloth, was "a sort of cotton stuff" sold on the Gold Coast and used "for clothing the common people." A Dutch map of the Gold Coast dated December 25, 1629 shows a region where clothes were woven like carpets and worn among the Acanists [Akans], and that people in this region made use of horses but had no firearms (Fynn, 1971, p. 3).

In addition to the *quaqua* cloth, "there were also cloths from Whyddah, Ardra and Benin to the east." The Whyddah cloth was a strip about two yards long and about a quarter of a yard broad. Several of the strips were commonly joined together to make a bigger band of cloth. The Ardra cloths were said to be small and narrow bands whereas the Benin cloths consisted of either three or four bands. "The color of the Benin cloths was blue or blue with white stripes" (Fynn, 1971, p. 11).

The first European traders on the Guinea Coast played the role of middlemen who carried commodities between such places as the Cape Verde Islands in the west and Benin and Angola to the east. As Alpern (1995, p. 10) points out, most of the cloths European ships carried to the Gold Coast "came from elsewhere in Kwaland, notably Yorubaland (Ijebu), Benin, the western Niger River delta and the southern Ivory Coast. But Senegal, Sierra Leone, and Cameroon also furnished cloth. So did the Portuguese island colonies of Sao Tomé and Cape Verde."

ADINKRA SYMBOL ORIGINS

Although various hypotheses have been developed to explain the origin of the symbols, the exact origin of the symbols used in the textiles of the Akan people is yet to be specifically determined. One hypothesis is that they are derived from talismans and scripts believed to have Muslim associations from North Africa as a result of the trans-Saharan trade (Rattray, 1927; McLeod, 1981; Mato, 1986).

This hypothesis has been premised on three factors: (a) some of the symbols and their names are alleged to have Islamic origins; (b) *adinkra* symbols are mostly of geometric and abstract shapes, something that conforms to Islamic art; and, (c) there exists an *adinkra* cloth as claimed by Bravmann (1974) and believed to have been seen by Roy Sieber that has Islamic or Arabic writings. Mato contends, for example, in an elaborate examination of historical sources (principal source being Rattray's work) that "islamic writing, amuletic symbols or kufic 'script' have been given as probable source for *adinkra* symbols"(Mato, 1986, p. 64). He further illustrates the Islamic sources thus: "A number of adinkra symbols have Islamic links either through their form: Mohammedan Lock (fig. 112) [that is, *mmra krado*—symbol #288], Wise man's knot (fig. 113) [that is, *nyansapɔ*—symbol #649], or *Nsaa*—the Northern cloth (fig. 141) [that is, *nsaa*—symbol #657]; or through related Asante proverbs" (pp. 64-65). This hypothesis has a number of inaccuracies that needs to be set straight.

First, from the production technique perspective it has been suggested that the *adinkra* symbols have Islamic origin. This line of argument is advanced with the "empirical evidence" that Sieber saw an *adinkra* cloth with Arabic or Islamic writing (Mato, 1986, p. 67). I raised this line of argument with Sieber in a personal interview on July 22, 1996 at Bloomington, Indiana. He told me that what he saw was a sick man wearing a cloth with Islamic inscription.[8] This was to ward off any evil spirits so that he would recover from the sickness. Sieber said this was not to suggest that *adinkra* symbols had Islamic origin. He further pointed out that the issue should not be whether the Asante created the symbols or adopted them from other people. Assuming the Asante borrowed or adopted symbols from others at all, the issue as Sieber pointed out, should be what the

Adinkraba
Apau - #189

Sunsum -
#35

Yesu wuo -
#100

Kramo bɔne
- #660

Nsaa - #655

Nyansa pɔ -
#649

Nam porɔ a -
#362

Owuo see fie
- #113

Asante did with what they adopted or borrowed.

Whether or not Bravmann or Sieber once saw an *adinkra* cloth, that line of argument does not hold water when one examines that claim more closely in relation to the *adinkra* production technique as used in the Asokwa and Ntonso areas near Kumasi. The *adinkra* cloth producers use the block-print technique in which they use carved blocks called *adwini nnua* (design blocks), a broad stick called *daban*, and a comb-like tool called *nsensan nnua*. This technique has not changed much from what Bowdich observed in 1817 nor from what Rattray observed in the 1920s. To make Islamic or Arabic inscriptions would require the use of a writing brush or stick. The cloth stamper does not use a writing brush nor a stick. Even when they stamp phonetically-based inscription (e.g., *owuo see fie*—#113–115), the letters are carved onto the *adwini nnua*. If the production technique has not changed much over the years, then there is no evidence from that angle to support the contention that the *adinkra* symbols have an Islamic origin.

The fact that some symbols look Islamic in form or have related names or proverbs does not provide a convincing evidence of Islamic influence, and for that matter, Islamic origins for the *adinkra* symbols. Articles by Wilks (1962, 1993) may be used here to show that Rattray and subsequent scholars like Mato are wrong in claiming that words like *nsaa* and *kramo*, and symbols like *nyansa pɔ* and *mmra krado* are of Islamic origin. Wilks points out that these words and others like *ponkɔ* (horse), *adaka* (box), *krataa* (paper), *kotoku* (sack), and *tawa* (tobacco) are Mande and not Arabic or Islamic in origin. These and other Mande words had been incorporated in the Akan (Twi) language as a result of commercial relations.

One of the fifty-three odd symbols that Rattray identified from the *adinkra* cloth is the *nkotimsefoɔ pua* (hairstyle of the queenmother's attendants—#233) which is likened to the swastika symbol (Rattray, 1927, p. 267). Should one construe some of the contemporary symbols that include the logos for Mercedes Benz (#606–607) and VW (#605) cars as German influence? The verbal form of the Akan language is full of words borrowed from other languages. For example, words like *bokiti* (bucket) and *kɔpoo* (cup) are borrowed from English, and *asopatere* (shoes) and *paano* (bread) are borrowed from the Portuguese (Wilks, 1993). The Akan are not unique in adopting and borrowing words and symbols from other languages and cultures. Why should scholars attempt to diminish the creativity of the Asante (and Akan in general) to adopt and borrow from other cultures? As Gilfoy (1987, p. 26) points out, the trans-Saharan trade that might have been the source of Islamic influence was "by no means one-way." It is possible, therefore, that the Moslems—be they Arabs or Mande, Hausa or Fulani—might have copied some of the Akan symbols.

The Akan have had close contacts with numerous other ethnic groups (from within and outside the continent of Africa) for many years and they have demonstrated a readiness to appropriate and utilize items produced by these other groups. In cultures as highly organized in pre-colonial times as the Akan had developed, it is foolhardy to engage in a futile discussion that seems to attribute originality and creativity to outsiders other than the people themselves. In this light, one will ask with Picton (1992, p. 28): "Why is it always assumed, however, that it was North Africa [or for that matter, outsiders] that influenced the sub-Saharan region rather than the other way around?" There are other more plausible hypotheses to explain the origins of the *adinkra*.

The Bron Hypothesis

The Bron (Abrɔn, Bono or Brong) is believed to be the first Akan state. Warren (1975, p. 3) writes, "historically the Bono claim—and this is substantiated by oral histories from other Akan states—to have originated the Akan crafts of goldsmithing and kente cloth weaving." Posnansky (1987) provides some archaeological evidence from Begho to substantiate the Bron hypothesis that cloth weaving and other Akan crafts must have first occurred in the Bron state. The Bron state was in a strategic economic location as it traversed the transition zone of the forest and savannah belts between the Sudanic nations

Gye Nyame - #5

Sankɔfa - #637

Asɛm pa asa - #671

Nkotimsefoɔ pua - #234

Mercedes Benz - #606

VW - #605

Donno ntoasoɔ - #413

Nkyinkyimiɛ - #499

on the edge of the Sahara. Bron towns such as Techiman were important early market towns on the Djenne trade route.

Long before the decisive war of 1699-1701 against Denkyira, the Asante under Osei Tutu defeated the Dormaa state to the north. The defeat of Dormaa gave rise to Gyaman. A reluctant group of subjects under Bofu Bini refused to accept Asante rule. This group moved farther north to establish what became known as "*Gya man*—they have left their nation" (Terray, 1987). Subsequent Asante–Gyaman wars were either to strengthen Asante domination and control over the resources (especially gold) of the area and the northern trade routes, or they reflected the resistance of the Gyamans to Asante domination.

Tne Asante conquests of Bron ensured access to the crafts and resources and control of trade routes. The power of Kumase manifested itself through the action of people known as the *ahenkwaa* (servants), *abɔfoɔ* (hunters), and *batadifoɔ* (traders) of the Asantehene. It was through these interactions that possibly cloth weaving and other crafts were transferred to Asante. Or Asante conquests of Bron resulted in the transfer of innovations in weaving that might have improved on existing local weaving industry.

The Gyaman Hypothesis

Another hypothesis is that the name adinkra is associated with Nana Kofi Adinkra, King of Gyaman, who replicated and dared to claim that he too, like the Asante King, had a Golden Stool.[9] In 1818, the Asantehene Nana Osei Bonsu declared a punitive war against Nana Adinkra as his claim was considered an act of insolence that violated the Asante assertion that the likeness of the Golden Stool should never be said to have existed before or after the historic descent of the Asante Golden Stool. Nana Kofi Adinkra was attacked and defeated for making such a claim. Among the war booty captured from Gyaman were the *adinkra* stool symbols, some craftsmen, and the technical know-how for making the *adinkra* cloth. This explanation for the origin of the *adinkra* cloth and its symbols, however, appears to be anachronistic when viewed in the light of Bodwich's written account. Bodwich (1819) witnessed the production of *adinkra* and *kente* cloths during his visit to Kumasi in 1817, that is, one year before the punitive war against Nana Adinkra of Gyaman.[10]

One informant from Asokwa related to me that when the Gyamans were defeated, the body of King Adinkra was found in a pile of dead people. When his body was retrieved from the pile, it was found to be covered with the *ntiamu ntoma* (stamped cloth). Thereafter, the *ntiamu ntoma* became known as *adinkra ntoma*.[11] This explanation suggests that *ntiamu ntoma* (stamped cloth) must have existed prior to the 1818 Gyaman-Asante War. The cloth became associated with the name *adinkra* after the war. Such possibility may also be inferred from the explanation offerred by Opoku (1987, p. 194) thus:

> When Adinkra was subsequently defeated and taken prisoner, he appeared in a parade before the Asantehene, wearing a cloth with abstract symbols describing the depth of sorrow for his defeat, the loss of brave warriors, and his reduced status. As is the Asante practice, the cloth and the symbolic imprints, with several additional motifs, are still remembered as "Adinkra cloth."

People in the Asokwa and Ntonso areas continue to differentiate *adinkra* cloth from *kente* by referring to *adinkra* as *ntiamu ntoma* (stamped cloth) and kente as *nwentoma* (woven cloth).[12] The adinkra cloth is further distinguished as being *ntiamu* or *nhwemu* (stamped or whisked painting) and *nwɔmu* (embroidered). Three stages are employed in the making of the *adinkra* cloths: (1) dyeing (*ntoma aduro hyɛ*), (2) printing or stamping (*ntiamu*) and whisked painting (*nhwemu*), and (3) embroidering (*nwɔmu*) or simple sewing of the pieces together.

Koryɛ - #319

Dua afe -
#378

Mmra krado
- #288

Hwehwɛ mu
dua - #650

Nsaa - #658

Adinkraba
Apau - #188

Pagya - #267

Adinkrahene
- #178

The Denkyira Hypothesis

Another view, however, suggests that the art of printing the adinkra cloth was known in Denkyira and other Akan states that existed long before the "Osa-nti" war which occurred around 1700. This war ended the rule of the Denkyira over the Asante, and also gave rise to the Asante kingdom. The Asante, according to this explanation, learned the art of weaving and printing cloth from the Denkyira craftsmen and specialists who either defected or were captured during the war (Agyeman-Duah, n.d. no. 13). Wilks (1975, p. 456) writes: "The first and second Asokwahenes, Nuamoa and his full brother Akwadan, were among the many Denkyira who voluntarily transferred their allegiance to Osei Tutu in the late seventeenth century." When Akwadan defected he was said to have carried a trumpet that was made of gold. This must refer to a gilded abɛntia—gilded state horn (called nkrawobɛn—#173).[13] These Denkyira people are said to have introduced several innovations not only in textile and other crafts but also in government and military organization.

If one accepted this hypothesis, then the 1818 Gyaman war must have resulted in bringing to Asokwa war captives[14] that introduced additional technological improvements (e.g., the use of carved apakyiwa in stamping as compared to the use of feathers in the painting technique that Bowdich mentions in the quote below) in the textile industry. In the adinkra production process, Asokwa informants maintained that it was Nana Adinkra's son, Apau (or Apaa) who introduced innovations such as the use of calabash for carving out the stamps.[14] He is also believed to have introduced the very first symbol (adwini kane), adinkrahene (king of the adinkra symbols—#178–185; 186–187). He is remembered and honored with the symbol Adinkraba Apau (Apau, Son of Adinkra—#188–189). Other symbols are believed to have been copied from the carved column (sekyedua) of the stool and other regalia of Nana Adinkra of Gyaman (Kyerematen, 1964). This hypothesis is problematic because the Bowdich collection of 1817 has the adinkrahene symbol that is believed to have been introduced by Nana Adinkra's son after the 1818 Asante-Gyaman War.

Etymological Explanation

Yet another view presented by Danquah (1944) is that the word adinkra derives from the Akan word nkra or nkara which means message or intelligence. This message or intelligence is what the soul takes with it from God upon obtaining leave to depart to earth, that is, enter the human being upon birth. The Akan call the soul of the person kera or kra, and the soul is the spiritual aspect of God that enters the human being upon birth and leaves the person at death. Adinkra is the parting or send-off message or intelligence that the soul carries to and from God. Perhaps the association of adinkra with kra (soul) as parting message provided the basis for the view that the adinkra cloth was a cloth for mourning.

One informant[15] also explained that the name adinkra became associated with the ntiamu toma (stamped cloth) that was given to Prempeh I to take with him into exile. He was given several ntiamu ntoma as adi nkra ntoma (parting cloth) to mark his taking leave of his people. One of the adinkra cloths he took with him was stamped the ɔsrane (moon—#509). This was to symbolize that the king may come and go, but the people as nation will forever be there. From then on ntiamu ntoma became known as adinkra. This hypothesis seems to be based on the etymological hypothesis because at Ntonso and Asokwa, the cloth producers continue to refer to adinkra as ntiamu ntoma. The problem with this explanation is that Prempeh carried not only adinkra cloths; he also took several kente (or nwentoma) cloths with him. If the cloth (ntiamu ntoma) he took with him into exile was to mark his taking leave of his people, then one will surmise the nwentoma (kente) should also mark the occasion of his taking leave of his people. And, therefore, such kente cloths should be called adinkra ntoma. But of course, kente is nwentoma not adinkra or ntiamu ntoma.

Another etymological explanation offers that the term adinkra is a corruption of the word adwini kane (first design or first symbol). Each of the designs or symbols in the

Sankɔfa -
#646

Nyansapɔ -
#649

Gye Nyame -
#7

Adinkrahene
- #182

Adinkraba
Apau - #188

Nkrawoben -
#173

Krapa - #62

Nkrabea -
#75

adinkra cloth is called *adwini* (design) and the cloth is referred to as *adwini ntoma* (designed cloth) or *ntiamu ntoma* (stamped cloth). Bowdich (1819, p. 310) wrote:

> The white cloths, which are principally manufactured in Inla and Dagwumba, they paint for mourning with a mixture of blood and red dye wood. The patterns are various and not inelegant, and painted with so much regularity with a fowl's feather, that they have all the appearance of a coarse print at a distance.[16]

Whatever the source of the name and the symbols, the *adinkra* is more than a mourning cloth. In one sense, it can be viewed in terms of the Akan symbolism of color encoded in the background of the adinkra cloth; in another sense, the symbols and the patterns of stamping them in the cloth constitute text that needs to be examined for what it encodes. We now discuss the Akan color symbolism encoded in the *adinkra* cloth.

COLOR SYMBOLISM

Among the Asante as well as all Akan, color classification is basically tripartite. These colors exist as complementary parts of triadic series. The three basic colors or ranges of color are *tuntum, fufuo* and *kɔkɔɔ*. *Tuntum* designates all very dark shades which approach absolute blackness. *Fufuo* covers pale, white, grey and cream colors; and *kɔkɔɔ* all red, brown and yellow shades (Antubam, 1963).

All shades of white (*fufuo*), for example, ivory, white glass, egg shell, white clay (*hyire*), are generally associated with coolness, innocence, peace, purity, virtue, virginity, victory, virtuosity, and rejoicing and happiness (Antubam, 1963). Spiritual entities such as God and deified spirits of ancestors that live in the spiritual world are associated with white; the lower world, abode of chthonic creatures and demons, is associated with black. Hagan (1970, p. 8) points out that *fufuo*

> is the ritually auspicious color and it has immediate association with victory and spiritual purity. It is associated with the sacred, and it is considered the color of gods and kings; the symbol of the purity and sacredness of their persons and estate. Fufuo also expresses joy and hope and well-being. That aspect of the human person which bears a man's destiny and directs his fortunes (kra) is associated with fufuo,... .

Rattray (1927, p. 175) points out a contrast: "The corpse of a dead priest is draped in white and sprinkled with white clay (*hyire*) or powder, symbolizing the antithesis of ordinary funerary customs, which possibly mark out the wearers as being in a state of sorrow or defilement."

Some shades of *kɔkɔɔ* (red for example, *memene* and *kɔbene*) are associated with heat, anger, crisis, grief, blood, danger, witchcraft, and warfare (Antubam, 1963; Hagan, 1970). Hagan (1970, p. 9) notes that "Akans generally point to blood as the paradigm of the red color cluster and much of the ambiguity in the symbolic meaning of the color derives from the mixed associations of blood. Blood stands for life and vitality… Akans believe that blood is the means by which a *kra* [soul or spirit—#35–36] might be given human form. But as blood stands for life, so does any blood which does not give life, or is spilled wastefully, stand for death."

On the other hand, some other shades of *kɔkɔɔ* (yellow and the color of juice of the ripe pineapple, for example) symbolize prosperity, royalty, glory, the prime of life, and maturity. Yellow also signifies the presence and influence of God in the society and the rule of a king (Antubam, 1963).

The broad connotations of *tuntum* are less precise, but are usually associated with night, death, loss, and ancestors (Antubam, 1963; Hagan, 1970). Black "does not," as Hagan (1970, p. 9) points out, " necessarily connote defilement or profanation. The Stool of kings or elders who die in battle or of old age while in office are consecrated and held

Ɔsrane - #509

Nkyɛmu - #675

Kyɛmferɛ - #698

Ananse antɔn kasa - #715

Aban - #143

Sitia bɛkum dorɔba - #584

Mako nyinaa - #614

Akokɔnan - #425

sacred to their memory, and they are black." Antubam (1963, p. 79) suggests that black symbolizes sp̲i̲r̲i̲t̲u̲a̲lity and age as "all objects which are dedicated to the spirits of the dead are purposely treated to appear black; and objects of war booty, except gold and silver, are blackened."

Some shades of *tuntum* have complex meanings. Bright blue, for example, is the color for love and feminine tenderness. According to Antubam (1963, p. 82), blue "is likened to the serene appearance of the crescent moon in the heavens. It is also often used to symbolize the role of a queen mother." On the other hand, *adinkra* cloth with indigo blue dye (*birisi*) is considered as *ntoma tuntum* (black cloth) for certain funeral purposes (e.g, *kunayɛ*—widowhood).

On a spatial and temporal plane, the Akan envision life as a circular continuum of colors. Life starts with white and runs clockwise towards youth and adolescence with yellow. During *abadintoɔ* (child naming ceremony) the child is dressed in white and is given *pokuaa* (gold nugget) as *kera sika* (gold for the child's soul) symbolizing continuous life and prosperity for the child. Adult life is reached with brown (*dansinkran*), and ends with black for death.[17] At the intermediary points, the main colors combine and gradually change shades; the center of the Akan life cycle, being the sum of all parts, is conceived as multi-colored.

During funerals brown, black and red (for example, *kuntunkuni, birisi,* and *kɔbene*) *adinkra* cloths are usually worn. When *adinkra* is used as a mourning cloth, three types of color backgrounds, *kɔkɔɔ* (all shades of red) and *tuntum* (all shades of black) on one hand, and *fufuo* (all shades of white) on the other hand are used. *Tuntum* and *fufuo*, when used together for funerary purposes, symbolize the Akan concept of dualism such as life and death, beginning and end, and crisis and normalcy, victory/peace and crisis/chaos, sacred/ profane, and mourning and rejoicing. Red (*kɔkɔɔ,* for example, *kɔbene*) and black (*tuntum,* for example, *kuntunkuni* and *birisi*) adinkra cloths are worn together by the immediate relatives of the deceased person, while only black (*tuntum*) *adinkra* is worn by the other mourners (see pictures #). As Hagan (1970, p. 10) explains, "at this level black and red refer to opposite categories and relationships": family and non-family members. Akan Christians have incorporated their color symbolism into their Christian religious rituals. Good Friday (*Yesu wuo*—#100) is marked by the wearing of *tuntum* and *kɔkɔɔ* mourning clothes, and Easter *(Yesu wusɔre*—#104)—resurrection, and thus beginning of life—is marked by the wearing of white to symbolize a new beginning made possible by the triumph of Jesus over death and his ascension to heaven.

Bright background colors of white and all shades of yellow are worn for all diverse occasions. White *adinkra* is usually worn when a very old person dies. This signifies the attainment of victory over death and the earning of glory and rest which is the lot of good ancestors. White *adinkra* is also worn to indicate a return to normalcy after mourning or to give thanks (*aseda*) for recovery from illness, and to mark victory or innocence during trial (Antubam, 1963; Sarpong, 1974).

As a signal for the end of the Odwira[18] festival, the king wears white adinkra to mark the return to normalcy. White adinkra is also worn by the Asantehene-elect for some stages in the ritual of enstoolment at Pampaso and also in the Bampanase Courtyard (Agyeman-Duah, 1962).

Cloth Patterns

Another way in which *adinkra* cloth may be understood is to examine the name given to each cloth pattern (e.g. *Kwasiada adinkra*—Sunday *adinkra*), and the constituent symbols in each cloth. In other words, the type of symbols predominantly stamped into the cloth together with the background colors carries messages and also determines the occasion for which the cloth is to be used. In general, the printing of the symbols does follow particular patterns which give specific names to the finished cloth. Examples of the names for the finished cloth are: (1) variations of adwinasa such as *Kwasiada adinkra, adinkra akyi adinkra, mmaa ma*; and *ɔhene kɔ hia* (the king is gone to the women's

Anyi me ayɛ
a - #564

Sunsum -
#36

Daban -
#681

Nsensan -
#706

Dɛnkyɛm -
#217

Dwantire -
#281

Gye Nyame -
#5

Owuo sɛe fie
- #113

quarters [harem]—picture— #); (2) *m'akoma mu tɔfe* (my sweetheart — picture—#); (3) *abete ntema*; (4) *ɔsrane ne nsoroma ntoma* (moon and stars cloth); and, (5) *kontonkurowi* (rainbow—picture—#). Also on demand, a particular symbol or set of symbols will be used to meet customers' requests (for example, *koroyɛ*—#319 and mercedes benz—#606–607). The cloths may be named after individuals, events, and social messages, including proverbs (Rattray, 1927, pp. 236–268), as well as tell stories.

When used by officials of the king's court, for instance, the adinkra cloth may present a message in lieu of the spoken word. In such usage the wearer of the cloth can rely entirely on the rhetoric of his visual icon to state, in very general terms, the official policy he represents.[19] For example, in connection with the grand funeral rite (*ayikɛse*) for his immediate predecessor, Nana Agyeman Prempeh I, Otumfuo Sir Osei Agyeman Prempeh II wore *adinkra fufuo* with the *dɛnkyɛm* (crocodile—#215–218) motif. The white background color signified the installation of a new king as return to normalcy vis-a-vis the crisis situation the state had been thrown into by the death of the predecessor. The *dɛnkyɛm* motif signified adaptation to the changing circumstances following the colonization of Asante by the British.[20] Nana Opoku Ware II, the successor to Prempeh II, on the other hand, wore *adinkra fufuo* with the *mframa dan* (wind resistant house—#435–436) motif. Polakoff (1982, pp. 98, 100) notes: "The choice made by Opuku [sic] Ware II was especially appropriate for the stormy political mood of African countries." The use of *mframa dan* motif in this instance might have signified chieftaincy and the indigenous political system it represented as being more stable and secure than the Westminster parliamentary system colonialism had imposed on the country. When Nana Opoku Ware II was installed as Asantehene, Ghana had just returned to civilian rule under the Progress Party led by Dr. K. A. Busia after a three-year military rule. Before he became the Asantehene, Nana Opoku Ware II, as J. Matthew Poku, had served as a Commissioner (Minister) for Transport and Communications in the 1966-1969 military government and Ghana's ambassador to Italy.

I witnessed similar use of the cloth to make oblique statements at a funeral ceremony I observed in Kumasi on May 28, 1994. Some immediate family members of the deceased wore factory-made and hand-printed a d i n k r a cloth with the symbol *owuo sɛe fie* (death destroys the home—#113–115). When I asked why the use of that particular symbol, one of the people wearing that cloth responded that it was their father who had passed away and they wanted to convey their feelings about how poorly they had been treated by the dead man's *abusua* (matriclan) members.

PRODUCTION PROCESSES

Adinkra is a printed cloth that utilizes the block-print technique. The technique used by the Asante is indigenous. The original fabrics onto which the symbols were printed were locally woven cloth produced from locally grown and hand-spun cotton. The cloth serves as the 'canvas' on which the symbols are printed. The background color, in the past, was usually either plain white, indigo, rustic red, or brown. Sources of natural dyes included barks of trees and roots, leaves and flowers, and fruits. For example, green dye could be extracted from papaya (pawpaw) leaves, and brown could be obtained from cola nuts. The most common background dye is *kuntunkuni* produced from the bark of the roots of the *kuntunkuni* tree, obtained from the savannah regions to the north. The bark is soaked first and then pounded, and water is added and strained. The liquid is then boiled, strained again, and cooled after which the dye-stuff is ready for use. After dyeing and drying, the cloth is stretched out on a printing table or the ground padded with foam or old sacks for the stamping. Contemporary adinkra cloths have varied back-ground colors and the fabrics that serve as the canvas for printing are usually factory-made. Locally hand-woven fabrics continue to be used at Ntonso. With the use of screen printing, the hand-woven adinkra cloth is enjoying increased demand from both local and foreign consumers.

The pigment which is used as ink for the block print is prepared from the bark of the *badeɛ* tree (bridelia micranta of the natural order euphorbiaceae). The epidermis is first

Yesu wuo -
#100

Yesu wusɔre
- #104

Nsoromma -
#117

Nkyɛmu -
#674

Ɔhene kɔ hia
- #194

Koryɛ - #319

Dɛnkyɛm -
#217

Mframa dan
- #435

removed and the rest of the bark is pounded. After soaking in a barrel for three days, it is then pounded and strained, and lumps of iron slag (ɛtia) are added to the solution to hasten evaporation as it is boiled till it is gluey thick, yielding a black fabric paint which the craftsmen call *adinkra aduro*.[21]

The stamps (*adwini nnua*) used for the block printing are made from pieces of old calabash or gourd (*apakyiwa* or *koraa*—lagenaria vulgaris) on which are carved the different symbols.[22] A small handle is made from sticks (*praeɛ*) which are tied into a knot and pegged into the back of the calabash pieces. To apply the stamps the cloth is laid out on a dry flat clean piece of ground padded with foam, old sacks, or board, and it is held taut with pins or wooden pegs. The cloth[23] is divided into rectangles, squares or parallelograms (panels) by using either a wooden comb (*dua afe*—#378–384), *daban* (iron bar or a measure—#681), or *nsensan nnua* (line-making sticks). The *dua afe* or the *nsensan nnua* is dipped into the *adinkra aduro* and applied free hand to draw the line patterns[24] (see picture). These initial line designs are known as *nsensan* (lines—#704–706), *kɛtɛwa* or *kɛtɛpa* (good bed—#418), *ɔwɔ aforo adobɛ* (snake climbs the raffia palm tree—#345–346), *nhwemu*, or *nkyɛmu* (divisions—#674–675), or *daban* (a measure—#681).[25] The other *adinkra* symbols are then printed in each of the rectangles on the cloth. Some of the symbols are designed by using the *dua afe* (for example, asambo—#374–376), *nsensan nnua* (e.g., mframadan—#435–436), the heads of different sizes of nails (e.g., sumpie—#174), and the *prae* handle of the carved *adinkra* stamp (for example, tuo aboba—#352). Sometimes no lines are drawn and the stamps are applied in freehand style to the cloth. In this method, one or two symbols (usually donno—#406, nsoromma—#116–121, and donno ntoaso or donno nta—#407–415) are used to serve as boundary lines within which the other symbols are printed. Or the *nwɔmu* (embroidery) design is utilized as lines to divide the cloth into sections for printing.

The production process is differentiated by sex and age. Young and middle-aged women usually prepare the dye-stuff and the *adinkra aduro* and they also dye the cloth prior to it being block-printed. Men tend to prepare the *adinkra aduro* and do the block printing. While young boys are often given the embroidery (*nwɔmu*) part to do, older men and women tend to carve symbols onto the calabash pieces. Even though the production of the cloth tends to be carried out with family members as the production unit, hired labor on a piece rate basis is also utilized to carry out some of the major stages of the cloth production (dyeing, printing, sewing, and embroidery) for bulk sales to retailers. Asokwa producers tend to make cloth to order, while Ntonso producers tend to produce on a commercial scale for the market. Producers at Asokwa tend to be full time workers producing *adinkra* cloths, whereas some of the producers at Ntonso tend to split their time between producing *adinkra* and farming. There are machine-printed *adinkra* cloths being produced in Ghanaian, British, Dutch, Japanese, and French factories. The machine-made prints are color fast and may be washed very often, whereas adinkra cloth produced by the indigenous block-print process is not color fast and may not be washed frequently. Some of the indigenous producers at Ntonso and Asokwa are stamping on commercial print cloth, resulting in what has been termed as "fancy" *adinkra* cloth. A new development that I observed at Ntonso in 1999 is the use of the silk-screening technique for printing adinkra cloths. The silk screening technique uses imported fabric dye that is fast. Despite these inroads into the Akan indigenous textile tradition, consumers prefer the aesthetic quality of the hand stamped cloth.

Dua afe -
#378

Kɛtɛpa -
#418

Mframadan -
#436

Daban -
#681

Nkyɛmu -
#675

Nsensan -
#705

Donno
ntoasoɔ -
#407

Asambo -
#375

1. Ɔkyeame, singular (akyeamefoɔ, plural) has been interpreted as a linguist or spokesman for the chief.

2. Nana Antwi Buasiako, personal interview at Ayigya, Kumasi, May 30, 1996.

3. The origins of the Akan as a group of people has been heatedly debated. In 1965 this debate was joined by a series of seminars at the University of Ghana. Papers presented in the series have been published in the journal Ghana Notes and Queries and elsewhere.

4. Kiyaga-Mulindwa (1980, p. 503) writes: "The origin of the term 'Akan' is obscure. The term has been appearing in print for over 400 years, and its usage has changed with time." Daaku (1970, p. 3) notes that there once existed a loose confederation of states known as Akani of which Denkyira and Adanse were part. These states were found in the area washed by the Oda, Ofin and Pra rivers.

5. In addition to weaving and printing, embroidery and applique techniques for utilizing textile are also well known by the Akans.

6. Raffia was in time replaced by cotton yarns spun from locally grown cotton. It was soon discovered that cloth could be woven from the silk material out of the long silky yarns produced by a species of spider, ɔkɔmantan (Kyerematen, 1964). Later the Akan weavers would unravel the colored silk cloths obtained through trade with the Europeans and use the threads for weaving. This enabled the Akan weaver to increase the number of colors available to him.

7. Portuguese travelers to the West African coast in the fifteenth century reported that Africans wore loin cloths and wrapping cloths. Linguistic, archeological, and documentary evidence suggests that cotton spinning and weaving existed widely if unevenly in West Africa prior to contact with Europeans (Schaedler, 1987; Brooks, 1992).

8. One swallow does not a summer make. What Sieber is believed to have seen must be the work of an itinerant Hausa or Mande cloth producer. There is a factory-made cloth called Kramo nte Hausa (the Muslim does not speak Hausa) that has Arabic (Islamic) inscription. This cloth does not resemble an adinkra cloth at all. There is a hand-made imitation of this cloth in the Berlin Museum fur Volkerkunde that I have seen personally. This Berlin sample does not resemble in either shape or form an adinkra cloth.

9. The Asante nation had been formed following the nkabom (unity) meeting of various chiefs called together by Osei Tutu and ƆkƆmfo AnƆkye. Ɔkɔmfo Anɔkye conjured from the sky a Golden Stool for the Asante king and decreed that no other king should have a golden stool or the likeness of it (see the discussion of stools in Chapter 5 and the discussion of the nkabom meeting in Chapter 6).

10. Kusi Boadum, personal interview at Asokwa, May 23, 1994.

11. Asante-Gyaman Wars.

12. Teacher Nsiah and Agya Yaw Nyamaa, personal interviews at Ntonso, May 22, 1994; Appiah and Agya Ampɔfo, personal interview at Asokwa, May 23, 1994.

Owuo sɛɛ fie
- #114

Nsoromma -
#118

Nyame dua -
#54

Owuo mpɛ
sika - #98

Awia - #30

Mframa dan
- #436

Abusua pa -
#447

Asam bo -
#375

13.   In relating the history associated with the *nkrawɔbɛn*, Appiah told me in a personal interview on May 24, 1994 at Asokwa that his ancestor, Nana Gyetua brought this horn from Denkyira to serve the Asantehene. When I checked with the record by Wilks (1975, p. 458), Nana Gyetua (Gyetoa) was the ninth Asokwahene. One should note that Wilks' record is derived from oral history.

14.   The Asante had a population policy of settling skilled war captives in craft towns (see Chapter 9).

15.   Appiah and Boadum, personal interviews at Asokwa, May 24,1994.

16.   A reader of a draft of the manuscript, who asked to remain anonymous, offered this explanation. This explanation may be based on the etymological hypothesis and does not seem to register with other informants. One informant intimated that it was a kente cloth that was later created and named *ɔhene aforo hyɛn* (the king travels in a boat to mark his exile from Ghana.

17.   Even though Bowdich claims that the *adinkra* cloth was painted with fowl's feather, the sample he collected (now at the British Museum) was definitely produced with the block-print technique.

18.   Death is not an end but a transition to life in a spiritual world.

19.   Odwira is an annual festival that signify regeneration and renewal of life. The ancestors are remembered in statewide ceremonies during which the sub-chiefs renew their oath of allegiance to the king.

20.   Nana Antwi Buasiako, an Asantehene Kyeame, explained to me in a personal interview (May 24, 1994) that the wearing of an *adinkra* cloth by the Asantehene to make a policy statement, is a deliberate decision made by the king in consultation with his counselors. When the decision is made with regards to what policy statement the king wants to make, the *Manwerɛhene*, the chief public servant in charge of the king's clothing and personal effects, then charges the *Asokwahene* to commission the production of the cloth to suit the occasion.

21.   The British captured Kumasi in 1896 and exiled Prempeh I to the Seychelles Island in the Indian Ocean. The Asantehene was reduced to the status of Kumasihene and the Asanteman Nhyiamu was abolished. When Prempeh I was returned from exile in 1924 the British would only allow him to rule as Kumasihene. He died in 1931 and was succeeded by Prempeh II under whose reign the Asanteman Nhyiamu was restored in 1935 and, thence, ruled as Asantehene.

22.   Some printers at both Asokwa and Ntonso said they had experimented with factory-made fabric paint but abandoned its use because it does not have the shining appearance as *adinkra aduro*. One will also imagine that the fabric paint is more expensive, and to minimize costs, the printer is better off using the local product. There is also the attachment to "tradition" and the printer does not want to take risks regarding customer taste. However, since about 1999, screen printing has become the vogue at Ntonso, Tewobabi and neighboring villages. According to Teacher Kofi Nsiah (interviewed, April 29, 2000),this technique was introduced by artists at the University of Science and Technology, Kumasi and popularized through workshops at the National Cultural Centre, Kumasi. This technique has given rise to the use of many more symbols, and also the use of various printing ink colors in addition to the traditional black printing ink.

Mo no yɔ -
#520

Anyi me ayɛ
a - #564

Dua afe -
#384

Fihankra -
#433

Ɔdɔ aniwa -
#370

Blɔk dan -
#438

23. In comparison to the prints on old cloths, the prints on recent cloths seem much bigger. Such blocks as the *dwenimɛn ntoaso* (#212), *abeteɛ ntema* (#619) and *adinkrahene ntoaso* (#186–187) are examples of the bigger sized prints.

24. There are two types of cloth sizes, one for the man and one for the woman. The man's cloth varies from a young man's (that is, small) size of 90" X 216" (usually called half piece— *po fa*) to a full grown man's size that varies from a medium size of 90" X 288" (what is usually called the 8 yard-size) to a large size of 135" X 432" (what is usually called the 12 yard-size or full piece— *po*), and the woman's may be three pieces of 45" X 72" each or two pieces, of which one is 45" X 72" and the other is 45" X 144" (called the *dansinkran* and worn in toga-style similar to the man's). The man-size cloth is divided into six horizontal fields (rows) by eight vertical fields (columns) forming forty-eight panels. One symbol is usually printed in each panel and the symbols in each panel may be repeated in some order to form a pattern for each cloth. It is in the system of patterning and the creative use of symbols and colors that the variety of *adinkra* cloths arises.

25. The *dua afe* (wooden comb) or *nsensan nnua* has two, four, six, eight, or ten "teeth." The numbers of lines made by the *dua afe* and *nsensan nnua* have symbolic meanings themselves. One symbolizes the indivisible, the *kra* (soul) of *Nyame*. *Nsatea kor* means the same as *Gye Nyame* (except God). Two symbolizes Nyame as a duality, divisible by birth. Nsateanu means *Memma mo mmo ne yɔ me man* (I congratulate you people of my state). Three symbolizes Nyame as the creator and ruler of the universe that is a continuum of the sky (*ewimu*), earth (*ewiase*), and the underworld (*asamando*). Three is also considered a lucky number. Four symbolizes *Nyame* as the creator and ruler of the four cardinal points of the compass and the revolving heaven. Five symbolizes Nyame as a Supreme Being. Six symbolizes the dialectical processes of life, death and resurrection or rebirth. It is the symbol of strength, vitality and rejuvenation. Seven is the symbol for the universe and the state. It represents the seven planets each of which presides over the seven days of the week, and the seven abusua (family) that form the state. Eight symbolizes procreation, fertility and fecundity. Nine (i.e., 3+3+3) symbolizes the triad comprising *Nyame*, *Nyankopɔn*, and *Ɔdomankoma* that rules the universe (Meyerowitz, 1950; Antubam, 1963).

26. Sometimes a brush-like tool is used to make these lines and the whisked painting effect of the brush work gives rise to the type of *adinkra* cloth called *nhwemu*.

The coat-of arms of Ghana as an adinkra symbol - # 368

CHAPTER 3

Ɔbɔadeɛ te sɛ obi a oretwa puru; ɔno na onim n'ahyease ne n'awieɛ.
Only the Creator of the universe, like the creator of the circle,
knows its beginning and its end.

ONIPA BE
WUNASIKA
TE ASE
Onipa bɛwu
na sika te
ase - #112

Asɛm pa asa
- #671

Anommaa ne
ɔwɔ - #347

Nsakorɔ -
#364

Nsakorɔ -
#366

Nsakorɔ -
#365

ADINKRA SYMBOLS

STYLIZATION

The adinkra symbols are graphic either in a pictographic or ideographic form. They are based on various observations of and associations between humans and the objects they use, floral and fauna scenes, the human body and its parts, and elements of nature and abstract ideas. There is an increased use of phonological script in recent years. Examples of the use of phonological script are to be found in such symbols as *asɛm pa asa* (the truth is gone—#671), *owuo bɛgya hwan* (who will be spared by death?—#99), and *onipa bɛwu na sika te ase* (one will die and leave one's wealth behind—#112).

Adinkra symbols have been classified in the past on the basis of the sources of their derivation—fauna, flora, geometric and so forth. Ofori-Ansah's chart (1978, 1993), for example, classifies the adinkra symbols from these sources of derivation. "But symbols," Cohen (1979, p. 90) explains, "are highly complex socio-cultural phenomena and can therefore be classified according to a variety of criteria, depending on the purpose of the classification, which in turn depends on the theoretical problem that is being investigated and the variables that are considered in the study."

In this book the adinkra symbols are viewed as a form of writing made up of ideograms and pictograms and, increasingly in recent times, phonograms. This classificatory system is illustrated in Table 2. In rows 1–4 are examples of symbols that are pictograms based on parts of the human body; flora and fauna; celestial bodies; and human-made objects. Rows 5–7 contain ideograms that are in part combination of pictograms that suggest action. For example, the symbol in the quadrant 5a represents a bird holding a snake by the neck (*anommaa ne ɔwɔ*—bird and snake—#347), and 5b represents a mythical bird that flies with the head turned backwards (*sankɔfa*—go back and retrieve—#644). On the other hand, the symbols in Columns 7b–7h are modifications of the symbol in Column 7a. Each modification is based on an addition of another symbol to the *Gye Nyame* (except God—#2) symbol. The symbol in quadrant 7g, for example, is a combination of the *sepɔ* (dagger—#299) with what is essentially the *Gye Nyame* symbol. In Row 8 are examples of phonograms that are based on alphabets in the English and Twi languages. The rise of alphabetic writing dates to contact with Europeans in the 15th century (Gerrard, 1981).

The symbols in Table 3 show some of what Frutiger (1991) sees as the main stages of stylization or degrees of iconization. These stages include the first level of schematization in which the drawing is a recognizable drawing, e.g., *dɛnkyɛmfunafu* (siamese twins crocodiles—#311), *nsakorɔ* (one hand—#364), *sankɔfa* (go back and retrieve—#644), *adwa* (stool—#163), *akofena* (state swords—#164–169), *ɔhene tuo* (king's gun—#258–260), and *ɔsrane* (crescent—#509). The second stage is a cross-cut representation of the object, e.g., *dɛnkyɛmfunafu* (siamese twins crocodiles—#312), *nsakorɔ* (one hand—#366), *sankɔfa* (go back and retrieve—#647), *adwa* (stool—#154), *bese saka* (bunch of kola nuts—# 575–581), *akokɔ nan* (hen's feet—#424–427), *ɔhene kyiniiɛ* (king's umbrella—#170), and *mframa dan* (wind-resistant house—#435–436). The other level of schematization is one in which the outward form of the object completely disappears and only a part of the function of the object is explained, e.g., *dɛnkyɛmfunafu* (siamese twins crocodiles—#308), *nsakorɔ* (one hand—#365), *sankɔfa* (go back and retrieve—#646),

Gye Nyame
- #2

Denkyɛmfunafu
- #311

Adwa - #153

Gye Nyame
- #3

OWUO
BƐGYA
·HWAN

Owuo bɛgya
hwan - #99

Adwa - #154

Adwa - #163

Owuo mpɛ
sika - #98

adwa (stool—#153), aban (castle—#138–147), gye Nyame (except God—#2–9), and owuo mpɛ sika (death accepts no money—#98). As Frutiger points, out "in the progressive course of schematization, verbal explanation becomes essential. The stronger the degree of iconization, the more dependent it becomes upon explanatory language" (Frutiger, 1991, p. 230).

AKAN WRITING

Abraham (1962, p. 111) indicates that the Akan "expressed their philosophico-religious ideas through art." The themes of the Akan art tended to be associated with the origins and structure of the universe, life, and social organization. As art, the well known adinkra symbols embody manifold religious, political, philosophical, ideological, and historical associations. They make reference to personal grandeur, political solidarity, prosperity, the peace of the nation, and economic constraint, among other ideas and concepts. The adinkra symbols together with other Akan symbols such as those found in gold weights and wood carvings incorporate a considerable amount of material from the various oral genres that include maxims, proverbs, songs, funeral dirges, folktale, anecdotes, and everyday expressions. These genres reflect many important aspects of Akan society such as the aesthetic, religious, ethical, and social values. They record everyday events and social interactions.

The adinkra symbols, as well as the other Akan visual symbols and images, were used for communication. "An Asante," writes McLeod (1976, p. 89), "on being shown a particular image, will attempt to recall or discover the verbal formula to which the image corresponds." The adinkra symbols were used to communicate not only among human beings but also between human and spiritual beings. The latter use was probably even more important in the early development of Akan writing. For example, from Rattray's (1927) pioneering study in which he identified about fifty three symbols (see Appendix A), as well as from the samples of the adinkra cloth collected by Bowdich in 1817 (now in the British Museum), Prempeh I's cloth (now in the National Museum of African Art, Washington, D. C.) and the cloth sent to King Willem 1 of Holland in 1825 (now in Rijksmuseum voor Volkenkunde, Leiden), one can see that several of these symbols were used for communication between human and spiritual beings. Table 4 illustrates some of the early symbols for spirituality that are incorporated in the adinkra cloth. Nyame dua (God's altar—#53–60), for example, symbolized the presence of God, God's protection and spirituality. This altar was placed in front of houses to serve as a medium for communicating with God and the spirits of one's ancestors. The mmusuyideɛ or kerapa (sanctity or good fortune—#61–69) symbol was woven into place mats that were placed beside the king's bed so that he would step on three times each night before going to sleep (Rattray, 1927, p. 266). This was to wish himself good luck and God's protection as he slept. In the morning, before the king stepped out to undertake his routine for the day, he would touch three times the biribi wɔ soro (there is something in the heavens—#126–128) symbol that hung from the lentil of the bedroom door. Each time he touched the symbol he would repeat : Nyame, biribi wɔ soro na ma ɛmmɛka me nsa (God, there is something in the heavens, let it reach me). The king did this to wish himself good luck, high hopes and high expectation for the day (Rattray, 1927, p. 266).

A recent development in the use of adinkra symbols for communication between human and spiritual beings has been the incorporation of some of the symbols into the liturgical arts of the Christian Church in Ghana. Quarcoo (1968, pp. 55–56) illustrates this incorporation of adinkra symbols into the liturgical arts of the Emmanuel Church (Methodist) at Labadi, a suburb of Accra thus:

Worked actually into the walls are motifs usually referred to as Adinkra designs. All along the walls of two long sides of the building are the patterns; namely, the Gye Nyame—God is the answer—or except God [# 2]; the eight-ray sun or star [# 116]; the Mmusuyide [# 61]—sacrifice; the 'Dwennimmen [#

34

Gye Nyame
- #2

Kera pa -
#62

Nsoromma -
#116

Dwɛnnimɛn
- #205

Fihankra -
#434

Akofena -
#164

Mmeramubere
- #22

Adwa - #156

205],' the sign of a lamb, humility and divinity; and the '*Fihankra* [# 434],' the household. For the first time, at least in recent times, the attempt has been made to use signs in such sequence as to run as a 'sentence.' God; son of the sky, sacrifice, ram and household. When verbs are supplied, we get something like this— 'God's son became a sacrificial lamb for the household.' This is the core of the Christian message. There is, of course, the cardinal point of the Resurrection on which faith stands.[1]

Other adinkra symbols that Quarcoo identifies as having been incorporated in the liturgical art of the Emmanuel Church are *Nyamedua* (God's altar—#53–60), *akofena* (state swords—#164–169), *mmeramubere* (female cross—#22–24), *mmeramutene* (male cross—#20–21), and *adwa* (stool—#151–163). He writes the following about the *adwa* (stool—#151–163) symbol:

> it is a symbol of solidarity, and love; at the same time an artifact whose association with government and politics, magic and ritual, the world of the living and the ancestors, is very significant. It is meaningful to the Ghanaian and it could be made meaningful to the Ghanaian who already know of the black stools, both as altars of the ancestors and the mundane things which help to remind them of their history, unity, solidarity, continuity and link with the dead, the living and the yet-to-be born. This is why it may be a useful visual art to help people to comprehend the teaching of the church about the nature of the Christian Spirit world (Quarcoo, 1968, pp 60-61).

Similarly, the Our Lady of Mercy Catholic Church at Community One, Tema has a front wall with several adinkra symbols in relief form. The symbols on the wall include *Gye Nyame* (except God—#2), *Nyame dua* (God's altar—#53) and *Mmusuyideɛ* or *Kerapa* (Sanctity or good fortune—#61). Also, the Ghana Christian Council of Churches has incorporated the *dɛnkyɛmmireku funtumireku* (Siamese-twin crocodiles—#308–315) symbol in its corporate logo in order to emphasize the view that the denominations may differ but they can work together to achieve the common goal of bringing the salvation of Christ to all human beings.

Concurrent with the Churches incorporating Akan symbols into their liturgical arts, adinkra cloth makers are increasingly utilizing Church icons as new symbols for the cloth. Examples of Church icons that have been incorporated in the adinkra cloth include *Yesu asendua* (Cross of Jesus—#102–103), *Yesu wuo* (Jesus' death—#100) and *Yesu wusɔre* (the Resurrection of Jesus—#104).

Another recent development in the use of the adinkra symbols is their utilization by the Ghana Publishing Corporation and other publishing companies as book cover designs. Also, the symbols have been incorporated in the logos of institutions like the universities, secondary schools and public and private corporations such as the banks. The Ghana Standard Board, for example uses the *hwehwɛmu dua* (measuring rod or standard of measure—#650–651) symbol obviously to depict the nature of the mission of the Board— to set and verify high standards of product quality for the locally produced or manufactured products.

Other adinkra symbols reflect some social interactions. One of my informants at Asokwa explained the story behind the symbol *Onyame adom nti* (by the grace of God— #124) to me thus: Opanin Kwasi Dwoben was commissioned to print adinkra cloths for the wife of a prominent national political leader in the early 1960's. After the work had been completed, the woman refused to pay the previously agreed upon price. Opanin Dwoben politely asked the woman to take the cloths for no fee at all. As the woman left, he remarked *Onyame nti me nwe ahahan* (by the grace of God, I will not eat leaves— #124). Eating leaves among the Akan is associated with sheep and goats in the house and animals living in the wild. He then later came up with the design, *Onyame adom nti* (by the grace of God—#124) to remind himself and tell the world about his encounter with

Denkyɛmfunafu
- #308

Yesu wusɔre -
#104

Yesu
asɛnnua -
#102

Hwehwɛmu
dua - #650

Nyame
adom nti -
#124

Ma w'ani
nsɔ - #465

Dadeɛ bi twa
- #565

Seantie yɛ
musuo -
#714

the woman.[2]

There are several of the adinkra symbols that are linked to *anansesɛm*—folk stories. Some of these stories were told to me by some of the cloth producers or bystanders as I interviewed the cloth producers at Ntonso and Asokwa. I will illustrate with three of the many stories that are linked to some of the adinkra symbols: *ma w'ani nsɔ dea wowɔ* (be content with your lot—#465), *dadeɛ bi twa dadeɛ bi mu* (some iron can break others—#565) and *seantie yɛ mmusuo* (disobedience is disastrous—#714).

The symbol *ma w'ani nsɔ dea wowɔ* (be content with your lot—#465) is linked to the story in which a man decides to commit suicide rather than live in poverty. The man looks for the tallest tree in the forest to hang himself so that no one will find him out. He decides to leave his clothes under the tree for he came to this world naked and he would leave it naked. As soon as he gets to the top of the tree and he makes the noose to put around his neck, he noticed someone running away with his clothes which made him realize that there is someone else poorer than he is. The man quickly climbs down the tree to chase after the other person to get his clothes back. When he catches up with the other person, the other person gives back the clothes and tells the man: *ma w'ani nsɔ dea wowɔ na nea ahia no ne nea wɔawu*—"be content with your lot for the poor person is the dead person. While one has life, one has to make the best of it for life is an opportunity the Creator has given us to do something that is worthwhile."

The story linked to the symbol *dadeɛ bi twa dadeɛ bi mu* (some iron can break others—#565) is a metaphor the Akan use to express the idea that no one is unconquerable. This image derives from the use of chisel or hacksaw (metal) to cut another metal. The story is told of how the leopard taught its cubs to cry: "There is nothing in this world that can overcome us." One day when the mother leopard left to go hunting to feed her cubs, a deer stopped by the leopard's den. He taught the cubs to cry: "There is something in this world that can overcome us." When the mother leopard returned and heard her cubs cry the way the deer had taught them, she was very angry. She decided to teach the deer a lesson in minding his own business. The next day as mother leopard left to go hunting, she encountered the deer. Mother leopard demanded an explanation from the deer why he would teach her cubs to cry: "There is something in this world that can overcome us." Before the deer could utter a word of explanation, the mother leopard jumped to attack him. The deer was nimble-footed and was able to jump to the side, making the leopard miss him. The nd mother leopard fell into a thicket of thorns and was fatally injured. As she lay bleeding to death, the deer went to call the cubs to come and see what had happened to their mother. When the cubs came to the scene, they realized that their mother had died. The deer then told the cubs: "If there is nothing in this world that can overcome everyone, your mother would not have died. There is something in this world that can overcome everyone." The story teaches the lesson that no one in this world is unconquerable.

The *seantie yɛ mmusuo* (disobedience is disastrous—#714) symbol incorporates lessons of respect for the elderly and social control as contained in the *anansesɛm* (folk story) of the same title. In this story a beautiful young woman refused the suggestion of her parents to marry a young man of their choice. This young woman then set some very stiff requirements to be fulfilled by a young man who wanted to marry her. One such requirement was that the man should be able to shoot an arrow through a fresh egg without cracking the egg-shell. Many a young man who courted her failed to meet these stiff requirements. One day, a monster turned itself into a handsome looking young man and went to court this young woman. He was able to meet the requirements set by the woman so he married her. A week after the marriage rites had been performed the young man decided to take his wife to his 'town.' When the newly-wed couple reached the groom's 'town,' he turned himself into the monster that he really was. The night that the monster was going to eat up the young woman, there came to her rescue none other than the young man who her parents had chosen for her and she had rejected. He rescued her from the monster and took her back to her home where they got married. Her parents admonished her with the proverb: *obi nware ne kuromanni nnu ne ho*—no one does regret from marrying

36

Ananse
antɔn kasa -
#715

Ma w'ani
nsɔ - #465

Dadeɛ bi twa
- #565

Mercedes
Benz - #606

Seantie yɛ
musuo -
#714

Mercedes
Benz - #606

Ɔdɔ bata
akoma ho -
#395

Akoma -
#385

from one's own town. In essence, the devil (that is, one's townsfolk) you know is better than the angel (that is, the stranger) you do not know.

There are numerous accounts of how some of these symbols were developed, particularly in recent years. There is the story of the man who could not afford to buy a Mercedes Benz. He asked for a cloth that is made up of the internationally known logo of the giant automobile manufacturer. If he could not afford to ride in the prestigious car, he could afford to wear its logo in his cloth, hence the benz symbol—#606–607. Mato (1986) catalogues several of these accounts of historical and everyday events.

Sometimes, two or more symbols are placed together to express an idea or a proverb. An example of this is given by the symbol ɔdɔ bata akoma ho (love is in the heart—#395) in which the akoma (heart—#385) and nkotimsefoɔ pua (hairstyle of the queenmother's attendants—#233) are combined. Other examples include owuo kum Nyame (death killed God—#94) and aboa ɔbɛyɛnnam no (predatory animal—#132). Owusu-Ansah (1992), son of Asantehene Prempeh II and a research fellow at the College of Art, University of Science and Technology at Kumasi, has developed several new symbols. Many of his symbols are modifications or adaptations of some of the old symbols, such as gye Nyame (except God—#2–9). In the symbol Onyankopɔn dɔ wo (God loves you—#81), for example, the gye Nyame symbol is modified to incorporate the heart symbol. In the case of symbols such as owuo sɛe fie (death destroys the household—#114–115), asɛm pa asa (the truth is gone—#671), and ɛkaa nsee nkoa (the weaver bird wishes—#491) pictorial signs are combined with alphabetical writing.

The question of authorship of the old adinkra symbols is a very difficult one. Though they might have originated from individuals, no helpful information regarding the authorship of old symbols could be gathered from the cloth producers or from other people who know about the symbols. The authorship of contemporary symbols is, of course, easier to determine. The cloth producers generally come up with the symbols, and several of these have been catalogued by Mato (1986). The court of the Akan chief required each new chief to created new symbols to add to the repertoire of the regal paraphernalia. The chief would request the artisans to create new symbols for certain occasions. Occasionally, individuals may bring their own symbols to be carved and stamped. Examples of symbols that were brought by some individuals to the cloth producers include the koroyɛ (unity—#319) and the benz symbols. Owusu-Ansah's (1992) work is an example of the ingenuity of contemporary artists to modify and add to the time-honored adinkra motifs.

Some of these symbols show direct relationship between the objects they represent, and show less abstraction. Other symbols represent something else other than themselves. For example, nkuruma kɛse (big okra—#195–203) is used to symbolize the benevolence associated with the practice within the Akan extended family system in which adults raise not only their own biological children, but also the children of others. Children are highly treasured, and being able to bear and raise several children successfully gives one status and prestige in the Akan society. In this sense, the adinkra symbols as ideograms and pictograms are to be read in a cultural context. Some of the meanings of the symbols as given by their sources of derivation are described in the following sections in this chapter.

FLORA AND FAUNA

The adinkra symbols include examples of diverse varieties of flora and fauna. By using plants as symbols, Akans recognized the sense of beauty in the realm of vegetal life. They also used these examples not so much as ornaments or decoration but much more as drawings with a symbolic content to express life, growth, fertility, procreation, development, and so on. The indigenous flora is mainly represented by fruits (e.g., nkuruma kɛse—#195–203, bese saka—#575–581), leaves (e.g., ahahan—#701, Nyame adom nti—#124, and adwerɛ—#108), and seeds (e.g., wawa aba—#502–506, and fofoo aba—#481–484).

The symbols based on fauna show how animals have played a very important role as the essential archetypes of all that is instinctive, and as symbols of the principles of material,

Nkotimsefoɔ
pua - #233

Owuo kum
Nyame - #94

Nkotimsefoɔ
pua - #233

Gye Nyame
- #2

Onyankopɔn
dɔ wo - #81

OWUOSEEFIE

Owuo sɛɛ fie
- #114

Koroyɛ -
#319

Nkuruma
kɛse - #195

spiritual, and even cosmic powers. The *ananse ntontan* (spider's web—#32–34), for instance, symbolizes orderliness, architectural creativity, the structure of dwellings and settlement, and the structure of life and society. This symbol also stands for the sun and its rays and the vitality and creative powers of God. In some Akan stories God is referred to as *Ananse Kokuroko* (the Great Spider or the Great Creator). The *ɔkɔdeɛ mmɪwerɛ* (eagle's talons—#263) and *akoo mmɪwerɛ* (parrot's talons—#261–262) also symbolize the snatching abilities and the strength in the claws of the eagle and the parrot.

For earth-bound human beings, birds with their ability to fly were seen as more than an embodiment of earthly faculties. Domestic birds like the chicken must have been an exception. But even the chicken was seen as an archetype of all that is instinctive. The *akokɔ nan* (hen's feet—#424–427) symbol, for example, depicts the motherhood instincts: tender care, firmness, protection, love and discipline. *Akokɔ* (fowl or rooster—# 694–696) depicts gender division of labor (*akokɔbedeɛ nim adekyeɛ nso otie onini ano*—a hen could herself discern the break of the day yet she relies on the cock to announce it), or matrilineage (*akokɔbedeɛ na ne mma di n'akyi*—the chicken follows the hen rather than the rooster). The chicken egg (*tumi te sɛ kosua*—power is like the egg—#329–330) is likened to power as a precious yet delicate thing: it is a source of life that must be handled delicately and firmly. Too much firmness or careless handling may crush the egg. Other human characteristics are still projected onto animals today, in a manner that finds expression in commonly used similes and metaphors. Thus, Akans speak of someone being as "humble as a dog" (*kraman ahobrɛaseɛ*), "dumb as sheep" (*woagyimi te sɛ odwan*), and "as eloquent as a parrot" (*n'ano ate sɛ akoo*).

THE HUMAN FORM AND ITS PARTS

The heart, eye, hand, mouth, and the head are some of the parts of the human body that are used as adinkra symbols. The head is reflected in the symbol *tikorɔ nkɔ agyina* or *tikorɔ mmpam* (one head does not constitute a council—#325–326). This means one person cannot rule a nation by oneself. The eye is used to symbolize love (*ɔdɔ aniwa*—#370), sleepiness and the fragility of the physical self (*anikom nnim awerɛho*—#109–110), self-discipline or being in a state of agitation (*ani bere a, ɛnsɔ gya*—#466–475), agreement (*ani ne ani hyia*—#550), and vigilance (*ɔhene aniwa*—#190–192). The heart is used to express love and devotion (*ɔdɔ firi akoma mu*—#390–392) and patience (*nya aboterɛ*—#385–389). The teeth and tongue symbol (*se ne tɛkerɛma*—#320–322) depicts, in one sense, the interdependence of members of a society in working together to achieve a common goal. In another sense, the symbol represents the reconciling and adjudicating role played by the tongue between the two sets of teeth (Yankah, 1995, p. 49). The hand symbol (*nsa korɔ*—#364–366) represents cooperation or power.

Hairstyles (*pua*) for both men and women served as symbols of status. Women wore varied coiffures to express their social status in terms of age and marital status. Old women wore closely shaven hairstyles (*dansinkran*). The queenmother's attendants wore various kinds of hairstyles (*mmodwewafoɔ pua*—#238–239, and *nkotimsefoɔ pua*—#233–237). Men wore various hairstyles to identify themselves as members of special groups, for instance executioners (*adumfoɔ*), key bearers (*nkwantanan*—#230), and court heralds (*nseniefoɔ*). Before major festivals and ceremonies men would grow their hair long so that status coiffures and special hairstyles would be made for the occasion. Some of the courtiers had coiffures such as *mpuaansa* (three tufts), *mpuaanum* (five tufts), and *mpuankrɔn* (nine tufts). The adinkra symbol, *gyawuatikɔ* (Gyawu's hairstyle of bravery—#246–252), is one such coiffure that was first worn by the war hero Bantamahene Gyawu.

GEOMETRIC AND ABSTRACT FIGURES

Geometric figures were obviously drawn from observations of nature. For example, the full moon representing circle (*bosom* or *ɔsrane abɔ puru*—#15) and the crescent moon (*ɔsranefa*—#509) representing the semi-circle presented themselves constantly to the Akan's observation. But in nature itself it was difficult for the eyes to meet really straight

Ɛka nsee nko
a - #491

Bese saka -
#575

Asɛm pa asa
- #671

Nkuruma
kɛse - #196

Akokɔ nan -
#425

Akokɔ -
#695

Tikorɔ
mpam - #326

Ɔdɔ aniwa -
#370

lines, with precise triangles or squares, and it seems clear that the chief reason why Akan gradually worked out conceptions of these figures is that their observation of nature was an active one. To meet their practical needs, they manufactured objects that were more and more regular in shape. They built dwellings, stretched bowstrings in their bows, modeled their clay pottery, brought them to perfection and correspondingly formed the notion that a pot is curved, but a stretched bowstring is straight. In short, they first gave form to their material goods and only then recognized form as that which is impressed on material goods and can therefore be considered by itself as an abstraction from the material goods. In similar ways notions of geometric magnitudes of length, area and volume as well as fractional parts (e.g., *abunu*—half and *abusa*—third) and numbers arose from practical activities and observation of nature.

Antubam (1963) explains the symbolic significance of the circle, semi-circle, oval, triangle, squares and rectangles, and other geometric and abstract figures. The circle (*puru*— #15) symbolizes "the presence and power of God, and sanctity in the male aspect of society"(p. 105). Sarpong (1974, p. 101) writes that "the circle is the symbol of the presence and power of God." It also "stands for the life-stream which, as it were, flows continuously." The notion of a circle is embodied in such symbols as *Nyame dua* (God's altar—#53–60), *ananse ntontan* (spider's web—#32–34), *mate masie* (I have heard and kept it—#652– 654), *mpua anum* (five tufts—#223–229), *adinkrahene* (king of the adinkra symbols— #178–185), and *sunsum* (spirit or soul—#35–36). The concentric circles signify the universe and its creator. Only the Creator of the universe, like the creator of the circle, knows its beginning and its end (#178–185).

The square and the rectangles stand for "sanctity in the male aspect of both God and man" (Antubam, 1963, p. 106). They depict such qualities attributed to the nature of God as perfection in wisdom, honesty, justice, courage, fairness, mercy, perpetual growth, or incarnation. The square or rectangular notion (*anannan* or *ahinanan*) is embodied in such symbols as *kerapa* (#61–65, 67–69), *nsaa* (#655–659), *aban* (#138–147), *fihankra* (#429– 434), *mframadan* (#435), *nkyɛmu* (#674–675), *kurontire ne akwamu* (#327), *funtumfurafu* (#308–314), *dame dame* (#669) and *blɔk* (#438–443).

The semi-circle as represented by the crescent moon (*ɔsrane* or *ɔsranefa*—#509) symbolizes the female aspect of society. It is a symbol of fertility. "It bears with it all the bounty of the female, tender kindness, grace, and sereneness" (Antubam, 1963, p. 108). Sarpong (1974, p. 102) says the crescent moon shape "bears with it all the beauty and female qualities of the woman—tender kindness, gracefulness and serenity." The adinkra symbols *ɔsrane* (or *ɔsranefa*) and *ɔsrane ne nsoromma* depict this notion of the semi-circle.

The straight or upright cross (*mmeramutene*—#20–21 or *asennua*—#102–103) appears in several adinkra symbols such as *mmeramutene* (male cross—#20–21), *aban* (castle—#138–147), *kerapa* (sanctity—#61–69), *Nyame nwu na mawu* (I die only when God dies—#46–49), *akomantoaso* (joined hearts—#401), *Yesu asennua* (cross of Jesus— #102–103), and *donnontoaso* (doubled drum—#407–415). It symbolizes "the rightful or pious interference of a male parent on earth" (Sarpong, 1974, p. 102). The female cross (*mmeramubere*—#22–4) in the form of X represents "ill-will, negative attitude or evil intention." From this basis "it is a taboo to cross legs; it is bad manners and regarded as contempt of court if one is in an Akan traditional court," and if one is caught sitting with the legs crossed in the Akan traditional court, one may be charged with contempt of the court (Sarpong, 1974, p. 102). The two crosses (*mmeramutene* and *mmeramubere*) symbolize the various attributes of the two sexes which form the very core of Akan gender beliefs and sexual behaviors in the society. These beliefs affect almost all aspects of Akan behavior, from marital relations, care of menstruation and pregnancy, adultery beliefs, and ideas about kinship relations, to details concerning the nature of ancestral propitiation, inheritance, and funerary rites.

The triangle (*ahinansa*—#717–718), as incorporated in the medallion called *adaeboɔ*, symbolizes *Nyame* (God) as the ruler of the universe which is a continuum of the sky

Ɛse ne
tɛkerɛma -
#322

Nsakorɔ -
#364

Nkotimsefoɔ
pua - #233

Gyawu atikɔ
- #250

Puru - #15

Nyame dua -
#56

Sunsum -
#35

Mpua anum -
#223

(*ewimu*), the earth (*asase*) and under the earth (*asamando*). The triangle also symbolizes the pride of state. The triangle is depicted by such other symbols as Ɔdomankoma (creator—#12–13), *Nyame aniwa* (God's eyes—#174), and *Onyankopɔn bɛkyerɛ* (God will provide—#129).

Other geometric and abstract figures include the chevron or inverted V, which represents growing anew or the vitality of fresh growth (Antubam, 1963). The chevron shape is incorporated in symbols like the *mmodwewafoɔ pua* (hairstyle of the queen's attendants—#238–239), *asambo* (chest feathers of the guinea fowl—#374–376), and *ɔwɔ aforo adobɛ* (snake climbs the raffia palm tree—# 345–346).

SOCIAL CHANGE

Hunter and Whitten (1976, p. 409) point out that "writing systems are rich sources of information about language change in general, about the history of specific languages, and about the structures of past languages." Changes occurring in the society serve as sources for new ideas and new symbols. As language, the adinkra system of writing has built on tradition and incorporated new ideas, symbols, and words. There is the increased use of the phonological scripts. This is evidenced, for example, by the use of symbols such as ABCD (#700), *asɛmpa asa* (the truth is gone—#671), and *ɛkaa obi nkoa* (someone wishes—#489).

As a record of history, the adinkra symbols show evolutionary developments in the cultural, historical, and social relationships that have occurred and continue to occur in the society. With time, the adinkra cloth has absorbed most of the existing symbols from other Akan arts and created new ones; it has tended to add and accumulate and appropriate symbols from other cultures to reflect the dynamic nature of the language of the Akan. As a reflection of the changes society is experiencing, the adinkra symbols themselves have undergone changes in size and design.

Akan believe that society is dynamic. This belief is implied by the expression associated with the symbol *mmerɛ dane* (time changes—#685). The dynamic forces that impinge on society result in changes in the society. These changes may be due to fundamental laws of nature and demographic and technological developments, among other factors. The fundamental laws of nature that are encoded in the adinkra symbols include development and self-preservation. Development is indicated by symbols such as *mmofra bɛnyini* (the young shall grow—#421) and *woyɛ abofra a* (while you are young—#461). Self-preservation is encoded in several symbols such as *nni awu* (thou shall not kill—#478) and *ɔbra yɛ bɔ'na* (life is a struggle—#547). One is also urged to adapt one's self to suit the changing times and conditions as indicated by the expression *mmerɛ dane a, dane wo ho* (when times change, adapt yourself—#692).

Several of the symbols in the adinkra cloths record social changes that have been brought about by both external and internal factors. For example, the *aban* (castle, fortress—#138–147), *kurontire ne akwamu* (council of state—#327), *ɔhene tuo* (king's gun—#258–260), *UAC nkanea* (UAC lights or chandeliers—#621), benz—(#606–607), television—(#608–612), and *sedeɛ* or *serewa* (cowrie shell—#591–596) symbols record specific technological developments and historical events that led to particular changes and factors that influenced the direction of such changes in the Asante (Akan) and Ghanaian society. Some symbols point to selective borrowing of ideas from other societies. *Ɛtuo* (gun—#258–260), for example, came with the Europeans. It has been incorporated not only in the language, but also into important political as well as funeral rituals of the Akan. When the king-elect takes the oath of office he is given the *ɔhene tuo* (king's gun—#258–260) which he fires to demonstrate his ability to honor his responsibility as the military commander-in-chief to ensure protection, security, and peace of the society. During funerals the gun is fired in the morning to signal the beginning of the funeral, and is fired again in the evening to mark the end of the funeral for the day. The gun salute also serves "as an important means of announcing the event of death and the journey of the deceased to both the living and the dead, near and far" (Nketia, 1969, p. 144, fn 2).

Aban - #140

Blɔk dan -
#438

Ɔsrane -
#509

Mmermutene
- #20

Yesu
asɛnnua -
#102

Puru - #15

Ahinansa -
#717

Mmɔdwewafoɔ
pua - #238

The symbol *kurontire ne akwamu* (council of state—#327), for example, records the military and governmental structural changes introduced by Osei Tutu in the 17th century. Osei Tutu underwent *ahemfie adesua* (palace training) in statecraft and governance in Denkyira and Akwamu prior to becoming the Asantehene. During his reign he applied some of the knowledge and skills he had acquired from his "schooling" in Denkyira and Akwamu. He was superbly supported in this venture by the legendary Ɔkɔmfo Anɔkye. These changes not only resulted in the strengthening of the Asante military capacity, but also in laying the foundation for increased bureaucratization of the governmental system (Wilks, 1975, 1993).

The *aban* or *abansoro* (fortress, palace, castle or two-story building—#138–147) symbolizes, in the words of McCaskie (1983, p. 28) "an iconic representation of Culture as an idea." It also records the special relationship between Asante and Elmina. As Yarak (1986) suggests, "wealthy Ɛdena [i.e., Elmina], *vrijburgher* [free citizens] and Dutch merchants placed skilled artisans at the disposal of the Asantehene to aid in the construction of the king's 'stone house' at Kumasi during 1819–21." This castle was made of carved stone and was completed in 1822 during the reign of the Asantehene Osei Bonsu. It was roofed with brass laid over an ivory framework, and the windows and doors were cased in gold, and the door posts and pillars were made of ivory (McLeod, 1981). Wilks (1975) referred to the *aban* as "The Palace of Culture." The 'stone house' or two-story building (*abansoro* or *abrɔsan*) represented an adaptation of the structural form of the European castles and forts and architectural designs on the coast. This castle was ransacked and destroyed by the British during the 1874 British-Asante War.

The social changes that the adinkra symbols record are not limited to the changes of the past; contemporary changes taking place in the larger Ghanaian society have been and continue to be captured by the adinkra symbols. The adinkra symbols for Mercedes Benz (# 606–607), television (#608–612) and Senchi bridge (#628–632), for example, show some of the new technological changes and the new vocabulary that have been introduced into the country. They serve as new status symbols and indicators of economic development in the society. Even though the television was introduced into Ghana only in 1965, it has had a tremendous impact on the entire nation. On the other hand, the UAC *nkanea* symbol (UAC lights or chandeliers—#621) does not merely depict the introduction of street electric lights. It also points to the ubiquitous presence and dominant influence of the UAC (Unilever) Group of Companies and other foreign companies in Ghana as a result of the incorporation of the Ghanaian economy into the world capitalist system.

Kookoo dua (cocoa tree—#573), *bese saka* (bunch of cola nuts—#575–581), and *abɛ dua* (palm tree—#574) are examples of symbols that record about crops that have played important roles in the economy of the society at different times over the years. *Bese* (cola nut) was very important in the trans-Saharan trade long before Europeans had direct contact with the Akan. *Abɛ dua* became a very important source of vegetable oil for making soap and greasing machines in the industrialization of Europe. Cocoa became important only after the 1880's. Since then it has played a very significant role in the incorporation of the Ghanaian economy into the global system. It symbolizes new sources of wealth and the enterprise of the Ghanaian farmer. In the late 1950's and early 1960's, Ghana supplied about 25–50 percent of the world's cocoa. Cocoa has brought tremendous changes in land ownership and tenure systems, inheritance rights, and some disastrous family relations as well as changes in political developments in the country. Between 1903 and 1930, cocoa production brought both land and labor into the market, and radically transformed the relations of production (Kay, 1972). Busia (1951, p. 127) stated as a measure of what the Asante considered to be the disastrous effects of cocoa on family relations that "cocoa *sɛɛ abusua, ɾaepae mogya mu*—cocoa ruins the family, divides blood relations." Cocoa production has given rise to very destructive land disputes that have wrecked families and villages. Chiefs became willing accomplices in the new scramble for land that disrupted the unity and integrity of traditional society. Ninsin (1991, p. 24) writes:

41

Ɔwɔ aforo
adobɛ - #346

Asɛm pa asa
- #671

Ɛka obi nko
a - #489

Mmerɛ dane
- #685

Mmɔfra
benyini -
#421

Ɔbra yɛ
bɔna - #547

TV - #610

Ɛtuo - #259

In the wake of this new scramble, the value of land as a commodity soared. Chiefs responded by, once more, turning communal lands into a source of private wealth: they alienated communal lands to prospective cocoa farmers under various forms of tenancy arrangements.

By the 1920s, these developments had seriously disturbed social peace. For example, the extensive involvement of chiefs in land disputes and destoolments had severely breached the authority of chiefs as well as the stability of the institution of chieftancy itself.

Furthermore, the devastating effect of the cocoa disease that afflicted acres of farms in the 1940s and 1950s gave rise to the expression: *Sɛ wo yɛ kookoo na anyɛ yie a, san konu wo abɛ*—If you fail as a cocoa farmer, you better turn to the palm tree. For Ghana, cocoa has accentuated the country's fragile economy as vicious cocoa price fluctuations on the world commodity market have had devastating effects on the country's balance of payments position particularly in the 1960s and 1970s.

In religion, *asɔredan* (place of worship—#89), *Yesu asennua* (cross of Jesus—#102–103), *Yesu wuo* (Jesus's death—#100) and other symbols about Christianity also point to the pervasive influence of Christianity in the country. The Akan who in the past did not build temples in order to worship the Creator have no problem now going to the *asɔredan* (place of worship—#89) on Fridays, Saturdays, or Sundays to worship the Creator. Indigenous religious festivals such as Odwira and Yam Festival have been overshadowed by new religious festivals such as Christmas (*Abibirem Buronya*—#107) and Easter, symbolized by *Yesu wusɔre* (Jesus's resurrection—# 104). In some instances, traditional religious practices such as naming ceremony and funerals have come under severe attacks by Christian religious leaders who at the same time have appropriated some of the Akan symbols, for example, *gye Nyame* (#2-9) and *Nyame dua* (#53-60) as their own. On the other hand, there has been similar influence of Akan symbols on Christianity in Ghana. I have already mentioned in the early sections of this Chapter how the Christian Church has adopted some of the adinkra symbols into its liturgical arts. Obeng (1991, 1995) also shows how the Catholic Church, in at least the Kumasi diocese, has incorporated some of the adinkra symbols and their ceremonial usage into the annual Corpus Christi celebrations of the Church. The work, **Adinkra Oration** by Angela Christian published in 1976 further illustrates the effort by the Church to incorporate Akan symbols into the Christian theology. Christian uses twenty-seven symbols for which she quotes passages from the Bible to express similar thoughts and sentiments conveyed by the Akan with their symbols.

Some symbols have been utilized to reflect and comment on contemporary political developments in the greater Ghanaian society. Even though some of these symbols might have been designed and used long before they became associated with new political developments in the country, such political developments made these symbols more popular or notorious. The *akofena* (state sword—# 164–169), *aban* (castle—#138–147) and *kookoo dua* (cocoa tree—#573) symbols have been incorporated into the Ghana national coat-of-arms, which is itself carved as an adinkra symbol (*ɔman asɛnkyerɛdeɛ*—#368). Other examples of the adinkra symbols that have been associated with contemporary political developments include the use of *akokɔnini* (rooster or cockerel—#694–696), *ɛsono* (elephant—#219–220), *kookoo dua* (cocoa tree—#573), *abɛdua* (palm tree—#574), *awia* or *ewia* (sun—#27), and *ɔhene kyiniiɛ* (king's umbrella—#170) as emblems and signs for various political parties from about the 1940s. *Ebi te yie* (some people are better seated, or better placed—#600–602) gained popularity in Ghanaian political discourse during the interregnum of the National Liberation Council (NLC) military junta from early 1966 to late 1969.

Some of my informants at Asokwa, Ntonso and Bonwire explained how the *akokɔnini* (rooster or cockerel—#694–696) symbol was popularized and identified with the

Kurontire ne
Akwamu -
#327

Ɛtuo - #260

Aban - #146

UAC nkanea
- #621

Aban - #142

TV - #608

Kookoo dua
- #573

Senchi Bridge
- #628

Convention People's Party's (CPP) red cockerel symbol in the late 1950's and early 1960's; the *kookoo dua* (cocoa tree—#573) together with *kɔtɔkɔ* (porcupine—#264–265) was identified with the National Liberation Movement (NLM) in the 1950's; *awia* (sun—#27) with the Progress Party (PP) in 1969-1972; and *abɛdua* (palm tree—#574) with the People's National Party (PNP) in 1979-1981.

On the other hand some of these informants were quick to deny any relation between *ɔhene kyiniiɛ* (king's umbrella—#170) and the National Democratic Congress's *akatamanso* umbrella symbol. The informants pointed out that what was in the adinkra cloth was the chief's umbrella, hence the name *ɔhene kyiniiɛ*. When asked why one of the Asantehene's umbrella had the name *akatamanso*, one of the informants quickly explained that in the adinkra cloth he made sure that he deliberately turned the umbrella symbol upside down to show his indignation at the NDC party for appropriating "sacred" chieftaincy symbolism in order to gain legitimacy.

In the adinkra cloth production process one notices changes in the types of fabric used, but very little or no change in the dyeing and stamping processes. No longer do the printers use locally woven fabric, but more and more use is made of factory-produced cloth that already has some designs on it. Some printers make use of rubber foam padding in place of old rags. In 1999 during a quick visit to Ntonso, I witnessed the use of screen-printing technique in the production of adinkra cloths. The fabric is woven on a broad loom (about six inches wide) using the plain weave technique. The fabric is screen-printed using factory-made fabric paint; and, then the strips are sewn together by hand (*nwɔmu*) or on an overlock (interlock) or regular sewing machine.

MULTIPLE MEANINGS

Symbols are sometimes ambiguous and therefore open to several interpretations. This characteristic of symbols gives rise to fluidity of meanings. That is, a symbol does not have fixed and, therefore, static meaning. A symbol takes on meaning in some context. This characteristic of symbols may be illustrated by the word "school." There are several views and assumptions held about this word by different people. Some people view it as a place of learning, a process of learning (e.g., formal vis-a-vis informal learning), place of work, place of domination, an authority system, a group of fish, or a group of persons who hold a common doctrine or follow the same teacher. Another example is the word mouse. In everyday usage, a mouse is some type of rodent. In computer usage, mouse is an input device.

A symbol need not have a single agreed upon meaning. However, though the meanings individuals attribute to symbols will vary, interpretations are not entirely random or personal. "One characteristic of the symbol," as Saussure (1966, p. 68) points out, "is that it is never wholly arbitrary; it is not empty, for there is a rudiment of a natural bond between the signifier and the signified. The symbol of justice, a pair of scales, could not be replaced by just any other symbol, such as a chariot."

Cultural symbols evoke different meanings and feelings for different groups of people in any given society. For example, the Statue of Liberty in the U. S. means different things for various groups of immigrants in the country. For American Indians and African Americans, this cultural symbol evokes mainly negative feelings or lack of reverence. The use of the statue to portray female and maternal images in depicting human ideals: liberty and justice exposes some irony in French and American politics—women had no vote in either France or America in 1886 when the statue was unveiled.

Within a society there is a range of associations and meanings that are attached to most symbols. As participants in a common social order, each member interacts with other members of that order. Through these interactions the members of the society encounter ideas and phenomena, and the members learn from each other definitions for such ideas and phenomena. Meanings and interpretations peculiar to each member become part of the social meanings and interpretations. Through social interaction a society ensures general agreement on how symbols will be interpreted. Within that broad agreement,

Kurontire ne
Akwamu -
#327

Abɛ dua -
#574

Bese saka -
#580

Asɔre dan -
#89

Yesu
asɛnnua -
#103

Abibirem
buronya -
#107

Akokɔ -
#694

Awia - #27

each individual member may develop specialized refinements of meanings. The result is that there is enough general agreement to communicate with each other, yet there is enough individual variation to make the meaning of any symbol ambiguous. This is because "it is the very essence and potency of symbols," as Cohen (1979, p. 87) puts it, "that they are ambiguous, referring to different meanings, and are not given to precise definitions."

Adinkra symbols, as cultural symbols, are no exception to this characteristic of symbols. Some adinkra symbols have precise and unambiguous meanings. Other adinkra symbols have multiple meanings. In this respect, the adinkra cloths function in a way that is similar to certain aspects of language as described by such linguists as Ferdinand de Saussure. He identifies what he calls the quality of "mutability," by which he means that the linguistic sign, being dependent on a rational principle, is arbitrary and can be organized at will (Saussure, 1966). This suggests that linguistic signs change their meaning over space and time. Similarly one sees that the messages communicated by the symbols shift in meaning depending on the context in which they operate.

The meanings of adinkra symbols are heavily context dependent and there is considerable variability in how the symbols are understood by different social strata and taste groupings. The meaning of some of the symbols slightly changes from place to place, while some symbols represent more than one proverb or maxim in the same locality. This characteristic of ambiguity is sometimes exploited to strategic advantage. For example, the *dɛnkyɛm* (crocodile—#215–218) symbol is used to express "adaptability," a view that is based on an observation of the fact that the crocodile lives in water, yet it does not behave like fish; it breathes oxygen directly through its nostrils unlike the fish that absorbs oxygen from water through its gills. From this observation the symbol means adaptability of one to changing circumstances in life. The same symbol expresses "greatness of power," a view that is based on another observation of the way the crocodile carries its eggs in its mouth. This behavior of the crocodile is taken to symbolize the idea that the crocodile is powerful to the extent that it can swallow a stone. A king wearing an adinkra cloth with the symbol will be communicating to his subjects how powerful he is.

The symbol *nkyinkyimiɛ* (zigzag—#499–501) is interpreted as zigzag in one sense or change and adaptability in another sense. Cowrie shells (*serewa* or *sedeɛ*—#591–596) were once used as currency and, therefore, symbolize wealth and affluence. They are also used by priests for religious purposes, and they, therefore, symbolize sanctity. On the other hand, *bese saka*—(#575–581)—expresses wealth when *bese* is used as currency or seen as an important cash crop. *Bese*, when used to welcome visitors, symbolizes hospitality. In another context *bese* is used as a symbol of wisdom and knowledge as in the aphorism: *Bese pa ne konini ahahan yetase no ɔbanyansafoɔ* (It takes the knowledgeable and wise person to distinguish between the very similar looking leaves of the red and white kola tree—#575–581).

Also, the meaning of a symbol is often obscure because it involves time and space, cultural, and historical relationships which are not always clearly understood. Since the symbolic meaning is obscure and subject to various interpretations, a few particular symbols have more than one name and meaning in different localities. For example, some people call the *blɔk* (cement or cinder block—#437–443) *dame dame* (checkers—#668–669) and vice versa. *Ahahan* (leaves—#701) has been associated with different interpretations in different areas and/or at different times such as *wodu nkwanta a, gu me ahahan* (leave me a sign at the intersection), *yenkɔte aduro a, ɛne ahahan* (when we gather material for herbal medicine, it is none other than a leaf), or *bese pa ne konini ahahan, yɛtase no ɔbanyansafoɔ* (it requires skill and experience to distinguish between the similar looking leaves of the red kola and white kola leaves).

In this chapter, I have given examples of how the adinkra cloth producer used signs and symbols to translate concrete information into abstract markings. Such usage served to remove the data from their context. For example, the sighting of the moon as *ɔsranefa* (crescent moon) or *ɔbosom abɔ puru* (full moon) was abstracted from any simultaneous events such as atmospheric or social conditions (e.g., partly cloudy night). These signs

Ɔhene
kyiniiɛ -
#170

Ɛsono -
#219

Ebi te yie -
#600

Akokɔ -
#696

Dɛnkyɛm -
#218

and symbols also separated the knowledge from the person presenting data. For example, the *Onyame adom nti* (by the grace of God—#124) symbol presented the encounter between the cloth producer and his customer in a "cold" and static form, rather than the "hot" and flexible oral medium which involved voice modulation and body language.

In the rest of this book the adinkra symbols are classified on the basis of the concepts inferred from the narratives that are associated with the symbols. In order to discuss what the adinkra cloth producer wrote about Akan political beliefs, governmental organization, social values and family relation several adinkra symbols are grouped together into these broad concept areas. The discussion of these concepts is constrained by the number of adinkra symbols I have been able to identify. This deficiency is not limited to the adinkra system of writing. Hunter and Whitten (1976, p. 409) note that

> Writing systems which depend heavily or exclusively on any one of these three principles—pictograph, ideograph, logograph—are subject to "overloading": unless the range of information to be represented is narrowly limited, a tremendously large number of signs is required.

Adinkra symbols as either a pictographic or ideographic system require a wide number of symbols to represent the wide range of ideas and thoughts of the Akan. This poses an "overloading" problem. The constraints of "overload" and not being able to identify all the adinkra symbols that have ever been used pose problems for a fuller examination of Akan thinking on the various concepts discussed in the following chapters. Cloth, as a main medium in which several of the adinkra symbols have been encoded, is a perishable product. Besides, more new symbols are being created as part of the dynamics of a living language creating the possibility that other adinkra symbols exist somewhere that I have not been able to identify. Or, perhaps I have not been able to draw on the extensive Akan oral literature to provide a more elaborate synthesis of what adinkra cloth and its symbols communicate. Therefore, the discussions that follow in the subsequent chapters should not be construed as limitations of Akan thinking.

ONIPA BE WUNASIKA TE ASE

Onipa bewu - #112

Gye Nyame - #7

Akokɔ - #695

Aban - #138

Ɔhene kɔ hia - #194

Asomdwoeɛ fie - #361

TV - #610

Benz - #607

1. Quarcoo's reference to a sequential arrangement of the adinkra symbols into a sentence is obviously based on the assumption that all writing systems are of a linear form.

2. Appiah, personal interview at Asokwa, May 24, 1994.

3. Boadum, personal interview at Asokwa, May 24, 1996.

4. Appiah, personal interview at Asokwa, May 24, 1994.

5. Yankah (1995, p. 70) writes, "the same [symbol] now stands for the proverb: *Akokɔbere nso nim adekyeɛ* (The hen also knows the dawn of day), conveying a sense of equality [of woman] with man."

6. Akan *ahemfie adesua* is the subject of discussion in the classic, *Forosie* by Efa (1968, 1944).

7. This symbol is said to record the construction of a stone castle in Kumasi that was completed in 1822. Variants of this symbol pre-date the construction of this castle. For example, the cloth collected by Bowdich in 1817 has one of these variants of the *aban* symbol. Other people say aban refers to the British Fort in Kumasi that was built after the !874 Asante-British War. During the 1896-1900 Asante-British War this fort was besieged by Asante soldiers. The siege gave rise to the expression: *Oburoni bɛka abansoro do* - The whiteman will remain trapped in the fort. The word *aban* also refers to the king's palace and the word *abansinase* refers to the area of the ruined palace or the old place of settlement.

8. The *vrijburgher* were mulatto children descended from African mothers and Dutch fathers. They were considered free citizens as they were subject to Dutch law and not to the traditional law of the Elmina (Feinberg, 1969).

9. The King's personal residence in the Manhyia Palace is known as *Abr]sanase*. The word *abr]nsan* is derived from the word *abrɔnsan* (European-styled house). *San* is another word in Akan for *dan* (building or house) as explained to me by Rev. Joseph Yedu Bannerman in a personal interview at Winneba, May 13, 1993. For example, *aburosan* (corn barn), is a raised structure or granary for storing corn.

10. Dantzig (1980, p. vii) refers to the castles and forts along the coast as "a collective historical monument unique in the world: the ancient 'shopping street' of West Africa." In having a castle built in Kumasi, the Asantehene, apparently wanted to redirect the geography of trade once more through Kumasi rather the coastal area.

11. The radio was introduced in Ghana in 1935 as part of the colonial government's effort to control the media in the country.

12. UAC stands for United Africa Company. The Company is a subsidiary of the giant multinational corporation Unilever. One of the first street lights in Kumasi was placed in front of the UAC store in the Adum section of the city and

Koforidua
nhwiren -
#626

UAC nkanea
- #621

Asɔre dan -
#89

Ɔhene
kyiniiɛ -
#170

Ɔman
asɛnkyerɛdeɛ
- #369

Ɔdɔ aniwa -
#370

became an important landmark in the commercial center of the city, hence the name UAC lights (Kusi Boadum, personal interview at Asokwa, May 24, 1994).

13. UAC and other European companies that operated in West Africa formed the Association of West African Merchants (AWAM), through which the companies operated rings and pools to control the West African market to the chagrin of the Africans. "*Awam*" has come to mean collusion and trade malpractice in the Akan language in Ghana. Webster and Boahen (1967, p. 267) indicate that so widespread was the influence of the UAC in the AWAM group of companies that Ghanaians made this remark about the UAC: "The earth is Lord Leverhulme's [head of Unilever, the parent company of UAC] and the fullness thereof."

14. The asøredan was modelled after one of the church buildings at Asokwa according to Appiah in a personal interview at Asokwa, May 24, 1994.

15. The Dutch coat-of-arms (# 369) that is found on the cloth that was given as a gift to King Willem I seems to have been drawn not stamped with a carving.

16. Teacher Nsiah and Agya Yaw Yamaa, personal interview at Ntonso, May 26, 1993; Appiah and Kusi Boadum, personal interviews at Asokwa, May 24, 1994; and Mr. Afranie Duodu and Nana Osei Kwadwo, personal interview at Bonwire, May 24, 1994.

17. In an interview on May 25, 1994 of five cloth stampers at Asokwa who wanted to remain anonymous. The National Democratic Congress (NDC) led by Flt. Lt. J. J. Rawlings came to power in a political party-based election 1992 after nearly eleven years of PNDC military rule under Rawlings. Apparently, their request to remain anonymous lest they may be intimidated explains the seeming silence for adinkra producers to create new or utilize old symbols that directly address the rule of the military in Ghana for the greater part of the country's existence as an independent nation.

18. Compare the meaning of the word "eye" in each of these shifty sentences:
She has a good eye for judging distances.
He poked the thread through the eye of the needle.
Winds whirled around the eye of the hurricane.
An eye for an eye and a tooth for a tooth.

CHAPTER 4

Nyame nwu na mawu
If human beings cease to exist, God ceases to exist

Abɔde
santaan - #1

Gye Nyame -
#2

Puru - #15

Ɔdomankoma
- #12

Asase - #25

Awia - #27

CONCEPTS OF THE UNIVERSE, GOD, SELF, AND SPIRITUALITY

THE UNIVERSE AND GOD

An essential basis of a people's cultural heritage is found in their views of the nature and structure of reality with regard to what is the meaning of existence, what is the nature and structure of the universe (does order exist out there in the world or do humans invent it?), and freedom or the lack thereof to make choices. The Akan view the universe as a creation of a Supreme Being, whom they refer to variously as *Ɔbɔadeɛ*,[1] *Nyame*, *Nyankopɔn*, *Ɔdomankoma*, *Ananse Kokuroko*, *Ɔmaowia*, *Nana*, *Ɔmansuo*, *Toturobonsuo*, and *Twedeampɔn Kwame*.[2] This creator was viewed as being androgynous, that is, the creator was simultaneously male and female, possessing both the masculine and feminine qualities. Yet God is beyond both male and female.

There are several *adinkra* symbols that encode the Akan cosmology regarding beliefs about the origin, structure, and destiny of the universe. There are also symbols that depict Akan beliefs about death and afterlife. The Akan believe that the Creator first created the Heavens, Earth and, the underworld (*Asamando*). The creator then populated the heavens with the sun (*awia*—#27–31), moon (*ɔsrane* or *ɔsranefa*—#509) and stars (*nsoromma*—#116–121), and populated the earth with human beings, plants, rocks, the sea, rivers, and animals. In time, the creator made day and night (*hann ne sum*—#18–19).

The Akan concept of the totality of the universe is depicted by the symbol *abɔdeɛ santaan* (totality of the universe—#1). This symbol incorporates the eye, the rays of the sun, the double crescent moon all of which are part of nature, and the stool which is human made. The universe, according to the Akan worldview, is a natural as well as a social creation.[3] The natural aspect of the universe includes the celestial bodies[4] like the sun (*awia* or *ɛwia*—#27–31), the moon (*ɔsrane*—#509), the stars (*nsoromma*—#116–121), and elements like wind,[5] lightning and thunder (*anyinam ne aprannaa*—#37–38) and water (i.e., rain, *nsuo*—#39–41), as well as human beings and plant and animal lives. One of the expressions the Akan use to express this totality of the universe is: *Ɔdomankoma Ɔbɔade, ɔbɔɔ soro ne asase; ɔbɔɔ ɛwia, ɔbɔɔ ɔsrane ne nsoromma, ɔtɔɔ nsuo, ɔbɔɔ nkwa, ɔbɔɔ nipa, ɔbɔɔ owuo, na ɔte ase daa.* This means God the Creator, He created the cosmos—the heavens and the earth; He created the sun, the moon and the stars and rain; He created life, the human being, and death; the Creator is immortal. The Akan, therefore, believe in a God they regard as the Great Ancestor, the true high God. He is the Creator who has always existed, and will always exist as symbolized by *hye anhye* (unburnable—#42–45) and *Nyame nwu na mawu* (I die only when God dies—#46–49). The Creator is also represented by other symbols such as *Ɔdomankoma* (Creator—#12–13), *puru* (circle—#15), and *Ananse Kokuroko* (spider—#32–34). The circle (*puru*—#15) represents the universe and its creator. Only the creator of the universe, like the creator of a circle, knows its beginning and its end. The *ananse ntontan* (spider's web—#32–34) represents the orderly structure and organization—the grand architectural design—of the universe.

Ɔsrane -
#509

Nsoromma -
#116

Hye anhye -
#42

Nyame
aniwa - #16

Ananse
ntontan - #33

Nyame bɔ
yɛn ho ban -
#76

Asase - #26

Akokɔbdeɛ
ne kosua -
#106

Attributes of God

The symbol *Gye Nyame* (Except God—#2–9) is used to express the view that no one lived who saw the beginning of the universe and no one will live to see its end except God. God is further seen as the Creator par excellence, the Great Beginner or infinitely manifold God (Danquah, 1944). He is also personalized as *Onyankopɔn Kwame Atoapem*, the Great one who appeared on Saturday (Busia, 1954).

In Akan belief, the Creator is the source of all things (*Ɔdomankoma*—#12–13) and there is nothing beyond Him (*Onyankopɔn bɛtumi ayɛ*—#96). No one knows what the day will bring forth except God the Creator (*obi nnim adekyeɛ mu asɛm*—#50). *Nyame yɛ ɔdɔ* (God is love—#81). He has great love for His creatures and He shows His care and compassion for them by providing for their needs (Opoku, 1978, p. 28). It is by the grace of God that we live as depicted by symbols such as (#77; 124; 131). God provides us with sustenance (*Onyankopɔn ma yɛn aduane daa*—God, feed us always—#79). He sees all things (*Brɛakyihunadeɛ, Nyame yɛ huntahunuiɛ*—#16–17), and protects us (*Onyankopɔn bɔ yɛn ho ban*—#76). And He fills the pot of the poor with water (*Nyame na ogu ahina hunu mu nsuo*—#39–41).

Land – Mother Earth

To the Akan what is real is of a dual nature with corporeal-spiritual[6] and male-female components. The Akan see reality as "unity in duality comprising two conflicting elements" (Dzobo, 1992, p. 130). *Nyame* is the Spiritual component—the creator and giver of life. Mother Earth (*Asase Efua* or *Asase Yaa*) is the physical component of the duality—the sustainer of life. The Akan have an image of a masculine God and feminine Earth (hence the female name *Asase Yaa* or *Asase Efua* for Earth and *Onyankopɔn Kwame* or *Kwame Atoapem* for God).[7] The Akan regard *Nyame* as the Elder vis a vis Earth, hence the expression: *Asase tre, na Onyame ne panin* (Of all earth, God is the Elder—#25–26). Akan believe that no one created God, thus God is referred to as *Obiannyɛwo* (The Uncreated One). The Akan believe there is some order to God's creation and they express this in statements such as *bosompo bɛtoo abotan*—the sea was created after rocks. On the other hand, Akan wonder about what God created first in other instances as posed in questions like: *akokɔbedeɛ ne kosua, hwan ne panin?* (the hen and the egg, which came first?—#106).

The symbol *asase yɛ duru* (the Earth is mighty—#25–26) signifies the importance of land. The expression *tumi nyinaa wɔ asase so* (all power is in land) underscores the importance of land to the Akan. *Asase* (land) is not only the sustainer of life, it is also considered as the source of power. It has the power of fertility and it is her spirit that makes plants grow.[8] Mother Earth receives the newly born, sustains the living, and receives the dead back into her womb on internment. Before a grave is dug, a prayer is offered to ask permission of Mother Earth for her child to be buried in her womb (Opoku, 1978).

Akan custom teaches that the way God's gift of land is utilized reflects the spiritual and social fabric of society. For example, Akan consider it an abomination and crime to have sexual intercourse in the fields. People are advised to refrain from polluting the land and its rivers, streams, lakes and the sea or contaminating nature in any way that can be deemed adverse to human life. Proper land use is evidence of faithfulness to God and Mother Earth and is reflected in the health or prosperity of the society. Unjust land use or pollution of the land, on the other hand, is believed to spell social, economic or spiritual disaster, crop failure, and epidemics. The logic here is simply that one cannot expect to do harm and violence to nature and Mother Earth, the bearers of life and existence, without precipitating crises in our economic, social, spiritual, animal, plant and human life.

The Akan believe that land, as sustainer of life, ought to be owned communally.[9] Membership in the matriclan family entitles one to usufruct right in land. This belief has been punctuated and undermined by recent developments in land ownership and tenure that have resulted in individual appropriation and ownership of land. For example, the development of farms on which are planted perennial crops such as cocoa, citrus, and oil

Hye anhye -
#42

Woyε hwan
- #111

Sunsum -
#35

Nyame yε
Ɔhene - #11

Gye Nyame -
#5

Hye anhye -
#45

Agya, Ɔba
ne Sunsum -
#74

palm trees has resulted in individual ownership of land. Urbanization and development of housing for rent have also affected the traditional land ownership.

Self

An important aspect of the Akan cosmology encoded by some of the *adinkra* symbols is the human being's relation to the universe and the Creator. There are symbols that, for example, depict the forces of nature on human beings; the role of humans in the maintenance of life; and Akan attitudes regarding responsibility and initiative as the Akan envision their place within the universe.

The Akan belief is that the human being is made up of a physical part—a system of tissues and bones (*honam* or *nipadua*). The human being is also made up of a system of traits, habits, and attributes; that is, a personality. The Akan believe that while one is a system of tissues and bones and a personality, one is more importantly an enduring unity of experiences, a self.

In the Akan thought, anything which exists in its natural state has *sunsum* (spirit or soul—#35–36). *Sunsum* is the essence of the being or object; its intrinsic activating principle. *Sunsum* is derived ultimately from the Supreme Being, the Creator and source of all existence. The symbol *Onyankopɔn adom nti yεte ase* (By God's grace we live—#77) conveys the Akan belief that without the life-giving force from God, the human being ceases to exist. Another symbol that captures this idea is the one that alludes to the essential nothingness of human beings (*woyε hwan?*—who are you?—#111). Without the spiritual essence, the physical aspect of the human being is fragile and mortal as indicated by the symbols *owuo bεgya hwan* (who will be spared by death?—#99), *owuo de dɔm bεkɔ* (death will claim the multitude—#95), *owuo atwedeε* (death's ladder—#90–93), and *anikum nnim awerεhoɔ* (sleep does not know sadness—#109–110). The *anikum nnim awerεhoɔ* symbol conveys the idea that the spirit may be willing, but the body may be weak.

Akan believe that the human being is created in the image of God and the birth of a child marks the infusion of the spiritual and the physical aspects of life into the human being. The human being as an image of the Supreme Being is born sacred and free of sin (Antubam, 1963). The human being has both a physical body and spiritual part—the soul (*ɔkra, kra* or *sunsum*).[10] This soul is believed to enter the body with the child's first breath at birth. The spiritual part is indestructible (*Nyame nwu na mawu*—#46–49) and imperishable (*hye anhye*—#42–45) and, therefore, lives on after the copreal part of the human being dies. Hence the belief in life after death and reincarnation.

The concept *sunsum* has often been translated from the psychological perspective as personality, ego or character (Busia, 1954; Meyerowitz, 1951). Danquah (1944, p. 22) describes *sunsum* as "the power that sustains a person's character or individuality." Busia (1954, p. 197) writes: "*Sunsum* is that which you [the man] take with you to go to the side of the woman and lie with her; and then the *Onyankopɔn*, the Great One, will take his *kra* and bless your union." Akan view the human being as a trinity (*agya, ɔba ne sunsum krɔnkrɔn*—#74) or triadic composite of *mogya* (blood) which is received from the mother; *sunsum* (spirit, personality) which is received from the father; and *kera* or *kra* (soul, spirituality) which is received from God, the life-giving force. This trinity[11] gives rise to the following relationships:

Mother	Father	God
Mogya	*Sunsum*	*Kra* (*Ɔkra*)
Abusua	*Ntorɔ*	Spirit(Soul, Spirituality)
	(or *Egyabosom*)	

Nkonsa, woyε hwan? Ahemfo koraa yεwo wɔn (Nkonsa, who are you? Even kings are born—#111) symbolizes the Akan idea that without God's grace and the life giving force of God, the human being is essentially nothing. And, what God has ordained no

OWUO
BƐGYA
HWAN

Owuo bɛgya
hwan - #99

Anikum
nnim
awerɛhoɔ -
#110

Nyame nwu
na mawu -
#49

Sunsum -
#35

Nyame yɛ
Ɔhene - #11

Woyɛ hwan
- #111

Nkrabea -
#75

Gye Nyame -
#8

human being can change (*nea Onyankopɔn aka abɔ mu no*—#88, or *asɛm a Onyankopɔn adi asie no*—#72).

Destiny

God is also believed to give to each individual, *nkrabea* (destiny, fate—#75). *Nkrabea* (destiny) is believed to determine the uniqueness and individuality of a person. The unique characteristics of individuals reflect the differences in individuals' destiny. This view is expressed thus: *esono onipa biara ne ne nkrabea* and is indicated by the symbol *nkrabea* (destiny—#75). This view is also indicated by the aphorism: '*Nyame amma akyemfra hwee no, na ɛnyɛ ne ntware ho a*—if God did not give anything at all to the swallow, it is not its swiftness and turning ability' that is associated with the *akyemfra* (swallow—#136–137) symbol. That is, God gave each individual some ability, talent or potential. No one can change the destiny God gives to one (*asɛm a Onyankopɔn adi asie no*—#72). Also, the Akan believe that when God was giving destiny to one no one else was there—*obi rekra ne Nyame na obi foforoɔ ngyina hɔ bi* (Gyekye, 1987).

SPIRITUALITY

Even though the Supreme Being is the ultimate Spirit and the human being has been created in the image of God, the Akan believe that there are lesser spirits (*abosom ne asaman*), some good and some evil. The good ancestors serve as the good spirits that protect the living from the misdeeds of the evil spirits. The Akan believe in the abiding presence and protection of God, the Supreme Being who is always available as an ultimate recourse for those in difficulty. The Akan religious thought is essentially theocentric and theistic, with God at the center of it all. This view is expressed by the symbols Adinkrahene (king of the *adinkra* symbols—#178–185;186–187) and God is king (*Nyame yɛ Ɔhene* —#11).

When prayer is offered to God, He is approached without priests or intermediaries. The Akan believe that everyone has direct access to God, and one's relationship with God is personal and does not require an intermediary or temple. Prayer may be offered at any place for God is Almighty, All-seeing (*Onyankopɔn aniwa hu asumasɛm biara* or *Nyame yɛ huntahunni*, also *Brɛakyihunadeɛ Nyame, ohu asumasɛm biara*—#16–17), and Omnipresent. He is believed to hear the slightest voice and the humblest cry (Sarpong, 1974). The Akan say that if you wish to say something to God, you tell it to the wind. God is invisible, but He is believed to be everywhere just as the air we breathe is everywhere and is invisible.

Akan sacred praises or praise poems are acts of worship and offering to the Supreme Being. The sacred praises of God offer the Akan the opportunity to share in God's strength and glory, His beneficence and beauty and in His creation and His active care of it. The Akan praise God as King (*Onyame yɛ ɔhene*—#11). God rescues the humble and helps the needy. The Akan, in this respect, say: *Ankonam boafoɔ ne Onyankopɔn* (God is the helper of the lonely—#270) and *aboa a onni dua no, Nyame na ɔpra ne ho* (God cares for the destitute). Also, God fills the pot of the lonely (*Nyame na ɔgu ahina hunu mu nsuo*—#39–41). The Akan also praise God as the physician that has the cure for all diseases. God is believed to look out for the interest of the disadvantaged. An example of this attribute of God is depicted by the symbol *wobu kɔtɔ kwasea* (if you fool the crab—#623) which is associated with the maxim: *wobu kɔtɔ kwasea a, Nyame hunu wo to* (If you fool the crab God sees your rear end).

To say that the Akan did not establish temples for worship of God nor did they have a hierarchy of priests is not to suggest that God was not regularly mentioned in prayer. Almost every Akan prayer begins with the mention of God. The Akan also see the need to make periodic and occasional supplication and sacrificial offers (*Mmusuyideɛ*—#61–69, *Nyame Dua*—#53–60) not only to invoke the good spirits to protect them from the machinations of the evil, but also to atone for any misdeeds and evil intentions of one or the community. *Nyame dua* (#53–60) is the altar from which *Nyankonsuo* (God's water)

51

Asɛm a
Onyame -
#72

Krapa - #62

Nyankopɔn
aniwa - #17

Gye Nyame -
#3

Adinkrahene
- #178

Ankonam
boafoɔ -
#270

Asɔre dan -
#89

Nyame dua -
#60

was used to bless members of a household when purification and propitiation ceremonies were performed. On such occasions, the head of the household (if it is a household ritual) or the abusuapanin or his deputy (head of the family, if it is a family ritual) serves as the "religious leader" or master of ceremony.

When the Akan pray, as reflected by the symbols (*mesrɛ nkwa tenten ne nkɔsoɔ ma wo*—#52, and *momma yɛmmɔ mpaeɛ*—#70), they invoke the powers of *Nyame* and *Asase Yaa*.[12] Life, fertility, abundance, prosperous and long life, peace, God's grace and protection—these basic virtues form the recurrent theme of most Akan prayers. These prayers show that Akan value human life above all material things. Some of the ideas expressed in an Akan prayer are best captured by the following:

> *Yɛsrɛ wo nkwa,*
> *Yɛsrɛ wo adom;*
> *Ɛmma yɛnwu awia wuo,*
> *Ɛmma yɛnwu anadwo wuo;*
> *Yɛkɔ nnae a, yɛnwo ba;*
> *Yedua aduadeɛ a, ɛnso aba pa;*
> *Ma asomdwoeɛ mmra wiase;*
> *Ma nkɔsoɔ mmra ɔman yi mu,*
> *Ma ɔman yi nyɛ porɔmporɔm.*
> We pray for life and pray for grace
> Let not death be with us by day or by night;
> May we be blessed with children,
> And may what we plant bear good fruit.
> Let there be peace in the world,
> And may there be prosperity
> In this land abundantly.

In the past a ritual, *mmusuyideɛ*[13] (a purification as well as a protective ceremony), was performed for the township or village. As part of the ritual all streets of townships were swept each morning and evening to remove mystical danger and to prevent disease or death from entering the townships. Even though the Akan pray to God, they did not institutionalize a public practice of building temples and a lineage of priests to worship Him. The Christian and Islamic ways of worship have become prevalent and these days there are places of worship (*asɔre dan*—#89). According to Sarpong (1974, p. 13), it needs to "be pointed out that the contention of a few nineteenth century writers who raised doubts about the originality of the Ghanaian conception of God is completely inadmissible." Christian teaching has, for example, confirmed the Akan conception of the soul. The Christians teach that God made the human being in His own image and the Akan belief is that the Creator gives a bit of His spirit to everyone whom God sends to the earth.

There are some religious rituals associated with the *kra* (soul)—one's spiritual being. *Akradware* (soul washing) ceremony is celebrated on one's *kra da* (soul day)—the day of the week on which one was born. It is a cleansing ceremony and is celebrated on one's birth day because that is when one's soul (*kra*) can be communed with. There is also another ceremony, *ntorɔ adware* which the father and his children used to observe. *Adwera adware*, on the other hand is a cleansing ceremony one celebrates to mark the escape from misfortunes such as a long bout of illness. *Adwera* (watery shrub—#108) leaves may be used in both *akradware* and *ntorɔ adware*.

Hope and God's Grace

Nyame dua (God's altar—#53–60) symbolizes the dependence of human beings on God as God is the source of life and hope. Opoku (1978, p. 33) has observed that: "Among the regalia of the Asantehene is an Onyamedua stump covered with leopard skin, which is

Mesre nkwa
tenten - #52

Momma
yɛmmɔ
mpaeɛ - #70

Adwera -
#108

Adepa bɛba -
#125

Krapa - #63

Onyakopɔn
bɛkyerɛ -
#129

Anidasoɔ
nsoromma -
#123

Nsoromma -
#117

often carried by an attendant following closely behind him in procession. This symbolizes the dependence of not only the Asantehene but also the entire Asante nation on God."

The Akan believe that the human being is like the star that is dependent on God (*Ɔba nyankonsoromma te Nyame so na ɔnte ne ho so*—#116–121). There is the hope that one's star will shine one day (*da bi me nsoroma bɛpue*—#693). This serves as a motivating factor for one to keep on in life with the expectation that there is light at the end of the tunnel. Other expressions of hope and expectation captured by adinkra symbols include *ade pa bɛba* (some-thing good will be forthcoming—#125), *Onyankopɔn bɛkyerɛ* (God will provide—#129), *Onyankopɔn adom nti biribiara bɛyɛ yie* (by God's grace all will be well—#131), *Onyankopɔn bɛyɛ me kɛse* (God will make me great—#130), and *biribi wɔ soro* (there is something in the heavens—#126–128). In the past the *biribi wɔ soro* symbol was hung above the lintel of a chamber door in the king's palace for the king to touch three times repeating each time the expression: *Nyame biribi wɔ soro na ma ɛmmɛka me nsa* (God there is something in the heavens, let it reach me). This was to wish the king God's blessing, good luck, high hope and good expectation as he went out to carry out his duties each morning. On the other hand, the symbol *kerapa* (sanctity or good luck—#61–69) was woven into a bedside mat on which the king would step three times for God's protection and good luck before going to bed at night (Rattray, 1927). Another symbol used to depict hope and expectation is *anidasoɔ nsoromma* (star of hope—#122–123) which is associated with the expression: *anidasoɔ wɔ wiem* (there is hope in the heavens above).

DUALISM AND DIALECTICS

Spiritual and Physical

The Akan belief is that the universe, as well as the human being, is both spiritual and corporeal (that is, physical), and that while the corporeal aspect may perish and die, the spiritual aspect is immortal and imperishable. Akans also believe in a physical world (the earth—*asase*) and spiritual world (soro - sky) that form part of a continuum: heaven and earth (*soro ne asase*—#14). These beliefs of dualism and the imperishability of the spiritual part of the human being are marked by such symbols as *sunsum* (spirit or soul—#35–36), *hye anhye* (unburnable—#42–45), *Nyame nwu na mawu* (I die only when God dies—#46–49).

A significant aspect of the Akan dualism is reflected in the relationship between the physical and the spiritual. The spiritual component is the life force in the human being. While the spiritual part of the human being is indestructible (e.g. *Nyame nwu na mawu*—#46–49), the physical part is capable of being destroyed if proper care is not taken or when death occurs. The physical part decays or goes back to the womb of Mother Earth and the spiritual part goes to *Asamando*. The spiritual part is later reincarnated in another child. In this sense, Akan believe in life after death and reincarnation.

Male and Female

Another significant aspect of the Akan dualism is reflected in the relationship between the male and female. Male is associated with the right, spirit of conception (*ntorɔ*), auspicious omens, normalcy and coolness, strength, superiority, and the center. The female is associated with blood of conception (*mogya*), red, warmth and heat, inferiority, weakness, inauspicious omens, and witchcraft. The right hand, associated with the male, is used in greeting,[14] eating, and in giving gifts. The left hand is associated with the female. It is the hand that is used for cleaning oneself after defecating and for unpleasant tasks. It is considered an improper manner for one to point with one's left fingers. While the male is associated with the center, the female is associated with the hearth (*bukyia*). There is ambivalence in the concept of femininity as it is associated with fertility, life, and continuity as well as danger, destruction, evil spirits, and death.

The two crosses (*mmeramutene*—male cross—#20–21, and *mmeramubere*—female

53

Da bi me
nsoromma
bɛpue - #693

Onyankopɔn
adom - #131

Biribi wɔ
soro - #127

Biribi wɔ
soro - #126

Hye anhye -
#43

Soro ne
asase - #14

Hann ne sum
- #19

Hann ne sum
- #18

cross—#22–24) symbolize the various attributes of the two sexes which form the very core of Akan beliefs about their society. These beliefs affect almost all aspects of Akan behavior, from marital relations, care of menstruation and pregnancy, adultery, and ideas about kinship relations, to details concerning the nature of ancestral propitiation, inheritance, funerals, and categorization of death.

Death and Life

The Akan view of reality as "unity in duality comprising two conflicting elements" is further illustrated by how they view death. Sarpong (1974, p. 20) sums it up thus:

> Any given existence may be defined as a dedication to, an immersion in death, not simply because it is on its way to meet death, but more essentially because it constantly realizes in itself the "situation" of death. The presence of death is so fundamental to existence that not one of its stirrings can be understood otherwise than in the light of the constitutive and systematic ordering towards   death.

Death provokes dualistic "thoughts of darkness and light, weakness and strength, evil and good, sorrow and joy, non-existence and life, war and peace, defeat and victory, vice and virtue, ignorance and knowledge, in short, confusion (Sarpong, 1974, p. 21).

Death is inevitable for all as symbolized by *owuo atwedeɛ* (death's ladder—#90–93) and *owuo de dɔm bɛkɔ* (death will claim the multitude—#95). It does not discriminate between the rich and the poor (*owuo mpɛ sika* - death accepts no money—#98); *yɛbɛdane agya* (we shall leave everything behind—#599), or the old and the young. This inevitability of death is conveyed by the following stanza in the drum poetry cited in full below:

> We have, since we arose from ancient times,
> Been exposed to incessant suffering.
> The *Ogyapam* tree and its ants are from antiquity
> (Nketia, 1969, p. 125).

The ants not only harass the *ogyapam* tree, they kill it; yet the ants and the tree were created together from the beginning. That is to say, the tree was destined to die; it is the law of the Creator. The Creator made man to die; and when the destined time comes, nothing can stop death because what God has ordained, no human being can change (*asɛm a Onyankopɔn adi asie no, onipa ntumi nnane no*—#72).

Death, by natural circumstances, is not a curse or the loss of a dear one, but is considered as going home to God—a victory. Death is a transition in life—a passage from the visible world of the living physical beings into the invisible world of spirits of ancestors and God. That is, the Akan view death as a phase in the biography of persons, after which the dead resume existence as spirits which interact with the living and affect the lives of the living in a variety of ways. In this sense, some of the dead are feared and venerated, and extensive recurring rituals (e.g., *fundahɔ, nnawɔtwe nsa, adaduanan ayie, afenhyia ayie, ahobaa*) are (or were) performed for them. These rituals of veneration were erroneously termed ancestor worship by European writers.

When a very, very old person dies the body is laid in state in white before being buried. The white signifies victory over death and/or peaceful transition to the spiritual world. The power of death is so irresistible that even Jesus Christ, who Christians believe as the Son of God and therefore has the antidote to death's venom, could not avoid it (*Yesu wuo*—#100).

The manipulation of dead bodies served as dominant political symbols. For example, *Asɔneɛ, banmu*, and *nananompɔ* served to associate the dead with supreme state power. The royal mausoleums (*asieɛ* or *banmu*—#101) at Banpanase (*Asɔneɛ*) and Bantama (*Banmu*) for the Asante and *Nananompɔ* for the Fantse at Mankesim serve to illustrate the manipulation of dead corpses as dominant political symbols. Kyerematen (n.d., p. 11)

Mmeramutene
- #20

Mmeramubere
- #22

Owuo
atwedeɛ -
#90

Owuo kum
Nyame - #94

Nyame nwu
na mawu -
#48

Asɛm a
Nyame - #72

Hye anhye -
#42

Nyame nwu
na mawu -
#47

Owuo sɛɛ fie
- # 114

Hye anhye -
#43

Onipa bɛwu
na sika te ase
- #112

Ɔdomankoma
- #13

writes:

> it [Asɔneɛ] is the Ashanti equivalent for the process of embalming dead monarchs. A chamber, of a hall and bedroom, is kept for each of the successive Kings, furnished and equipped as for a living monarch. There is the bed, constantly made with a regular change of the bedding; supply of variety of cloth for different occasions; food and drink are provided and palace officials and a wife are detailed for service. After a year the skeleton is removed to the Bantama Mausoleum…Every year at a special ceremony at this Mausoleum, called the Annual Service (Afenhyiasom) the reigning King goes to inspect the skeletons to make sure that the gold joints are in place and to order replacements for those damaged or missing.

It is believed that the spirits of the ancestors come back to life everyday a child is born. Akan, therefore, have no difficulty with the Christian view of life after death and resurrection. In the symbol (Yesu wusɔre—#104), Akan believe the resurrection of Christ is a demonstration of God's power to overcome the venom of death—Nyame na ɔte nankaduro.

The naming ceremony for a baby, a week after birth, is to mark the transition from the spiritual world to the physical world of the living. It is believed that during the first week after birth the child is a spirit in transition. If it is an inauspicious spirit, it may return to where it came from before it is a week old. Such an inauspicious spirit that returns as a child may be given a funny or unusual name (kɔ-san-bra-din—go-and-come-back-name) to make it stay in the physical world.

The Akan dialectical understanding of life and death as polar opposites complementing each other is best illustrated by the following Akan prayer to God:

Ɛmma mennwu awia wuo,
Ɛmma mennwu anadwo wuo;
Ɛmma mennwu koraa;
Na ma me nwu.
Don't let me die in the day,
Don't let me die at night,
Don't let me die at all,
But let me die.

In this dialectic, as Dzobo (1992) explains, one expresses one's desire to see and appreciate the beauty of life and nature (line 1) and to be sexually active (line 2) in order to fulfill one's creative and reproductive being and have many children who may perpetuate one's name, beliefs, traditions, and philosophy of life (line 3). After one has fulfilled one's destiny one would be happy to die and join one's ancestors (line 4).

Furthermore, the Akan say that Ɔdomankoma bɔɔ owuo na owuo kum no—God created death and death killed Him (#94). Yet God knows the antidote for the serpent's venom (death) as indicated by the following quality of God: Nyame na ɔte nankaduro— God has the antidote for the venom of death.

The following drum poetry taken from Nketia (1969, p. 125) is pregnant with Akan dialectical views on the Creator, life and death:

Noble Ruler,
Condolences!
  Condolences!
  Condolences!
Noble ruler, we share your grief.
We sympathize with you in your bereavement.
We have, since we arose from ancient times,
Been exposed to incessant suffering.

55

The *Ogyapam* tree and its ants are from antiquity.
The Creator created death and death killed Him.
Thou Deceased,
Condolences!
  Condolences!
  Condolences! (Nketia, 1969, p.125).

Akan believe that the Creator Ɔdomankoma, is one who is infinite, eternal, having no beginning and no end. Yet the drummer says "The Creator created death, and death killed Him." This statement must be juxtaposed with another statement: *Nyame nwu na mawu* (could God die, I will die or when a man dies he is not really dead—#46–49) for one to understand the cryptic message of the drummer. The drummer is saying in effect that as long as God is not dead, death is not an end, but a new beginning. The Akan belief is that the human soul is in the image of God, the Creator, the Eternal One. Thus the human soul does not die, or the human soul dies only when God dies. That is, if human beings cease to exist, God ceases to exist. It is the drummer's way of conveying the Akan belief that there is life after death. That is why the drummer ends his message with an address to the deceased. The deceased is offered condolences, for he is able to hear it in the other life just begun.

Owuo mpɛ
sika - #98

Yɛbɛdan
agya - #599

Ban mu -
#101

Yesu wuo -
#100

Yesu wusɔre
- #104

Mema wo
hyɛden -
#105

Ɔdomankoma
- #12

Awia - #27

NOTES

1.   This Creator is envisaged as fire. The life-giving spirit or power that animated the fire and caused the birth of the universe is the vital force (*kra* or *ɔkra*) which enters the human being at birth.

2.   Akan give the following names and appelations to God:
Onyankopɔn—Alone; the Great One; the Supreme Being
Bɔrebɔre—Creator; Excavator; Hewer; Carver; Architect; Originator; Inventor
Ɔbɔadeɛ—Creator
Ɔdomankoma Infinite; Boundless; Absolute; Eternal; Prometheus; Inventor
Obiannyɛwo—The Uncreated One
Tetekwaframua—He who endures from time immemorial and forever; One whose beginning and end are unknown; Alpha and Omega
Tweduampɔn—The Dependable One
Brɛakyirihunuade—All-knowing; All-seeing; Omniscient
Otumfoɔ—The Powerful One; Omnipotent
Atoapem—Ultimate; Final; Unsurpassable; Problem-solver
Ɔmaowia—Giver of Sunshine; Source of Warmth and Vitality
Nana—Grand Ancestor
Toturobonsu, or *Ɔmansuo*—Giver of Rain; Rainmaker
Ananse Kokuroko—The Great Spider; The Wise One; The Great Designer
Amaɔmee—The Provider; Giver of Sufficiency
Ɔpamboɔ—The One who does the impossible
Nyaamanekɔse—The One to appeal to in times of adversity

3.   Akan have various stories to explain the beginnings of the universe. Each story attributes the universe to a spiritual creator. The drummer, for example, believes God created the word and the drummer first. The drummer, in turn, created the drum with which the drummer spreads the word.

4.   The Akan knew of other celestial bodies (*okyin nsoromma* - planets) like Mars, Venus, Jupiter, Mercury and Saturn in addition to the moon, stars and the sun (Meyerowitz, 1951). *Wimu* or *ewimu* is the space encompassing the earth (*asase*). Ewia or awia is the sun, and ewiase or wiase is the visible world under the vault of heaven. Dunn (1960) also indicates that the *kyɛkyɛ* star is the planet Venus and that Fantse fishermen knew about the Milky Way.

5.   The wind is believed to be the messenger of God; hence the expression: *Wopɛ asɛm aka akyerɛ Nyame a, na wo ka kyerɛ mframa* (when you want to send a message to God, you tell it to the wind).

6.   There is no corresponding Akan word for 'matter' in the abstract sense. The missionaries invented the word *famadeɛ* (*famu adeɛ* - literally thing of the ground) to translate matter in the Bible. The Akan words for body or form cannot be generalized to mean matter as the opposite of spirit.

7.   Akan give first names to their children according to the day of the week

Sunsum -
#35

Asase - #25

Hye Anhye -
#42

Agya, Ɔba ne
Sunsum - #74

Adwera -
#108

Mmeramubere
- #23

on which the child is born and the sex of the child. There are seven first names for girls and seven for boys. Yaa is the name for a girl born on Thursday and Efua (or Afia) is the name of a girl born on Friday. Kwame is the first name for a boy born on Saturday. The name is said to be the soul name (*kradin*) indicating the day of the week the soul (*sunsum* or *ɔkra*) entered the child at birth or the day of the week on which the spiritual being entered the physical world (see the section on Time in Chapter 10).

8. Akan do not regard *Asase* (Earth) as a deity to be worshipped as indicated by the maxim: *Asase nyɛ bosom, ɔnkyerɛ mmusuo*—The earth is not god, she does not divine.

9. The Akan society is a continuum that comprises the dead, the living, and the yet-to-be-born. Land is used by the living members in such a way that it will be preserved for use by the yet-to-be-born members of the society.

10. *Sunsum* and *ɔkra* are often used interchangeably and may appear to be synonymous. Another aspect of one's spirituality is the concept of *ntorɔ*. *Ntorɔ* is traced patrilineally, and the following is a list of some of the ntorɔ groups: *Bosompra, Bosomtwe, Bosommuru, Bosomafram, Bosomayensu*, and *Bosompo*.

11. The Akan view of trinity is also to be seen in the ahinansa (triangle - # 717-718) symbol.

12. Asante refer to Earth as *Asase Yaa* and Fantse refer to her as *Asase Efua* (Afua). In Asante Thursday is the "rest day" while Friday is the "rest day" among Fantse for Mother Earth. On these days it is forbidden to go the farm.

13. Among the Fantse similar rituals (e.g., *ahobaa* and *akwambɔ*) were celebrated annually to purify the community and ward off bad spirits and bad omens. *Ahobaa* is more of a memorial service to remember the family's ancestors. It si a sad occasion marked by mourning and the singing of funeral dirges (*nsudwom* or *nsubaa*). *Akwambɔ* is more of a new (or end of the) year celebration. It is a joyful occasion marked by a parade of the *asafo*.

14. When there is a seated gathering of people, one is supposed to shake hands in the proper way, from left to right of the seated. The Akan is supposed to know this proper way of greeting. The one who does not know and greets from right to left of the seated is said to be greeting in the female way (*okyia mmaa mu* - he greets in a direction like a woman does).

CHAPTER 5

Sɛ ɔman mu yɛ dɛ a, yɛn nyinaa te mu bi.
If there is peace and stability in a state, we all live in it.

GOVERNMENTAL ORGANIZATION

Adwa - #156

STATE AUTHORITY

Authority may be defined as the right of one or a group to make decisions and to command the actions of others within a socially defined sphere. The authority system in a society may be inferred from the political organization that prevails in a given society. The Akan have a centralized state system headed by a monarchy chosen from a royal family.

The sovereignty and power of Akan rulers are expressed through many objects that constitute the royal regalia. The palace, stools, swords, crowns, umbrellas, musical instruments, military accoutrements and other items all together play a significant role in enhancing the ambience of the ruler and in calling attention to his authority. The adinkra cloth producers make use of some of these items of regalia to chronicle the political organization and history of the nation, and functions of individuals in the political system of the society. These adinkra symbols also testify to the technical excellence of the people and the highly complex bureaucratic organization the society developed.

Sunsum - #36

In Asante, as in other Akan societies, the most important item of the regalia of the royalty is the stool (*ɔhene adwa* or *akonnwa*—#151–163). Before discussing the symbolism of the king's stool, we need to point out that there are several types of stools used by all manner of people. Stools may be "classified according to the sex of the user," writes Sarpong (1971, p. 17). He points out that men have their stools as do women. "The social status of the persons who use stools for official purposes," Sarpong continues, "affords still another purpose of stools." There are the king's stool (*ɔhene adwa*), queenmother's stool (*ɔhemmaa adwa*) and the poor person's stool (*adammadwa*—literally two-penny stool). In everyday sense, the stool is also a symbol of hospitality. When one goes to another's house one is first offered a stool to sit on and then water to drink to signify that one is welcome to the house.

Asase - #25

Ohene Adwa — King's Stool

The *ɔhene adwa* (king's stool—#151–163) encodes the Akan philosophical construct of state territoriality. As Preston (1973, p. 81) points out, the *ɔhene adwa* "exists only in relation to specific laws of custody of the earth [*asase*—# 25–26] and this custody has its origins in prime occupancy of territory which is considered a de facto sacred act." That is, the existence of *ɔhene adwa* carries a territorial concept with it. This territory may be *kuro* (town) or *ɔman* (state). In essence, where there is no stool, there is no town or state.

Aban - #138

There are two types of stools associated with the political system: the blackened stools of the ancestors and the white stools of the reigning king.[1] The stool of the reigning king is white or the natural color of the wood from which it is carved. The stools of the kings who proved to be great leaders are blackened and preserved in a special ceremony to honor them after they have passed away. The blackened stools are believed to inhabit the spirits of the ancestors, and are, therefore, believed to constitute the soul (*sunsum*—#35–36) of the nation.

Adwa - #155

These blackened stools are kept in the temple of stools (*nkonnwafieso* in Twi; *nkongua dan* in Fantse) as symbolic memorial and shrine of the great ancestors. As Sarpong (1971, p. 38) explains: "the stools are blackened firstly, in order that they may not appear too

Tumi Afena - #148

Adinkrahene
- #182

Akofena -
#164

Adwa - #163

Adwa - #162

Ɔhene
kyiniie -
#170

Adwa - #160

Akofena -
#166

Nyansa pɔ -
#649

nasty; secondly, so that they may properly represent the dead and signify the sorrow of the living at the death of their chiefs; thirdly, so as to produce a feeling of awe in those who appear before them; and lastly, to render the stools durable since they must be perpetually present to receive the sacrifices and offerings of the people."

The stool of the ɔhene is the sacred symbol of his political and religious authority as it represents the permanence and continuity of the nation (Busia, 1954). When a successful king dies in office his stool is blackened and added to the ancestral stools.[2] The reigning monarch serves as the link between the living, the yet to be born, and the dead members of the society. In the olden days when there was a natural catastrophe, the incumbent ruler would deliberately stand on top of the stools of the ancestors as a sign of desecration in order to enrage and wake up the spirits of the ancestors to help the living deal with the catastrophe (McLeod, 1981, p. 117).

Because the stool of the king is believed to enshrine the ancestral power, it is considered sacred and religious, and its occupant is expected to be pure in heart and to hold high ethical and moral standards. As a symbol of state power it embodies the past, present, and the future of the nation, that is, it marks continuities across generations and groups and close solidarities between the living and the dead. The king has the responsibility to preserve the stool for posterity. The stool binds all the members of the family (and thus the nation) together. These views about the Akan stool is succinctly summed up by Preston (1973, p. 81) thus:

> Stools are the symbolic axis of the leadership complex. Stools enshrine the collective spiritual essence of past, present, and future generations of the state's populace, and the collective ancestral kra of the royals past, present, and future. The ɔmanhene symbolically sits on the consecrated stool of the founder of the state, who indeed actually did sit upon the stool before its ritual elevation.

Each king decides on the symbol to be incorporated in his stool.[3] For example, Asantehene Nana Prempeh II chose the nyansapɔ (wisdom knot—#649) to convey the notion that he would solve the nation's problems by sagacity rather than by the power of the sword. Other king's stool symbols that have been incorporated in the adinkra cloth include dame dame (checkers—#668–669), ɛsono (elephant—#219–220), mmeramubere (female cross—#22–24), kɔtɔkɔ (porcupine—#264–265), dɛnkyɛm (crocodile—#215–218) and, ɔsrane (crescent moon—#509). Sarpong (1971) provides a catalogue of several of the king's stools.

The most important ɔhene stool of the Asante nation is the Sika Dwa Kofi (Golden Stool). The Sika Dwa is believed to be the abode of the soul (sunsum—# 35–36) of the Asante nation. It symbolizes the power, health, and wealth of the Asante nation. It is exhibited only on the installation of the Asantehene, at durbars such as the Adae and Odwira festivals, and on special occasions for the formal presentation of the Asantehene to his people. Such occasions present assurances of the stool's safekeeping and an opportunity to enjoy the hospitality and munificence of the leader. More discussion on the Sika Dwa will be provided in Chapter 6.

In the Asante society, as Wilks (1975) points out, the ultimate fount of all political authority (tumi) has been symbolized by the Golden Stool (Sika Dwa Kofi), and the ultimate assignee of the wealth of the nation was symbolized by the Golden Elephant's Tail (Sika Mena). "As a 'natural' feature of society ... political-jural authority flowed downwards from the Asantehene to the people under the Golden Stool, and as an equally 'natural' feature of society… wealth flowed upwards from the people (by various forms of taxation) to the Asantehene, under the Golden Elephant's Tail" (Wilks, 1975, p. 430). Thus, the custodian of the Sika Dwa (the powerful—otumfoɔ) was he who legitimately exercised tumi (political power). The Sika Mena symbolized the highest level of government at which wealth was appropriated and redistributed (ɔgye); thus in addition to being otumfoɔ the Asantehene was also ɔgyefoɔ—the taking one (Wilks, 1975, p. 430). The Golden Axe

Mmeramubere
- #22

Kɔtɔkɔ -
#264

Aban - #147

Sunsum -
#35

Akuma -
#567

Sumpie -
#174

Ɔhemmaa
papa - #176

Ɔhene papa -
#175

(*Sika Akuma*) symbolized the power of the Asantehene to resolve disputes peacefully, that is, serve as the chief judge. This is depicted by the following expression: *Dua biara ni hɔ a ɛyɛ den sɛ akuma ntumi ntwa, nanso asɛm biara ɛyɛ den no, yɛmfa akuma na ɛtwa, na yɛde yɛn ano na ɛka ma no twa*—There is no tree that is so hard that it cannot be felled with an axe; however, no matter how difficult an issue may be, it must be settled by counseling and negotiations, not with an axe. There is further discussion on the Golden Axe (Sika Akuma) in Chapter 6.

Ɔhemmaa adwa—Queenmother's stool

The queenmother as a co-ruler, has joint responsibility with the king for all affairs of the state (Rattray, 1923; Meyerowitz, 1951; Busia, 1951; Aidoo, 1981; Arhin, 1983; Manuh, 1988). This important constitutional role of the queenmother is illustrated by the Asante political organization in which the *ɔhemmaa adwa* (queenmother's stool) is the *akonnua panin*, the senior stool in relation to the *ɔhene adwa* (king's stool). As Aidoo (1981, p. 66) points out: "As a full member and co-chairman of the governing council or assembly of the state, the queen mother's presence was required whenever important matters of state were to be decided." This is incorporated in the *sumpie* (pyramid—#174) symbol. The queenmother sitting side by side with king on the *sumpie* is one the significant occasions for the public display of the constitutional role of the queenmother. The queenmother who successfully carried out her constitutional and other responsibilities was honored as *ɔhemmaa papa* (good queenmother—#176). More will be said in Chapter 6 about this power-sharing arrangement between the king and the queenmother.

Akofena—State Swords

Next in importance to the stools are the gold hilted state swords as indicated by the adinkra symbols *akofena* (state swords—#164–169) and *tumi afena* (sword of power—#148–149). *Akofena* symbolizes state authority, power and legitimacy. *Akofena* is also known as *nsuaefena* (oath sword) as it is used by chiefs to swear the oath of office and by sub-chiefs to swear allegiance to a higher authority. There are various state swords that are used for specific functions. Kyerematen (1964, p. 34, 36) distinguishes as many as six categories and sub-categories of state swords. Two major categories are the *kɛtɛanofena* and *akofena*. *Kɛtɛanofena* swords are either *akrafena* or *bosomfena*, which are carried respectively on the right and left sides of the king in state processions. Each Asantehene is required by custom, dating back to Opoku Ware I (who reigned around 1731–1742), to create their own two swords: *akrafena* and *bosomfena*. State swords known as *akrafena* (literally, soul sword) are used in the rituals for purifying the chief's soul and various blackened ancestral stools. The "*akrafena* and *bosomfena* together are representative of the spiritual and physical, masculine and feminine, individual and political dualities necessary to form a complete society in both royal and non-royal classes" (Erlich, 1981, p. 43).

The four principal state swords of the Asantehene are the *Bosommuru*, *Mpomponsuo*, *Bosompra* and *Bosomtwe*. The *Bosommuru*, first made for Asantehene Osei Tutu, is the state sword with which every Asantehene dedicates himself to the service of the nation. It represents Osei Tutu's *sunsum* (soul—#35–36) and is one of the *bosomfena* or the left-hand swords. The *Mpomponsuo* (symbolizing responsibility—#150) belonged to Asantehene Opoku Ware I. This is a special *akofena* with which the Asantehene swears the oath of office. The *amanhene* in turn use this state sword to swear the oath of allegiance and loyalty to the Asantehene. "The oath system as known today in Ashanti," according to Hagan (1971, p. 49, n. 21) "perhaps dates back to Opoku Ware who instituted the use of the Mpomponsuo for oath taking." *Mpomponsuo* (responsibility—#150) is the foremost example of the *akrafena*, or the right-hand swords (Fraser, 1972, p. 145).

Akofena -
#167

Tumi afena -
#149

Mpomponsuo
- #150

Akofena -
#167

Sunsum -
#36

Dεnkyεm -
#217

Akofena -
#168

Dεnkyεmfunafu
- #312

Asantehene Kwaku Dua I made the third most important state sword, Bosompra as his *bosomfena* and Kraku as his *akrafena*. Bosompra is one of the foremost examples of the left-hand state swords. It is used by the Asantehene to send messages to the Queen Mother. The embossment (*abɔsodeε*) on this state sword is a treasure container (*kuduo*). It symbolizes the responsibility of the King to ensure provisions from the hearth (*bukyia*), represented by the queenmother, for his people's material needs, hence the expression: *εsεn kεseε a ɔgye adididodoɔ*—the big pot that provides for many.

The fourth most important Asante state sword in the *kεtεanofena* group of swords is the Bosomtwe, which is linked with a deity that resides in Lake Bosomtwe. The embossment on this sword is the *dεnkyεm* (crocodile—#215–218) which symbolizes power, greatness, and adaptability. There are a variety of state swords with symbols embossed on the blade for use by the state functionaries according to their rank or status in the governmental structure (Ross, 1977; Fraser, 1972; Kyerematen, 1964). Examples of symbols that are encoded in the adinkra cloth that may be found as *abosodeε* (embossment) on state swords include *kɔtɔkɔ* (porcupine — #264–265), *bese saka* (bunch of kola nuts—#575–581), *nkatehono* (groundnut shell—#582), *akuma* (axe—#567), and *nsoromma* (star—#116–121).

State swords known as *asomfena* (service or courier swords) are carried by state traders, royal messengers and ambassadors as tokens of credibility and credentials on diplomatic and other state missions. The *ahoprafoɔafena* (fly whisk bearers sword) is an example of service sword. Other specialized swords included the *abrafoɔafena*, *sepɔ* (dagger—#299–301) and *afenatene*. The *abrafoɔafena* looked more like a bayonet than a sword and was used by the constabulary, *abrafoɔ*. The *sepɔ* was a small knife "used in the past by executioners for thrusting through the cheeks of their victims to prevent them [from] uttering a curse [on the king]" (Kyerematen, 1964, p. 36).

The "*afenatene*, literally the long sword, is differently shaped and is not carried about but planted in the ground. It has a triple blade, much shorter than that of the other swords in proportion to the rest of the sword, and between it and the hilt is a long shaft of various decorative forms such as plaits and spirals" (Kyerematen, 1964, p. 34).

Chiefs maintain a group of sword-bearers, each of whom carries one of the various state swords on public occasions. While swords were an important military weapon in the past, their use these days is ceremonial as they have unsharpened blades. An example of such swords is the *domfonsan* which was "used on the battlefield for swearing the oath of fidelity and for leading the army" (Kyerematen, 1964, p. 36).

Other State Regalia

Other important symbols of state authority that have been encoded in the adinkra cloth include the umbrella (*ɔhene kyiniiε*—#170), king's gun (*ɔhene tuo*—#258–260), king's crown or head band (*ɔhene kyε* or *ɔhene abotire*—#171), horns (*mmεntia* or *ntahera*—#172–173),[4] iron bells (*dawuru*—#241–242; 243–245), drums (e.g. *donno*—#406, *donno nta*—#407–415, *atumpan*, *kete*), and palanquins. The king's gun (*ɔhene tuo*—#258–260) symbolizes the military responsibility of the king to guard and ensure the security and defense of the nation. The symbolic importance of the gun is to be inferred from the following text used in the swearing of the king-elect to become the Asantehene:

> I am the descendant of Osei and Opoku of Bonsu and Agyeman
> I am direct nephew of Prempeh.
> Today the soul of Agyeman Prempeh has gone whence it came and his gun lies idle.
> By your grace and the grace of Kumasi people
> You have presented the gun to me
> If I do not protect and govern you well as did my forbearers
> I swear the Great Oath (Kyerematen, n.d., p. 18).

Bese saka - #575

Nsoromma - #116

Sepɔ - #300

Akofena - #165

Ɔhene kyiniiɛ - #170

Ɔhene tuo - #259

Agyin dawuru - #241

Abɛntia - #173

The Asantehene-elect later fires the *ɔhene tuo* (the king's gun—#258–260) to demonstrate his capability of commanding the state's military forces on the battlefield. Soon after being formally sworn into office, he holds the *Mpomponsuo* (responsibility—#150) sword in his right hand and the *ɔhene tuo* (king's gun—#258–260) in the left, and steps out to dance to the *atoprɛtea* rhythms of the *fɔntɔmfrɔm* ensemble (Kyerematen, n.d.). This ceremonial use of the instruments of national defense and security is also encoded by an *adinkra* symbol called *afena ne tuo* (sword and gun—#268).

The umbrella (*ɔhene kyiniiɛ*—#170), on the other hand, indicates who the king is among a gathering of people as reflected in the aphorism: *Nea kyiniiɛ si no so na ɔyɛ ɔhene* (He who has the umbrella over his head is the king). The umbrella is also symbol of the protection the king is believed to provide for the nation. Fraser (1972, p. 145) notes that "these huge objects are both practical sunshades and symbolic, quasi-architectural, space-defining forms that help express the chief's role as ruler." When the king dies it is metaphorically said that "Nana has removed his umbrella; we shall be scorched to death by the sun" (*Nana atu ne kyiniiɛ; awia na ɛbɛku yɛn*).

The Asantehene has no less than 23 different umbrellas each of which is used on a particular occasion (Fraser, 1972). Some of these umbrellas are the *Bɔaman, Akatamanso, Nsaa kyiniiɛ,* and *Akroponkyiniwa*. On the top of the umbrella is usually placed a carved symbol (*ntuatire*) with a specific meaning. These include symbols like *sankɔfa* (go back and retrieve—#633–648), *babadua, akobɛn* (war horn—#253–257), *akokɔbaatan ne ne mma* (the hen and her chicken—#424–427), and *tikorɔ nkɔ agyina* (one head does not form a council—#325–326). These symbols are deliberately displayed as part of the king's regalia on festive occasions so that "all who see them may read, mark and inwardly digest what they stand for" (Kyerematen, 1964, p. 1). Even though the first published illustration of the state umbrella was by Muller in 1673, the use of state umbrellas in West Africa had been the subject of commentary by Arab chroniclers who observed them in ancient Mali (Fraser and Cole, 1972, p. 308).

The drums (symbolized for example by donno— #406) and the horns (symbolized for example by *abɛntia*—#172 and *nkrawobɛn*—#173) are the divine media that give vocal expression to the existence of the soul of the nation and its continuity. These media are used in providing music and to transmit ancestral history and other sacred texts. Drum texts are utilized as (a) invocation of ancestral spirits and to recall ancestral history; (b) eulogy; (c) proverbs; and (d) to communicate greetings, praises, congratulations, warnings, emergency calls and general announcements. Particular drums and horns are used to extol the praises of the king. There are several types of drums, for example, *atumpan* (talking drum), *donno* (bell drum—#406), *mpintin*, and *fɔntɔmfrɔm*. The drum messages, for example, may be used to refer to the king as the powerful one, the benefactor, the people's mother (*nkuruma kɛse*—#195–203), the valiant one, and the vigilant and all-seeing one (that is, *ɔhene aniwa twa ne ho hyia*—#190–192). The *ɔhene* is also referred to in various contexts by the drummer as *nkuruma kɛse* (#195–203), *ɛsono* (#219–220) or *dɛnkyɛm* (#215–18). The good king may be referred to as the elephant (*ɛsono*—#219–220) that provides shelter, security and protection to his subjects so that they do not get wet, that is, they are not harmed.

Some drums are used for special purposes. For example, *asuboa* drum is used to imitate the cry of the crocodile, the *etwie* drum is used to imitate the roar of the leopard, and the *aworobɛn* was in the past played behind a thief to disgrace him publicly (Sarpong, 1974; Nketia, 1969). The *etwie* drum was used in the past in military campaigns to deceive the enemy.

The horns (*mmɛnson, ntahera* or *mmɛntia*—#172–173) are used by the hornblowers of the various horn ensembles to allude to the power of the king thus: "He is like the hawk that roams all nations, he will come home with victory." Or, It is the horns that make us know who is a king or a chief," is another well known adage spoken in relation to the king. The horns are also used to mention very witty historical events or to draw attention to the king in very few words. They are also used to call attention to the skill and power of

Akofena ne
tuo - #268

Ɔhene
kyiniiɛ -
#170

Akobɛn -
#254

Sankɔfa -
#636

Akokɔ nan -
#425

Ti korɔ -
#326

Donno -
#406

Ɔhene aniwa
- #190

the king. An example of this is as follows: *Woahunu mmoa nyinaa brɛboɔ, woahunu ntɛtea brɛboɔ pɛn?* This literally means: You have seen the liver of all animals, but have you ever seen the liver of the ant? This alludes to the power and skills of the king to minute details.

Ahemfie—Palace

The seat of government is called *ahemfie* or *aban* (palace, castle, fortress, or stone house—#138–147). The *aban* or *ahemfie* is usually a massive and monumental piece of architecture which appears, in its relative permanence, to symbolize the enduring character of divine kingship (Fraser and Cole, 1972, p. 308). The palace tends to create an isolating spatial envelope that provides shelter for leaders.

During the reign of Asantehene Osei Bonsu, a magnificent palace (*Aban, Ahemfie, Abrɔsan,* or *Abansoro*—#138–147) was built. This palace was made of carved stone and was completed in 1822. It was roofed with brass laid over an ivory framework, and the windows and doors were cased in gold, and the door posts and pillars were made of ivory. Wealthy merchants of Elmina are believed to have aided in the construction of the king's stone house at Kumasi (Yarak, 1986). The *aban* has been referred to as the Palace of Culture. This fortress was ransacked and blown up by the British in the 1874 war (McLeod, 1981; Wilks, 1992).

Attached to the *ahemfie* would be the harem (*hia* or *hyiaa*), quarters for the women. There is an adinkra symbol called *ɔhene kɔ hia*, and one of the names of the adinkra cloths is also called *ɔhene kɔ hia* (The king is gone to the harem to visit his wives— #194). The Asantehene's palace is called Manhyia. The personal residence of the king within Manhyia is called Abrɔsanase.

There is a raised platform or dais *(sumpie*—#174) that stands in the front yard of the king's palace. This is used by the king for making public addresses. At Manhyia Palace there are two such royal daises: *Sumpie Kumaa* (also known as *Bogyawe*) and *Sumpie Kɛseɛ* (also known as *Dwaberem*).

GOVERNMENTAL STRUCTURE

In this section, I use the Asante governmental structure to discuss Akan political organization as encoded by the *adinkra* symbols. The Asante people developed a highly structured state organization with systems of rules and regulations that were used to govern the society. The authority and power systems set out the statuses within the social structure indicating who must take and receive orders. The Asante political structure was based on corporate kin groups with the primary unit being the family. The head of the household, usually the man, served as the head of that political unit. The household head was mirrored in instituted officers of progressively larger political units with basic unit as the extended family (or matriclan—*abusua*), to the town (*kuro*),[5] and the highest unit being the nation-state (*ɔman* or *ɔmantoɔ*). This is depicted in Table 2 as follows:

Table 2: Akan Political Units

The head of each unit serves as the religious, legislative, judiciary, and administrative leader for the unit. At the *kuro* and *ɔman* levels of government, the leader is considered as the supreme priest of all the gods in his dominion, and he represents the priests in the legislative council. He also has the duty to see to it that all the rituals and ceremonies connected with all the gods of the dominion are carried out so that the welfare of his people is not endangered. The *ɔhene* who carried out his responsibilities and ensured peace and progress in the state was considered *ɔhene papa* (good king—#175). The *ɔhene papa* (good king—#175) represents *Nyankopɔn* the masculine aspect of the Supreme Being on earth. The *ɔhemmaa papa* (good queenmother—#176) represents *Nyame, ɔma*

64

Abɛntia - #172

Nkuruma
kɛse - #199

Aban - #145

Aban - #138

Ɔhene kɔ hia - #194

Sumpie - #174

Aban - #146

Abusua
panin - #453

awia (giver of the sun), the feminine aspect of the Supreme Being on earth. At the higher levels of the political system, the *ɔdekuro* and *ɔmanhene* also serve as the military leaders. Membership in the military organization (*asafo*) is patrilineally determined. At the higher levels of the political system, the *ɔdekuro* and *ɔmanhene* are chosen by the queenmother subject to the approval of the masses. Leadership at the household and *abusua* levels is based on seniority.

At the *kuro* level there is a village or town council (*nhyiamu* or *kuro manyimfo* or *apamfo*) made up of the *ɔdekuro* and *abusua mpanyimfo* (heads of the various matriclans in the town/village) and *ɔhemmaa*. The council regulates the village/town affairs such as settling disputes arising among members of different lineages. The council also carries out such welfare services as ordering the periodic cleaning of the village/town, the clearing of bushes around streams and ponds that were the main sources of water for the community, and the maintenance of paths leading to the main farm areas or to the capital (*ahenkuro* or *akropɔn*) of the state (Busia, 1951, pp. 63–65).

The village/town council also serves as the channel of communication between the village/town, the division, and the state. It transmits orders (a) to make contributions in cash and/or in kind for state funeral rites and toward installation expenses of the heads of the division and the state; (b) to levy fighting men for war; and, (c) to execute policies relating to divisional and national concerns.

Orders are transmitted to the general public through public announcements by the *dawurobɔni* (town crier) depicted by the adinkra symbol *Agyin dawuru*—Agyin's iron bell (#241–242; 243–245). In emergency situations such as fire or some natural disaster, the *asafo* drum or *akobɛn* (war horn—#253–257) would be sounded to call every able-bodied person to action. Answering such clarion calls was considered an honorable and patriotic duty. One was considered a coward who was able but would not volunteer one's services in times of national crisis. *Kɔsankɔbi, wokasa ɔbaa ano a, Kobiri nku wo* (deserter, may Kobiri [a deity] kill you if you dare speak as a man to a woman—#253–257 was a way of deriding cowards).

Governmental Structure in Asante

The Asante Constitution was such that at the head of the Asante governmental structure stood the Asantehene (Asante king) and Asantehemaa (Asante queenmother). He was considered the guardian of the temporal and spiritual unity of the kingdom. Although the Asantehene had enormous powers that clearly gave him the potential of becoming an autocrat, his exercise of those powers and his independence in decision-making were, in fact, closely circumscribed by the legal and customary norms of the polity and the Seventy-seven (77) Laws given to the state by Ɔkomfo Anɔkye. Blatant violations of these laws and norms could result in public and formal charges leading to impeachment and destoolment. The queenmother had the constitutional responsibility to advice and guide the king, and she had the right to criticize and rebuke him in public (Aidoo, 1981; Manuh, 1988).

Below the Asantehene are the *amanhene* of the confederate states (*amantoɔ*), and under these are the *adekurofoɔ*—chiefs of the various towns and villages. The Asantehene is the primus inter pares (first among equals) as far as the *amanhene* were concerned. The *amanhene* had their obligations to the Asantehene, but they also had compensating rights. The *amanhene* had to swear oath of allegiance and loyalty to the Asantehene promising to heed his call by day or night; they were obliged to supply him with fighting men when so required and contribute to a war tax (*apeatuo*) or a national levy imposed by the Asantehene for some specific purpose; and they recognized a right of appeal from their own courts to the Asantehene's court at Kumasi.

The *amanhene* were expected to attend the Asantehene's Odwira festival. They also recognized certain trade regulations of the Asantehene and his conduct of foreign affairs. The *ɔmanhene* combined executive, judiciary and legislative as well as religious functions. The *ɔmanhene* also served as the commander-in-chief of the army. In assuming office,

Ɔhene papa -
#175

Ɔhemmaa
papa - #176

Awia - #27

Nea ɔpɛ sɛ
ɔbɛdi hene -
#177

Ɔhene kyɛ -
#171

Agyin
dawuru -
#242

Nkotimsefoɔ
pua - #233

Akobɛn -
#255

the chief will swear the oath of office using *akofena* (state swords—#164–169).

The Asante Empire comprised a confederacy and the tributary states. The confederacy consisted of the sovereign states (amantoɔ) of Mampon, Bekwai, Nsuta, Dwaben, Kumawu, Kokofu, Kumasi, Offinso, Asumegya and Ejisu where each one of them had its own *ɔmanhene* and a council of state. The Kumasihene is also the Asantehene, a primus inter pares. Each of these *amanhene* swears the oath of allegiance and loyalty to the Asantehene. In Kumasi, for example, the council of state is headed by the Kumasihene (who is also the Asantehene). The Bantamahene, who is also the Kumasi Kontirehene, is the senior ranking functionary and presides over the affairs of the council in the absence of the Asantehene. The Kumasi Kontirehene is the commander-in-chief of the Kumasi army. Next in command in the Kumasi army is Akwamuhene who also serves as the Asafohene.

The Asantehene presided over two important decision-making councils of state: Asantemanhyiamu (Assembly of the Asante Nation) and the Council of Kumasi.[6] The origin of the Asantemanhyiamu presumably dates from the formation of the Asante kingdom in the late seventeenth century.

Originally the Asantemanhyiamu was intended to function as the supreme legislative and judicial body of the Asanteman. However, the unwieldiness of the convocations of the Asantemanhyiamu and its inadequacy for the management of the complex day-to-day affairs of government became such that the Council of Kumasi gradually assumed, de facto, the powers of the Asantemanhyiamu. With time, especially after the 1874 war in which the British defeated Asante, dissenting local politicians in the various *amantoɹ* reacted against Kumasi's highly centralized style of governing and its dominance in nearly all phases of political life—decision-making, appointments, control over the public sector of the national economy, instruments of coercion, and foreign policy.

The hierarchy in the Akan governmental structure as exemplified by the Kumasi system of government (Council of State) comprised the King, the Queen Mother, the Kontire ne Akwamu and Mpanimfoɔ (Elders), and Gyaasehene, and Gyaasewahene. The Mpanimfoɔ (Elders) consisted of Abusua Ahemfo (Clan Chiefs), viz: Oyokohene, Beretuohene, Aduanahene, and Konahene. The remaining members of Mpanimfoɔ comprised the leaders of the various military divisions in the state, namely, Benkumhene, Nifahene, Twafoɹhene, Adɹntenhene, Ankɔbeahene, Kyidɔmhene, and Akyeamehene.

The Kumasi Council of State was presided over by the Asantehene and operated as the highest court of justice and chief advisory body to the Asantehene. By the middle of the nineteenth century the Kumasi Council of State had extended its influence over Asante domestic administration, the conduct of foreign policy, and central government operations in trade, public works, guild craft, and fiscal and monetary regulations. Membership in the Council of Kumasi varied over time and according to the type of business under discussion. Senior Kumasi *ahemfo* occupied seats on the Council. Heads of the civil and military organizations and other appointive bureaucratic and princely offices were also members of the Council. Other members included the *abusua ahemfo*. The Council brought in outside expertise by making people with specialized skill and knowledge in specific areas of governmental affairs adjunct members without voting rights. The Asante Nkramo (Asante Muslims), who served under the administrative supervision of the Nsumankwaahene of Kumasi as scribes (*ɔhene krakye*), physicians, and spiritual advisors, constituted a very important group of such experts.

PUBLIC SERVICE

Public administration (*amammuo*) was developed into specialized service in which individuals acquired training and expertise. *Ahemfie adesua* (literally court learning) was the means by which individuals acquired the training and expertise to render public service. Public administrative roles in Asante society are described by the term *ɛsomdwuma*— literally public service work. Those employed in such roles are known as *asomfoɔ* and *nhenkwaa* (the king's courtiers). In the Asante society public service was developed into a highly complex hierarchy that initially was based on ascriptive characteristics but later

Agyin
dawuru -
#241

Dawuru -
#243

Kurontire ne
Akwamu -
#327

Asase aban -
#354

Akofena -
#166

Kɔtɔkɔ -
#264

Ti korɔ -
#325

Nea ɔpɛ sɛ
obɛdi hene -
#177

developed to include individuals who earned their positions by achievement. The hierarchy ranged from the chief at the top through a layer of advisors (*akyeamefoɔ*, *mpanimfoɔ, akɔmfoɹ*, etc.) to the courtiers (*nhenkwaa*). Later as the political economy of the Asante empire expanded other public service positions were created and these included *akwamufoɔ* (road constructors), *nkwansrafoɔ* (road guards who collected tolls), *asokwafoɔ* (drummers, hornblowers) and *nsumankwaafoɔ* (scribes, medicinemen and herbalists). A new division of chiefs was created—the *gyaasewa* division—to be responsible for palace administration, public works and public trade (*bata fekuo*). Some of these public servants distinguished themselves successfully and were promoted to the status of chiefs, military leaders, envoys, governors, and *aberɛmpon*.

Rattray (1969) distinguished the following offices of public servants in the Asantehene Palace in Kumasi, capital of Asante: *akyeame* (spokesmen); *akonnuasoafoɔ* (stool carriers); *asokwafo* (drummers, horn blowers); *akyiniiɛkyimfoɔ* (umbrella carriers); *banmufoɹ* (caretakers of the royal mausoleum); *adwarefoɔ* (bathroom attendants); *akradwarefoɔ* (soul-washers); *ahoprafoɔ* (elephant tail switchers); *papasoafoɔ* (fan bearers—#231–232); *soodofoɔ* (cooks); *asoamfoɔ* (hammock carriers); *akokwafoɔ* (floor polishers); *sanaafoɔ*; *fotosanfoɔ*; *adabrafoɔ* (eunuchs); *nsɛniefoɔ* (heralds); *afonasoafoɹ* (sword bearers); *atumtufoɔ* (gun bearers); *akyɛmfo* (shield bearers—#269); *kwadwumfoɔ* (minstrels); *asumankwafoɔ* (scribes, medicine men and herbalists); *abansifoɔ, akwansrafoɔ*, or *akwansifoɔ* (highway policemen or road guards)—responsible for the protection of state traders, regulation of state trade, and control of immigration; *akwammofoɔ* (road maintenance group)—responsible for felling trees obstructing highways, clearing the highways of weeds, building bridges across rivers; and *abrafoɔ* (executioners). These various public servants were distinguished from one another by their haircuts (e.g., *mpua anum*—#223–229, *nkotimsefoɔ pua*—#233–237, *nkwantanan*—#230, and *mmodwewafoɔ pua*—#238–239), by the state swords (*akofena*—#164–169) they carried, helmets and medallions they wore, and the keys (*nsafoa*—#240) they carried.

In the royal household the king is served by four senior public servants who are responsible for his well-being. These are the *Gyaasehene*—chief of the royal household; *Daberɛhene* — the chamberlain in charge of the king's bed chamber; *Manwerɛhene*—the chief in charge of the king's clothing and personal effects; and the *Soodohene*— the chief of the royal cooks and culinary matters. Under these senior public servants served various people as the *abenasefoɹ* (king's wardrobe attendants), *mmɔwerɛbufoɔ* (barbers and manicurists), *mansufoɔ* (providers of drinking water), *patamufoɹ* (caretakers of drinks), *somesisifoɔ* (waist-holders), *kaneasoafoɔ* (lamp bearers), and *aburamfoɔ* (goldsmiths). From these various positions functionaries were appointed to conduct diplomatic negotiations and the resolution of possible military disputes in the conquered territories and provinces administered from Kumasi. These provincial administrators were known as *nhwɛsofoɔ*—literally, overseers.

MILITARY

The king's gun (*ɔhene tuo*—#258–260) as pointed out earlier, signifies the military leadership of the king. This military responsibility is also signified by the symbol *ɔkɔdeɛ mmɔwerɛ* (eagle's talons—#263). Even though the Asante, like the other Akan societies, had no standing army, the *asafo*[7]— i.e., a people's militia—was a well established social and political organization based on martial principles. Every able-bodied person belonged to an *asafo* group; every child automatically belonged to his or her father's company. Internal sub-divisions within an individual company included the main fighting body, the scouts[8], reserves, and the minstrel unit whose main job it was to sing patriotic and war songs to boost the morale of the military.

In Asante, major reforms undertaken by Asantehene Osei Tutu in the late seventeenth century included the reorganization of the military by creating the Kontirehene and Akwamuhene as the military generals. Even though they were equals, the Kontire was regarded as the first among equals. The original Kontire (also known as *atuo nsɔn*—

Mmɔdwewafoɔ
pua - #239

Nkotisemfoɔ
pua - #234

Mpua anum -
#223

Nkwantanan
- #230

Ɔhene papa -
#232

Mmɔdwewafoɔ
pua - #238

Ɛkyɛm -
#269

Mpua anum -
#226

seven gunners) was composed of Amankwatia, Safo Pasoam, Gyedu Kumanini, Akyampon Kofi, Brefo Apaw, Firam Gyereba, and Awua Kokonini. The Soaduru division created by Obiri Yeboa was reorganized and renamed the Akwamu in commemoration of Osei Tutu's sojourn and education in Akwamu (Wilks, 1975, 1992). These military and political reforms are encoded in the symbol *kuronti ne akwamu* (council of state—#327).

The *asafo* companies forming the Asante or any other Akan state national army[9] were organized into main fighting divisions thus: *adjnten* (vanguard—main body, under the *adɔtenhene*), *twafoɔ* (advance guard, under the *twafohene*), *kyidɔm* (rearguard—under the *kyidɔmhene*), nifa (right wing, under the *nifahene*),[10] *benkum* (left wing, under the *benkumhene*), *akwansra* (scouting division), *ankɔbea* (home guard, under the *ankɔbeahene*), and *gyaase* (the king's bodyguard, under the *gyaasehene*). *Asafo* companies were also differentiated by the different colors of headgear and hairstyles worn by members, exclusive drums, horns and other musical instruments, appellations, flags and emblems. Other units within the main divisions included *afenasoafoɔ* (the carriers of spears and shields), *sumankwaafoɔ* (the herbalists and medicine men), and the *asokwafoɔ* (heralds).

The *adinkra* cloth symbols that relate to the military organization of the state include *ɔhene tuo* (#258–260), *gyawu atikɔ* (#246–251), *akobɛn* (war horn—#253–257), *akoo mmɔwerɛ* (parrot's talons—#261–262), *pagya* (strikes fire— #266–267), *ɔkɔdeɛ mmɔwerɛ* (eagle's talons—#263), and *tuo abobaa* (gun bullets—#352). In times of war or other national crises the *akobɛn* (war horn—#253–257) or war drums would sound, and every able-bodied person was expected to respond to the call to action. Answering the clarion call was deemed an honorable and patriotic duty.

In the past Asante warriors could be summoned from all areas to Kumasi by drum beat and the sound of the war horn (*akobɛn*—#253–257) with the message: *Asante kɔtɔkɔ monka ntoa*—Asante porcupines, seize your gun and powder-cartridge belts. The Asante military's fighting strategy was likened to the porcupine's strategy of shooting its quills in barrages and how quickly it would reproduce them for protection against its predators. The *kɔtɔkɔ* symbol (porcupine—#264–265) and the expression: "*Asante kɔtɔkɔ, kum apem a, apem bɛba*—Asante porcupine, you kill a thousand, a thousand more will come" has become synonymous with Asante bravery, military prowess and gallantry. In present times the *asafo* continues to play an important role in emergency situations and in providing welfare services (e. g., fire, floods, or search parties for someone lost in the bush or drowning) especially in the rural areas.

Military titles of honor that were conferred on individuals for their heroism and bravery included *ɔsabarima, baafoɔ, ɔsahene, katakyie, aberɛmpɔn, ɔsagyefo*, and *ɔgyeatuo*. The *ɛkyɛm* (shield—#269) symbol depicts heroic deeds and bravery. Such heroic deeds were treasured long after the death of the hero as implied in the following maxim: *ɛkyɛm tete a, ɛka ne meramu* (When a shield wears out, the framework still remains—#269). The prestigious title of *ɔberɛmpɔn* was conferred on individuals who not only rendered but also excelled in military service. This title was later conferred on successful *batafoɔ* (state traders). Chiefs who earned the *ɔberɛmpɔn* title were allowed to carry *sika mena* (gilded elephant tails). The highly prestigious title of *ɔberɛmpɔn* was seldom conferred for other than valor, but later it became one with which distinguished service to the state might be rewarded. Hence the expression: *ɔbarima wɔyɛ no dɔm ano, na wɔnyɛ no wɔ fie*, meaning a manly deed is made facing the enemy on the battlefield, not in the home.

JUSTICE, LAW, AND ORDER

The Akans did not separate in different individuals or institutions the functions of the executive and the judiciary. To understand the Akan system of justice, law and order encoded by the adinkra symbols the Kumasi state organization will be used here for illustrative purposes. The Council of State in Kumasi, for example, functioned as a court both of legislation (*amansɛm*) and of justice (*asɛnnie*). Its sessions were in the *Pramakeseeso*—the great courtyard of the Asantehene's palace. The Council was the

Nkotimsefoɔ
pua - #236

Pagya - #267

Akobɛn -
#257

Akofena ne
tuo - #268

Ɔkɔdeɛ
mmɔwerɛ -
#263

Ɔhene tuo -
#260

highest court of justice. Legal hearing or trial session was referred to as *asɛnnie*, and the court of justice was known as *asɛnnibea*; courtiers who gave advice during legal cases were known as *atrankonnwafoɔ*.

The court proceeds with the litigants stating their cases and calling their witnesses. They are then examined by the assessors (*akyeame*). After consultation the assessors advise the chief as to his decision. The decision of the lower courts could be appealed to the higher courts. In the capital of the *ɔman* the *akyeame* could hold supernumerary courts of their own to relieve the pressure of work upon the regular courts. The decisions of the Council of State were publicized by the *nseniefoɔ* (heralds) and *dawurofoɔ* (gong-beaters, as in *Agyin dawuro*—# 241–242; 243–245). State executioners (*adumfoɔ*) carried out public executions when one was sentenced to death. Condemned prisoners were held with handcuffs (*ɛpa*—#295–298) and executions were carried out with *sepɔ* (executioner's knife or dagger—#299–301) during annual public ceremonies. *Abrafoɔ* (police) maintained public order and patrolled the streets at night and enforced curfew allowing no one to leave the town after nightfall. The *abrafoɔ* and *adumfoɔ* effectively enforced the *mmara* (law) promulgated by the *Asantemanhyiamu* and/or the Council of State.

A dispute within a household was regarded as *afisɛm* or *abusuasɛm* (e.g., slander, insults and other abuses, assault, and cases regarding personal property), and such disputes fell to the jurisdiction of the *ɔhemaa* (queenmother), *abusuahene* or *abusuapanyin* and his council of elders (*badwafoɔ*). If the dispute involved acts hateful to the state or the gods (such as invocation of the Asanteman Ntam also known as the Ntam Kɛse—Great Oath and *ɔman akyiwadeɛ*—state taboos such as treason, invocation of a curse on a chief, incest and adultery) the case would fall to the jurisdiction of the Asantehene's or *ɔmanhene's* court or a court of officeholders (e.g., *akyeame*) delegated by the Asantehene to sit on such a case.

The *ɔhemmaa* had her own *ntam* (oath) which was the formula for invoking the judicial process. She had her own court with female counselors and akyeame who acted as prosecutors and judge. The *ɔhemmaa's* court served as a refuge for a fugitive from the *ɔhene's* court. The fugitive could successfully seek the *ɔhemmaa's* intervention (*dwantoa*) in cases carrying the death penalty. While the king's court dealt with *amansɛm* (matters of state), *ɛfisɛm* (domestic matters) were dealt with by the *ɔhemaa*. In certain cases, however, male litigants could apply to have their civil cases transferred from the king's court to the queenmother's court where fees and fines were generally lower (Aidoo, 1981; Arhin, 1983b; Manuh, 1988).

In Akan legal practice, one was presumed innocent until proven otherwise as symbolized by *dwantire* (ram's head—#279–285). Fairness was also presumed to prevail in the society, and no one should provoke another without just cause (*obi nka obi kwa*—#272–278). The symbol (*ankonam boafoɔ ne Onyankopɔn*—#270) points out the Akan belief that God ensures that there is justice and fairness for all, irrespective of their social class, status, or condition in life. Even though God ensures fairness and justice, the individual is required to do unto others what she or he would want others do unto him/her (*nea wopɛ sɛ*— #271). Litigants were also urged to be conciliatory to each other for in the Akan belief, *obi nkyɛ obi kwan mu si* (to err is human—#302).

Gyawu atiko
- #252

Akobɛn -
#253

Etuo abobaa
- #352

Kɔtɔkɔ -
#265

Etuo koraa -
#355

Gyawu atiko
- #248

Ɛpa - #297

Kɔtɔkɔ -
#265

1. Chiefs have added to their collection of stools adaptations of chairs believed to be based on the *aketɛnnua* or European chairs. These adapted chairs are the *asipim* and *konkromfi*.

2. The stool is oftentimes made from white wood such as *ɔsɛsɛ (funtumia* sp.), (*Apoctnaceae Alstonia*), and *tweneboa* or *kodua* (cedar). Occasionally colored wood such as mahogany may be used in carving stools.

3. There are three parts to the stool: the base, the middle, and the top. The middle portion usually incorporates a symbol which may be associated with a proverb, a maxim or some phenomenon (Rattray, 1969; Sarpong, 1971). The symbols incorporated in the stool served to give names to the stools. In the past the symbols served to determine social class and status, age and sex of the owner.

4. Sarpong (1990) explains that the horns are of great variety and serve several purposes. The Amoakwa has been detailed by the Asantehene for the Asantehemaa, and together with *dawuro* (bells—#241–242) and *atumpan* drums it forms part of the Queen mother's ceremonial orchestra (*ɔhemaa agorɔ*). Other horns include the *nkrawobɛn* (#173—which is believed to have been brought to Asante by some Denkyera defectors during the 'Osanti' War), *asikabɛn, kwakorannya, nkofe, nkontwewa, durugya,* and *atɛntɛbɛn*, and these are grouped into various ensembles.

5. There is also the *akuraa* (hamlet or farmstead) which is considered a temporary settlement usually of members of a household on a farm. This is headed by the head of the household.

6. Each of the confederate states had its own Council of State. For example, the Dwabenhene was the head of the Dwaben Council of State.

7. Asafo companies existed in all the Akan states. The Fantes went a step further by incorporating some European customs in their Asafo companies. The typical Asafo company in a Fantse township, according to Aggrey (1978), was headed by the *Tufohene*, the military advisor to the chief of the township. Next in line was the *Asafobaatan. Supi* was the commanding officer, and the divisional captain within a company was called the *Safohene* (for the male) or *Asafoakyerɛ* (for the female). Other ranks in the Asafo were the *Asafokɔmfo* (the priest), *ɔkyerɛma*—head of the *akyerɛmafo* (the drummers), *frankaakitani* (flag bearer), *sekanbɔni* (sword maker), *ɔkyeame* (spokesperson or linguist), and *abrafoɔ* (executioners). Datta (1972) distinguishes between formal and informal offices, the former being characterized by a specific ritual with which the assumption of the office was marked. Among these offices are the *tufohene, asafobaatan, supi, safohene, frankaakitani, sekanbɔni,* and *ɔkyeame*. These office-holders take the appropriate oath on the assumption of office at formally organized ceremonies.

8. The Akan Asafo scouting system is what Baden Powell is believed to have used as the model for the Scout Movement (Tufuo and Donkor, 1989).

9. The Mampɔnhene served as the Kontirehene of the Asante national army, the supreme commander of which was the Asantehene.

10. The Asante national army differed from the *amantoɔ* (state) armies in that each

Akofena ne
tuo - #268

Ɛkyɛm - #269

of the *nifa* and *benkum* wings had two sub-divisions *nifa* (right) and *nifa moase* (right-half), and *benkum* (left) and *benkum moaase* (left-half) (Busia, 1951).

CHAPTER 6

Pempamsie se: Bebirebe ahɔɔden ne koroyɛ.
The strength of the multitude lies in unity.

ASPECTS OF AKAN POLITICAL BELIEFS

UNITY

Nkɔnsɔnkɔnsɔn
- #303

Adwa - #156

Abusua
panin - #453

Pempamsie
- #324

Adwa -
#155

Nkabom -
#318

Several adinkra cloth symbols point to Akan views about political concepts such as unity, diversity, peace, war, diplomacy, pluralism and democracy. There are symbols that encode how state authority is legitimated, and other symbols encode sanctions and other social control mechanisms and rights and responsibilities of both leaders and the led. This chapter will decode some of the adinkra symbols in order to shed some light on Akan views about these concepts. The Akan state is made up of loosely knit matriclan families (*abusua*, singular, *mmusua*, plural) that comprise individual households. The diversity in the society is obvious in many respects other than the plural matriclans: political views, sex, age, occupation, and differences in individual as well as group ability. The need for social cohesion, cooperation, unity, and national integration in the pluralistic society is paramount.

The Akan ideological belief indicates that the cohesive force of the family (*abusua*) is spiritual. The cohesive force of the family is expressed by the belief in the descent from a common ancestress and the belief in a community of the living, the spirits of the dead, and the yet-to-be-born members of the family. This idea of the cohesive force of the family is also symbolized by the *nkɔnsɔnkɔnsɔn* (chain—#303–307) symbol and expressed thus: *Yɛtoatoa mu sɛ nkɔnsɔnkɔnsɔn; nkwa mu a, yɛtoa mu, owuo mu a, yɛtoa mu. Abusua mu nte da.* This translates thus: We are linked together like a chain; in life we are linked, in death we are linked. Family ties are never broken. Or, people who share common blood relations never break away from one another. Membership in a family is permanent. The individual members of the family form something similar to the links in a chain. This symbol emphasizes the view that each link in a chain is important and that each one must be strong and ready to play his/her role effectively. No one in a society is a "left-over" and so everyone should be ready to fill that "space" which he/she alone, but no one else, can occupy.

Similarly, the cohesive force of an alliance of families forming the *ɔman* (nation-state, country or empire) is believed to be a spiritual one. The cohesive force holding the state together has been achieved through the institutionalization of the king's stool (*ɔhene adwa*—# 151–163). In Asante, this alliance of nation-states to form the Asanteman under one king, Asantehene, was achieved by the institutionalization of the Golden Stool (Sika Dwa) as will be discussed below.

Unity within the family (*abusua*) and national integration are based on the continual reconciling of diverse individual and group interests. Reconciling individual and group interests within the family is encoded in the symbol *abusua panin kyerɛ wo dɔ* (family head assert your affection—#453). The *abusua panin* serves as the family's delegate to the council of elders or council of state (*kurontire ne akwamu*—#327). The *abusua panin* is also the chief arbiter in household disputes and quarrels in order to ensure peace and harmony in the family.

Reconciling national interests vis-a-vis family and individual interests is also emphasized by such adinkra symbols as *koroyɛ* (unity—#319), *pempamsie* (preparedness in unity—#323–324), and *nkabɔmu ma yɛtumi gyina hɔ* (united we stand—#318). The *pempamsie* symbol is associated with the expression: *Pempamsie se: Bebirebe ahɔɔden ne koroyɛ; ɔman si mpoma dua dadebo a, ɛkɔ akɔterenee* (Antubam, 1963). This literally

Nkɔsɔnkɔnsɔn
- #303

Kurontire
ne Akwamu
- #327

Koroyɛ -
#319

Funtumfunafu
- #309

Nsa korɔ
- #365

Ese ne
tɛkerama -
#320

Kokuromotie
- #317

Asase - #26

means that the strength of the many lies in unity; once people are resolved in unity, nothing can stop them from reaching their goal. Or, in unity lies strength. Another expression that best summarizes the emphasis on unity is embodied in the *nkabɔm* (unity—#318) symbol: *Nkabɔmu ma yɛtumi gyina hɔ, mpaapaemu ma yɛhwe ase* (United we stand, divided we fall). The symbol emphasizes the need for united action, unity in diversity, and national unity.

The mythical siamese twin crocodiles symbol (*funtumfunafu dɛnkyɛmfunafu*—#308–315) also stresses the problems of trying to reconcile individual and group interests and places emphasis on cooperation and unity of purpose. Two-headed crocodiles joined at the stomach fight over food that goes to the common stomach no matter which one of them eats the food. They fight over the food because each relishes the food in its throat. The two heads signify individuality while the common stomach symbolizes the common good of all the individual members of the society. This symbol stresses the oneness of humanity in spite of cultural diversity. It also emphasizes the need for unity in the family or state. Members should not quarrel or fight for selfish interests, for what each gains is for the benefit of all.

Even though people are born into a social setting, communal membership does not diminish the reality of individuality. In this sense, the individual has character and a will of his/her own. The *funtumfunafu* symbol (siamese twin crocodiles—#308–315) depicts how the desires, interests, and passions of individual members of a society differ and may conflict with that of the common good. The two heads of the crocodiles with a common stomach symbolize the inherent conflicts in reconciling individual interests with the common good of the society. The social good must not, and cannot, be achieved at the expense of individual rights, responsibilities, interests, and desires. Gyekye (1987, p. 160) says the following about this symbol:

(1) at least the basic interests of all members of the community are identical, and
(2) the community of interests forms the basis for the maximization of their interests and welfare.

While it suggests the rational underpinnings of the concept of communalism, it does not do so to the detriment of individuality. The concept of communalism, as it is understood in Akan thought, therefore does not overlook individual rights, interests, desires, and responsibilities, nor does it imply the absorption of the individual will into the "communal will," or seek to eliminate individual responsibility and accountability.

Individuality may give rise to social conflicts. Since the nation is made up not only of individuals, but also of diverse groups of matriclans, there is the need for national unity and integration. The siamese twins crocodile symbol also gives rise to the expression: *ɔdɛnkyɛmmɛmu nhwere papam korɔ* also, *ɔdɛnkyɛmmɛmu wuo ama dua mono so awu* or *ɔfuntum wuo sane mmatatwene*—the death of the siamese twin crocodile affects the tree and the creeping plant. When the crocodile is killed by hunters it is carried by being tied to a pole. The creeper is used as rope to tie up the dead animal. The death of the crocodile spells death not only for the tree that serves as the pole but also the creeper that is used as rope in tying the crocodile to the pole. In this analogy it is clear that the well-being of one depends on the well-being of others. The notion that something is "for me" is meaningless unless it is linked with the total idea that it is "for us,"—this is the cardinal principle of Akan communal life.

National Integration and Cooperation

National integration is also emphasized by the use of such symbols as *ese ne tɛkrɛma* (teeth and tongue—#320–322), *nsa korɔ* (one hand—#364–366), and *koroyɛ* (unity—#319). The teeth and tongue not only live together; they also work and complement each other. As they work together the teeth bite the tongue sometimes, yet they continue to live in harmony. The symbol depicts the complementary nature of human beings as well as

Funtumfunafu
- #312

Ese ne
tɛkrɛma -
#321

Nsa koro
- #366

Boa w'aban -
#336

Koroyɛ -
#319

Nsa koro
- #364

Adwa -
#157

Dwenimmɛn
- #204

nations.

The *koroyɛ* symbol is based on a story of three baby birds that had lost their mother. Their joint wailing from a tree near a farm developed a beautiful harmonious piece of music that attracted the attention of a farmer. The farmer decided to nurse the birds. The farmer became a mother to the birds. Very soon, the birds fought among themselves because each wanted the nest all to itself. Eventually two of them left to be on their own. The next day as the farmer came to feed them he could only hear a forlorn melodic piece of music. As he got closer to the nest he found out that the birds had broken up, he urged the remaining biɔd to go and look for its siblings before he, the farmer would feed them together. The bird flew away and very soon returned with the other two. The farmer fed all three birds together, and they lived together in unity happily ever after.

Unity is a source of strength as suggested by the symbol of *nkabɔmu* (unity—#319) and the saying that is associated with it: united we stand, divided we fall (*nkabɔmu ma yɛtumi gyina hɔ, mpaapaemu ma yɛhwe ase*—#319). Akans illustrate this view with the strands of the broom. When taken individually, the strands of the broom can be broken easily. But when all the strands are tied together to form the broom it is nearly impossible to break. The symbol *nsa korɔ* (one hand—#364–366) encodes this view of united action. The Akan say: *ɔbaakofoɔ nsa nso Nyame ani hata*—one man's hands cannot cover the sky. Even though the individual's hands may not be big enough to cover the sky, when all unite and join hands together, there is the possibility of covering the sky.

Power

Political power is believed to emanate from the people (both the living and the spirits of the dead ancestors). This source of political power is depicted by the *adwa* (stool—#151–163) symbol in the political organization of the Akan society. In Asante, there developed, as part of deliberate political reforms to devolve power through a hierarchy of stools: *abusua dwa* (matriclan stool); *ɔhene* or *ɔhemmaa dwa* (king's or queen's stool—i.e., stool of the royalty)—based on ascription; and *ɛsom adwa* and *mmamma dwa* (service stools, i.e., stools for public servants, administrative officers, or stools of sons and grandsons of chiefs)—based on achievement criteria.

Power is also believed to emanate from land ownership as indicated by the expression associated with the *asase yɛ duru* or *asase trɛ* (mighty earth—#25–26) symbol which says: *tumi nyina ara ne asase* (all power emanates from land). Even though land is communally owned by the *abusua* with the *abusua panin* as the trustee, land ownership by groups or individuals is an important source of power. At higher levels of the Akan political organization, the king as custodian and grantor of land can alienate land for sale or as a gift to citizens and non-citizens.

Power must be exercised judiciously and carefully by the king and his counselors and administrators. The king must rule by consensus to ensure democracy. This view of exercising political power is depicted by the *kokuromotie* (thumb—#316–317), *tikorɔ mpam* (one head does not constitute a council—#325–326), and *nea ɔretwa sa* (the path-maker or trailblazer—#363) symbols. The thumb represents the king; and the other fingers on the hand represent the individual members of society, who are free, unique and independent. But they are all firmly rooted in the whole, which is the hand, and derive their being and importance from their relatedness in the whole, individually, and collectively.

The community, symbolized by the whole hand, derives its existence from the interrelatedness of its fingers. Without the fingers there will be no hand, without the hand there will be no fingers. There is no king without subjects, and there are no subjects without a king. One cannot tie a knot without the concerted action and functional interdependence of all the fingers, big and small. On the other hand, when a leader tries to misuse or abuse his power, the masses will rise against him. This is implied in the maxim: *wode kokuromotie kj ayie a, wɔde sotorɔ gya wo kwan* (when one throws one's weight about at a funeral, one is bound to get slapped in the face—#316–317).

Tumi afena -
#149

Asase - #26

Nea ɔretwa
sa - #363

Tikorɔ
mpam - #325

Kokuromotie
- #317

Ɔsrane ne
nsoromma -
#404

Dwenimmɛn
- #205

Ɛsono - #219

In the *nea oretwa sa* symbol, the leader is urged to involve his followers in decision-making and consult with his elders in governing, for the followers are better placed to realize the mistakes of the leader. The king, as a path-maker does not know whether his actions and behaviors are right or wrong. It is the people as followers who see the mistakes of the king.

Another symbol that encodes the Akan belief that power emanates from the people is the *nsoromma ne ɔsrane* (stars and moon—#402–404). *Nyankonsoromma na ɔman wɔ no na nyɛ ɔsrane a*—the state belongs to the stars not the moon. The stars represent the people and are contrasted with the moon, representing the king. The people, like the stars, are permanent and always there; the king, on the other hand, may come and go just as the moon waxes and wanes.

Yet another symbol that chronicles the Akan belief about power is the *ɛsono* (elephant—#219–220). In the expression: *wodi ɛsono akyi a, hasuo nka wo* (when you follow the elephant, you do not get wet from the dew on bushes), the symbol uses the analogy of the elephant to stress, in one sense, the might of and the protection offered by the king. In the expression: *ɛsono kokuroko, adoa na ɔman wɔ no* (the elephant may be big and mighty, the nation does not belong to the elephant but to the deer), the symbol uses the analogy of the elephant, in another sense, to portray the view that power derives not from the king but the people. Also, in the expression: *ɔbaakofo na okum ɛsono ma amansan* (when the individual hunter kills the elephant, it benefits the entire community), the elephant symbol is used to suggest the interdependence of the individual members of the community. Despite the size and might of the elephant it can be brought down by an individual. The success of the individual in bringing down the elephant benefits the entire community of people.

Power sharing is an important aspect of the Akan political beliefs. The king and queenmother are co-rulers. Even though the female ruler has been conspicuously absent from local administration under the various colonial and post-independence laws and ordinances, that does not mean that the female ruler has not carried out her constitutional responsibilities. Oduyoye (1979) suggests that it is due to the tenacity of the queenmother in administering protective regulations for women that matrilineal inheritance has survived in Asante and other Akan communities and has been guaranteed in national laws.

Power is not only shared between the king and the queenmother. It is also shared among the rulers and their councilors. The power sharing guarantees that the ruler does not become despotic and dictatorial. In Chapter 5 we saw how the queenmother is the only person who can publicly rebuke the king. Adinkra symbols that encode the Akan belief of power-sharing include *tikorɔ nkɔ agyina* (one head does not constitute a council—#325–326), *kurontire ne akwamu* (council of state—#327), and *nam porɔ a* (when the fish rots—#362). In the *nam porɔ a* (when the fish rots—#362) symbol, for example, the Akan indicates that corruption in society starts from the leadership—*nam porɔ a, ɛfiri ne ti* (when fish rots, it first rots from the head). This implies not only power sharing, but also indicates that the head is still responsible for upholding high ethical and moral standards that will promote the well-being of the society.

Democracy and Akan democratic practices

The views discussed in the preceding section about power and authority underpin Akan belief in democracy and the practice of democracy. Akan hold the view that democratic rule must be based on consultation, discussion, consensus building, and coalition formation. Democratic practices are found in family relations as well as in the advanced forms of governmental organization at the state and national levels. *Tikorɔ mpam* (One head does not constitute a council—#325–326), *tikorɔ mu ni nyansa*, or *ɔbaakofoɔ mmu man* (wisdom abounds not only in one head, or one person does not rule a nation—#325–326), and *wo nsa da mu a* (if your hands are in the dish—#328) are some of the adinkra symbols that depict Akan views on democratic rule in the family as well as the *kuro* (town) and *ɔman* (nation-state). These symbols depict the value of consultation

Tikorɔ
mpam - #326

Tumi te sɛ
kosua - #330

Ɛsono
anantam -
#221

Kurontire
ne Akwamu
- #327

Nam porɔ a -
#362

Tumi te sɛ
kosua - #329

Wo nsa da
mu a - #328

Funtumfunafu
- #308

and discussion in arriving at decisions especially at the court of the king.

Underpinning the democratic practices is the view that power is fragile as symbolized by *tumi te sɛ kosua* (power is like an egg—#329–330). This symbol depicts the fragility of power. As a symbol of democracy it suggests the virtue of sharing political power, for it is not safe to hold power in one hand. Power sharing is symbolized by the *kurontire ne akwamu* (council of state—#327). At the *abusua* (family), *kuro* (town) and *ɔman* (nation-state or empire) levels of government, use is made of variations of the council of state to devolve and share political power through the following structures: *abusua mpanimfoɔ, kuro mpanimfoɔ* (made up of *abusua mpanimfoɔ, ɔdekuro, asafohenefoɔ, akyeamefoɔ,* and the queenmother), and *ɔman mpanimfoɔ* or *aberɛmpɔn* (made up of various chiefs, elders, and military leaders). The council of state notion of governance is incorporated in the symbol called *kurontire ne akwamu* (council of state—#327).

Akan believe in participatory democracy. The participatory democracy is evidenced by the process for the selection (election) of the king. The prospective candidate to occupy the king's stool (*ɔhene adwa*—#151–163) is nominated by the queenmother subject to the approval by the council of state (*kurontire ne akwamu*—#327), and the masses of the people (*nkwankwaa* or *asafo*—symbolized by *asase aban*—#354). This participatory system of government has an inherent defect. It has a monarchical basis which opens up opportunity for only royal members from the matrilineage to become kings. This problem is compounded by the fact that, within any given royal family, succession to stools is ill-defined and eligibility is broad (Henige, 1975). There does not exist a law of primogeniture in Akan societies so within any given royal family there can be several eligible candidates who can contest for the stool.

Resolving the constitutional problem posed by these defects in the indigenous Akan political system is very difficult, and has occasionally resulted in constitutional crises. This may be illustrated by the political crises that resulted in a civil war and interregnum of what Wilks (1975) describes as "republican form of government: *kwasafoman*" in Kumasi in the mid–1880s. Wilks (1975, p. 540) writes: "The *nkwankwaa* ... remained unconvinced of the virtues of a monarchical system, and for a brief period of time Kumasi existed under a republican form of government: *kwasafoman*." The commoners group made up of *nkwankwaa*—sometimes referred to as *mmerante* (commoners, masses or young men), some *asikafo* (a nascent class of rich traders), and some chiefs established *kwasafonhyiamu* (council of commoners and chiefs). Ironically, their claim to legitimacy was the *ɔhene adwa* (the king's stool—#151–163)—the Golden Stool. This period is marked by a *kente* cloth that is called *Oyokoman na gya dam* (crisis in the Oyoko nation).

The belief in participatory democracy is depicted by the symbol *wo nsa da mu a, wonni nnya wo* (if your hands are in the dish, people do not eat everything and leave you with nothing—#328). This implies participatory democracy and ensures a sense of ownership in the decision reached in the political process. In Akan society, participatory democracy is also exemplified by civic responsibility and service (e.g., in participation in *ɔman dwuma*—communal labor) to the community. This is implied in the expression attributed to the monitor lizard that his is to help build, but not to destroy his state (*ɔmampam se: me deɛ ne sɛ merepam me man, ɛnyɛ mammɔeɛ*—#336).

Cooperation and unity of purpose are not only important at the communal level, they are also important at the individual level. When one undertakes a good cause, one is given all the support one would need. This is captured by the expression *woforo dua pa a, na yɛpia wo* (when you climb a good tree, you are given a push—#331, 712). Also, just as one hand cannot wash itself, so it is difficult for an individual to provide everything for himself/herself. Similar view is implied in the maxim: *nipa nyɛ abɛ dua na ne ho ahyia ne ho so* (the human being is not like the palm tree that she\he should be self-sufficient—#574). Other symbols that depict this notion of interdependence is *boa me na memmoa wo*—#332 and *boafo yɛ na*—#334). As one tree does not constitute a forest, and one tree cannot withstand a storm, it is necessary for one to join with others to work to achieve what is good for the individual as well as the community of individuals. People and

Dua koro -
#343

Adwa -
#158

Kurontire
ne Akwamu
- #327

Asase aban -
#354

Wo nsa da
mu a - #328

Woforo dua
pa a - #712

Boa w'aban -
#336

Abε dua -
#574

countries depend on one another for much that they require in order to survive. The world would be a difficult place to live in, if people did not agree to cooperate with one another.

Another symbol that depicts this notion of interdependence is *boa w'awofoɔ* (help your parents—#459). In this regard, the Akan say: *sε w'awofoɔ hwε wo ma wo se fifiri a, εwɔ sε wo nso wohwε wɔn mmere a wɔn se retutu*—if your parents take care of you as you grow your teeth, you should take care of them as their teeth fall out. This the interdependence between parents and their children. Yet another symbol for interdependence and fellowship is *nnamfo pa baanu* (two good friends—#337). The proverb associated with this symbol is: *hu m'ani so ma me nti na atwe mmienu nam daa no* (the deer is always seen in pairs so that one will help the other out in case of any emergency).

Nationalistic and Patriotic symbols

Akan are enjoined to be patriotic. Crisis situations such as war and natural disaster offered opportunities for the Akan to display his/her patriotic responsibilities. One symbol that encodes this sense of patriotic responsibility is *boa w'aban* (help your government—#336). Another symbol implies that the one who is bringing success in the form of wealth to his/her society should not be stopped. This is conveyed in the following maxim: *Yεrepere adeε a, yεpere ba fie; na obi a ɔrepere adeε akɔ kɔtɔkɔ no, yεnsi no kwan* (When we strive for wealth, we bring it home; and we don't stop him or her, who strives for wealth for the land of the porcupine—#344). Also, the Akan is urged to be patriotic in the saying that *apεsε yε kεse a, ɔyε ma dufɔkyeε* (when the hedgehog grows fat, it benefits the wet log—#367). In contemporary times the adinkra cloth makers have incorporated the flag (*frankaa*—#684) and the Ghana coat-of-arms (*ɔman Ghana agyiraehyεdeε anaaso asεnkyerεdeε*—#368) in order to promote nationalistic and patriotic feelings.

Unity in Diversity in Asante

The founding of the Asanteman (confederacy) required the highly complex system of integrating individual and group interests at various levels of the political structure. *Asanteman nkabom* was achieved by various means of integration including spiritual, military, political and economic means. Spiritually, the Golden Stool (Sika Adwa) represents the soul (*sunsum*—#35–36) of the Asante nation. This reliance on the soul is in consonance with the Akan belief system in which the soul (*sunsum*—#35–36) is the medium through which one's affiliation to one's relationship group is achieved and validated. Through the Golden Stool, the *ɔman adwa* (state stool of the Asante), the Asante forged national integration and group unity. The following story is one version of how the Golden Stool was institutionalized.

In Asante mythology, Osei Tutu and Ɔkɔmfo Anɔkye are said to have called all the chiefs of the other paramountcies to an assembly (*nhyiamu*) in Kumasi on a Friday. Anɔkye is said to have given an inspirational speech on the principles and advantages of unity by drawing an analogy of the broom. The individual strands of the broom are easily broken, yet when the strands are put together to form a broom, the broom is unbreakable. Based on this analogy he pointed out that in unity is strength and disunity spells fall and oppression. He then pointed out the dangers inherent in the subsidiary position of the Kumasiman and the other *aman* (states) at the meeting vis-a-vis Denkyera.

The mythology goes on to illustrate how Anɔkye is believed to have called down from the skies a supernatural stool of solid gold. He ordered the surrender of nail-parings and hair clippings of the kings and queenmothers gathered at the meeting and set some of the clippings afire together with the surrender of the regalia (state swords, ancestral stools, etc). In the midst of the smoke, Anɔkye is believed to have conjured a Golden Stool (Sika Dwa Kofi) from the heavens. He then smeared on the stool some of the concoction he had made from the remaining nail-parings and hair clippings and mixed the remaining part of the concoction in palm wine and gave the mixture to the kings and the people in the gathering to drink. Anɔkye then told the kings and queenmothers at the meeting that their spirits (*sunsum*—#35–36) had entered the Golden Stool. The Golden Stool enshrined the

77

Boa me -
#331

Boa
w'awofoɔ -
#459

Adwa -
#161

Ghanaman
asɛnkyerɛdeɛ
- #368

Frankaa -
#684

Kɔtɔkɔ -
#264

Apɛsɛ - #367

Adwa - #156

essence of the nation, and its destruction would mean the destruction of them all as a people. He decreed that the custodian of the Golden Stool, the Kumasihene, would become the Asantehene. The institution of the Golden Stool also required the *amanhene* to swear allegiance, that is, surrender part of their sovereignty to the Asantehene and observe a code of moral laws (*mmara ahoroɔ aduosuon-nsɔn*—seventy-seven laws) said to have been decreed by Anɔkye.

When the reigning Denkyirahene at that time, Boamponsem heard about this meeting, Wilks (1992, p. 111) writes, he "mocked the attempts of Kumasiman to build up its strength: '*osa nti na ɛyinom aka wɔn ho abɔm yi*' hence the name *osa nti fo* or *Asantefo*—the because of war people."

The Kumasiman (rather the Oyoko family) needed to forge unity and integration of the various matriclan groups. Rattray (1929, p. 273) says of the mythology of the founding of Asanteman thus:

> What Komfo Anotche now achieved was the amalgamation of the other clans—Beretuo, Asona (Offinsu and Ejisu), and Asenie (Amaku)—under Osai Tutu, to fight the Dominas, whose chief was an Aduana. So remarkable did this achievement seem to the Ashanti, who were accustomed to the isolation and strict independence of the numerous petty chiefs, that they ascribed the feat to Anotche's magical powers.

If the unity (*nkabom*—#318) ritual performed by Osei Tutu and Okomfo Anɔkye resulted in a military coalition to bring together the matriclans or the separate *amantoɔ* in order to fight the Denkyira, then after the Denkyira War the military coalition was transformed into a political union. In this union the Golden Stool became the single most important unifying symbol of the people. It is believed if the *sunsum* (soul—#35–36) of the nation is enshrined in the Golden Stool, then it must be more important than any one person or group of persons, even the king. It is believed to be the shrine of the Asante nation.

The symbolic importance of the Golden Stool is described by Fraser (1972, p. 141–2) thus:

> The honors accorded the Golden Stool are, broadly speaking, those rendered to an individual of the highest rank. The Stool must never touch the bare ground, and, when it is exhibited on state occasions, it rests on its own special throne, the silver-plated Hwedomtea, an elaborate chair… Not only does the Golden Stool have its own throne, it also has its own set of regalia, including state umbrellas, elephant-skin shield and rug (Banwoma), a gold-plated drum, a lute, and its own bodyguard and attendants. Indeed its name, Sikadwa (or Adwa) Kofi, "The Golden Stool That Was Born on Friday," conforms to the Akan custom of naming people, in part, according to the day of the week on which they are born. The Stool is viewed as a living person, a sacrosanct being that houses the soul and spirit of the Ashanti people.

Other significant symbols that became politically manipulated to foster national unity and integration included the various uses of the *akofena* (state sword—#164–169) as discussed in Chapter 5. The various *amanhene* forming the Asanteman have to use the Asantehene's state swords to swear allegiance to him. Every year the *amanhene* have to attend the Asantehene's Odwira in Kumasi where the mumified bodies and stools of past Asantehene are manipulated as political symbols. See Chapter 4 for a brief discussion on the political symbolisms associated with the mumified bodies and stools of past Asantehene.

Diplomacy, Conflict Resolution, War and Peace in Asante

The Asante people have been portrayed in the past as "war-like people." This description was based on the view that the Asante empire rose from the desire of the people to merge together for the purpose of fighting the Denkyiras. The war against the

Nkabom -
#318

Pempamsie -
#323

Fa wo ho die
- #342

Adwa -
#160

Kɔtɔkɔ - #265

Fa woho die -
#339

Tuo aboba -
#352

Mpaboa -
#353

Denkyiras was to assert the Asante people's right to self-determination, independence and freedom *(fawohodie—#338–342)*. War was not only directed at an external enemy. The enemy could come from within as indicated by the symbol *fie aboseaa* (household pebbles—#356–358). And the enemy from within is more dangerous and destructive than the enemy from without.

Furthermore, the Asante symbol of *kɔtɔkɔ* (porcupine—#264–265) and the war cry: *kum apem a, apem bɛba* (when you kill a thousand, a thousand more will come) have been said to describe the warlike nature of the Asante people. No animal dare meet the porcupine in a struggle is the apparent motto of the Asante. Other symbols that are suggestive of war as an instrument for attaining political ends include *tuo aboba* (gun bullets—#352), *tuo koraa* (even the gun—#355), *ɔhene tuo* (the king's gun—#258–260), *akofena ne tuo* (sword and gun—#268), *ɛkyɛm* (shield—#269), *pagya* (strikes fire—#266–267), *ɔkɔdeɛ mmɔwerɛ* (eagle's talons—#263), and *mpaboa* (sandals—#353). Declaration of war would be signaled, for example, by sending gunpowder and bullets (*tuo aboba*—#352) and sandals with the statement: *wonni mpaboa a, pɛ bi; wonni atuduru a, pɛ bi na me ne wo wɔ bi ka wɔ ɛseramu* (prepare for war and meet me on the battlefield).

If the Asante were militaristic at all, they used their military genius and strategy to stand up against external aggression, oppression and suppression and to fight for their freedom and independence (*fawohodie—#338–342*). The Asante also saw war as the natural extension of diplomatic activity and the army as the chief instrument in the conduct of foreign policy.

The Asante were peace-loving people in the past as they are now. The Asante valued the use of diplomacy and peaceful conflict resolution as a valid instrument of political action. The symbol—*ɔwɔ aforo adobe* (the snake climbs the raffia palm tree—#345–346)—which was incorporated into almost every piece of regalia of the king, provided a basis for the development of a negotiating principle: tactfulness and patience. The snake does not possess limbs yet it is able to climb trees. It does so through tact and patience even though it recognizes it has to go through twists and turns in the process of climbing. The symbol extols the importance of diplomacy and prudence as the necessary ingredients of real valor.

Another basis for the development of a negotiating principle is incorporated in the maxim: *Dua biara nni hɔ a ɛyɛ den sɛ akuma ntum ntwa nanso asɛm biara a ɛyɛ den no, yɛmfa akuma na etwa, na yɛde yɛn ano na ɛka ma no twa*—there is no tree so hard that it cannot be felled with an axe; yet, however difficult or intractable an issue may be it must be settled by counsel and negotiation not with an axe. As Dupuis (1824) indicated, it was "a maxim associated with the religion" of the Asantehene, "never to appeal to the sword while a path lay open for negotiation." This maxim is encoded in the adinkra symbol *akuma* (axe—#567).

The elaborate protocol associated with diplomacy was accepted and practiced by the Asante government and its envoys. "Thus, notification of the dispatch of embassies, requests for audiences, the holding of the audience itself, and the message delivery all followed prevailing conventions and accepted formats" in diplomacy and the conduct of foreign affairs. "To a society that was used to formality even in private receptions and greetings, and to members of a profession that was drawn largely from a group that was well acquainted with the art of court ceremony, diplomatic protocol must have seemed a normal and familiar practice" (Adjaye, 1984, p. 235). Asante diplomats and emissaries performed various functions as ambassadors-at-large, roving ambassadors, and resident ambassadors. Their functions were both covert and overt.

The Asante government did not set up an office for foreign service as a distinct branch of government. However, there developed with time the specialization of certain individuals and *afɛkuo* (bureaus) in diplomatic appointments, the standardization of procedures regulating appointments and conduct regarding diplomatic and foreign service, and individual experts and territorial specialization for the conduct of foreign affairs.

There developed four distinct bureaus (English, Dutch, Danish, and Arabic) for

Sunsum -
#35

Adwa - #163

Tumi afena -
#148

Adwa - #156

Sunsum -
#36

Fie abosea -
#358

Etuo koraa -
#355

Ɔwɔ akɔforo
adobɛ - #345

formulating and carrying out foreign policy. The Butuakwa Stool, for example, specialized in Fantse affairs,[1] and the Boakye Yam Kuma Stool specialized in Elmina and Dutch affairs. At the individual level notable experts included Akyeame Boakye Tenten and Kofi Bene (peace negotiators) and Bosommuru Dwira and Kofi Afrifa (British affairs) and the Owusu Ansas. Yaa Akyaa (also known as Akyaawa), daughter of Asantehene Osei Kwadwo, distinguished herself as a diplomat. For her pioneering role as a diplomat, she acquired the nickname Yikwan (path-maker or trailblazer). She headed the Asante mission that negotiated and signed the Treaty of Peace and Free Commerce with the British on April 27, 1831 (Adjaye, 1984).

Asante diplomatic service personnel utilized a set of emblems which served as their credentials and ranking. The highly ranked akyeame were associated with their golden staffs (akyeamefoɔ poma); the "large crooked sabres with golden tilts" (tumi afena—#148–149 or akofena—#164–169) were associated with the afenasoafoɔ; nseniefoɔ were identified by their monkey skin caps; and the round, gold plates identified the akradwarefoɔ. These emblems were recognized as symbols of authority not only by the appointing government but also by the host governments that received them (Adjaye, 1984).

The Sika Akuma (Golden Axe) was carried only by the Afenasoafohene or his immediate deputy or representative. The Sika Akuma symbolized resolution of conflict through peaceful negotiation. It signaled that the message carried by the bearer of the Golden Axe was the final one, the last resort to conciliatory processes on the part of the government before turning over the conduct of affairs to the military authorities. This occurred, for example, in 1807, when Fantse militants rejected any negotiated settlement of differences and actually seized the Golden Axe. War inevitably followed.

The conduct of foreign service gave rise to the use of other written forms such as Arabic, Dutch, and English as means of communication with foreigners. The ɔhene krakye (the King's scribe), for instance, emerged as the official specializing in the English correspondence of the Asantehene. However, "written diplomacy" was not regarded as a substitute for "oral diplomacy;" the written communication was only employed as a supplement to the traditional oral medium (Adjaye, 1984).

Peace (asomdwoeɛ—#349; 360) is highly treasured by the Akan. The king's palace is referred to as asomdwoeɛ fie (house of peace—#361). Newly installed chiefs were required to plant a tree as a sign of peace, continuity of state authority and proper succession. During the planting ceremony, the trees planted by his predecessors were decorated with white cloth or hyire (white clay), and before them the new chief would swear an oath to rule well and guard his people and maintain peace in the state. Thus, these trees symbolized the spiritual coolness or peace (adwo—#349) and orderliness of the state. They also serve as shady areas in towns and villages (nnyedua ase) where people gather for festivals, games (ɔware, ntɛ, and dame), and for town meetings. As McLeod (1981) points out, before going to war, a chief would swear an oath that he would not permit the enemy to cut down the trees. "Being a symbol of political unity and therefore also of military strength," Platvoet (1985, p. 183) writes, "the Akan gyedua featured not only in the political processes of concluding peace, but also in those of waging war … Before going to war, the ruler of a town might visit the central gyedua of his town and swear to it that he would not take to flight nor allow the enemy to capture the town and cut down its gyennua."

On the other hand, "rebellion against a ruler was often proclaimed by the 'young men' [nkwankwaa] striking off leaves and twigs from the (central) gyedua, thus stating their intention to depose him, with, or at times without, the due processes of law…Such an attack upon the gyedua and the king was possible only if it expressed a widespread feeling" of disaffection (Platvoet, 1985, p. 190). When the chief died, the werempefoɔ would tear down some of the branches of the gyedua trees as a sign of disorder which had come upon the Asante nation following the chief's death.

The masses of the people form what may be referred to as asase aban (earth fortress—#354). When the masses rise, as they did in the Yaa Asantewaa War of 1900 and the civil war of the 1880s, they cannot be restrained. In 1896 Asantehene Prempeh I prevented his

Ntease̱ - #348

Adwo - #349

people from fighting the British in a war which, he, in his judicious foresight, felt must be avoided. Of his own volition he chose to be taken prisoner and be exiled rather than lose thousands of his people. However, in 1900 when the Governor went to Kumasi and demanded the surrender of the Golden Stool (Sika Dwa) so that he could sit on it as the representative of Queen Victoria, the masses were no longer restrainable. They listened to the speech in utter silence, dispersed quietly, and prepared for war against the British. The war effort by the masses to save the Golden Stool from falling into the hands of the British was led by Yaa Asantewaa, queenmother of Edweso (Boahen, 1972).

NOTES

1.   In his autobiography, Nana Baafour Osei Akoto (1992, p. 20) indicates that "The Butuakwa Stool serves as the liaison between the Asantehene and some paramount chiefs in the country namely, that of Juaben State, Kokofu State, Nkoranza State, Agona-Asante State, Akim Abuakwa State, New Juaben State, Yendi in the Northern Region, and the Adonten Clan of Kumasi."

CHAPTER 7

Akokɔ nan tia ne ba so a, ɛnku no.
Parental admonition is not intended to harm the child.

BEAUTY, LOVE, AND FAMILY (ABUSUA) RELATIONS

Nkɔnsɔnkɔnsɔn - #305

Abusua te sɛ kwaeɛ - #451

Fihankra - #433

Ɔbaatan awaam - #422

Ɔbaatan - #420

Abusua te sɛ kwaeɛ - #450

Akan (Abusua) Family

The human being, to the Akan, is a communal being. The expression, *Onipa firi soro bɛsi a, obɛsi onipa kuro mu* (When a person descends from heaven , i.e., when one is born, she/he descends into a human society) suggests an Akan conception of the person as a communitarian being by nature. This also presupposes the priority of the cultural community in which one finds oneself. The communitarian nature of the human being is also expressed in the Akan belief that one is a member of an indivisible continuum of ancestors, the living, and the yet-to-be-born. As noted earlier, this is depicted by the *nkɔnsɔnkɔnsɔn* (chain—#303–307) symbol. Even though the Akans believe a person is by nature a social (communal) being, they also believe one is by nature other things (e.g., an individual) as well (Gyekye, 1992).

The center of the Akan social system is the family. The family is an extended one which may comprise the head of the household, usually a male (*agya*—father, or sometimes *wɔfa*—uncle); the wife (*yere* or *yerenom*—wives) of the head; their unmarried children; married sons and their wives; and possibly nephews and nieces of the head. The head of the household wields both political and spiritual (religious) power. He acts as the intermediary between his household members, the larger society, and the spirits of the ancestors and the yet-to-be-born. The head of the household is the administrator of all family property, and the arbitrator of household disputes.

The household—*i.e. efie*, forms the basic unit of the *abusua*. Membership in the *abusua* is matrilineal. Within the *abusua* the mother-child (*mogya*—blood) relationship is of paramount importance, hence the expression: *Woni wu a, na w'abusua asa* (when your mother dies that is the end of your lineage). The *abusua* is said to be analogous to the bunch of palm nuts which has clusters (*mmɛtema*, pl.; *abɛtema*, sing.). One's *abɛtemasofoɔ* implies a unit of one's closest relatives, the cluster that forms a segment of the lineage as a whole. Thus, Akan say that *abusua mu wɔ mpaee*—the family lineage has branches or segments based on the *abusuafoɔ mmaa*—the female members of the lineage. Another analogy for the segments within a family is implied in the symbol *abusua hwedeɛ* (#449) in which a grass field is depicted as clusters of grass. *Hwedeɛ* is a species of grass that grows scattered in little tufts. In this symbol the *abusua* is seen like this grass, and like grass it burns in the typical wildfire manner when set ablaze by family disputes. The *abusua* is made up of clusters of sisters and their children. Sibling rivalry, family disputes, and petty jealousies can set sisters apart as if they are enemies not family members; hence the expression: *abusua hwedeɛ gu nkuruwa, me nko me deɛ na egya da mu*—every family has its internal crisis or dispute that may be smoldering, mine is ablaze. Another expression that expresses the divisions and dissension within a family is: *fie moseaa twa wo a, ɛsene sekan*—the smooth pebbles of the husehold when they cut they cut sharper than a knife—#356–358.

The *abusua* is the basic social group for most aspects of institutionalized social interactions, including success to high state offices (e.g., queenmother and king), inheritance of property (especially of land and other immovables), one's status as a citizen (commoner

Abusua
hwedeɛ -
#449

Fie abosea -
#357

Abusua
panin - #453

Abusua te sɛ
kwaeɛ -
#451

Ɔbaatan -
#419

Ɔbaatan
awaam -
#423

Abusuafoɔ
ho te sɛn -
#445

Abusua dɔ
funu - #455

or royal), and one's links with the spiritual world, especially where one's body is interred after death (Busia, 1954; Fortes, 1950).

Family Head

The head of the *abusua* is known as *abusua panin* (male) and *abusua ɔbaa panin* (female). The *abusua panin* has certain responsibilities and obligations as implied by the symbol *abusua panin kyerɛ wo dɔ* (family head assert your affection—#453). He sees to it that enmity and strife, quarrels and dissensions do not occur among relatives in the *abusua*. Such incidents are inevitable as the Akans recognize that the *abusua* is like a forest (*abusua te sɛ kwaeɛ*—the family is like forest—#450–452) made up of a variety of individual trees. From a distance the trees seem clustered together. When one gets closer to the family or one enters the forest, one finds individual trees or individual persons. Dissensions and quarrels may bring disunity and create factions within the *abusua*. The *abusua panin* is responsible for managing these social conflicts from exploding into open disputes and quarrels. The *abusua panin* watches over the welfare of the whole group. He has the power and the duty to settle private disputes between any of his fellow members so that peace and solidarity can prevail in the group. As the following expression implies the *abusua panin* is expected to be fair and firm, protective of all members, and to be benevolent, kind and sympathetic: *Woyɛ damprane a ase yɛ nwunu; abusua panin kyerɛ wo dɔ* (You are like the giant shade tree in the desert; family head assert your affection—#453). Also the benevolent *abusua panin* may be referred to as *abasatea a adɔeɛ wɔ mu* (the slender arm full of benevolence).

The *abusua panin* is the chief representative of the *abusua* in its political and legal relations with other *abusua* and the greater society. He is the custodian of the ancestral stools of the lineage and he takes the lead in organizing corporate obligations, such as the funeral of a deceased member of the *abusua*.

Family and Funeral

Funeral is an occasion during which the unity and solidarity of the lineage receive public expression, as funeral expenses are shared among adult members of the lineage. This public display of *abusua* unity and solidarity is depicted by the symbol *abusua dɔ fun* (the family loves the corpse—#454–458). Decent, elaborate and expensive funerals constitute a strongly marked goal for the Akan. *Abusua panin* is the chief mourner. If the deceased person is a husband and father, his *abusua panin* formally presents two sets of *nkaansa* (notification drink) to the family of his wife and children on the one hand and to the head of his *ntorɔ* or *asafo* group on the other hand. The *nkaansa* to the *asafo* group requires the group to provide services in the form of grave digging, bearing the coffin to the cemetery, and performing other mortuary rites to honor the deceased member. The *nkaansa* to the wife and children requires their matriclan to present *esiedeɛ* for the burial of the deceased husband and father. The *esiedeɛ* usually consists of material things which include the coffin, clothing,[1] toiletries, and drinks, and cash to be used to defray other expenses incurred because of the funeral.

Family Dissension

An *abusua* that is rife with open disputes and dissensions is depicted by symbols like *abusua bɔne* (malevolent family—#448) and *abusua hwedeɛ* (family dispute—#449). The inherent sibling rivalry within the clusters of sisters and their children (*abɛtemasefoɔ*) is one major source of disputes within the Akan family. Other sources of dissensions within the family include chieftaincy disputes; individual interests versus the common good; new sets of economic incentives that have forced the youth to migrate to urban areas in search of jobs, thus reducing the number of family members in the rural areas to shoulder the family's obligations; Akan inheritance laws that result in conflict between a man's wife and his children on one side and his *abusua* on the other, and property rights over real estate (developed and undeveloped land).

83

Abusua pa -
#447

Abusua bɔne
- #448

Abusua
hwedeɛ -
#449

Momma
yɛnnodɔ yɛn
ho - #462

Fie abosea -
#358

Nkɔnsɔnkɔnsɔn
- #303

Fihankra -
#434

Abusua pa -
#447

Akan inheritance law requires that unless there be a deed of gift by a man to his wife and children of which the lineage (*abusua*) approves, the property of a man who dies intestate goes to his matrilineal heir and not to his own children and wife. Conflicts around the Akan inheritance law has done much to bring into the open the rival claims of matrilineal kinship and paternal responsibility. A popular expression that decries the Akan inheritance law is: *wɔfa wɔ hɔ nti merenyɛ adwuma* (the maternal uncle is there for me to inherit so I won't work).[2]

If the family is the royal or ruling family, chieftaincy disputes may center around competition by potential candidates to occupy the stool of the ruling family. There is no well-defined succession line to the chieftancy in a given royal family. A number of eligible candidates may have "parties" formed around them to contest for the position. Such a contest may rift the family into hostile camps. One famous situation centered around who should become the next Asantehene after the death of Kwaku Dua II in 1883. The conflict resulted in a civil war in the royal Oyoko Family. This civil war became known as *Oyokoman na gya dam* (Crisis in the Oyoko nation) for which a *kente* cloth has been named.

Family Totem

Each *abusua* is identified both by its own proper name and its common emblem (*nsɛnkyerenɛɛ*—totem or symbol, see Table 5 below). The Akan *abusua* groups are: *aduana* (also known as *atwea, ntwaa, aowin, aborade, aboradze* or *adwinade*); *agona*; *asinie*; *asona* (also known as *nsɔna, odum, odum-na, dwum,* or *dwumina*); *berɛtuo* (also known as *twidan*); *ɛkoɔna* (also known as *asɔkɔre, kɔna,* or *adɔnten*); and, *oyoko* (also known as *daku, yogo, yoko, owɛko,* or *anɔna*). All persons bearing a common clan name (that is, belonging to the same *abusua* or *abusuakuo*), resident however widely apart, are considered to be related by blood. In this regard, the *abusua* or *abusuakuo* functions "as a kinship charter for any Akan outside his [her] natal home or state—a visa, so to speak, for temporary or permanent residence" (Chukwukere, 1978, p. 136). All *abusua* members are expected to observe mourning taboos on funeral occasions.

A patrilineal lineage grouping known as *ntorɔ*[3](*egyabosom* among the Fantse) also exists among the Akan. Among the Akan the *ntorɔ* is what determines one's characteristics like personality and disposition, and the spiritual bond between father and child. It is the father's *ntorɔ* or *sunsum* and the mother's *mogya* (blood) together with *kra* (soul) from God that forms the human being. While the father-child (*ntorɔ*—spirit) relationship is considered spiritually based, the mother-child relationship is considered biologically (or physically) based. The patrilineage determines one's membership in *asafo* companies and societal responsibilities (civic and military). Among the Asante and other Akan groups the *ntorɔ* lineage gives rise to the use of particular surnames. Thus, one could to some extent tell a person's *ntorɔ* by the surname one uses. Examples of some of the names which are commonly but not exclusively found among people of the same *ntorɔ* group are:

Ntorɔ Group	Names
Bosommuru	Osei, Owusu, Poku, Saakodie, Amankwaa, Safo, Nti, Anim
Bosompra	Dua, Boakye, Boaten, Akyeampon, Agyeman, Ofori, Bediako
Bosompo	Duko, Bafi, Adom
Bosomafram	Afram, Peasa, Dame, Amponsa, Awua, Anokye

(Source: Mensah, 1992)

HOUSING

The Akan's nature as beings-in-relation results in a societal system in which none is left in want of basic human needs for shelter, clothing and food. The house (*fie*) is one's identity: *wo firi fie bɛn mu?*—which house are you from? is a common question used to establish one's identity. The house is a symbol of security and happiness. It provides elderly people respect and security. In return, the elderly give back protection to the very

Sunsum -
#35

Abusua te sε
kwaeε -
#452

Adwera -
#108

Fihankra -
#434

Blɔk dan -
#438

Εban - #428

Mframa dan
- #435

Blɔk dan -
#439

young, and also allow the young to drink from the elderly's fountain of knowledge and wisdom. The house is a concrete representation of social relations and the sentiments that accompany such relations. Building a house constitutes building a powerful symbol not only to express one's identity and status. It also serves as important measure of achievement in one's personal life; hence the expression: *Yεbisa wo fie a woasi, na nyε wo sika dodoɔ a woanya*—we ask to be shown the house you have built, not how much money you have accumulated.

The houses Akan build to provide shelter are usually of the *fihankra* (compound house—#429–434) type in which live all family members. The *fihankra* is a kind of house design with an open central quadrangle with rooms on each of the four sides. The uncompleted *fihankra* will have a fence (*εban*—#428) built to complete the unfinished sides.

These days, the *εban* is built around completed houses, especially in the urban areas for decorative purposes as well as for additional security and as a status symbol. The traditional wattle and daub houses have been replaced by cement or cinder block houses (*blɔk dan*—# 437–443). To build a house is seen as a measure of accomplishment more valuable and enduring than money. This may be inferred from the Akan expression: *Yebisa wo fie a woasi, na nyε wo sika dodoɔ a woanya*—we ask to be shown the house you have built, not how much money you have accumulated. The block house is not only a symbol of protection, security and shelter as all houses are so regarded. The block house has also become a new status symbol. This is indicated by the expression: *wonni sika a, wonsi blɔk dan* (if one does not have money one cannot build a cement or cinder block house—#437–443).

This display of affluence as suggested by the preceding expression is further seen in the extensiveness of the cement or cinder block wall that people build as a fence (*εban*—#428) around their houses. The wall, as a decoration and communication device, tends to incorporate some of the adinkra and other symbols (see picture —#). Interestingly, the wattle and daub houses were very cool and therefore suited better to the tropical climate of Ghana. The cement or cinder block houses, on the other hand tend to be very warm and humid. Whether one builds a wattle and daub or a block house, a well-built, reinforced and well-ventillated house symbolized in the adinkra cloth as *mframadan* (well ventilated or breezy house—#435–436) is highly regarded by the Akan. The *mframmadan* also symbolizes stability and security.

The multi-room rectangular building with an open courtyard found in Akan houses, as captured by the *fihankra* symbol, marks the Akan concept of private and public space. The Akan *fihankra* building used as a home demarcates between the *fie* (inside, private) and *abɔnten* (outside, public). The *fihankra* symbolizes protection, security and spirituality. In front of the house is placed a stump called the *nyame dua*—God's altar which represent's God's presence and protection. When one enters the house, the open courtyard (*adiwo* in Twi; Fantse call it *paado*) represents the public space within the house. This open courtyard has multiple uses. It is usually surrounded by a verandah where guests may be received. A bigger group of guests will usually be received in the *dampan*. The *dampan* (literally, empty room) is semi-private and has multiple uses: from receiving guests, and holding court to laying the dead in state during funerals. Then, there are the private rooms: living room, bed rooms, bathrooms, etc. There is also the kitchen, which very often extends into the open courtyard. In a big Akan house, there is the women's quarters (*mmaa mu*) which will have its own open courtyard and a number of private rooms. The kitchen and the bathrooms will usually be in these quarters. In the Asantehene's Palace the women's quarters is called *Hia* or *Hyia*. The concept of *fihankra* reinforces the idea of close family ties and unity.

The home as the first agency of socialization is very crucial in the instruction of children in selecting and adjusting their relations from their age-set playmates to their mother's food circle, the immediate kinship group (*abεtesemafoɔ*). The child who strays into a playmate's house and eats there is admonished to stay at home (*tena fie*—#446) as

Mframa dan
- #435

Tena fie -
#446

Fihankra -
#429

Nyame dua -
#53

Blɔk dan -
#438

Tena fie -
#446

Ahoɔfɛ ntua
ka - #543

Afafrantɔ -
#371

indicated by the following expression: *Wonam nam a, ohyia na wohyia; aboa antena fie a, ɔgye abaa* (when one does not stay at home one gets into trouble; the animal that roams is often beaten). The same idea is expressed also by the proverb: *Akokɔba a ɔbɛn ne ni na onya abɛbɛ serɛ di*—The chick which keeps close to mother-hen gets the benefit of the best part of the cricket.

BEAUTY AND LOVE

Beauty (*ahoɔfɛ*) is seen in terms of physical characteristics as well as certain social and moral qualities such as humility, etiquette, elegance, and gracefulness. A round face, a smile, and white, clean set of teeth, and well groomed or coiffured hair are some of the physical characteristics considered beautiful. A well-mannered person is also considered beautiful. In fact, good character, to the Akan, is more valued in a person than mere physical beauty as encoded by the symbol *ahoɔfɛ ntua ka*—(beauty does not pay—#543). The symbols such as *afafrantɔ* (butterfly—#371–373), *mampam se* (monitor alligator teeth—#377), *asambo* (chest feathers of the guinea fowl—#374–376), and *dua afe* (wooden comb—#378–384) also depict the Akan view of a beautiful person. A man may, for example, express his love and admiration of a beautiful woman thus: *Ne se nwɔtwe a ɛsisi nyaaanyaa sɛ mampam se; ɔbaa ahoɔfɛ, amampamma, mepɛ wo nkonse* (Her teeth have gaps between them like the young alligator lizard; beautiful woman with spirals around your neck, I love you—# 377).

Love (*ɔdɔ*) emanates from the heart not from the head as encoded by the symbols *ɔdɔ firi akoma mu* (love is from the heart—#390–392) and *ɔdɔ bata akoma ho* (love is close to the heart—#395). First love is like madness; it is illogical (*ɔdɔ foforo*—#370). Love will make one cry tears of joy or sorrow as suggested by the symbol *ɔdɔ nisuo* (love tears—#394). In Akan love relationships, the man takes the initiative in courting a woman. Courtship is very discreet. Courtship romance is illustrated by the following expression associated with the *ɔdɔ aniwa* (Love eye—#370) symbol: *ɔdɔ, mehu wo a, mebɔ m'ani asu; mefa wo a, mefa siadeɛ*—my love, when I look at you, my eyes are sanctified; I bound in good luck when I touch you. The following poem by Aquah Laluah (1960) called *The Serving Girl* further illustrates the meaning attached to the *ɔdɔ aniwa* (love eye—#370) symbol:

> The calabash wherein she served my food
> Was polished and smooth as sandalwood.
> Fish, white as the foam of the sea,
> Peppered and golden-fried for me.
> She brought palm wine that carelessly slips
> From the sleeping palm tree's honeyed lips.
> But who can guess, or even surmise
> The countless things she served with her eyes?

During the courtship the woman will urge the man not to deceive her (*nnaadaa me* —#398) and will encourage him to go forward to her people and ask for her hand in marriage. A man in love may give gifts to the woman he admires. Gifts that were developed into symbolism of their own were the *dua afe* (wooden comb—#378–384) and *akuaba* (wooden dolls). Young men in love would present wooden combs to their girlfriends. On the handle of the comb would be carved symbols with such names as *kae me* (remember me—#397), *megye wo awodɔm* (I wish you to be a mother of several children), and *ɔdɔ yɛ wu* (love survives till death or love-unto-death, or love is everlasting). Women would also give gifts and use their musical groups to sing the praises of their lovers. The *donno* (bell drum—#406) is prominently played by women in these musical groups. The women composed their love songs to praise or make references to loved ones, brothers or some outstanding men in the community. In the past, any man who was thus honored was supposed to give the women presents. An example of such love songs sung by a women's musical group as translated by Sarpong (1977, p. 24) is

86

Dua afe -
#384

Asambo -
#375

Ɔdɔ aniwa -
#370

Ɔdɔ nisuo -
#394

Nnaadaa me
- #398

Kae me -
#397

Akoma -
#388

Ɔdɔfo nyera
fie kwan -
#393

Osee yei, yee yei!
Ɛtwɛ Adwoa ei!
Obi di wo na
Wamma wo ade a
Ku no oo!
Ose yei, yee yei!
Ata Kwasi Adwoa ei!
Otoo too too.
Yɛrepɛ kɔte atɔ oo!
Sɛ mmarima nni kuro yi mu?

Translation:
Rejoice, rejoice!
Vagina of Adwoa
If someone 'eats' you [has intercourse with you]
And fails to reward you,
Slay him!
Rejoice, rejoice!
Ata Kwasi Adwoa!
Good for nothing!
We are in search of penis to buy!
Any wonder that this village is devoid of men?

Success in courtship depends to a very great extent on winning the girl's mother's favor. Winning the mother's favor may be done through giving gifts such *ɔtwee serɛ* (deer's thigh) and *nkyene* (salt) or by rendering services such as clearing the farm of the girl's mother—indications of the man's skills and ability to shoulder responsibility. Yet, without the father's approval the match will not be allowed. The father has to make sure that the suitor of his daughter will be able to support her. Parents must satisfy themselves that their future relations-in-law are agreeable with respect to certain characteristics that include the following:

wonyɛ ntokwakofoɔ—they are not quarrelsome
wonyɛ mansotwefoɔ—they are not litigious
wonyɛ bonniayɛfoɔ—they are not ungrateful
wonyɛ odifudepɛfoɔ—they are not greedy
wonyare yarebɔneɛ—they are not suffering from "taboo" diseases such as leprosy, epilepsy and cushion's syndrome.

The woman should be *ɔdeyɛfoɔ*—industrious; *obu nipa*—respectful; *ɔte kasa*—obedient; *ɔte ne ho ase*—sexually faithful; *ahoɔfɛ*—beautiful (beauty is not by any means a decisive factor).

The man should be *ɔsifoɔ*—industrious; *ɔyɛ ɔbarima paa*—manly and potent; *ne ho nni asɛm*—his character is without blemish.

MARRIAGE

Marriage (*aware* or *awadeɛ*) to the Akan is a configuration of beliefs and practices about the place of children, endogamy and exogamy, and the significance of the family in the society. For two people to get married to each other, they must fall outside the ring of prohibited marriages. One such prohibition is that the spouses should not be of the same lineage (*abusua*). The Akan considers it an abomination (*mmusuo*) for one to marry from one's *abusua*. This is viewed as incestous relationship as implied by the following maxim: *wo nuabaa aserɛ so a, wonna so* (if your sister has big and beautiful thighs, that is not where you sleep—#422–423). The husband and the wife must belong to separate clans or kindred groups (*mmusua*). The man proposes to the woman—*mɛware wo* (I shall marry you—#399). Upon favorable responses from the woman's parents, his people will arrange for a marriage ceremony.

Donno -
#406

Akoma
ntoasɔɔ -
#401

Ɔdɔ bata
akoma ho -
#395

Mɛware wo -
#399

Aware papa -
#416

Kɛtɛ papa -
#418

Fa w'akoma
ma me -
#396

Ɔsrane ne
nsoromma -
#404

Akan Marriage Ceremony

Aware-gye or *ɔbaa-ho-adeyɔ* is the term Akan use for marriage ceremony. The ceremony consists of the following steps: *kɔkɔɔkɔ nsa* or *serɛ nsa* or *abobomu-bɔdeɛ*; *akontan sekan*; *tiri nsa*; *tambobaa*; *ahyiade*; *bɔɔdo taa*; and *aseda nsa*.

Marriage is a union not only between the two people in love, but also of the two families (*mmusua*) of the lovers that is why future relations-in-aw must be found to be agreeable as indicated above. Marriage as a contract is not like the bond of blood in *abusua* relations. This view of marriage is associated with the symbol *aware yɛ ayɔnkoyɛ, ɛnʋɛ abusuabɔ* (the contract of marriage is a contract of friendship that can be broken; it is not like the bond of blood in family relationships—#400). Implied in this view is the possibility of divorce. However, this is not to suggest that divorce is a common practice among the Akan. To this Akan say *aware nyɛ aware na, na ne gyaeɛ*—getting into a marital relationship is not as difficult as getting out of it.

For a marriage to be considered legal it is required that the woman's father or *wɔfa* (maternal uncle) should accept *tiri nsa*[3] (head drink) from the prospective suitor and hand it to the head of her *abusua*. In return, the bride's father gives *aseda nsa* (thank-you-drink) to the groom and his people. The *tiri nsa* and the *aseda nsa* together make the marriage legally binding on both families as these drinks are drank by relatives of both the bride and the groom as witnesses to the union. *Tiri nsa* ensures marriage stability as it is refundable by the woman's family if she is blameworthy for the dissolution of the marriage. On the other hand, if the man is blameworthy for the dissolution of the marriage he loses both the woman and the *tiri nsa*. *Tiri nsa* gives the husband (1) exclusive sexual rights over his wife and the legal paternity of all children born to her while the marriage lasts; and (2) the right to essential domestic and economic services from the wife. The *tiri nsa* obliges the man to (1) provide the wife and her children with food, clothing and housing; (2) give her sexual satisfaction and care for her when she is ill, and be responsible for debts she contracts in the course of the marriage (*mmaa pɛ dɛ kyiri ka*—#444); and, (3) obtain the wife's consent if he wishes to take an additional wife.

The responsibility of the man for the wife's debt incurred during the marriage is enshrined in the time-honored Akan marital pledge: *Wode ɔbaa yi rekɔ yi, sɛ ɔkɔbɔ ka a, wo dea; sɛ ɛnso ɔkɔfa sadeɛ a, ɔde kɔ n'abusua mu. Wo pene so?* (As you take away this woman with you, should she incur any debt it will be your liability; but if she comes by a treasure she takes it all to her lineage. Do you agree?). If the husband wants to take a second wife, he has to give *mpata nsa* (pacificatory drink) to the first wife. This is in effect to ask the wife to share her sexual rights over the man with another woman. The first wife has the right to refuse the *mpata nsa* and thus stop the man from taking on an additional wife. If the first wife refuses to accept the *mpata nsa* and the man goes on to marry a second woman, the first wife can seek divorce for that reason.

Problems in Marriage

Marriage is viewed as a long journey (love survives till death or love is everlasting—#378–384), problematic (*aware yɛ ya*—#405), and not to be rushed into (*obi ntutu mmirika nkɔdɔn aware-dan dɔteɛ*—#399). The promise to marry someone carries such responsibility that one is urged not to rush into it as it is a commitment for life. One cannot sample it first to determine whether one likes it or not before one plunges into marriage (*aware nyɛ nsafufuo na yɛasɔ ahwɛ*—#405). It, therefore, requires patience (*nya akoma*—#385–389), truthfulness (*kyɛkyɛ pɛ aware*—#402–404), commitment (*fa w'akoma ma me*—#396), devotion and persistence (*ɔdɔfo nyera fie kwan*—#393), and cooperation (*akoma ntoaso*—#365). Akan marriages are either monogamous or polygynous, but polyandry is not practiced (Sarpong, 1974). Sarpong claims that polygyny accorded social status and economic advantage to the men.

A woman who has a good marriage is believed to benefit herself as well as her family (*abusua*) as indicated by the *aware papa* symbol (*ɔbaa nya aware pa a, ɛyɛ*

Dɛnkyɛm
dua - #400

Fa w'akoma
ma me -
#396

Ɔdɔ firi
akoma mu -
#391

Abirekyi
mmɛn ne
ɔdɔ - #444

Aware mu
nsɛm - #405

Nnaadaa me
- #398

Aware papa -
#416

Dɛnkyɛm
dua - #400

animuonyam ma ɔno ne n'abusuafoɔ—Good or a very successful marriage is beneficial for the woman as well as her family—#416). The woman who has a good and successful marriage is said to sleep on a good bed (*ɔbaa kɔ aware pa a na yɛde no to kɛtɛ pa so*—#418).

Some of the characteristics of good marriage include being able to produce children, an indication that she sleeps on a good bed. A fruitful woman may be compared with the fruit of okra plant containing many seeds as symbolized by *nkuruma kɛse* (big okra—#195–203). The lack of children in a marital relationship may be grounds for divorce.

On the other hand, a bad marriage is said to destroy or corrupt a good woman (*aware bɔne sɛe ɔbaa pa*—#417). The Akan also say that aware *bɔne tete ntoma*—bad marriage leaves one in tatters. A bad marriage may be characterized by infidelity, adultery, spousal abuse, laziness, incessant intereference by the spouse's relatives (especially by the man's sisters and mother), and impotence and infertility (*saadwe*).

Divorce (*Hyireguo* or *Awaregyaeɛ*)

Divorce, to the Akan, is neither anti-social nor religious sacrilege. Marriage is dissolvable only after relevant complaints have been stated and heard by arbitrators. Such complaints may stem from many factors including economic (e.g., incapability of maintaining wife), friction between the couple (e.g., owing to disrespect, disobedience, quarrels) or friction with spouse's kin (e.g., intereference from in-laws), and sexual deficiencies (e.g., infedility on the part of the husband, adultery or suspected adultery on the part of the wife, impotence of wife or sterility of husband). Either the man or the woman can seek divorce. A married woman can seek divorce from a husband who neglects her sexually or who can be proved to be impotent or sterile (*kɔte krawa*), or who neglects her and the children, or an abusive spouse. It is considered shameful and disgraceful for a man to physically assault a woman (*barima mfa n'ahooden nware*—#405); on the other hand, a woman is not supposed to say to a man that he is a fool and therefore, abuse (physical, psychological or otherwise) by the man or by the woman can be basis for divorce. Adultery was naturally a ground for seeking divorce. There were certain forms of adultery by the woman that were permissible in the past. The husband could only be in adulterous relation with another married woman, because he could have more than one wife.

Cruelty and neglect were also grounds for separation and divorce. Desertion by the man for a period of three years conferred on the wife the right to marry another man. Incessant interference by relatives (especially by those of the man) may be basis for divorce. The symbol *meso kɛntɛn hunu a na worehwehwɛ mu* (even when I carry an empty basket you search through it—#625) expresses the spouse's displeasure at the interference by the marital partner's relatives. The man's relatives, especially his mother and sisters may interfere in his marriage on the pretext that he is neglecting his *abusua* responsibilities towards his ŋephews and nieces, that is, his sisters' children.

Sometimes no definite reason may be given as the basis for divorce. When no definite reason or a vague one is given it is always to be understood that the man or the woman finds it embarrassing or degrading to reveal the actual cause for divorce. It may also be that a partner may not want to injure the reputation or cause harm to the other partner.

PARENTAL AND CHILDREN'S RESPONSIBILITIES

Paternity is acknowledged by the man's acceptance of responsibility of maintaining his lover during her pregnancy and by giving her and her child a number of customary gifts (e.g., *funumatam* —cloth to cover the navel) immediately after the child is born. The child's naming ceremony (*aba dintoɔ*) is the critical assertion of fatherhood by the man. The naming of the child gives the father the opportunity to honor his relatives, particularly his parents by naming his children after them. It was regarded a disgrace to the child and the mother if the child was not named by its father. The child without a known father is derided as "*onni sɛe kyiri botire*" (a child without a known father does not eat the head of

Kɛtɛ papa -
#418

Aware bone
- #417

Ɔbaatan -
#419

Mmɔfra
bɛnyini -
#421

Aware mu
nsɛm - #405

Aware bone
- #417

Menso wo
kɛntɛn -
#625

a slaughtered animal). The pregnant woman who could not name the man responsible for her pregnancy is derided as *wanhwɛ asukorɔ so ansa nsuo* (she did not collect her water from one source—that is, she slept with several men), consequently no one man could be held responsible for her pregnancy.

The norms and practices of socialization make differential demands and expectations on the parents. Parental admonition of their children is not intended to harm the children as symbolized by the way the hen may step on her chicks to protect them (*akokɔ nan tia ne ba so a, ɛnku no*—#424–427). It is regarded as the duty and the pride of fatherhood for the husband to bring up his children and to set them up in life. The father is dominant in the upbringing of the sons, while the mother plays a dominant and crucial role in the upbringing of the daughters. In the past the father took his son to farm and taught him how to farm, or taught him his craft if the father was a craftsman. These days the father is responsible for the schooling (and/or apprenticeship training) of his children. Even though the father is responsible for the upbrining of his children, Akan say that *ɔba nyin ɔse fie na ɔnka hɔ* (a child grows up in its father's house but never becomes a member of the father's lineage).

The mother is expected to teach her daughter feminine manners and skills for how successful or otherwise she is in socializing her daughter becomes evident when the daughter marries. This is expressed by the saying: *ɔbaa kɔ aware a, ɔde ne ni na ɛkɔ*—when a woman goes into marriage she goes with her mother. The daughter is socialized to be serviceable and submissive to her father, her sibling brothers, and older persons. The mother is expected to transmit her craft and occupational skills to her daughter. Among the crafts and industries in which women engage are pottery, manufacture of beads, soap-making, sewing, baking, and cooking.

A good mother is referred to as *ɔbaatan* (motherliness—#419–420). She is benevolent as she is considered a mother to all children. Sarpong (1974, p. 69) describes the Akan view of motherliness thus:

> Motherliness requires a woman to provide, by way of preparation, adequate food and shelter for her own children and when necessary, for those of others and for strangers. In some places in Ghana, a deceased woman who is known to have been benevolent is bewailed as: "The woman who gives to both mother and child." "Grandmother, the cooking pot that entertains strangers." "The mighty tree with big branches laden with fruits. When children come to you, they find something to eat."

Such praises may also be rendered to a man who is viewed as good father. Such a good father may be praised as "*agya a woyɛ mmɔfra ni*—the father who's a mother to children" or the "*abasatea a adɔyɛ wɔ mu*—slender arms that always take care of the needy and the vulnerable."

Children are taught to respect, support and protect the elderly. The respect for the elderly is indicated by the symbol: *woyɛ abɔfra a* (while you are young—#461). Children are responsible for the upkeep of their parents when the latter get old. This responsibility children have for their parents is indicated by the symbols—*Boa w'awofoɔ* (help your parents—#459) and *boa mpanimfoɔ* (help the elderly—#460). The bond between the father and his children is given tangible expression in funeral rites. The children are required by custom to provide the coffin for his burial. The following statement is said of children when they provide a coffin for their father's burial: *wosi dan ma wɔn akɔraa*—they put up a house/room for their father. This expresses the children's final filial obligation to their father. It is considered a serious failing on the part of a man if he dies with no child born to him to give him this last respect. It is derivisely said of such childless (and often regarded irresponsible) man: *n'adaka ayɛ no ka*—the cost of his coffin has become his own obligation, meaning he was left with no one with the obligation to pay for his coffin.

CHAPTER 8

Ahoɔfɛ ntua ka; suban pa na ahia.
Beauty does not pay; it is good character that counts.

SOME ASPECTS OF AKAN SOCIAL AND ETHICAL VALUES

Yɛ papa -
#463

Wobu kɔtɔ
kwasea a -
#632

Bu wo ho -
#464

Ɔbra te sɛ
- #498

Di mmra so -
#479

Nni awu - #478

The value system of a society consists of the explicit and implicit ideals shared by the members of the society. The values held by the members tend form a coherent system and these values influence the behavior of the group members. There may exist alternative or even conflicting conceptions of the desirable. The norms, mores, and values of the Akan people are derived in part from the Akan view of the nature of the universe. The Akan view the nature of the universe as a duality: spiritual and physical; the dead and the living; masculine and feminine; good and evil; the heavens and the earth; and natural and social. While the individual is a creation of a Supreme Being, the individual is also a social being. The Akan is a citizen of an undivided community of the dead, the living, and the yet to be born. Thus, to the Akan, morality and values have a spiritual source. God and the ancestors are believed to have keen interest in the moral order of the society. Ancestors are believed to be constantly watching over their living relatives, punishing those who break the customs or fail to fulfil their social obligations, and blessing and helping those who obey the laws and customs and fulfil their social obligations. God is believed to be all-seeing and has keen interest in the moral order of society. This belief explains why the Akan say: *wobu kɔtɔ kwasea a, Nyankopɔn hunu w'akyi* (when you fool the crab, God sees your rear end—#623).

One symbol, *ɔbra te sɛ ahwehwɛ* (life is like a mirror—#498), seems to provide a summary of the Akan basic ethical standard. One sees himself/herself reflected in a mirror. From this mirror image one is able to appraise one's self as being a unique person, different from all others. This mirror image enables one to imagine how one appears to other people. It also enables one to imagine how others judge one's appearance, and thereby enables one to experience feelings of pride or shame. In life, one's feeling of self is reflected in the mirrors of faces, words, and gestures of those around one. From this perspective, the Akan is taught early in childhood to do nothing that will bring disgrace to himself/herself as a member of the community. This is conveyed by the maxim: *animguaseɛ mfata ɔkanniba* (disgrace does not befit the Akan). The Akan is always aware that his/her well-being lies in the welfare of his/her society.

The salient features of the Akan value system include the value of life, the value of human being, and the value of the communal social organization.[1] Among the most important social values of the Akan are diligence and hard work, virtue, truthfulness, obedience, honor, selflessness, excellence, and respect. A child is taught very early to work hard and readily in the house, on the farm, or in following a particular trade or profession. *Adwuma adwuma o; adwuma yie* or *adwuma da wo ase* (Work, work; work is good or work is grateful to you) is a popular greeting the Akan exchange at the work-site.

There are certain norms and mores that are accepted by Akan as moral standards to which everyone is expected to conform in their everyday behavior. These forms of accepted behavior become the minimum morality that characterizes the behavior of the average citizen who endeavors not to violate the customs or social values or laws of his/her society. The basic ethical standards require one to behave, in one's relations with all persons, in such a way that nothing one does may bring discredit on one's family. One must do unto others what one will want others do unto him/her (*nea wopɛ sɛ nkorɔfoɔ yɛ ma wo no*—

91

Nea wopε sε -
#271

Nkyinkyimiie
- #499

Ɔbra yε bɔ na
- #498

Sesa wo
suban -
#496

Ahoɔfe ntua
ka - #543

Ye papa -
#463

Enni nsekuo
- #493

Nkyinkyimie
- #501

#271). Whatever one does—good or bad—is a pointer to what sort of family one comes from. Several adinkra symbols such as *nni awu* (do not kill—#478), *di mmara so* (observe rules—#479), *sesa wo suban* (change your character—#495–497), and *yε papa* (do good—#463) encode some of these moral standards of the Akan people.

Gyekye (1987, p. 147) notes: "The concept of character, *suban*, is so crucial and is given such a central place in Akan moral language and thought that it may be considered as summing up the whole of morality." He further points out that "moral virtues arise through habituation, which is consonant with the empirical orientation of the Akan philosophy" (p. 150). The Akan say: *ahoɔfe ntua ka, suban pa na ahia* (beauty does not pay, it is good character that counts—#543). In other words, good character is more valuable than physical beauty.

In Akan moral thought a person is not born with a settled tendency to be good or to be bad. Antubam (1963) indicates that the Akan do not believe one is born with an original sin. One's character is determined by one's deeds or actions which are learned. Since one can desist from certain actions, then one can certainly change one's character. This view is captured by the symbol, *sesa wo suban* (change your character—#495–497). Also, the expression *woyε papa a, woyε ma wo ho; woyε bɔne nso a, woyε ma wo ho* (when you do good you do it onto yourself; what you do that is bad, you do onto yourself—#463) implies that one lives with the consequences of one's actions. Therefore, one has the freedom to choose to be good or bad. It is on this basis that society has standards for punishing wrong-doers.

All Akan societies have their ethical and moral codes. Among the Asante, for example, Ɔkɔmfo Anɔkye is believed to have handed down to the society a code of seventy-seven laws to govern legal and moral judgement. The code covered such areas as sexual behavior, respect for old age and authority, honor, discipline and the value of life. Honor is a value treasured by the Akan either as an individual or as a community. The importance of this moral value is expressed by the following: *fεdeε ne owuo, fanyinam owuo* (between death and dishonor, death is preferable—#493).

Respect for Human Life and Humanity

The Akan belief that life is the most valuable thing in the whole world is expressed by the symbol *nni awu* (do not kill—#478). The aphorism associated with this symbol is: *nni awu na nkwa yεntɔn*—do not kill for life is priceless. This symbol depicts the high value Akan place on human life. Human life, to the Akan, is too precious to be wasted by senseless killing. Akan also say that *nipa yε fε sen sika* (the human being glitters more than gold; that is, the human being is more beautiful and more valuable than wealth or treasures). The Akan belief is that human life has within itself the power of change, growth and development. This dynamic, creative power in the human being must work towards building up instead of destroying as indicated by the aphorism: *mampam se, me deε ne sε merepam me man, εnye amammɔeε* (The monitor alligator says, mine is to help build up, but not to destroy my state—#377).

The Akan believe that all human beings are children of God as indicated in the maxim: *nnipa nyinaa yε Onyankopɔn mma*. From this perspective, the Akan believe in the basic equality of human beings. The symbol *woyε hwan* (who do you think you are?—#111) questions the very personhood of one. The Akan is deeply hurt when she/he is given cause to say, "s/he behaved toward me as though I were not a human being."

Exchanging greetings is not only a mark of showing respect but is also considered part of decency and decorum. The starting point of harmonious social relations is, to the Akan, the exchange of greetings. Greeting is more than showing courtesy; it is considered an acknowledgement, a recognition of the other person as a fellow human being. It is to confirm your very existence as a human being. To greet someone, that is, to recognize the existence of one whom you pass in the street as a fellow human is, to the Akan, an obligation. People exchange greetings verbally and/or by handshake. *Mekyia wo* (I salute you—#531), *nante yie* (goodbye—#542), *yεbεhyia bio* (we'll meet again—#539–540),

Aya - #519

Woye hwan - #111

Mekyia wo - #531

Akwaaba - #533

Abusuafoo ho te sen - #445

Mema wo hyeden - #105

Bre wo ho ase - #557

Anibere a - #466

akwaaba (welcome—#533), and *abusuafo ho te sɛn?* (how is the family—#445), and *wo ho te sɛn?* (how are you?—#534) depict some of the common Akan greetings and expressions of friendliness, hospitality, and forms of acknowledgement of the basic equality of human beings. *Mema wo hyɛden* (accept my condolences—#105) is the common way for one to express one's condolences and sympathy to a grieving family or individual.

Self-respect and Respect for the elderly and authority

The Akan is expected to respect one's self and also to show respect for the elderly and people in authority. Self respect is depicted by the symbol *bu wo ho* (respect yourself—#464). Not being arrogant (*nyɛ ahantan*—#477; 665–666), not being boastful (*ntwitwa wo ho nkyerɛ me*—#525), being humble (*brɛ wo ho ase*—#557), and having patience (*nya aboterɛ*—#385–389, 476) are examples of symbols that depict acts of self respect in the Akan society. The self-respecting person is one who knows how to control one's anger. It is said to such a person: *ani bere a, ɛnso gya* (no matter how flaming red one's eyes may be, flames are not sparked in one's eyes—#466–475). By this expression one is urged not to succumb to one's emotions, but to excersie restraint in trying and difficult moments.

The one who has self respect is also respectful of others, especially the elderly. The elderly are to be respected as they serve as the intermediary between the dead and the living. The chief as a person in authority, as well as the elderly, is considered to be sacred as he/she is thought to be in closer proximity to the ancestors (Sarpong, 1974). The elderly and the person in authority are regarded as the moral exemplar and are thus a standard which descendants should emulate. Respect for the elderly is depicted by symbols such as *boa mpanimfoɔ* (help the elderly—#460). Another symbol of respect for the elderly is *woyɛ abofra a* (while you are young—#461). One who is disrespectful is said to be arrogant. To such a person is said *ɛhuru a, ɛbɛdwo* (it will cool down after boiling—#544).

Selfishness and jealousy

The Akan also places emphasis on social conduct and carrying out one's social obligations as part of good character. Volunteering your time, that is, making yourself available in giving personal help, rather than donating money, in other words, generosity that consists of presonal service and hard work is more honorable and has wider application and can be useful to more people. This is captured by the symbol: *yɛ papa* (do good—#463) and the associated expression: *Woyɛ papa a, woyɛ ma wo ho*—When you do good you do it unto yourself. The Akan is taught to eschew selfishness and jealousy. The jealous person is said to be like the *mfofoo aba* (seed of the *mfofoo* plant—#481–483). This symbol is associated with the maxim: *sedeɛ mfofoo pɛ ne sɛ gyinantwi abɔ bidie* (what the *mfofoo* plant always wishes is that the *gyinantwi* seeds should turn black and die). The Akan must eschew jealousy and covetousness as the symbol indicates. Other symbols that convey to the Akan the need not to be jealous and covetous include *ɛkaa obi nko a* (someone wishes—#489) and *ɛkaa nsee nko a* (the weaver bird wishes—#490–492).

Envy and hatred are bad conducts that the Akan should steer his/her life away from. The envious person suffers shame and disgrace. *Atamfoɔ ani awu* (adversaries are ashamed—#546) and *atamfoɔ rebrɛ* (adversaries are suffering—#487–488) are examples of symbols used to indicate the sufferings the envious persons go through. The gossip is said to expose the shortcomings of others except his own (*kata wo deɛ so*—#485–486). The gossip is an envious person, so the Akan is urged not to gossip (*nni nsɛkuo*—#493). Rather than engaging in idle talk or gossip, the Akan is urged to think about herself/ himself (*dwen wo ho*—#561–563) and also to put herself/himself to productive work (*gyae me ho nkontabuo na pɛ wo deɛ*—#485–486).

Kindness

The Akan is socialized to value security, decorum, reciprocity, and benevolence. There are several symbols that depict the virtues of kind-heartedness and commitment to

ehuru a -
#544

ekaa obi nko
a - #489

Fofoo aba -
#484

Kata wo dee
so - #485

Eka nsee
nko a -
#491

Atamfoo
rebre - #487

Momma
yennodo -
#462

Nkuruma
kese - #200

the poor and the vulnerable. The symbol *momma yεnnodɔ yεn ho* (let us love one another—#462) conveys the Akan ethic that what is of value at the personal level is inseparable from that at the social level. This means that the practice of basic values is inseparable at the personal and social levels. Being a friend to the poor, providing shelter for the widow and the orphan, honoring one's parents and showing respect for the elderly and for the human personality are virtues that stem from knowing that *nipa nyinaa yε Onyankopɔn mma* (all human beings are the children of God). The *nkuruma kεse* (big okra—# 195–203) symbol also portrays the virtue of kind-heartedness as implied in the maxim: *Amoawisi, nkuruma kεse a ɔwo mma aduasa nso ɔgye abayεn* (Amoawisi, the benevolent one who bore thirty children of her own yet raised other people's children—#195–203). The good family head (*abusua panin*) who provides for the orphan and the widow in the family is also said to portray these virtues of kind-heartedness and commitment to the poor and vulnerable (*abusua panin kyerε wo dɔ*—#453).

Gratitude and Contentment

Ackah (1988, p. 34) writes: "The Akan is always particular about the behavior towards him of someone to whom he has made himself useful." This embodies the Akan concept of reciprocity, a central idea in Akan value system. There are essentially three forms of reciprocity: compensatory, obligatory, and initiatory reciprocity. The compensatory type of reciprocity is indicated by the symbol *pagya wo ti na gye aseda* (raise your head and accept thanks—#521). The symbol *woyε papa a, woyε ma wo ho* (when you do good, you do it unto yourself—#463) expresses the view that a good deed returns to those who do it. This also suggests the compensatory type of reciprocity. The obligatory type of reprocity is based on the demands of justice. This is conveyed by the symbols *nea wopε sε* (do unto others—#271) and *pagya wo ti na gye aseda* (raise your head and accept thanks—#521). The Akan says *onipa yε yie a, ɔyε gye ayεyie* (a good deed deserves praise). Also, when an Akan makes a present he accepts thanks (*Ɔkanni kyε adeε a ɔgye aseda*—#521). These expressions convey the view that one must offer thanks in anticipation of a favor or service that will be rendered. The ungrateful person is likened to a stranger who returns a good favor with ingratitude (*woyε ɔhohoɔ papa ɔde wo ti bɔ dua mu*—#522–523). Of the ungrateful person it may be said: '*kae da bi' yεde se boniayε* ('remember the past' is said to the ungrateful person). Also, to the ungrateful person may be said *anyi me ayε a, εnsee me din* (if you will not praise me, do not tarnish my good name—#564).

When young people take care of their elderly parents, they are expressing their gratitude to their parents for taking care of them in their childhood days. The gratitude children show to their elderly parents is depicted by the symbols *boa w'awofo* (help your parents—#459) and *boa mpanimfoɔ* (help the elderly—#460). These acts of service to one's parents and the elderly encompass the three aspects of reciprocity in the Akan value system.

The Akan are urged to be content with their lot as we saw in Chapter 3 of the story of the man who wanted to commit suicide rather than live in poverty. This is expressed by the following: *ma w'ani nsɔ nea wowɔ* (be content with your lot—#465). The following analogy is also given to illustrate the need to exercise contentment: if you have a small head and you try to increase the size by adding layers of mud onto your head, when it rains such layers will fall off. The Akan have to make do with the little they have. They have to capitalize on any least opportunity, for if a quantity of water does not suffice for a bath it will at least be sufficient for drinking (*nsuo anso adwareε a, εso nom*—#465).

Good Health

Good health as an important social value to the Akan is indicated by the recurring theme of health and long life evidenced in Akan prayers. The adinkra symbol, *mesrε nkwa tenten ne nkɔsoɔ ma wo* (I pray for long life and prosperity for you—#52), conveys the Akan's value for good health. When the Akan exchange greetings with each other the first thing enquired is the health of each other (*wo ho te sεn?*—#534) and the health of

Abusua panin
- #453

Pagya wo ti -
#521

Anyi me aye
a - #564

Woye]h]ho]
papa a -
#522

Boa
w'awofoɔ -
#459

Ma w'ani nso
dea wowo -
#465

Mesre nkwa
tenten - #52

Woho te
sem? - #534

family members (*abusuafoɔ ho te sɛn?*—#445). Good health is also signified by the symbol *mmɔ adwaman* (do not fornicate—#480). In this symbol the idea is conveyed that promiscuous lifestyle is not only immoral but also carries the risk of incurring sexually transmitted diseases. Akan believe in a sound mind and a sound body. One must not suffer from any "unclean" diseases like sexually transmitted diseases, leprosy, epilepsy, madness, sleeping sickness, smallpox and blindness. Such diseases were believed to be used by the gods to punish evil-doers and communities that failed to honor ancestral taboos.

Work Ethics

The Akan believe that when God created the universe, He created work as part and parcel of human beings. This belief is indicated in the following: *Ɔdomankoma bɔɔ adeɛ, Ɔde adwuma bataa nipa ho* (God created work as part and parcel of human beings). Work ethics of tenacity, diligence, industry and frugality are encoded in symbols such as *tabono* (paddle—#507–508), *ɔkɔtɔ* (crab—#588–590) *okuafo pa* (good farmer—#568), *aya* (fern—#510–519), *afa* (bellows—#569–572), *wo nsa akyi* (the back of your hand—#552), and *nsɛneɛ* (scales—#676). The symbol *tabono*, for example, suggests that hard work, like steady paddling, inspires confidence and industry. The *asɔ ne afena* (the hoe and the machete—#566) symbol, on the other hand, encodes the Akan view that *woansɔ w'asɔtia ne afena mu anyɛ adwuma a, ɔkɔm bɛde wo mawawu*—one must work or one will die frm hunger.

It is disreputable for an Akan to be regarded as lazy (*akwadworɔ*). *Akwadworɔ* means sloth, laziness, or tardiness. Akan popular maxim teaches that there is nothing in laziness except tattered clothes (*akwadworɔ mu nni biribi no, na nyɛ ntomago*). Parents are very particular about training their children to grow to be productive adults. Mothers are particularly burdened to cultivate proper work ethics in their daughters lest the daughters would grow up and turn out to be lazy wives. Laziness on the part of the wife would be grounds for divorcing her. Laziness as the grounds for the divorce of a woman is considered a disgrace to her and her mother.

The Akan is taught to believe that life is dynamic and problematic; one has to struggle all the time to make life meaningful. This is conveyed by the symbol *ɔbra ye bɔna* (life is a struggle—#547; 498; 499–501). This is because the life course is not straight (*ɔbra ne kwan yɛ nkyinkyimiiɛ*) as indicated by the symbol *nkyinkyimiiɛ* (zigzag—#499–501). To follow a winding path one needs to critically assess one's bearings and direction from time to time. The winding path represents life's obstacles. We must stop at each obstacle, we must think and reorient our steps in order to attain our goal in life. There are many encounters in a person's life. One may encounter ups and downs, joyous and sad moments (*ani hunu yaa*—#526–529), and wonderful and ordinary events. It is the duty of the virtuous person to bear the vicissitudes of life patiently by enjoying the happy and wonderful moments as well as having the perseverance and hardiness of the *wawa aba* (seed of the *wawa* tree—#502–506) to withstand the adversities of life. Failure in life is more painful than the pain one might feel when being cut with a saw. This is encoded by the symbol *ɔbra twa wo a* (life's agonies—#560).

The foregoing discussion suggests there is the possibility of making mistakes in the decisions one will make in life's choices. Akan say *nea ɔretwa sa nnim sɛ n'akyi akyea* (the path-maker or the trailblazer does not know that the path is crooked or curved behind him—#363). For that reason, one should not only be self-critical, but one should be able to listen to criticism, advice and suggestions from others. The Akan say *wo nsa akyi bɛyɛ wo dɛ a, ɛnte sɛ wo nsa yamu* (the back of your hand does not taste as good as the palm—#552). For one to be able to tolerate criticism and take other people's advice, one needs to be humble (*brɛ wo ho ase*—#557).

The symbol *gye w'ani* (enjoy yourself—#537) suggests that life must be enjoyed to make it worthwhile. The symbol urges one to make the best out of life. The symbol *nya aboterɛ* (be patient—#476) conveys the idea that with patience one can move mountains

Ani hunu yaa
- #528

Obra twa wo
a - #560

of difficulties. Another symbol that portrays the need for patience and persistence in life is the ɔsrane (crescent moon—#509) which suggests that the moon does not form a circle hastily.

There has been institutionalized a system of rewards and punishments to encourage individuals to avoid vices and to pursue certain virtues. One virtue cherished by the Akans is success in life. Success in life has its own reward. The Akan say that ɔbrane twa apɔ a, yɛma no mo (recognition and praise come with good deed—#520). Some of the rewards may come after one is dead as the Akan say apɔnkyerɛne wu a, na yɛhunu ne tenten (it is when the frog dies that we see its full length—#545). Similarly, Akan say ɛkyɛm tete a, ɛka ne meramu (when a shield wears out, the framework still remains—#269).

CHAPTER 9

Mmirikisie a yɛanntumi annɔ na yɛfrɛ nonsamanpɔ.
The farm that is not tended is referred to as a sacred burial ground.

ASPECTS OF AKAN ECONOMIC VIEWS, AND SOCIAL INEQUALITY

Okuafoɔ pa - #568

Kookoo dua - #573

Bese saka - #579

Ɔbohemmaa - #587

Sitia bɛkum dorɔba- #584

Asase yɛ dur- #26

INTRODUCTION

The pre-colonial Akan economy had passed the stage of simple subsistence economy as the development of centralized government, the local and long distance trade, and the use of money had led to the intensification of production. The principal sectors of the economy were agriculture, hunting, fishing, mining, crafts and trading. Nonetheless, production for domestic consumption was the dominant feature of the economy. Economic organization was largely based on the household whose productive activities were mainly oriented towards own use rather than for exchange. There was some limited government involvement in the economy. The centralized Asante government, for example, greatly influenced at least trade and gold production.

I briefly discussed in Chapter 3 *kookoo dua* (cocoa tree—#573), *bese saka* (bunch of kola nuts—#575–581) and *abɛ dua* (palm tree—#574) as examples of symbols that identify crops that have had significant impact on the Akan as well as the greater Ghanaian economy. The adinkra cloth also encodes several other symbols that relate to the nature of the pre-colonial Akan and contemporary Ghanaian economy as well as some of the economic activities of the people. Symbols such as *ɔbohemaa* (diamond—#587) and *okuafo pa* (good farmer—#568) and *afena ne asɔ* (cutlass and hoe—#566) suggest mining and farming as forms of economic activities. Other symbols such as TV (#608–612), *sitia bɛkum dorɔba* (the driver may die at the steering-wheel—#584–586), Senchi bridge (#628–632), benz (#606–607) and VW (#605) also point to economic activities of more contemporary times.

AGRICULTURE

Land, one of the important inputs for agriculture, was believed by the Akan to be the sustainer of life. On the basis of this belief, every Akan was entitled to usufructuary rights to land for the purposes of raising food crops. Agriculture was undertaken on small plots of land over which the effective or usufructuary rights of cultivation were vested in the *abusua* as a corporate body. Cultivation was carried out by the nuclear family on relatively small plots. The Asante make a definite distinction between land (*asase*) ownership and the usufruct right to land (*didi asase so*—right to eat from the soil). This distinction is embodied in the Asante maxim: *afuo yɛ me dea, asase yɛ ɔhene dea*—the farm, that is, the usufruct right to the land is mine, but the land belongs to the king). Thus Ollennu (1962) describes usufructuary title to land as the right of the individual citizen to the enjoyment of cultivation rights and even to the right of transmitting his individual enjoyment either by gift, will or inheritance to others.

Akan believe that land (*asase*—#25–26) is the sustainer of life and, therefore, it ought to be owned by the *abusua* as a corporate body so that every member of the *abusua* would have access to the use of land for raising crops for one's subsistence. Members of the *abusua* acquired portions of the *abusua* land through enterprise, effective occupation, and grants from the *abusua panin* or the king (McCaskie, 1980). The cultivator had exclusive rights to such naturally propogated economic trees as the kola and rubber. The

97

Abɛ dua -
#574

Bese saka -
#580

Mako nyinaa
- #613

Asɔ ne afena
- #566

Akuma -
#567

Afa - #572

Nkatehono -
#582

Kwadu hono
- #711

cultivator did not pay dues, levies, or rents for the usufruct rights to the land.

The state could not alienate land effectively held by the *abusua* lineages and individuals (Busia, 1951, pp. 42–50). Even though the state cannot alienate land already occupied by a subject, the king as custodian and grantor of land can assume the right of alienating, by sale or gift or otherwise, unoccupied lands to foreigners and companies for economic exploitation. In certain instances, some chiefs have unilaterally assumed the right to alienate land in order to promote national development. "This action by chiefs has been regarded as a breach of the traditional principles governing tenure" (Kyerematen, 1971, p. 37).

Cultivation was based on the use of such principal farm tools as cutlass or machete and hoe (*afena ne asɔ*—#566), axe (*akuma*—#567) and digging tool (*sɔsɔ*). These farming tools were manufactured by the local blacksmith (*ɔtomfoɔ*). The blacksmith shaped these tools from *daban* or *dade bena* (iron bar or measuring rod—#681) with the aid of *afa* (bellows—#569–572) and other tools. In general, localities were able to grow enough food for their own consumption, and in some areas, for example, around Kumasi and other large towns surplus food was produced for the market.

Food crops cultivated included yams, cocoyam (taro), corn (maize), groundnuts—as indicated by *nkatehono*—#582, bananas—as indicated by *kwadu hono*—#711, and vegetables (peppers—as indicated by *mako nyinaa*—#613–615, beans, okra—as indicated by *nkruma kɛse*—# 195–203, egg plant/garden eggs, etc.). After contact with Europeans other food crops were introduced into the Akan (and the greater Ghanaian) society. These crops included vegetables (e.g., tomatoes), plantain and varieties of cassava (manioc). Crops like the oil palm and rubber that grew wild became increasingly important as cash crops, and new cash crops like cocoa and coffee were introduced later. From the middle of the nineteenth century the missionaries, especially of the Basel and Wesleyan Missions opened agricultural stations for experimentation and extension of agriculture.

Oil palm tree (*abɛ dua*—#574) was valued for various uses. One could make the assertion that the Akan had a nascent integrated industry based on the oil palm tree. The oil palm industry initially consisted merely of picking the fruits from wild palm groves and extracting oil from the pericarp. The oil was in the early years used principally as cooking oil and also for soap-making and was put in *kyɛmferɛ* (potsherd—#698–699) as fuel for oil lamps. The oil from the kernel (alluded to by the symbols *mmɔdwewafoɔ*—#238–239 and *mede me se abɔ adwe*—#616) was used as pomade for the skin and as cooking oil. Both the palm and kernel oils were also used for medicinal purposes. The shell of the kernel was used as active charcoal by blacksmiths for various purposes including iron smelting and forging and the making of gun-powder. The palm branches were used as building materials and also for weaving baskets (*menso wo kɛntɛn*—#625) and making *apa* or *apata* (drying mats or storage barn—#583). The dry palm branches were used for making light (*ɔtɛn*) for use at night. Palm wine tapping was an important occupation for a number of men. As the slave trade ended, the oil palm industry expanded to satisfy growing demands in the soap and margarine factories in Europe. There entered into the oil palm industry several European companies to buy the oil palm products (particularly palm oil and kernel oil). The giant UAC (UAC *nkanea*—UAC lights—#621) first entered the Ghanaian market as Lever Brothers to buy oil palm products.

Cocoa

Kookoo dua yɛ sika dua (cocoa is a money tree—#573) signifies the importance of this cash crop in the Ghanaian economy. The *kookoo dua* symbol also encodes important historical, political, and economic text in the affairs of the greater Ghanaian society. Until the 1880s, the palm oil, rubber, and kola nuts that entered into the international trade were produced mainly through collection and gathering. As demand for these crops increased their cultivation was intensified. Cocoa and other crops were introduced and cultivated, especially after the abolition of the slave trade (Reynolds, 1973). The success of cocoa farming as an industry bears eloquent testimony to the entrepreneurial skills of the Akan and other Ghanaian farmers. It also suggests that the pre-colonial Akan economy, contrary

Apa - #583

Kɛntɛn - #625

UAC nkanea - #621

Kookoo dua - #573

Bese saka - #581

Koforidu nhwiren - #626

TV - #610

Mercedes Benz - #607

to the view expressed by Szereszewski (1966), was not "essentially static." The pre-colonial Akan economy did respond to market demands by being innovative. "Innovation," as La Torre (1978, p. 11) puts it, "should be understood here to include not only technological change, but rather any deliberate alteration in accustomed modes of economic activity, such as, for example, the rearrangement of social relations to acquire control over labor."

Indigenous modes of production such as nnɔboa[1]; labor market forms such as awowa (pawn labor), atabrako and apaadie[2] forms of daily wage or annual (afenhyia apaadie) wage, and forms of sharecropping like abusa (one-third of profit from sale of produce), abunu (half of profit from sale of produce) and nkotokuo ano (a fraction of the sale price of a bag load of produce); and capital accumulation methods such as susu and hazu were not only incorporated, but were intensified in the cocoa industry and other agricultural production. The colonial government's labor conscription laws to recruit labor from the north of Ghana for public works and mining in the south helped to intensify the use of the indigenous sharecropping system of tenure such as afenhyia and abusa (see Robertson, 1982; Aidoo, 1983). The failure of labor conscription laws in Ghana may be attributed in part to the intensified use of the traditional wage and sharecropping systems by Ghanaian farmers in the cocoa industry. Conscripted laborers from the north, and from French territories to the north and west, and German territory to the east who ran away from government labor camps or taxation schemes had alternative jobs with better wages and better working conditions on cocoa farms in the Akan areas.

Cocoa was first introduced on experimental basis by the Basel Mission at Akropong in 1859 with cocoa pods imported from Surinam. The experiment failed. Tetteh Quarshie is credited with the successful introduction of cocoa into Ghana from Fernando Po Island in 1879. Its production grew and Ghana's export of 13 tons in 1895 rose to 40,000 tons in 1911 (Dickson, 1971).

The success of the cocoa industry has resulted in significant structural changes in the political economy of the Akan as well as the greater Ghanaian society. The success of the cocoa industry has also resulted in the intensification of the market economy. Land purchase and leasing have increased as a direct result of the expansion of the cocoa industry. The success of the industry also hastened the process of capital accumulation and stimulated labor migration and labor market.

The success of the cocoa industry needs to be viewed in relation to its devastating effect on the religious and political unity of the traditional state or community. As Ninsin (1991, p. 23) notes: "The cocoa and mining industries severely disrupted this exclusiveness of the political and economic orders through the pressure for land and labour—independent or self-employed labour, and wage or semi-wage labour that was unleashed by these industries."

CRAFT INDUSTRY

Craft industry (adwindie) symbolized by, for example, afa (bellows—#569–573),[3] adwa (stool—#151–163), kɛntɛn (basket—#625) akofena ne tuo (sword and gun—#268) and kyɛmferɛ (potsherd—#698–699), covered such activities as weaving of baskets and textiles, wood-carving, pottery, metalworks (gold-smithing and black-smithing, indicated by afa—#569–572), and soap-making. Craft production was carried out on individual basis, as well as on family basis, and apprentices were close kin.

Basket weaving, encoded in the kɛntɛn (basket—#625) symbol, was the work of men. Baskets were woven from palm branches, canes and creepers. One of the important products of basket weaving industry was the palanquin for carrying the royals. Pottery, indicated by the kyɛmferɛ (potsherd—#698–699) symbol, was exclusively a woman's industry. However, men had exclusive monopoly in making the smoking pipe (taasɛn). Cloth weaving, dyeing and printing, suggested by the nsaa (hand-woven blanket—#655–659) symbol, involved men as well as women.

Symbols such as akokɔ (rooster—#698–696), akokɔnan (hen's feet—#424–427), dwenimmɛn (ram's horns—#204–211), dwantire (ram's head—#279–285) and ɛsono

Ebi te yie -
#600

Kookoo dua
- #573

Afa - #569

Kyεmfere -
#699

Kεnten -
#625

Akokɔ -
#696

Daban -
#681

Etuo
abobaa -
#352

(elephant—#219–220) suggest the possibility of the raising of livestock in addition to hunting. Such possibility would give rise to tanning and leatherwork. The possibility of tanning and leatherwork may also be inferred from other symbols such as ɔhene kyε (king's crown—#171) and mpaboa (sandals—#353). Other products of the leather works included afa (bellows—#569–572), cushions (atε) and soldier's belts and pouches

Smithing (gold-smithing, black-smithing, and the casting of goldweights), suggested by symbols such as afa (bellows—#569–572), asɔ ne afena (hoe and cutlass—#566), and daban (iron bar or measuring rod—#681), was a very important craft industry. Probably the most important products of the blacksmiths were agricultural implements of various sorts (axes, hoes, and cutlasses). Other items produced by blacksmiths included hinges, bolts, swords, knives, rings, chains, and musical instruments. The blacksmiths also repaired firearms as well as manufactured small quantities of firearms, gun-powder and bullets (tuo abobaa—#352).

Goldsmithing seems to have been under the close control of the political authorities in the Asante area. The courts of the Asantehene and certain other bureaus (fεkuo) contained a number of offices occupied by goldsmiths (e.g., adwomfoɔhene and buramfoɔhene), who supervised the work of the smiths (aburamufoɔ) employed by the court. Goldsmiths worked the gold into a variety of personal ornaments (bracelets, chains, breastplates, rings, trinkets, and so on).

As part of deliberate population policies of various Asantehene, craft villages were founded around Kumase with war captives or refugees in such places as Bonwire and Anawomase (textile weaving), Asokwa, Hemang and Ntonso (textile dyeing and printing), Breman, Fumesua and Adum (metalworks and goldsmithing), Pankrono, Tafo (pottery), Mamponten (soap making), Daaba (beadmaking), Sewua and Adwumakase Kεse (metalworks, textile weaving and drum-making), Banko and Nsuta (umbrella-making), and Ahwia (wood carving). The craftsmen and women were apparently free to make and sell anything except for items reserved for the king's palace.

HUNTING AND FISHING

Hunting (ahayɔ) and fishing were carried out on both individual and communal basis. These economic activities are suggested by symbols such as bomokyikyie (the river fish—#679), ɔkɔtɔ (crab—#588–590), nam porɔ (fish rots—#362), afidie (trap—#617), and etuo ne akyekyedeε (the gun and tortoise—#350). As part of the Asante population policy, many coastal Fante war captives were settled around Lake Bosumtwe, where their skills as fishermen could be put to good use. Hunting required special skills as suggested by the expression: gye akyekyedeε kɔma agya nyε ahayɔ—taking a tortoise to one's father is not considered hunting. Towns such as Sunyani grew as important meat processing centers for hunters.

MINING

Adinkra symbols that incorporate ideas about mining include ɔbohemmaa (diamond—#587), ɔkɔtɔ (crab—#588–590) and nsεneε (scale—#676). The chief methods of gold and diamond production were panning of alluvial streams and wetlands, and in the case of gold, quarrying or surface mining of gold-bearing ore (mmoaboa), and shaft mining (amenapeaa nkorɔn or nkorɔntu). "Akan miners in the eighteenth century dug slanting pits with broad steps to a depth of as much as 150 feet. The miners at the bottom dug out the ore and loaded it on trays, which were then passed to the surface by means of a human chain" (Hopkins, 1973, p. 46). The pit or shaft mining was known as nkorɔn dwuma, and the miners were known as nkorɔntufoɔ. Gold extraction by pit minig was shrouded in secrecy.

Panning of alluvial streams and wetlands is alluded to by the adinkra symbol ɔkɔtɔ (crab—#588–590). The crab in the wetland areas where there were prospects for alluvial gold, in digging its hole, would expose gold nuggets. This was one of several methods of prospecting the Akan used to identify possible sites for panning or digging along the

Nsɛnee -
#676

Bomokyikyie
- #679

Afidie - #617

Etuo ne
akyekyedeɛ-
#350

Kɔtɔ - #588

Ɔbohema -
#587

Nsɛnee -
#676

Serewa -
#595

banks of such rivers as the Ankobra, Pra and Offin. The panning method of production, now popularly known as galamsey, is increasingly making a comeback in recent years. Other minerals from contemporary Ghana include bauxite, manganese, and diamonds.

MONEY AND PUBLIC ACCOUNTING SYSTEM

In Asante, the state's involvement in the economy was manifested in the following ways:

1) intentional intervention of the state in economic processes through
   a) the protection and encouragement of trade
   b) the prosecution of warfare that brought skilled persons to be settled in craft villages
   c) the conduct of foreign relations to ensure trade stability
2) taxation and government expeditures such as tributes; taxes on trade; death duties; court fees and fines; and taxation on gold production
3) the use of gold dust as currency.

Some adinkra symbols such as *bese saka* (bunch of kola nuts—#575–581), *serewa* or *sedeε* (cowrie shells—#591–596) and *daban* (iron bar—#681) suggest the monetization of the Akan economy long before the contact with Europeans. Kola nuts, cowrie shells, beads, and gold dust were used as currencies at one time or another. European traders also introduced other currencies such as manillas, iron bars and rods (called *nnabuo* or *nnaredwoɔ*—see Garrard, 1980, p. 3), and copper rods. New forms of accounting based on indigenous systems were developed as part of trade with the Europeans. These new forms of accounting included the bar, sorting, and the ounce (Hopkins, 1973, p. 111).

In Asante, as in other Akan communities, there once existed a very complicated and elaborate accounting system based on gold dust (*sika futuro*) and goldweights (*mmrammoɔ*). The value of the gold dust was assessed by weight and the Gyaasehene controlled the Asantehene's treasury by keeping the weights (*mmrammoɔ*), spoons (*nsaawa*), scoops or shovels (*mfamfa*), scales (*nsɛnee*—# 676), and other appliances of the accounting system. Gold dust was demonetized as currency in Ghana in 1912.

The goldweights were kept in a bag called *futuo* and the functionary responsible for keeping the state treasury bags was known as the *fotuosanfohene*. The most important *futuo* of the chief was called *sanaa futuo* and the weights in this bag were used on special occasions like the Adae and Odwira festivals. The functionary responsible for this bag was called *sannaahene*. The chief's weights served as the standard and were usually heavier than ordinary people's weights. By this mechanism the state was able to transfer surplus from the people to the state treasury. The weights served as denominations[4] for exchange and other monetary transactions (Bowdich, 1819; Reindorf, 1895). Rattray (1969a, p. 117) provides the following description of how the Asantehene's Treasury operated:

> A large box, known as the *Adaka kεsie*, divided by wooden partitions into three compartments of equal size, was kept in the room in the 'palace' known as Dampɔn kεsie. This box was in joint charge of the Chief and Head-treasurer. The key of the chest was in the charge of three persons, the Chief, Head-treasurer, and the Chief of the Bed-chamber (the Dabere Hene); it was kept underneath the chief's sleeping mat. The three partitions of this box contained packets of gold-dust, each containing one *preguan* [*peredwan*] (i.e., about £8). This chest represented a kind of 'capital account.' All moneys paid into the Treasury were weighed, made up into bundles of a pereguan, and deposited in it. There were at least three witnesses to every transaction, and a fourth, if necessary, in the person of the official who first received the payments. Nothing less than a *pereguan* was deposited in this box, and nothing less was withdrawn; the Sana[a] Hene (Head-treasurer) accumulated receipts for lesser amounts in another box, for which his subordinates were responsible, until these sums

Sika tu sɛ
anomaa -
#597

Bese saka -
#577

Serewa -
#592

Kɔtɔ - #589

Toa - #598

Nsɛneɛ -
#676

Serewa -
#594

Bese saka -
#576

amounted to a *pereguan*, which was then transferred to the *Adaka kesie* [*Adaka kɛseɛ*] (big box).

Funds were transferred from the *Adaka kɛseɛ* to the *Apem Adaka* (the Great Chest—literally Box of thousand peredwans). The system was basically a simple one that required that each time a peredwan was removed from the apem adaka (the Great Chest) it was replaced by a cowrie and a cowrie was removed each time a peredwan was paid in (Bowdich, 1819). Accounts were balanced at the end of each day. Major audits were carried out once in each Asante month, at the end of the Great Adae (Akwasidae), for it was at that time that the greatest volume of Treasury business was transacted (Wilks, 1975). In Kumase, the Gyaasewahene was responsible for keeping the state accounts[5]. Batafoɔhene (Minister of Trade), Sanaahene (Minister of the Treasury), and Gyaasewahene (Minister of Finance) were some of the appointive posts created by the Asantehene to promote and control, especially, external trade. The following chart shows the organizational structure of the Exchequer in the Asantehene palace.

Asantehene s Exchequer Court

Gyaasewa—Exchequer
       Gyaasewahene (Treasury Minister)
Sanaa—Household (Treasury)
       Sanaahene (Household Head Treasurer)
Ahwerewamuhene: Custodian of the Golden Elephant Tail — Head of the Ahoprafo
Akyeame—Counselors
Damponkɛse—Treasury
       Fotosanfohene — Treasurer

Bureau	Ebura	Atogye	Bata Fekuo
	Royal Mint	Revenue Collection	State Trading
Head	Adwomfohene	Kotokuokurahene	Asokwahene
	Head of the Smiths		Minister of Trade
Civil Servants	Buramfoɔ	Togyefoɔ	Batafoɔ

AKAN ATTITUDES TOWARDS MONEY

Money is seen by the Akan as a resource either to be invested or consumed. This attitude towards money is best conveyed by the *bese saka* (bunch of kola nuts—#575–581) symbol. The red ant on the pod of kola nuts; it does not pluck the kola nuts to eat or sell. The meaning of the symbol alludes to the dog in the manger attitude that some people have towards economic resources like money. Some other proverbs give further clue to how money was viewed in the society. For example, *wonni sika a, anka ɛyɛ anhwea kwa* literally meant if gold (dust) was not made use of (in an exchange), then one would simply consider it as sand. Also, *sika nkɔ adidi nsan mma kwa* literally translates into money is not put out to come back with no profit. Thus, gold as money was viewed and used (1) as a form of savings, and thus as a mark of secured prosperity; (2) as a form of investment in the purchase of land and labor for food production; and (3) in the promotion of trade in the form of finance capital—a mark of risk-taking enterpreneurship (Wilks, 1993).

The symbol *sika tu sɛ anomaa* (money flies like a bird—#597) suggests the Akan view of money as something like a bird that can fly away from its owner if the owner does not handle it properly. This implies that investment must be made wisely so that a good return will be made on it. From this perspective individuals were provided with a capital outlay or seed money (*dwɛtire*) by their parents and relatives, or through borrowing (*bosea*)

Sika tu sɛ
anomaa-
#597

Onipa bɛwu
na sika te ase
- #112

Yɛbɛdan
agya - #599

Bese saka -
#579

Nsaa - #657

Nsɛnee -
#676

Ebi te yie -
#600

Firi ha kɔ -
#538

on which an interest (nsiho or mmɔho) was charged. Traders and other business-people would extend credit (ade firi) in which case markers such as nsensan (lines—#704–706) would be used to indicate the magnitude of the credit. This gave rise to the accounting system of san dan ho (make lines on the wall).

Akan also have the view that human beings are more important or more valuable than money. The Akan hold the view that money is something that can be used to buy almost everything, except one's life. Although money is important the Akan is encouraged to be benevolent towards the poor, for when one dies one leaves one's money behind (onipa bɛwu na sika te ase—#112). In this regard a story is told of how a spirit disguised herself and her child into human beings in tattered clothes to test a rich man. When the woman and her child approached the rich man, he made them feel very unwelcome. He refused them water to drink and sent them away from his house by screaming at them momfiri ha nkɔ (go away—#538). The woman called out to her child: bɛdan agya, ma yɛnkɔ (you'll leave everything behind you; let's go). Two days later, the rich man died of headache. His money could not save his life, and he left all his wealth behind him. To the Akan, the honest acquisition of money is not a sufficient moral claim for one to be regarded as a good person. The rich must demonstrate their goodness by being generous to their friends and family as well as the poor stranger. This social obligation on the part of the rich stems, in part, from the view that one would leave one's wealth behind when one dies (yɛbɛdan agya—#599).

STATE ENTERPRISE SYSTEM
Trading

Trading was carried out by either private and individualized local enterprises and/or state and long distance enterprises. The long distance trade to the north, which had links to the trans-Saharan trade networks, was based on the exchange of kola nuts (bese saka— #575–599), salt and other forest products for a variety of savanna natural and craft products and items from the Mediterranean regions for example, nsaa (hand-woven blanket made from camel hair—#655–659).

The long distance trade to the south with Europeans from about the mid-15th century was based on the exchange of gold, ivory, war captives, and rubber, oil palm products, and much later, cocoa for a variety of products including guns and ammunition, textiles (especially silk) and liquor. While long distance trade in rubber, kola nuts and oil palm products were undertaken largely by private individual entrepreneurs (akonkosifoɔ and adwadifoɔ), long distance trade in gold, ivory and war captives was undertaken by state traders organized into various state enterprises called bata fekuo. Local retailing (dwadie) was carried out by both men and women in local periodic markets. Kumasi, with its two daily markets, was the main Asante market town (Bowdich, 1819, p. 330, 334).

At least by the beginning of the 18th century the Asante economy had become highly monetized as shown in the adoption of units of gold dust (sika futuro)[6] as currency (Reindorf, 1895, p. 17). Bowdich (1819, p. 330) points out that in the Kumase daily markets the medium of exchange was units of gold dust as neither barter nor cowrie (sedeɛ or serewa—#591–596) was permitted.

The Asantehene was not only the ultimate fount of all political authority as symbolized by the Golden Stool, but also as the ultimate assignee of the wealth of the nation as symbolized by the Golden Elephant's Tail (Sika Mena). "As a 'natural' feature of society ... political-jural authority flowed downwards from the Asantehene to the people under the Golden Stool, and as an equally 'natural' feature of society ... wealth flowed upwards from the people (by various forms of taxation essentially on trade) to the Asanatehene, under the Golden Elephant's Tail (Wilks, 1975, p. 430).

State trade was promoted through the bata fekuo (state traders) using a form of public financing in which the king provided the seed capital (dwetire) and collected interest (mmataho, mmɔho or nsiho) on the capital outlay. Batahene (Minister of Trade), Sanaahene (Minister of Household Finance), and Gyaasewahene (Treasury Minister) were some of

Aya - #511

Kymferɛ - #699

Senchi bridge - #630

TV - #611

Abusua dɔ funu - #454

Mpua anum - #229

Ɔhene aniwa - #190

Ɔhene tuo - #260

the appointive posts created by the Asantehene to promote and control, especially, external trade.

The following account in the newspaper, *The Gold Coast Aborigines* (June 30, 1900, p. 3) describes the public financing of trade:

> The chiefs of Kumasi acted as Mercantile Agents for the King, each receiving from 500 to 1000 perequines [*perɛdwan*] yearly which they in turn distributed to their subchiefs or captains and other subjects, who took it to the coast for goods which they took into the interior; and made thereby fabulous profits: they rendered account to the King at the end of each year. With these resources, there is no wonder that they were immensely rich and could afford to meet the exactions of the King who knew well their various wealth (Wilks, 1993, p. 134).

STATE REVENUE SOURCES

The king imposed taxes, fines, fees, and tolls (*toɔ*) to finance his administration. Even though the taxes and fines levied were not very extensive as they were mainly limited to trade, they served to appropriate and reallocate surplus from the king's subjects. In Asante the taxes, fines, and levies imposed included the following:

(i) Death duties—these were monies paid to the king by the successor or lineage of the deceased as the king was regarded as the heir to the personally acquired property of his subjects. In return the king contributed to the deceased's funeral expenses. The death duties included

(i) death duties

ayibuadeɛ (burial money),

awunnyadeɛ (applicable to the self-acquired movable property of a deceased citizen)

muhoma

(ii) court fees and fines

aseda (thanks-offering, paid by the party found innocent in a suit)

atitɔdeɛ (blood-money, being a fine in lieu of the death penalty)

(iii) Levies on special occasions—these included

ayitoɔ (levy to cover the expenses of a chief's funeral)

apeatoɔ (war tax to cover war expenditures)

fotuobɔ (a levy for the enstoolment of a new chief)

asadeɛ (war booty)

ɔmantoɔ (a national levy for some specific purpose; in recent times this levy has been used to construct roads, bridges, street drains, schools, community centers, health clinics, and market stalls in the villages).

(iv) Other tolls and fees—for example tolls and interest charges levied on traders

highway tolls—*akwanmofoɔ* and *nkwansrafoɔ* levied tolls on the highways (*akwantempɔn*) to control external trade of the *adwadifoɔ* (private entrepreneurs) in order to promote the activities of state traders (*batafoɔ*); traders in the Kumasi daily markets were taxed by the toll collectors called *dwaberesofoɔ*

mmataho, *mmɔho* or *nsiho* (interests paid by state traders on the capital outlay from the king).

ECONOMIC DEVELOPMENT

Economic development in the Akan society is evidenced by several adinkra symbols that depict modern modes of transportation including Senchi bridge (#628–632), VW (#605), mercedes (#606–607), and *sitia bɛkum dorɔba* (the driver may die at the steering wheel—#584–586); technological advancements in media indicated by such symbols as TV (# 608—612), rapid urbanization as indicated by Koforidua *frawase/nhwiren* (Koforidua flowers—#626–627), and new forms of energy as indicated by UAC *nkanea*

Pagya - #266

Koforidua
nhwiren -
#627

Sitia bɛkum
dorɔba -
#585

Firi ha kɔ -
#538

Aya - #511

Kymferɛ -
#699

Senchi
bridge - #630

TV - #611

(UAC lights—#621).

After slave trade was abolished the increase in trade and other economic activities such as mining, logging, and cash crop farming of cocoa and other crops gave rise to the rapid development of new urban centers. Koforidua and towns like Agona Swedru rose rapidly as a result of cocoa farming and diamond mining. Newly rich people flaunted their wealth as indicated by such expressions *anya-wo-ho, asikafoɔ amma ntɛm* and Koforidua flowers (Koforidua *nhwiren*—# 626–627).

To facilitate trade and governmental administration in Asante, an array of highways (*akwantempɔn*) and bridges (*atwene*), with Kumasi as the center, were developed and maintained by the state. State officials who built and maintained the highways were known as *akwammɔfoɔ* and *akwansrafo*. The special levies that were imposed on specific occasions served as the source of capital accumulation for national development. In recent years special levy, *ɔmantoɔ*, has been used to construct roads, bridges, schools, community centers, health clinics, and market stalls in the villages.

The modern bridge over the Volta River at Senchi (Senchi bridge—#605–609) has been incorporated into the adinkra symbols to depict this function of the state to direct and facilitate national development. The rapid changes in the economic activities of the people and the increased and varied sources of state revenue have resulted from the introduction of cocoa, timber, mining, service and manufacturing industries. Economic development activities have become the concern of a more centralized national government.

SOCIAL INEQUALITY

The Akan society was stratified by either social classes: *asikafoɔ, adehyee* and *abrempɔn* (wealthy people and the royalty—the bourgeoisie), *nkwankwaa* (young people—the petty bourgeoisie) and the *ahiafoɔ* (the proletariat or underprivileged) according to Wilks, 1975) or by "status differentiation:" *abrempɔn, adehyeɛ* and *mpanimfoɔ* (the royalty and the elders of state), *asikafoɔ* (the wealthy), *nkwankwaa* (the free born, young people), and *ahiafoɔ, nkoafoɔ* and *nnɔnkɔfoɔ* (free born, but poor and servants and slaves) according to Arhin (1983). The distribution of wealth and income based on the Akan stratification system is alluded to by the symbols *abeteɛ ntema* (portioning *abeteɛ* meal—#619–620) and *gye kɔdidi* (take this for subsistence—#603). There was also conspicuous consumption in the midst of poverty as alluded to by the symbol *asetena pa* (good living—#604).

Social inequality in the Akan society is indicated by adinkra symbols such as *ebi te yie* (some people are better seated, or better positioned—#600–602), *gye kɔdidi* (take this for subsistence—#603), *asetena pa* (good living—#604), and *mako nyinaa* (all the peppers—#613–615). *Ayɔnkogorɔ dodoɔ nti na ɔkɔtɔ annya t ire* (too much of playing around with friends cost the crab its head—#588–590) expresses the outcome of wasteful use of one's resources in conspicuous consumption. Wasting time in playing around with friends did not only cost the crab money, but it literally cost him his head. In Akan mythology, that is why the crab does not have a distinguishable head as many other animals do.

Ohia (poverty) and *ahonyadee* (wealth) are two words Akan use to comment on social inequality, as well as comment on success from hard work and failure from laziness. Social inequality may stem from unequal natural endowment as implied in the expression: *mako nyinaa mpatu mmere* (all the peppers on the same tree do not ripen simultaneously—#613–615). But one's diligence and hard work determines one's station in life as implied in the expression: *mmirikisie a yeantumi annɔ no na yɛfrɛ no nsamanpɔ* (the farm that is not tended is referred to as a sacred burial ground—#566). *Ohia ne gyimi* (poverty is foolishness) and *ohia yɛ adammɔ* (poverty is madness) are judgements directed "against those who had access to the rewards of business and office but nevertheless failed to achieve prosperity," according to Wilks (1993, p. 139).

Social inequality was also determined by social norms and values in such instances as one's position in life based on membership in a royal family (as *ɔdehyeɛ, nkwankwaa, sikani,* or *akoa*), gender, and age. All these factors contribute to a social structure in which

Mercedes
Benz - #607

UAC nkanea
- #621

TV- #612

Abeteɛ
ntema - #620

Gye kɔdidi -
#603

Mako nyinaa
- #614

Menso wo
kfntʃn-
#625

- #602

some people are better situated or better off than others (*ebi te yie*—#600–602).

The world capitalist economy has dominated the Akan and the greater Ghanaian economy ever since the local economy was fully integrated into the world economy after the nineteenth century. Gold mining, lumbering, cocoa farming and agriculture continue to dominate the economy. The incorporation and domination of the Ghanaian economy by multinationals is indicated by symbols such as UAC *nkanea*, Benz and VW. This foreign domination of the Ghanaian economy has been resisted from time to time from the beginnings of the direct contact with the Europeans through such tactics as hold-ups and boycotts. The most spectacular hold-ups of produce by Ghanaian farmers against European company-dominated price rings include the 1858–1866 oil palm boycott and the 1937–38 cocoa hold-up (Wolfson, 1953; Howard, 1978).

Integration into the world capitalist economy is not the only source of social inequality in the Akan and the greater Ghanaian society. Social inequality also stems from various forms of economic exploitation and oppression. One form of economic exploitation is the appropriation of the fruits of one's labor by another. This is encoded by the symbol *mede me se abɔ adwe ma obi abɛfa* (I have cracked open the palm nut with my teeth—#616). The symbol portrays the exploitative situation in which one cracks the hard palm nut with one's teeth only for someone else to enjoy the kernel. It suggests that one should enjoy the fruits of one's labor but unequal social structure makes it possible for the powerful to literally take the food out of the mouths of the powerless.

Another form of economic oppression is alluded to by the symbol *meso nanka mentumi* (I cannot even carry the puff adder—#618). When one cannot carry the much lighter puff adder, it is oppressive to ask one to add on the much heavier python as the carrying pad. A story is told about an elephant that mounts the deer and rides him through the forest over the hills and through the swampy valleys. When the deer frantically groans about a breaking back, the elephant retorts angrily: "I wish I weighed a little less! Fancy yourself carrying the puff adder with the python for a carrying pad. A dream like this will kill your pain."

Yet another source of inequality may be seen in the system of injustices that stems from the unequal power relations endemic in the social structure. This is encoded in the symbol *ebi te yie* (some people are better seated, or better positioned—# 600–602). There is a story, popularized in the late sixties and early seventies by a song of same title (*Ebi te yie*) by the African Brothers Band, which alludes to social injustices in Ghana thus:

> There was once a meeting of all animals to discuss the problems of the animal world. All animals, including the leopard and the deer, were present at the meeting. It so happened that the leopard got seated directly behind the deer. As the meeting progressed the leopard continually harassed the deer. He clawed the tail of the deer to the floor and prevented the free movement of the deer and thus his active participation in the proceedings. Even when the deer attempted to raise his hand to be called to speak the leopard would pull down his hand or comment that the deer was too talkative or gibberish. It got to a point when the deer could no longer put up with the harassment he was being subjected to by the leopard. He mustered courage and yelled out above the din: "Petition please on a point of order. Chairman, secretary and honorable members of the assembly, the deliberations so far have been satisfactorily conducted, I would move for immediate adjournment; for not all of us here have good seats. Some are conveniently seated, others are not." The meeting saw beyond the words of the deer, for everybody knew the maltreatment he was being subjected to. The deer's motion was unanimously carried and the meeting was adjourned sine die.

In the Asante, as in the wider Akan social stratification system, social mobility was

Tabon - #507

Okuafoɔ pa -
#568

Abusuafoo
ho te sen -
#445

Nkyinkyimiiɛ
- #499

Ɔbra yɛ bona -
#547

determined by such factors as (1) military achievement; (2) outstanding service in the Asante bureaucracy (for example, Asante Agyei who originally was a salt carrier in the *bata fekuo* rose to the rank of *ɔhene kyeame*); (3) accumulation of wealth (for example, Yamoa Ponko and Kanin Abena (Wilks, 1975, pp. 693–4); and (4) craft skill (Arhin, 1968; LaTorre, 1978). These perspectives about social stratification in the Akan society suggest the need to critically examine the view held by several writers that the Akan society is egalitarian. If in the past the Akan society was egalitarian, recent economic developments in the country suggest a re-examination of the social structure of the Akan and the greater Ghanaian society.

NOTES

1. Nnɔboa (reciprocal labor) is system of cooperation in which a group of people pull their labor together to help each member of the group in turns on each one's farm. In this system no wage is paid, the one on whose farm the group will work on during the day provides food.

2. The one who hires his/her labor for monetary consideration is called *ɔpaani* (laborer, sing. - *apaafoɔ* - pl.). The laborer may be paid on daily basis (usually by the piece rate method) or on annual basis (*afenhyia apaadie*).

3. Bosman (1705) noted that the bellows used by the Akan were an invention of their own.

4. Peredwan was the highest denomination and was about three and one half ounces of gold dust. Other denominations included *poahuu, poa, pesaa* (or *pesewa* - which is the name given to the smallest unit of the currency in use in present-day Ghana), *daama, taku, takufa, soa, agyiratwe,* and *benaa* (Garrard, 1972, 1980; Ott, 1968).

5. The Gyaasehene also had a functionary detailed to check off the months by dropping a cowrie shell into a bag each new moon. The calendar kept by this functionary was based on *adaduanan* (forty days) or six weeks. The month was known as *bosome,* and *adaduanan mienu* (two 40-day periods) meant the same as *abosome miensa* (three months). The first new moon after the Odwira festival marked the beginning of the new year (*afe foforɔ*).

6. Gold dust ceased to be used as currency in the Akan and the greater Ghanaian society in 1912.

CHAPTER 10

Ɔkyena nhyehyɛe gyina deɛ yesua firi yɛn nkyiri; ɛno nti sɛ wo werɛfi na wosan kɔfa a, yɛnkyi.
The past serves as a guide for the future; so there is nothing wrong with retrieving the gems of our past as we march forward.

KNOWLEDGE AND EDUCATION

KNOWLEDGE

Hwehwɛmu
dua - #650

Mate masie
- #653

Nsaa - #656

Dame dame -
#668

Nyansa pɔ -
#649

Hwehwɛmu
dua - #651

Dame dame -
#669

Implicit in many of the verbal expressions associated with adinkra symbols is the concept of education in the Akan society, and, thus the importance of knowledge to the Akan. This is perhaps best exemplified by the symbol *mate masie* (or *ntesie*—I have heard and kept it—#652–654) derived from the aphorism: "*Nyansa bunu mu ne mate masie*" which literally means "in the depth of wisdom abounds knowledge and thought" (Antubam, 1963, p. 159). The Akan knowledge system is based on the view that the preservation of a people's culture has its basis in oral tradition. Akan oral literary forms that serve as sources which either embody the society's knowledge or provide an insight into the people's attitude to knowledge include proverbs, riddles and quizzes, drum poetry, funeral dirges, and story-telling. The adinkra cloths encode several of these oral literary forms, especially the proverbs, drum poetry, and funeral dirges.

The Akan word for knowledge is *nimdeɛ*, and a knowledgeable or learned person is known as *nimdefoɔ*. The Akan word for wisdom is *nyansa*,[1] and the wise person or sage is known as *nyansafoɔ* A word that is used interchangeably with *nyansa* (wisdom) is *adwen* (thought). Thus the wise person is a thinker (*ɔdwendwemfoɔ* or *ɔbadwemma*, hence the following expression used to describe the wise person: *ɔyɛ obi a n'adwen mu dɔ*—literally, she/he has deep thoughts). The wise person is one who can analyze or critically examine problems of people and society with a view to suggesting answers (*ɔpaepae asɛm mu*, or *ɔyɛ mpɛnsɛmpɛnsɛmu*, or *ɔyɛ nhwehwɛmu*) as depicted by the *hwehwɛmu dua* symbol (searching or measuring rod—#650–651). The expression: *Nananom nyansa pɔ yesiane no abanyansafoɔ*, symbolized by *nyansapɔ]* (wisdom knot—#649) also alludes to this view. *Nyansa* also means skill, dexterity, art, artfulness, learning, and knowledge. Various adinkra symbols (e.g., *dame dame*—#668–669, *nsaa*—#655–659, and *kyerɛ me kwan no*—#678) depict these meanings.

Education is termed *adesua*.[2] *Adesua* embraces all aspects of education: formal and informal, and institutionalized and non-institutionalized educational processes. There are two steps involved in the knowing process: (1) sense experience of the natural world (both physical objects and social relationships)—the empirical processes, and (2) the logical organization and interpretation of sensory data into ideas—the intellectual and intuitive processes (Dzobo, 1992). To have a good ear and to retain everything heard from the master is a mark of excellence in learning as indicated by the *mate masie* (I have heard and kept it—#652–654) symbol. The common expression associated with this symbol is: *nyasa bunu mu ne mate masie*—in the depth of wisdom abounds knowledge and thoughtfulness; I consider and keep what I learn (Antubam, 1963). This is more than mere memorization. It encompasses deep reflection on what one learns.

Knowledge or wisdom is also gained through experience and this is emphasized by the proverb: *Nyansa yesua, na yentɔ* (wisdom or knowledge is something we acquire through learning; it is not something we buy). The one who does not learn a lesson or gain experience from one's mistakes is considered a fool as expressed by the proverb: *Kwasea na ne dwan te mprenu* (it is only the fool who allows his sheep to break loose twice).

The Akan believe that knowledge comes from various sources, including intuition,

Mate masie -
#652

Kyere me
kwan no -
#678

Sankɔfa -
#634

Saa? - #536

Sankɔfa -
#633

Bomokyikyie
- #679

Asantrofie
anomaa -
#707

Ɔbonsam a
wonim no -
#680

revelation, authority, experience, logical reasoning, and experiments. As Minkus (1980, p. 185) writes: "Extraordinary perception, divination, dreams, and possession provide means of acquiring some knowledge of spiritual reality and causality, although even then human knowledge is limited and inadequate to penetrate the mysteries of existence." The Akan view reality as having spiritual and non-spiritual dimensions, and thus to understand and know reality requires the reliance on multiple sources of knowledge. The various sources of knowledge, as the Akan believe, are complementary and not antagonistic in one's attempts to discover and comprehend reality.

The experiences and aphorisms of the elderly form one important source of knowledge to the Akan. This is symbolized by the mythical sankɔfa bird (go back and retrieve—#633–648). This bird is said to fly forwards by looking backwards. In order not to reinvent the wheel, this symbol reminds the Akan of the importance of learning from the past or using the past as a guide to the future.

The wisdom knot (nyansa pɔ—#649) is another symbol that reflects the Akan belief in the knowledge of the wise. However, authority as the sole important source of knowledge is dangerous, particularly when it leads one to surrender one's independent judgement and leads one to make no effort to search for what is true or false. This view is given credence by the expression: Woyɛ Kwaku Ananse a, meso meyɛ Ntikuma (If you are Kwaku Ananse, I am Ntikuma). In one anansesɛm (Ananse story) Kwaku Ananse pretends to die and requests to be buried in the family farm with all cooking utensils. He then asks that nobody goes to the farm until after six weeks following his burial. After six weeks, Ntikuma and his siblings go to the farm only to realize that someone was stealing the crops. All along, Ntikuma who was doubtful of his father's death suspected none other than his father. To find out the truth, Ntikuma puts a tar-baby effigy on the farm and catches his father as the thief. The whole set of anansesɛm (Ananse stories) in which Ananse is either defied or caught lying or being challenged by his son Ntikuma gave rise to the expression above. Ntikuma is not being disrespectful of the father as an authority figure, but he is making the effort to search for what is true or false.

The Akan regard ordinary sense perception as another important basis of knowledge. However, this sensory-based knowledge is limited in its applicability, and the Akan belief about knowledge requires one to examine sensory-based as well as all knowledge critically. A critical mind is skeptical as depicted by symbols such as saa? (is that so?—#536), bommokyikyie (river fish—#679), and abɔnsam a wonim no (the devil you know—#680). Hence, the symbol hwehwɛ mu dua or ɔfamfa (searching or measuring rod—#650–651) urges one to examine knowledge critically as implied in the following: wose fa na woamfa a, worenhu mu; wohwehwɛ mu a, na wohu mu; wopusu no a, na wote ne pampan—you miss the opportunity of knowing when you refuse to take it upon request; you know what it entails when you examine it critically; you know the smell when you shake it. It implies that the outcome of research depends on an intelligent, patient and critical examination of evidence. Knowledge must be subjected to critical enquiry.

That critical reasoning or intellectual ability—the ability to critically analyze multiple facets of a problem and to reach an informed conclusion—is valued over sensory-based, subjective, simple knowledge is depicted by several symbols. Dwennimmɛn (ram's horns—#204–211), nsaa (quality hand-woven blanket or carpet—#655–659), kramo bɔne amma yɛanhu kramo pa (the fake prophet or sophistry makes it difficult for the good prophet or the truth to be known—#660–664), dame dame (checkers—#668–669), and kuntunkantan (egocentricism—#665–666) are examples of symbols that encode Akan views about critical reasoning and rationality. The Akan sage warns that one must be careful not to extend the claims of the power of rationality too far. This warning is encoded by the asanturofie anomaa (the long-ailed night jar, the bird of dilemma—#707) symbol. This bird presents a puzzling situation: when you take it, you incur jeopardy; when you leave it, you will miss a golden opportunity. Deciding on whether to take or leave the asanturofie bird entails more than rational and critical thinking.

Also, the bese saka symbol (bunch of kola nuts—#575–581) suggests the importance

Dwennimen -
#205

Kuntankantan
- #666

Kramo bɔne
- #660

Bese saka -
#576

Kuntankantan
- #665

Kyerɛ me
kwan no -
#678

Nsaa - #659

of critical thinking and experience. This symbol is associated with the following aphorism: *Bese pa ne konini ahahan yɛtase no ɔbanyansafoɔ* (The leaves of the white and red kola plants are very similar and it takes skill and experience to separate them—#575–581). This reminds one to critically examine all the possible options in dealing with problems before making decisions. It also points to the Akan view that the various sources of knowledge are complementary and not antagonistic in the search for knowledge.

Attitudes to Knowledge

Dzobo (1992a) distinguishes the following as examples of specific indigenous Akan attitudes to knowledge. One attitude to knowledge is that there is a limit to what any one individual can know, even though there is no limit to what can be known in principle. From this perspective, any one person who claims to know everything is viewed as knowing nothing. Hence, the symbol *kuntankantan* (egocentricism—#665–666) serves to remind one not to be egocentric and boastful of the little knowledge one has as depicted by the following maxim: *Nea ɔyɛ ne ho sɛ menim menim, nnim hwee* (he who knows all, knows nothing).

Another attitude is that the individual has an active role to play in the acquisition of knowledge. Even though *nyansa* is inborn and everyone has the potential to be wise, one has to develop one's mental capacity. That is, whatever one knows is acquired through experience and through a deliberate effort on one's part to know. The Akan believe that the search for knowledge is a life-long process. The symbol *nea onnim sua a ohu* (he who does not know can become knowledgeable from learning—#667) incorporates this view of life-long learning.

Akan regard the elderly as wise and believe that experience comes with age. This association of knowledge and wisdom with age is incorporated in the *sankɔfa* (go back and retrieve—#633–648), *kyɛmferɛ* (potsherd—#698–699), and *nyansa pɔ* (wisdom knot—#649) symbols. The *kyɛmferɛ* (potsherd—#698–699) symbol depicts this belief that experience and wisdom come with age by posing the question: *kyɛmferɛ se ɔdaa hɔ akyɛ, na onipa a ɔnwenee no nso nyɛ dɛn?* (If the potsherd claims it is old, what about the potter who molded it?—#698–699).

However, the Akan does not necessarily consider knowledge as the preserve of a particular age group. The expression: *Akyin-akyin sen anyin-anyin* (the well traveled is more experienced than the elderly who has stayed in one place all his/her life) captures this view about knowledge. In this regard the Akan view the "stay-at-one-place" elderly person as being insular as compared with the traveled person who is said to be cosmopolitan in outlook and ideas.

That knowledge is not necessarily the preserve of the elderly is also illustrated by the Ananse story in which Ananse tries to collect all the wisdom and knowledge in the world to hide in the tallest tree so that he alone would be the knowledgeable and wise one. He puts the knowledge and wisdom he has collected into a pot and hangs the pot around his neck and tries to climb the tree with the pot hanging in front of him, that is, between him and the tree. After several futile attempts to climb the tree, his son, Ntikuma who is supposed to have lost all his wisdom, draws Ananse's attention to the folly in attempting to climb the tree with the way the pot is hanging. Ntikuma suggests that his father should tie the pot onto his (father's) back. Ananse then realizes that his son's suggestion makes a lot of sense. Ananse gets frustrated in knowing that there is some wisdom left in his child's head. Ananse then throws down and smashes the pot of wisdom and knowledge.

The Akan believe that knowledge knows no boundaries. All humans are born with an inate and unique capacity: the capacity to think, learn and relate - the basic ingredient to the creation of knowledge. Thus an individual with the capacity to think, learn and relate, in a conducive environment which recognizes knowledge as a product and facilitates its value-addition through education and training, is the foundation for a dynamic and progressive society.

Another Akan attitude about knowledge is that knowledge is a liberator. The one

Nipa mfon
kwa - #677

Nea onnim
sua a - #667

Dwennimen -
#205

Kyɛmferɛ -
#699

Ananse antøn
kasa - #715

Nkrabea -
#75

Adwera -
#108

Obi nka obi -
#277

Asem a - #72

resource that liberates people from poverty and empowers them is knowledge. Possessing knowledge is empowering while the lack of knowledge is debilitating. Knowledge when combined with other factors of production (capital, labor, existing knowledge and other inputs) produces goods and services to satisfy one's wants and needs and thus serve to liberate one. This liberating knowledge is attained through insightful understanding of situations and the relations between things. An enlightened and insightful individual is free and creative. This view is alluded to by the symbol *kyerɛ me kwan no* (show me the way—#678). The Akan believe that knowledge must have practical bearing on the conduct of life. This is portrayed by the aphorism: *Nyansa nyɛ sika na woakyekyere asie*—Wisdom is not like money which may be kept in a safe; or, one does not collect wisdom in a bag, lock it up in a box and then go to say to a friend, 'teach me something.'

CAUSALITY AND FREE WILL

The Akan believe that nothing happens without a cause (*onipa mfɔn kwa*—#677). Several adinkra symbols such as *obi nka obi kwa* (no one should bite the other without justifiable cause—#272–278), *abɛ dua* (palm tree—#574), *sɛ nantuo kɔsene serɛ a* (if the calf is bigger than the thigh—#713) and *nipa mfɔn kwa* (one does not grow lean without a cause—#677) incorporate this belief. These symbols suggest that causality, to the Akan, is an objective reality. For example, the proverb: *sɛ mmerɛnkɛnsono si ne ti ase a, na ɛwɔ dea asase reka kyerɛ no* (whenever the palm tree bends, it is because of what the soil has told it—#574), illustrates this objective reality. The palm tree is very resilient and does not bend or break easily. If a palm tree is found to be bent over, then something must have caused that.

A closer examination of the concepts *sunsum* (spirit or soul—#35–36) and *nkrabea* (destiny—#75) helps in further explaining the Akan causal theory. The Akan causal theory has it that all beings and forces act by virtue of their *sunsum*. All events are caused and are potentially explicable. In some events the causal agent is a spiritual being or force. However, not all causes are said to operate in a spiritual way. Some causes are non-spiritual such as something caused by the deliberate actions of people. In this sense, Akan have a conception of dual causality: cause that is attributable to spiritual (e.g., *sunsum*) and divine factors such as one's *nkrabea* (destiny—#75) and cause that is attributable to one's actions. This follows from the concept of dual reality. While spiritual causality is vertical with the causal direction going from a higher spirit to a lower one, non-spiritual causality is horizontal (Gyekye, 1987).

One's misfortunes in life may be said to be caused by spirits (that is, external locus of control of causality) or one's bad character, carelessness (for example in decision-making), or lack of industry on one's part (that is, internal locus of control of causality). In this regard some illnesses are thought to be spiritually induced (*sunsum yare*). Should the illness be found to have a spiritual cause, a *musuyidee* ritual has to be performed to deal with the precipitating spiritual cause before any medical attempt will be made to cure the illness (Minkus, 1980). When one recovers from a long bout of illness, one performs an *asubɔ* or *adwere adware* (pacificatory or cleansing) ceremony to sanctify one's soul. This ceremony starts with a bath of water that has been seeped in *adwere* (watery shrub—#108) leaves.

The Akan say *etire nyɛ borɔfere na yɛapae mu ahwɛ deɛ ɛwɔ mu* (the human head—i.e., the mind—is not like the papaya fruit to be split open to determine its content—#708). This suggests that even though there exist causal laws there also exist human actions and thoughts. This must not be taken as a contradiction to the concept of destiny (*nkrabea*—#75). Akan believe that one has the ability to choose between alternative possibilities in such a way that the choice and action are to some extent creatively determined by the conscious subject at the time. In the symbol *asanturofie anomaa* (bird of dilemma—#707), one is faced with choice between bad and good luck. When one chooses the bird, one is responsible for the bad luck one brings unto oneself by that choice. On the other hand, when one forgoes the bird and the good luck, one has to bear

111

Obi nka obi -
#277

Sɛ anantuo
kɔsene -
#713

Sankɔfa -
#635

Dwennimɛn
ntoaso -
#212

Asantrofie -
#707

Etire - #708

Yɟ papa -
#463

Nokware -
#670

the responsibility associated with that choice too. Akan use this situation of dilemma to point out that human being, as a self-conscious being, has the ability for personal initiative and response, and that within limits he/she is able to reshape himself/herself, to influence the behavior of his/her fellow beings, and to redirect the processes of the outer world. Also, self-consciousness makes reflective thinking and the sense of right and wrong possible. It enables a person to consider himself/herself as a subject and as an object of action; that is, it enables one to have freedom of choice. One, therefore, is responsible for the choice one makes.

The Akan view of causality also suggests temporal order and association. The temporal order implies direction which can be simple as well as complex. The causal agent antecedes the effect in a temporal sense. The Akan view of time is discussed further in the section on time below.

MORAL EDUCATION

Akan consider morality in terms of right and wrong conduct (*papayɛ*) or behavior (*nneyɛe*) and good and bad character (*suban*). Akan believe that irrespective of one's capacity, one can improve upon one's morality by learning to obey moral rules. Moral education and character training in the Akan society start from infancy. The child naming ceremony (*abadintoɔ*), for example, is the occasion for teaching even the young baby to distinguish between truth (*nokorɛ*—#670) and falsehood (*nkontompɔ*). The naming ceremony usually takes place eight days after the child is born. The officiant at the naming ceremony places the child on his/her lap and the child's name is called out aloud. The officiant dips his/her right index finger into water and let it drop onto the child's tongue. This is done three times with the saying each time: "If you say it is water, let it be water you are tasting." Then the officiant dips his/her right index finger into palm wine[3] for the child to taste saying, "If you say it is palm wine, let it be palm wine you are tasting." The child is then shown a black object and a white object followed each time by the saying, "If you say it is black, let it be black you are seeing and if it is white, let it be white you are seeing." By this ceremony the child receives his/her first moral instruction to speak the truth (*nokorɛ*—#670) all the time. The newborn is believed to have the ability to differentiate between sweet and non-sweet taste stimuli, and s/he is, therefore, expected to learn from this experience and grow up to be able to differentiate between truth and falsehood, and to be truthful.

In the past, in some farming communities, the baby boy was given a cutlass (machete—#566) and the baby girl was for a moment covered with a basket (*kɛntɛn*—#625). The cutlass was to signify to the child that he was expected to grow up to function as a hard-working individual who will not only sustain his family, but also become a productive member of the society. The basket signified to the girl that it was the task of the woman to collect foodstuffs from the farm, carry the load home and prepare food to feed her family and others.

The eight-day-old baby may not be cognizant of what the naming ceremony is all about. The full meaning and the educational value of the ceremony are learned gradually through the years at successive ceremonies. While the rudiments (for example, differences in tastes)[4] are learned by the individual at one's own naming ceremony, added knowledge is gained at successive ceremonies at which she/he is a parent, relative, or a participant in one way or the other. In this regard the naming of one is essentially not an individual but a social learning situation.

The ceremony serves to teach the ancestral history as the past accomplishments and qualities of the ancestor who bore that name are retold. The occasion reminds the participants that as individuals each has a contribution to make to the corporate life of the group. It also serves to emphasize to the newborn that she/he belongs to a lineage with tradition and history that she/he can be proud of.[5]

Another important moral belief taught to little children centers around goodness or virtue (*papa* or *papayɛ*—#463). The Akan child is taught that God is goodness or virtue,

Asɔ ne afena
- #566

Kʃntʃn -
#625

Nkyikyimiiʃ
- #499

Sankɔfa -
#638

Yʃ papa -
#463

Gye Nyame-
#4

Hann ne sum
- #19

Afe bi yɛ
asiane -#

and goodness or virtue is the first nature of God (*papayɛ yɛ Nyamesu a ɛdi kan*—#463). As Sarpong (1972, p. 40) puts it: "For it would appear that for the Akan what a man is, is less important than what a man does. To put it more concretely, a person is what he is because of his deeds. He does not perform those deeds because of what he is." From this basis, the Akan child is taught to do good.

Other situations used for moral education included story-telling, funeral dirges, games, quizzes and riddles (*ɛbisaa*). Games like *ɔware* and *dame dame* (checkers—#668–669) provided opportunities for teaching and learning rules important for developing children's sensibilities.

TIME

An important aspect of the Akan's body of knowledge is the time-space dimension. Time (*bere*) is indicated by multiple temporal structures. Time is, in one sense, a linear continuum and is infinite, as expressed by such words as *daa, daapem, mmeresanten,* and *afebɔɔ*—eternity). In yet another sense, Akan treat time as if it were a dimension of space in the relationship of distance between locations in space and the time taken to travel between them. This space-time dimension is marked by socially constructed quantitative measures for example, hour (*dɔnhwere*) and mile (*kwansin*).

In yet another sense, time, to the Akan, is cyclical in nature. It is associated with growth, movement, life, death and destruction and renewal. Thus an aspect of the Akan's view of time is based on the cyclical and rhythmic order in nature. The seasons follow one another in an orderly manner; life and death and renewal in plant and animal life move to the rhythmic movement of nature that occurs eternally. No point in a circle is beginning, middle, or end in the absolute sense; or else all points are these simultaneously. This is encoded in the concentric circles of the *adinkrahene* symbol (king of the adinkra symbols—#178–185). In other words, there can never, strictly speaking, be a beginning and end of the universe; it has always moved in an infinite succession of circles and is eternal and rhythmic. When Akan say '*abɔdeɛ santaann yi, obi ntenaa ase a onim n'ahyɛase na obi ntena ase nkosi n'awieeɛ, gye Onyame*' (this panorama of the universe, no one has lived who saw its beginning and no one will live to see its end, except God—#2–9), they are viewing time in its infinite sense.

The Akan had a lively appreciation of time. Not, of course, of clock time. There was great moral value attached to the productive use of time. Farmers, for example, made elaborate efforts to coordinate work in the house (e.g., house repairs, cooking, tool repairs, marketing) and on the farm (e.g., planting, weeding, harvesting, storage), and to stretch nature's constraints by the skillful use of early and late varieties of crops and other time-saving devices.

Time is viewed as a dynamic as indicated by the symbol *mmere dane* (time changes—#685). It is, therefore, imperative that one adapts oneself to the changing times (*mmere dane a, wo nso dane wo ho bi*—#692). Akans regard time as fleeting and precious as indicated by the following proverb: *Bere te sɛ anomaa; woanso ne mu na otu kɔ a, worenhunu no bio* (Time is like a bird; if you do not catch it and it flies away, you do not see it again—#686). That is, time must be used productively.

Time, to the Akan, is of three dynamic dimensions: a) various constructs of the past as depicted by remote past (*tete bere*), past (*kane no*), recent past (*nnansa*); b) present (*nnɛ mmere, seesei, mprɛnmpren*); and, c) future (*ɔkyena, daakye* or *da bi*). Even as the Akan lives in the present, she/he has the ability to move to the past through memory or roam the future through imagination. The symbol *sankɔfa* (go back and retrieve—#633–648) best illustrates this ability to traverse the various time dimensions: present plans for the future are based on past experiences. The Akan believe that there must be movement with times but as the forward march proceeds, the gems must be picked from behind and carried forward on the march. The symbol *dwene hwɛ kan* (think ahead—#673) also is suggestive of one's ability to transcend the present to speculate the future. The following words of a popular song in Ghana make use of the various temporal structures of the

Mmere dane
- #685

Adinkrahene
- #179

Gye Nyame -
#7

Mmere dane
a - #692

Mmomaa sf
#686

Sankɔfa -
#647

Dwene hwɛ
kan - #673

Hann ne sum
- #18

Akan:

Mmere retwam akɔ
Wobɛyɛ biribi a, yɛ no prɛko
Adeɛ rekye na adeɛ resa yi
Mmere ara na ɛrekɔ no
Ɔkyena wobɛka sɛ
Me huiɛ a anka
Nso na apa ho

Time is moving past
Do it now whatever you have to do
Day in day out
Time is on the move
Tomorrow you'll say
Had I known
That would be past.

In another sense, Akan view time as periodicity or duration, and hence divide it into segments such as day (*da*), week (*nnawɔtwe* or *dapɛn*), month (*bosome*), *adaduanan* (forty-two-day cycle), and year (*afe*). The day has two main parts: *adekyeeɛ*—day and *adesaeɛ* or *anadwo*—night (*hann ne sum*—#18–19). The *adekyeɛ* part is subdivided into seven units: *anɔpahema* (daybreak), *anɔpatutu* (early morning), *bɔme bosea awia* (mid-morning), *owigyinaeɛ* (noon time), *awiaberɛ* (early afternoon), *prɛmtoberɛ* or *mferɛtuberɛ* (mid-afternoon), and *anwummerɛ* (late afternoon or evening). The *adesaeɛ* or *anadwo* is subdivided into three segments: *ɔdasuo baako* (before midnight), *ɔdasuo mmienu* (around midnight), and *ɔdasuo mmiensa* (after midnight). There are also such expressions for nighttime as *anadwo dasuom* and *anadwo kɔnkɔn* and *hwanihwani* or *woyɛ hwan?* (who are you?—#111) for dawn when things appear as silhouttes.

Yet another way in which Akan depict time is by the cyclical and seasonal climatic changes and the activities associated with these time periods: *ɔpe berɛ* (dry season), *asusuo berɛ* (rainy season), *ofupɛ berɛ*, and *bamporɔ berɛ* (Mensah, 1992). Towards the end of the dry season and just prior to the onset of the rainy season is the time for the preparation of the land for farming.

The Akan believe in time as a natural phenomenon as well as a social construction. An example of natural time is indicated by the seven days of the week (*nna nsɔn*) that God is believed to have created. The Akan believe that God created the seven days, hence God is sometimes referred to as *Ɔbɔnna Nsɔn* (Creator of Seven Days). The seven days are each ruled by a planet (*okyiniwiemu*) each of which has its own distinct characters as follows: Kwasiada (Sunday), the day of Ayisi (Awusi, Awisi), is ruled by the Sun; Dwoada (Monday), the day of Awo, is ruled by the Moon; Benada (Tuesday) is the day of Abena (Mars); Wukuada (Wednesday) is the day of Aku (Mercury); Yawoada (Yaada, Yawda—Thursday) is the day of Aberao (Aberaw—Jupiter);[6] Fida (Fiada—Friday) is the day of Afi (Venus); and Memeneda (Saturday) is the day of Amene (Saturn).

Natural time, that is, God's time, is believed to be the best (*Nyame bere ne bere pa*—#133). Another example of the naturalness of time is depicted by the expression: *Adekyeeɛ nnyina akokɔ bɔneeɛ so; sɛ akokɔ bɛbɔn o, sɛ ɔremmɔn o, adeɛ bɛkye*—night and day are determined by nature; it is not cockcrow that changes night to day; whether the cock crows or not, night will turn into day (#694–696). Natural time is not limited to the present or the past alone; it also includes futurity. This idea of future is reflected in the expression: *da bi me nsoromma bepue* (my star will shine one day—#693). The Akan believe that in the future God will ask each one to render an account of his or her stewardship on earth (*daakye Onyame bebisa wo asɛm*—in future God will inquire something of you).

Time as natural phenomenon is also marked by the stages of life: birth, puberty,

114

Onyankopon
mmere -
#133

Odomankoma
- #12

Afe bi y*f*
asiane - #688

Sankɔfa -
#637

Abibirem
buronya -
#107

Da bi me
nsoromma -
#693

Akokɔ -
#694

Afe bi yɛ
asiane - #691

adulthood, and death. The stages of life are, in Akan thought, circulatory in form: life in the physical world, death as a transition to life after death in the spiritual world of ancestors (*asamando*), and reincarnation from the spiritual world into the physical world. Akan mark these time periods by various rituals: soul day (*kerada*), naming (*abadintɔɔ*), puberty (*bragorɔ*), marriage (*awareε* or *ayeforo*), and funerals (*ayie*). *Abadintɔɔ* (naming ceremony) marks the transition from the spiritual world to the physical world. The death rituals serve to mark the end of the physical aspect of human life and the beginning of spiritual life in the abode of ancestors. Time in the physical world is temporary and finite. On the other hand, time in its totality as circular natural phenomenon is infinite. The circular notion of time is also indicated in the end of year and beginning of new year song part of which runs:

> *Afe akɔ aporɔ abεto yεn so bio;*
> *Adom Nyame ankum yεn wama afe pa ato yεn;*
> *Afenhyia pa, afe nkɔ mmeto yεn bio*

> The year has made its circular journey and met us again;
> The gracious God spared us our lives during the year's circular journey;
> Happy new year, may the year go round and meet us again still alive.

The Akan view of time as a social construction is seen in their concepts of work scheduling, time-budgeting, and logistic planning in which time structures are linked with activities of the people and of the state. For example, the link between time and the activities of the people is illustrated by the expression: *Sε ɔbaa kɔ asuo anɔpa a, ɔdom ne ho anwummerε* (the woman who fetches water in the morning saves time for herself in the evening—#405). Implicit in this expression is the moral imperative to use time productively.

The social construction of time is also depicted by the calendars the Akan developed. The Asante, as well as other Akan groups, developed the forty-two-day calendar (*adaduanan* or *adapεn nsia*). Some of the Fantse on the coast developed a calendar based on their knowledge of the stars and lunar movements in relation to the fishing and farming seasons. In the *adaduanan* calendar system, a cycle of forty-two days recurring nine times (that is, nine Akwasidae ceremonies) makes a year. *Odwira* (also known as *Apafram* or *Apoɔ*), a purificatory ceremony, was celebrated as the New Year or First Fruits festival. Some of these Akan annual ceremonies have been superceded by such Christian temporal ceremonies as Easter (*Yesu wu sɔre*—#104) and Christmas (*Buronya*—#107).

Akan view time as having distinct characters. They believe that all the days are not equal or are not alike. This is depicted by the symbol (*nna nyinaa nsε*—#697). There are good or auspicious days (*nna pa*), bad or inauspicious days (*nna bɔne*), and days that are indifferent (*da hunu*). There are also *afe pa* (good year) and *afe bɔne* (bad or unlucky year). The symbol *afe bi yε asiane* (#687–691) also depicts this auspicious and inauspicious view the Akan have of time. The inauspicious days were used for religious rites. The days of the week have their own distinct characters as follows in the table below.

TRANSMISSION OF SPECIALIZED KNOWLEDGE AND SKILLS

The Akan's appreciation and quest for knowledge led to the development of some level of formalized education in various skills and specialties such as *ahemfie adesua* (statecraft), drumming (*ayan*), hunting (*ahayɔ*), priesthood (*akɔm*), oratory, accounting (*nkontabuo*), art and crafts (*adwinneε*), and herbal medicine (Akuffo, 1976; McWilliam and Kwamena-Po, 1978; and Oppong, 1973). Transmission of knowledge was premised on the view that he who does not know can become knowledgeable from learning (*nea onnim no sua a ohu*—#667).

Sankɔfa - #645

Akokɔ - #695

Afe bi yɛ asiane - #687

Nna nyinaa nsɛ - #697

Yesu wusore - #104

Wodu nkwanta a - #682

Abibirem buronya - #107

Nna nyinaa nse - #697

Akan Names Based on the Day of the Week the Child is Born

Day			Day Name		
Akan	English	Attribute	Male	Female	Appellation
Dwoada	Monday	Calmness Peaceful	Kojo Kwadwo	Adwoa Ajoa	Okoto
Benada	Tuesday	Compas- sionate	Kwabena Kobina	Abena Araba	Ogyam
Wukuoda	Wednesday	Advocate Hero	Kwaku Kweku	Akua	Ntonni
Yawoada	Thursday	Aggressive Courageous	Yaw Kwaw	Yaa Aba	Preko
Efiada	Friday	Adventurer	Kofi	Afua Efuwa	Okyini
Memeneda	Saturday	Problem- Solver; Valiant	Kwamena Kwame	Amba Ama	Atoapem
Kwasiada	Sunday	Protector	Kwesi Akwasi	Esi, Asi Akosua	Bodua

Source: Information derived from Opoku (1976), Gyekye (1987) and Mensah (1992).

The informal and formal processes of the apprenticeship system were utilized in the transmission of specialized knowledge and skills. Through informal processes the child was taught to know the history of the society (*abakɔsem* or *mpaninsem*); to show respect; to know the names of objects in the child's natural and social environment; how to count (*nkontabuo*); and various aspects of moral values such as not to smoke, lie, or steal. The child was given a well-rounded education and training (*nimdeɛ*). Besides the family's socialization processes, public storytelling (*Anansesem*—Ananse Stories),[7] games, songs,[8] drama, riddles, quizzes, and proverbs formed very important means for educating the child.

Logical reasoning, for example, is developed through riddles (*ebisaa*) and story telling. An example in the use of riddles as an exercise in logical reasoning is about a man who has a fowl, a basket full of corn, and a hawk to be transported across a river in a boat. The boat can carry only one of the three things at a time besides the man himself. The fowl cannot be left alone with the basket of corn, and the hawk will eat the fowl if he is not guarded. How can the man take the three things across the river? The solution lies in pairing the things that are not mutually attracted to each other, for example pairing corn and the hawk (Aggrey, 1977).

Riddles also teach one that knowledge is relative and context dependent. An example of this is in the following riddle: A man was traveling with three women—his wife, his mother and his maternal aunt. They came across a river on which was a very narrow wooden bridge. While they were crossing the river, the bridge collapsed and they fell into the river. Only the man could swim, and he could save only one woman. If you were the man, which of the three women would you rescue and why?

The Akan educational system utilizes formal and informal processes to stress three related goals: character, discipline, and wisdom. For example, knowing how to successfully incorporate proverbs into one's speech is a sign of wisdom and erudition; a young person who knows how to use proverbs uses them with tact and modesty when in the presence of the elderly. Whether it was to achieve technical skills or moral values, the Akan educational processes never failed to stress these three related goals.

INSTITUTIONALIZED KNOWLEDGE

In the Asante nation, as well as the other Akan communities, various bureaucratic

Mmere dane
- #685

Afe bi ye
asiane - #688

Hann ne sum
- #19

Wodu
nkwanta a -
#683

Bese saka -
#577

Nea onnim -
#667

Kramo bone
- #661

ABCD -
#700

and other governmental functions required technical and managerial skills and expertise. The buramfoɔ (goldsmiths), for example, used a complex smelting process to reduce worked gold to gold dust; the nsumankwaafoɔ (physicians and herbalists) had knowledge of both preventive and curative medicine; and the staff of the treasury (sannaa) were versed in the highly intricate monetary system of weights and gold dust, and in time-keeping and collecting taxes and fines. Similarly, the couriers and traders (batafoɔ) who plied the great roads (akwantempɔn) were versed in the intricate system for measuring distance, and rendering accounts after assessing and collecting tolls.

These varied skills and expertise required institutionalized knowledge. Various settings and structures were developed to disseminate broad ranges of values, attitudes, skills and various forms of specialized knowledge for the smooth functioning of the complex bureaucratic apparatus of the state. In these settings for dissemination of knowledge, the knowledge transmitted was highly institutionalized, decontextualized, deliberate and specific. The trainee was separated from home, placed under distinct authority, and put through a systematic program of instruction where fees (e.g. tiri nsa—admission or initiation fee, and mpɔnho nsa—graduation fee) were charged in some skill areas as the specialized knowledge and skills were often protected (sometimes hoarded) by particular individuals, professional groups, or institutions.

The Akan indigenous apprenticeship system (adwumasua, ntetee or esom)[9] constituted a very important means for transmitting formal and institutionalized or specialized knowledge. Various initiation ceremonies and rites were performed at major points in the institutionalized learning process. These rites of passage served to accept formally the prospective trainee into the appropriate trade, to mark major transitions from one grade to another during training, and to graduate and accept formally one into the professional practice and status. The major goal of these institutionalized learning settings was to impart, rather than hide, knowledge and skills to accredited learners.

Schooling of the King

The king himself undergoes ahemfie adesua (palace or court training—that is, political socialization) or amammuo ho adesua (political education) as depicted by the symbol nea ɔpɛ sɛ ɔbedi hene (he who wants to be a king—#177). During the six-week (adaduana) period of confinement, the king-elect undergoes formal education (ahemfie adesua). The curriculum of the ahemfie adesua comprises, among other things, the history and the political and military organization of the kingdom, the history of predecessor kings and their accomplishments, court etiquette, public speaking, drum language and poetry, music, dancing, and palace structure and administration. The ahemfie adesua is conducted in two phases: the intesive training during the the confinement period and the on-the-job training conducted when the kingassumes office. The on-the-job training takes place in the evenings so that it may not interfere with the normal engagements of the king. Highly specialized intructors and instructional materials are utilized as part of this formal education. "The schooling [of the king—that is, the Asantehene], particularly in the study of the palace structure and organization, is effected with the aid of wax models of palace officials and attendants and of the items of regalia. The models are called nkraba and the system of using them as visual aids for the schooling is called nkrahene" (Kyerematen, n.d., p. 20).

Training of hunters

In other specialized areas of learning, master craftsmen and experts ordered the distribution, acquisition, and recognition of knowledge. The curriculum of the hunter, for example, included astronomy, geography, plant and animal species and their nutritional and medicinal uses, animal movements, butchery and meat preservation. As McWilliam and Kwamena-Po (1978, pp.6 and 7) write:

A would-be hunter began his training as the apprentice of an experienced hunter, usually one who was well known for having killed the big animals, including the elephant. The new apprentice would follow his master through the woods.

117

Kyere me
kwan no -
#678

ABCD -
#700

Ahahan - 701

Sankɔfa -
#648

Seantie -
#714

Nea ɔpɛ sɛ
obedi hene -
#177

Adinkraba
Apau - #189

Sankɔfa -
#640

He would learn the use of the gun as the first step. He had to prove his ability as a first-class shot by killing a bird in flight—the hawk or any other wild bird. His course included acquiring a knowledge of edible fruits and the names of important and useful plants, particularly those for herbal use. Thus good hunters were invariably good herbalists... Similarly, the young apprentice must study the stars and know the changes in the climate and their effects on vegetation. This would enable him to predict the movement of the game and the right time to go hunting.

Lastly, he must learn and understand the 'road signs' in the bush so that he could find his way back to his village after a long stay in the woods lasting several nights. The symbol *wodu nkwanta a, gu me ahahan* (when you reach the intersection leave me a sign—#682–683) depicts the use of "road signs" (landmarks) or markers in the bush to give directions to people. The symbol also connotes time. One could tell from the freshness or dryness of the leaves or the sap from the stem of the leaf when the marker was left there. If the leaves were dry they suggested the marker was left there long time ago. On the other hand, if the leaves looked very fresh, that suggested that the marker was left there not so long ago. One was taught these markers and their meanings.

Priesthood

Another specialized skill area that may be used to further illustrate the Akan knowledge system and how knowledge was transmitted is priesthood (*akɔm*). Training was necessary before one could assume priestly functions. In this skill area there were well demarcated initiation and graduation ceremonies at which competence and knowledge were either confirmed or tested. Entry into the ranks of priesthood of the various shrines was preceded by a period of training under the tutelage of a senior priest or priestess for three or more years. The period and type of training varied with the nature of the functions of the particular deity that the priest served. The candidate for priesthood received a call either through illness or by being possessed by a deity. It was believed that refusal to obey the call would result in madness or death for the recalcitrant candidate. Relatives of the candidate could intercede on his/her behalf, and if their pleas were deemed valid the possessed person would be spared by a ritual of drawing out the deity from the body of the candidate.

The curriculum of the priesthood training included divination; diagnosis of diseases; prescription of cures; identification of herbs and roots and their medicinal qualities; moral lessons on respect of elders and the general public, equity of care, frugality, obedience, industry, cooperation, and chastity and abstinence; and songs and dance. Divination was based on the manipulation, usually by the casting of cowrie shells (*serewa* or *sedeɛ*—#591–596), pebbles, or some other divining devices and the recitation of specific oral texts and codes associated with particular configurations of the divining objects. Each configuration resulting from the casting of the divining devices is associated with a body of text and this text is recited after the tossing of the divining devices.

An experienced priest was able to diagnose a disease and fit it into one or more of the following principal categories of illness and disease: *honam yaree* (illness of the body— e.g., rheumatism, piles, boils); *nsane yaree* (infectious diseases—e.g., yaws, measles, chicken pox)); *abusua yaree* (illness of the matrilineal group); *mogya yaree* (illness of the blood, that is, genetical disease); and *sunsum yare* (spiritually-caused or psychological illness). If the illness is not a simple bodily ailment but 'something lies behind it' then a spiritual cause is attributed to it and the priest would specify what must be done to 'remove the misfortune' (*yi mmusuo*—to propitiate the god) that is troubling the patient. All medical attempts to cure the illness would prove futile if the precipitating spiritual cause were not first dealt with and the patient released from the misfortune that was troubling him/her. The priest (and herbalist) practised both curative and preventive medicine.

Advancement after the initial entry was dependent upon "a tenacious memory, a prudent discretion, and inviolable secrecy," writes Cruickshank (1853). After training, a day was set aside for the graduation ceremony during which the graduate performed the *akɔm* dance (possession dance). It is during this time that a name is believed to be revealed

Etuo ne
akyekyedee -
#350

Denkyem -
#217

Wodu
nkwanta a -
#682

Nsensan -
#705

Serewa - #596

Sunsum - #36

Nyame dua
#55

Nkron - #703

to the graduate. The graduate paid a graduation fee (*mpɔnho nsa*).

WRITING

The adinkra cloth symbols combine both pictograms (e.g., *dɛnkyɛm*—#215–218 and *akokɔ*—#694–696) and ideograms (for example, *Gye Nyame*—#2–9 and *mate masie*—#652–654). Besides incorporating the ideograms and pictograms on cloth, the symbols that form part of the adinkra writing may also be found in woodcarving, architectural designs, and metal casting. A more recent development in the adinkra form of writing has been the increased use of phonological scripts based on either English or Twi language. In recent times not only letters, but also words and sentences have been incorporated. ABCD (#700) symbolizes literacy that has come to be associated with contemporary formal schooling. Some of the phonological script is combined with the traditional ideographs and pictographs to create a whole new aesthetics.

Some examples of symbols that have words wrapped around motifs include the following: *Asɛm pa asa* (the truth is gone—#671), *ɛkaa nsee nko a* (the weaver bird wishes—#491), *ɛkaa obi nko a* (someone wishes—#489) and *owuo see fie* (death destroys the home—#114–115). Other symbols with words and sentences include *nipa bɛwu na sika te ase* (one will die only to leave behind one's wealth—#112), *owuo begya hwan?*, (who will be spared by death—#99), and *ɛkaa obi nko a* (someone wishes—#492).

Alphabetic Writing in Ghana

The use of the Roman alphabet in Ghana dates back to the Portuguese who are believed to have introduced the phonographic writing system with the establishment of trading post at the Elmina Castle, the building of which was completed in 1482. In 1503 the Portuguese made their initial attempts to convert the indigenous people of Elmina to Christianity and by 1529, a school had been set up to teach the children to 'learn how to read and write' in Portuguese ((McWilliam and Kwamena-Poh, 1975). When the Dutch routed the Portuguese out of Ghana, they did not only run schools in their castles in Ghana, the Dutch, (as well as the English, Danes and other Europeans who built castles in Ghana) also sent some African children to continue their schooling in Europe. Some of these children educated in the castle schools and in Europe later helped to write the Akan languages (Twi and Fantse) in the alphabetic form.

The development of the Roman alphabet for the Akan language dates to the seventeenth century according to European travelers' accounts. Between 1600 and 1602, for example, J. P. de Marees, a Dutch traveler on the Gold Coast, was able to compile a list of vocabulary of the Fantse and Ga-Adangme languages. The Danish chaplain in one of the first Danish settlements near Cape Coast, John Mueller listed 400 Akan (Fantse) words and their Danish translations as an appendix to his book *Die Africanische Landschaft Fetu* published at Hamburg in 1675. In 1743 Jacobus Capitein, an Elmina mullato who was sent to Leyden, Holland for schooling, translated into Fantse the Lord's Prayer, the Twelve Articles of Belief, and the Ten Commandments. In 1764, Christian Protten, a mullato from Christiansborg, translated the Lord's Prayer into Fantse. He also published a Ga-Twi-Danish catechism and a grammar book, *En nyttig Grammaticalsk Indledelse til Tvende hidinatil ubekiendte Sprog fanteisk ig Acraisk.* In 1785, P. E. Isert, a Danish botanist and traveller, prepared a list of Ga, Asante and Ewe (Krepi) words and their Danish translations. The two Asante princes Owusu Nkwantabisa son of Asanthene Osei Yaw (who ruled in 1824–34) and Owusu Ansah son of Asantehene Osei Bonsu (who ruled in 1800–24) were sent to England to go to school. They also published lists of Twi words ((McWilliam and Kwamena-Poh, 1975; Graham, 1976; Pawlak, 1985).

The Basel Mission from about 1840 modified the existing Roman alphabet to write the Akwapim Twi. This was used to translate the bible. Rev. H. N. Riis published two books on Twi grammar. One of the two books was entitled *Elemente des Akwapim-Dialekts der Odschi-Sprache (Elements of the Akwapim Dialect of the Twi language).* In 1854, Karl Richard Lepsius, a professor in Berlin and an Egyptologist, published *Standard*

Akoko - #694

Mate masie - #654

Serewa - #594

Bese saka - #578

Ahinansa - #717

Eka nsee nko a - #491

Mate masie - #652

Alphabet for Reducing unwritten languages and Foreign Graphic Systems to a uniform Orthography in European letter. This rekindled interest in writing some of the Ghanaian languages using the newly standardized Roman alphabet. In 1860 Timothy Laing, a Methodist missionary published the Fantse primer, *Fante Akenkan Ahyesie* (Pawlak, 1985).

Dan L. Carr and Joseph P. Brown published their book, *The Mfantsi Grammar* (in Fantse) in Cape Coast in 1868. In 1875, Rev. Johann Gottlieb Christaller wrote *A Grammar of the Asante and Fante Language called Tshi (Twi) based on the Akwapim Dialect with Reference to other Dialects.* In 1879, he published the *Dictionary of the Asante and fante language called Tshi* (Twi).

Despite the improvements, the Roman alphabet system still lacked sufficient letters to transcribe many languages. One solution has been to add new letters to existing ones. Another solution has been to create a new alphabet system, for example, the Cyrillic alphabet used in writing some of the Eastern European languages. In 1888, the International Phonetic Association (IPA) created in effect a new Roman alphabet, with lower case (small) letters only through the addition of a series of new letters (Dalby, 1986).

In 1930, the Government of Ghana (then called Gold Coast) adopted an official national alphabet for writing the languages in the country. This alphabet system has thirty-four (34) letters. Beginning from the end of the 19th century, the works of Rev. R. G. Acquaah (1884–1954), J. A. Annobil, C. A. Akrofi, J. J. Addaye, F. Safori, E. J. Osew, K. E. Owusu, S. K. Otoo, A. Crakye Denteh, A. A. Opoku, E. Effa, R. A. Tabi, Efua T. Sutherland, and J. H. Kwabena Nketia have contributed immensely in developing a corpus of literary classics in Akan (Asante-Twi, Akwapim-Twi and Fantse). The establishment of the Ghana Broadcasting Service in 1935 created a popular platform for young Ghanaian poets and writers (Pawlak, 1985). The establishment of the Bureau of Ghana Languages in the 1950's served as an important center for the development of Akan literature using the alphabetic writing system. In the 1950's and the 1960's there were several newspapers and magazines that were published in Fantse and Twi. Popular among these were *Amansuon, Nkwantabisa,* and *Dawuru.* Since then, the erstwhile School of Ghana Languages at Ajumako, the Linguistics Department and the Language Center at the University of Ghana have contributed to the development of alphabetized writing in Akan.

MATHEMATICAL KNOWLEDGE AND ACCOUNTING

Several mathematical ideas are vividly portrayed in the adinkra writing systems. The lines that are drawn with *dua afe* or *nsensan nnua* on the cloth before it is printed with various symbols are examples of Akan mathematical knowledge. The numbers of lines made by the *dua afe* and *nsensan nnua* have symbolic meanings themselves. One symbolizes the indivisible, the *kra* (soul) of *Nyame. Nsateaa koro* (one finger—#10) means the same as *Gye Nyame* (except God—#2–9). Two symbolizes Nyame as a duality, divisible by birth. *Nsateanu* means *Mema mo mo ne yɪ me man* (I congratulate you people of my state—#520). Three symbolizes *Nyame* as the creator and ruler of the universe that is a continuum of the sky (*ewiem*), earth (*ewiase*), and the underworld (*asamando*). Four symbolizes *Nyame* as the creator and ruler of the four cardinal points of the compass and the revolving heaven. Five symbolizes *Nyame* as a Supreme Being. Six symbolizes the dialectical processes of life, death and resurrection or rebirth. It is the symbol of strength, vitality and rejuvenation. Seven is the symbol for the universe and the state. It represents the seven planets each of which presides over the seven days of the week, and the seven *abusua* that form the state. Eight symbolizes procreation, fertility and fecundity. Nine (i.e., 3+3+3) symbolizes the triad comprising *Nyame, Nyankopɔn,* and *Ɔdomankoma* that rules the universe (Meyerowitz, 1951; Antubam, 1963).

The lines drawn on the adinkra cloth are usually drawn without a ruler and, as Frutiger (1989, p. 24) points out, "the drawing of a straight line without a ruler" is an abstract idea. The adinkra cloth designer is able to utilize this abstract idea to develop patterns that are not only aesthetically appealing, but also mathematically sophisticated. *Daban* (#681) is another line system in which the cloth printer uses a ruler.

Asem pa asa
- #671

Owuo begya
hwan - #99

ABCD -
#700

Nsensan -
#705

Nkyemu -
#674

Daban - #681

Nsatea koro -
#10

The Akan systems of numeration ranged from the few number words of the ordinary person to the extensive numerical vocabulary of traders, astronomers and specialized public servants. An example of Akan numeration systems is given by the expression: *Woamma wo yɔnko antwa nkrɔn a, wo nso worentwa du*—If you do not let your friend have nine you will not be able to have ten (nine— #702–703). Other symbols that depict the number concept include *nnamfo pa baanu* (two good friends—#337), *dua korɪ* (one tree—#343), *mpua anum* (hairstyle of five tufts—#223–229), *nkwantanan* (hairstyle of four tufts—#230) and *koroyɛ* (unity—#319). These few numbers that are incorporated in the adinkra symbols should not be construed as the extent of the mathematical knowledge skills of the Akan. Other Akan art work, for example the work of the goldsmiths, reveals very complex mathematical skills of the Akan.

There existed a very complicated and elaborate accounting and monetary system based on gold dust (*sika futuro*) and goldweights (*mmrammoɔ*. *Nsenɛɛ* (scales—#676) symbolizes this accounting system. The weights served as denominations for exchange and other monetary transactions. *Serewa* or *sedeɛ* (cowrie shells—#591–596) and *bese saka* (bunch of kola nuts—#575–581) were also used as currency. From *sedee* is derived the name cedi, the present currency in use in Ghana.[10]

The demands of commerce, bureaucratic and legal transactions at the king's court dictated the degree of standardization of weights and measures involving gold dust usage. There developed among traders counting systems based on five and ten. Traders for example, count fingers of plantain in multiples of five. Those who make a living fishing people on the coast count in multiples of five or ten depending on the size of the fish. Record keeping varied from knotted strings that were tied around the waist (*tɔmmaa* or *abɔsoɔ*) to the *san dan ho* (literally means "mark on the wall") and *susu* credit systems, and from the notched sticks to the treasury system of the king's court and the ritual of the annual census, carried out by the indirect methods that circumvented the taboo on counting living human beings.

The annual *Odwira* or *Afahyɛ* festival provided the means for taking a census of the population. Public accounts were balanced at the end of each day. Major audits were carried out once in each Asante month, at the end of the Great Adae (*Akwasidae*), for it was at that time that the greatest volume of Treasury business was transacted (Wilks, 1975). In Kumasi, the Gyaasewahene was responsible for keeping the state accounts. The Gyaasehene also had a functionary detailed to check off the months by dropping a cowrie shell (*serewa* or *sedeɛ*—#591–596) into a bag each new moon. The calendar kept by this functionary (timekeeper) was based on *adaduanan* (forty-two days) or six weeks. The month was known as *bosome*, and *adaduanan mmienu* (two forty-two days) was the same as abosome mmiensa (three months). The first new moon after the Odwira festival marked the beginning of the new year (*afe foforɔ*).

The *dapɛn* or *nnawɔtwe* system of counting days reflects the inclusive counting in some aspects of Akan numbering system which includes integers, fractions and operations like addition, subtraction, multiplication and division. Fractional ideas are expressed by words such as *fã* or *abunu* (half), *abusa* (third), *abunum* (fifth), and *nkotuku ano* (percentage). An example of symbols used to indicate Akan people's views about number concepts include *nnamfo pa baanu* (two good friends—#337), *ti korɔ nkɔ agyina* (one head does not constitute a council—#325–326), and *nkrɔn* (nine—#702–703). *Dame dame* (#668–669), *ɔware*, *ampe* and other games and quizzes provided opportunities for children to learn to count and to portray their mathematical abilities.

The ability to observe and reproduce and utilize patterns, both numerical and geometrical, was perfected by weavers, carvers, goldsmiths and other crafts people. The use of patterns was developed in housing construction and architecture, and for use in games like *ɔware* and *dame* (#668–669).

NOTES

EKAA NSEE NKOA

Eka nsee nko
a - #492

Gye Nyame -
#8

EKAA
OBI NKOA

Eka obi nko
a - #489

ONIPA BE
WUNASIKA
TE ASE

Onipa bewu
na sika te ase
- #112

1. The word nyansa is derived from the two words: *nya* (to gain, to find, to come by, or to expetience) and *nsa* (inexhaustible). Therefore, nyansa is literally "that which is obtained and is never exhausted," that is, a lesson which is learned from experience and is lasting.

2. *Nteteε* is another term that is indicative of education. It is used more in the sense of training.

3. In some communities salt or lemon juice and honey are used in place of water and palm wine. These days some people use soda pop (or any non-alcoholic beverage) or gin (or any alcoholic beverage) as a substitute for palm wine.

4. A study by Rosenstein and Oster (1988) demonstrated that within two hours of birth, infants with no prior taste experience differentiated sour and bitter stimuli as well as sweet versus non-sweet taste stimuli.

5. The dirges (*sudwom* or *subaa*) sung (or recited) by women and poetry (*awensεm*) recited during funerals serve similar purposes.

6. Fantse fishermen along the coast refer to this as Aberewa na mba (the old lady and her children).

7. These stories became known as Auntie Nancy stories in the New World when the slave trade transported African across the Atlantic Ocean. Ananse stories are a source of education, entertainment and humor.The stories reveal Akan socil construction of reality.

8. One song urges the indolent to go to the ant to learn its ways and be wise.

9. Εsom literally means to serve or to provide service. It is used to describe apprenticeship. Adwumasua literally means occupational training. A trainee or an apprentice is usually refered as ɔsomfoɔ. Public service was considered as εsomdwuma, which literally meant service work.

10. *Pesewa*, the basic unit of the contemporary Ghanaian currency is derived from *pεsewa* of the goldweight currency system, and *cedi* is derived from *sedeε*, the cowrie shell currency system.

CHAPTER 11

Bese papa ne konini ahahan yɛtasen no ɔbanyansafoɔ.

CONCLUSION

This study serves as an example of how the material culture of the Akan can be utilized as the context for both visual and verbal language learning. In this exploratory study, one can also discover that the links between the visual and the verbal make it possible for one to explore various themes in Akan thought and world view. It has been shown in this study that the *adinkra* symbols are more than visual representation of what the Akan verbalized. The *adinkra* symbols, when viewed as pictorial signs, ideograms, and phonograms, constitute a writing system. The symbols are linked to narratives that are drawn from the extensive Akan oral literature genres which include proverbs, stories, mythologies, poetry, funeral dirges, riddles and quizzes.

If we could exactly identify and interpret every single *adinkra* cloth symbol, every combination of symbols, and the various colors forming the background of the cloths and the narratives that are linked to these symbols we would be able to read the *adinkra* cloth as a "book." This "book" does not only serve as a store of social knowledge. It also serves to record knowledge that can be viewed as progressive and dynamic rather than static in quantity. By drawing on Akan verbal genres and also by appropriating symbols from other cultures the *adinkra* writing system does not only decontextualize every day interactional events.

The "book" also makes it possible for us to realize that literacy need not be associated only with formal schooling. Similarly, literacy based on writing systems that are phonetically-based is an important aspect of everyone's education in these times. However, alphabetical symbols alone have long been insufficient to record and convey human thoughts and knowledge. Therefore, being able to view, interpret and react to visual images such as those in the *adinkra* cloth is just as important for today's population. In the Ghanaian society where people have limited access to books that are based on the phonetically-based writing systems, the text incorporated in the *adinkra* system of writing can serve as basis of discourse in the classroom of both the young and the old. Such discourse can contribute to knowledge and thought. From this study we see that information can come in pictures as well as in words, and more usually in the kind of text that combines images with words. Literacy programs for adults, as well as the formal school curriculum for children, need to recognize that the visual element—be it pictogram, ideogram or phonogram—is a central part of complete literacy.

Adinkra symbols when read as a "book" supply considerably more than information about language; they can orient one toward the ways that all book learning makes possible: linking text to text, acquiring additional symbol and word meanings as symbol and word can have multiple meanings, relying on prior knowledge (e.g., from various Akan verbal genres) to help make sense of a text, and creating inferences based on information presented by a book (Smolkin and Yade, 1992, p. 439). These characteristics of learning are crucial to literacy for both school age children and adults.

What are some other educational implications of the *adinkra* system of writing? Is the knowledge encoded in the *adinkra* symbols the type of knowledge that is worth building into the formal educational curriculum of the school? The *adinkra* symbols have relevance for the work of writers and book illustrators as well as educators in general. Familiarity with these and other symbols and images of the society will play an important role in the culture's visual heritage. Writers and illustrators are recognizing that people of all ages, from toddlers to adults, enjoy and look toward illustrated books that reflect and convey the thoughts, ideals, and values of the society. School age children, for example, learn alphabets by first starting to read alphabet books most of which are picture books. As Smolkin and Yade (1992, p. 433) point out,

> children who participate in reading alphabet books are learning about at least two rather different sets of information. The first set is the "expected" set—children are learning about graphic form, how it operates and how people "talk about it." The second set may be, however, the more significant set—how people "use" books.

By reading *adinkra* cloth symbols as an illustrated "book," educators can gain new and important insight into the value of using pictures, illustrations, and other forms of visuals to accompany discussions. Comenius, the seventeenth century Moravian bishop and educator, became famous for his books *Orbis Pictus* and *Didactica Magna*, in which he astonished the educational world by suggesting that pictures as visual aids be used for instructing children in schools.

Adinkra symbols as visual representations suggest the importance of linking visuals with various abstract verbal concepts. This is of importance to subject areas like mathematics, science and literature. Morris and Pai (1993, p. 84) note that

> Mathematics, as the language of quantity, is the symbol system we use in studying the physical world of nature. Mathematics may be abstract, but is certainly not vague. What mathematics does is to render symbolic the absolute precision and regularity of the cosmos we live in.

Similarly, in literature, one is not only required to read text literally, but one is also required to be able to move to the interpretive level in understanding the visual symbols in metaphors, allegories, pun, and other figures of speech in a text.

Symbols are especially significant for understanding the changing and multicultural nature of the global community. From a cross-cultural perspective, one realizes that a symbol takes on different meanings in different social context. Some of the *adinkra* symbols have been borrowed or appropriated from other cultures. It will be interesting to undertake a comparative study to see what some of the *adinkra* symbols mean in other cultures that have similar symbols. In this study, for example, we see how the ram's horns (*dwennimmen*—#204) are used to symbolize strength in humility in the Akan social context. Gallant (1994, p. 704), on the other hand, makes us aware that in peasant societies in the Mediterranean region, to give a man the ram's horns "signifies the sexual conquest of his wife, thereby exposing the impotence of the husband and the power of the adulterer." That is, throwing down the ram's horns symbolizes cuckolding, and cuckolding is about loss of control and powerlessness.

At another level of comparison are various symbols that have been used to denote peace. The dove white with an olive branch has been used to symbolize peace in some societies. Yet in some other societies, the white flag symbolizes peace. In some American Indian societies the smoking pipe is the symbol of peace. In this study we see that when the Akan chief sent the axe (*akuma*—#567) he meant peace rather than war.

This study is just a first step in understanding the complexities of Akan and other Ghanaian symbolism. It points to the need for scholars to appreciate the importance of material culture as visual documents for research. More research is required in areas such as metal casting (particularly goldweights), wood carvings and other textiles and clothing designs in order to facilitate a better understanding of the connections between verbal strategies and the visual heritage of the Akan society. It is my hope, also that readers of this book and those who use African material culture in their work will be provoked to additional reflection on the interpretive possibilities these sources open up.

INDEX

1 *ABƆDE SANTANN* - TOTALITY OF THE UNIVERSE

Symbol of the **TOTALITY OF THE UNIVERSE - NATURAL AND SOCIAL CREATIONS**

From the expression: *Ɔdomankoma bɔɔ adeɛ; ɔbɔɔ awia, ɔsrane ne nsoromma, ɔbɔɔ nsuo ne mframa; ɔbɔɔ nkwa, ɔbɔɔ nnipa, ɛna ɔbɔɔ owuo. Ɔte ase daa.*

Literal translation: God, the Creator; He created the sun, the moon and the stars, the rain and the wind; He created life, the human being, and He created death. He lives forever.

The symbol incorporates the eye, the rays of the sun, the double crescent moon, and the stool. The stool depicts the socially created institutions and the authority human beings have over the environment.

2-9 *GYE NYAME* - EXCEPT GOD

Symbol of the OMNIPOTENCE and the OMNIPRESENCE OF GOD

From the Akan aphorism: *Abɔde santann yi firi tete; obi nte ase a ɔnim n'ahyɛase, na obi ntena ase nkɔsi n'awieeɛ, GYE NYAME.*

Literal translation: This great panorama of creation dates back to time immemorial; no one lives who saw its beginning and no one will live to see its end, EXCEPT GOD.

The symbol reflects the Akan belief of a SUPREME BEING, the CREATOR who they refer to by various names - e.g., ƆBƆADEƐ, NYAME, ONYANKOPƆN TWEREAMPƆN.

10 *NSATEA KORO* - ONE FINGER

Symbol of the OMNIPOTENCE OF GOD

From the expression: *Gye Nyame, mensuro obiara.*

Literal translation: Except God, I fear no one.

This symbol has the same meaning as the *Gye Nyame* symbol

11 *NYAME YƐ ƆHENE* - GOD IS KING

Symbol of the MAJESTY OF GOD, SUPREMACY and PREEMINENCE

From the expression: *Nyame yɛ ɔhene.*

Literal translation: God is king.

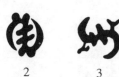

12-13 *ƆDOMANKOMA* - CREATOR

Symbol of the CREATOR OF THE UNIVERSE and DIVINE POWER

From the expression: *Ɔdomankoma a ɔbɔɔ adeɛ ɔno na nsɛm nyinaa firi no.*

Literal translation: God the Creator, all things depend on Him.

This symbol is often incorporated in the pendant called adaebɔɔ that forms part of a necklace (*ayanneɛ*) the king wears.

14. *SORO NE ASASE* - HEAVEN AND EARTH

Symbol of INDIVISIBILITY, CONNECTED and UNITY

From the expression: *Asase trɛ, na Onyame ne panin. Also, Nnipa nyinaa yɛ Onyame mma, obi nyɛ asase ba.*

Literal translation: Of all the earth, God the Creator is the elder. Also, All people are the children of the Supreme Being, God and no one is a child of the earth.

15. *PURU* - CIRCLE

Symbol of the OMNIPOTENT GOD, DIVINE POWER, ROYALTY, and THE SPIRIT OF GOD

From the expression: *Ɔsrane abɔ puru.*

Literal translation: The moon is in full circle.

The circle , with a point at the center, represents the turning universe and its pivotal point. The beginning and the end of the circle, like the creation of the universe, are only known to the CREATOR

16 17

16-17. *ONYANKOPƆN ANIWA HU ASUMASƐM BIARA* - GOD'S EYE SEES ALL SECRETS

Symbol of GOD'S ABILITY TO BE IN ALL PLACES, UBIQUITOUS NATURE OF GOD, EVER-PRESENT GOD, and OMNIPRESENCE

From the expression: Onyankopɔn afa boɔ sɛ ɔreto abɔ wo, wose merekɔtɛ. Also, Onyame yɛ ahuntahunii. Brɛakyihunadeɛ Nyame, onim asumasɛm biara.

Literal translation: When God attempts to throw a pebble at you, you say you are going to hide. Also, God sees all things. God, the Creator is all-seeing and is everywhere. There is nothing that can be hidden from the Creator. No one can hide from God.

18 19

18-19. *HANN NE SUM* - DAY AND NIGHT

Symbol of DUALISM, ORDERLINESS, DARKNESS AND BRIGHTNESS, and TIME

The Akan belief system has it that God's time is based on the concept of nna mmere nson (seven-day time). Hence another name Akans have for God is Abɔ-nna-nson (Creator of Seven Days). The seven days are each ruled by a planet as follows: Kwasiada (Sunday), the day of Ayisi (Awusi, Awisi), is ruled by the Sun; Dwoada (Monday), the day of Awo, is ruled by the Moon; Benada (Tuesday) is the day of Abena (Mars); Wukuda (Wednesday) is the day of Aku (Mercury); Yaoda (Yaada, Yawda - Thursday) is the day of Aberao (Aberaw - Jupiter); Fida (Fiada - Friday) is the day of Afi (Venus); and Memeneda (Saturday) is the day of Amene (Saturn).

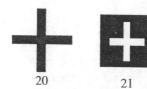

20 21

20-21. *MMERAMUTENE* - MALE CROSS

Symbol of the SUNLIGHT, WARMTH, ENDURANCE, and UPRIGHTNESS

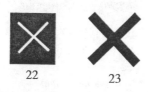

22 23

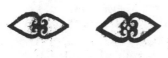

24

22-24. *MMERAMU BERE* - FEMALE CROSS

Symbol of WARMTH, SUNSHINE, and VITALITY

25 26

25-26. *ASASE YƐ DURU* or *ASASE TRƐ* - MIGHTY EARTH

Symbol of POWER, LIFE'S SUSTAINER, MIGHT, WEALTH, AUTHORITY

From the aphorism: *Tumi nyinaa ara ne asase.* Also, *Asaase trɛ, na Onyame ne panin.*

Literal translation: All power emanates from land. Also, Of all the earth, God the Creator is the elder.

This symbol reflects the importance of LAND (ASASE) to the Akan. Even though land is communally owned in the Akan society, land ownership (by groups or individuals) is an important source of power. The Akan believes ASASE (THE EARTH) is the feminine aspect of the duality of the universe with God, the CREATOR as the male. The EARTH, that is Land is the SUSTAINER OF LIFE.

27   28

29   30

31   32

33   34

35   36

37   38

39

40

41

27-31. *EWIA* or *AWIA* - SUN

Symbol of VITALITY, LIFE SPARK, WARMTH, and ENERGY

From the maxim: Ɔhene yɛ awia.

Literal translation: The king is the sun.

God as SUN'S ENERGY - ƆMAWIA - is the source of VITAL FORCE.

This symbol became associated with the Progress Party in the 1969 general elections in Ghana. To the Progress Party this symbolized the rising sun (*awia repue*) as progress.

32-34. *ANANSE NTONTAN* - SPIDER'S WEB

Symbol of CUNNING, INTELLIGENCE, CRAFTINESS, CREATIVITY, SHREWDNESS, and SAGACITY

The Spider is a principal character in Akan folk stories called Ananse Stories. The stories teach that God gave Ananse the meaning of order and God taught Ananse architecture, the structure of dwellings, and the structure of life and society. This perspective is symbolized by the spider's web, which also stands for the sun and its rays and the vitality and creative powers of God. In some stories God is referred to as Ananse Kokuroko (the Great Spider). Only the spider knows the beginning and the end of its creation, the web. Similarly, only God knows the beginning and the end of His creation. God's creation may be said to have the characteristics of the spider's web: orderliness and intelligence.

35-36. *SUNSUM* or *NTORƆ* - SOUL

Symbol of SPIRITUAL PURITY, and CLEANLINESS OF THE SOUL

The Akan belief is that *SUNSUM* is the part of ƆBƆADEƐ (God the Creator) that enters the human being at birth with the first breath. This *sunsum* is partly transmitted through the father to the child. While the male is capable of transmitting his *sunsum* to his offspring, the female cannot transmit her sunsum to her offspring. She transmits her blood (*mogya*) to her offspring.

37-38. *ANYINAM NE APRANAA* - THUNDER AND LIGHTNING

Symbol of the FIRE OF THE SKY, DESTRUCTION, PURITY, FLAME, VITALITY, and RENEWAL

From the aphorism: Sɛ anyinam te yerɛw ma apranaa bobɔ mu a, kae sɛ Onyame yɛ hene.

Literal translation: When it is thundering and lightning, remember God is King.

39-41. *NSUO* - WATER

Symbol of FERTILITY, LIFE FORCE, and FECUNDITY

From the expression: Ɔkwan atware asuo, asuo atware kwan; Ɔpanin ne hwan? Yɛbɔɔ kwan no kɔtoo asuo no, asuo no firi tete. Or, Sɛ ebinom nnya nsuo nnom na wonya bi dware a, kae sɛ Onyame yɛ hene. Also, Bea a nsuo wɔ no hɔ na nkwa wɔ. Also, Toturobonsu Nyame, no na ɔgu ahina hunu mu nsuo.

Literal translation: The path crosses the river and the river crosses the path; who is the elder? When we made the path to cross the river, the river was existing already from time immemorial. Or, If some people cannot have water to drink, but you have some to take your bath with, remember God is King. Also, Where there is water there is bound to be life. Also, God the Giver of rain, he fills the pot of the poor with water.

This symbol poses the question: the river and the path which was created first? Obviously, the river as God's creation preceded the path which is human creation. The symbol also forms part of the Akan people's explanation of the origins of the universe. Water was one of God's first creations. Water is also considered the source of life and vitality and fertility. Water in the sky (rain) and water on earth (rivers, sea, lakes) both make the earth fruitful and sustain plant and animal life. God as RAINGIVER (Toturobonsuo) is the source of life and fertility.

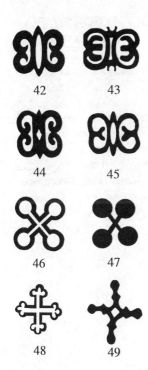

42 43

44 45

46 47

48 49

50

51

52

53 54 55

56 57 58

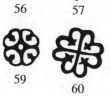

59 60

42-45. *HYE ANHYE* - UNBURNABLE

Symbol of the IMPERISHABILITY OF THE SELF, PERMANENCY OF THE HUMAN SOUL, and TOUGHNESS

This represents the idea that GOD the SPIRIT never dies, or God lives forever. The Akan belief is that the human soul, an image of God the Spirit, lives in perpetuity; thus, there is life after the death of the physical part of the human being in the Akan belief system.

46-49. *NYAME NWU NA MAWU* - I DIE ONLY WHEN GOD DIES

Symbol of the PERMANENCE OF THE HUMAN SOUL, THE INDESTRUCTIBILITY OF THE HUMAN SPIRIT, CONTINUITY OF HUMAN LIFE, IMMORTALITY, and RESPECT FOR OLD AGE

From the proverb: *Onipa wu a, na onwuiɛ.*

Or, *Nyame nwu na mawu.* Also, *Nyame bɛwu na mawu.*

Literal translation: When a man dies he is not really dead. Or, Should God die, I will die.

This symbolizes that there is something in a human being that is eternal, indestructible, imperishable, and that continues to exist in the world of spirits. The Akan belief is that the human soul is in the image of God, the Creator who does not die. Thus, the human soul does not die, or the human soul dies only when God dies. That is, if human beings cease to exist, God ceases to exist. Hence, the Akan believes in life after death.

50. *OBI NNIM ADEKYEEɛ MU NSɛM* - NO ONE KNOWS WHAT THE DAY WILL BRING FORTH

Symbol of UNCERTAINTY, VACILLATION, DOUBT, SKEPTICISM, and APPREHENSION

From the aphorism: *Obi nnim adekyeeɛ mu nsɛm, gye Nyame.*

Literal translation: No one knows what the day will bring forth, except God.

51. *OBI NKYERɛ AKɔDAA NYAME* - GOD IS NOT INTRODUCED TO A CHILD

Symbol of the GOODNESS OF HUMAN LIFE, RELIGIOSITY OF THE HUMAN BEING, and A PRIORI KNOWLEDGE

From the expression: *Obi nkyerɛ akɔdaa Nyame.*

Literal translation: God is not introduced to a child.

The child's knowledge of God occurs by intuition.

52. *MESRɛ NKWA TENTEN NE NKɔSOɔ MA WO* - I PRAY FOR LONG LIFE AND PROSPERITY FOR YOU

Symbol of GOOD WISHES, GOOD LUCK, PRAYER, and SUPPLICATION

From the prayer: *Mesrɛ nkwa tenten ne nkɔsoɔ ma wo.*

Literal translation: I pray for long life and prosperity for you.

53-60. *NYAME DUA* - GOD'S ALTAR

Symbol of the PRESENCE OF GOD, GOD'S PROTECTION, HOLY PLACE, and SPIRITUALITY

Similar to the biblical concept of the altar to the unknown God. The symbol signifies God's presence everywhere and every time.

61 62
63 64
65 66
67 68
69

61-69. *KERAPA* or *MMUSUYIDEɛ* - SANCTITY or GOOD FORTUNE

Symbol of SANCTITY OF SELF, SPIRITUAL STRENGTH, GOOD SPIRIT, GOOD LUCK, and GOOD FORTUNE

From the Akan aphorism: *Kerapa yɛ Nyame ahoboa; ɔte sɛ ɔkra, ɔkyiri fi na ɔkram fi te sɛ pɛtɛ nti na Nananom de no yi mmusuo.*

Literal translation: Sanctity is part particle of the good; it is like a cat; it abhors filth and it clears filth like the vulture that is why it is used to drive away evil and diseases.

The Akan believes that the human being is born sacred until the socialization or enculturation process corrupts him/her. The Akan does not believe in what other religions or philosophies call the original sin. This symbol was woven into the bedside mat on which the king would step three times for good luck before going to bed (see *BIRIBI WƆ SORO* also). Every year a ritual, *MMUSUYIDEɛ*, was performed. During the period all streets of townships were swept each morning and evening to remove mystical danger and to prevent disease or death from entering the townships.

70

70. *MOMMA YEMMƆ MPAEɛ* - LET US PRAY

Symbol of SPIRITUAL DEVOTION, SUPPLICATION, and PRAYER

The ideas expressed in an Akan prayer are best captured by the following:

Yɛsrɛ wo nkwa,
Yɛsrɛ wo adom;
ɛmma yɛnwu awia wuo,
ɛmma yɛnwu anadwo wuo;
Yɛkɔ nnae a, yɛnwo ba;
Yɛdua aduadeɛ a, ɛnso aba pa;
Ma asomdwoeɛ mmra wiase;
Ma nkɔsoɔ mmra ɔman yi mu,
Ma ɔman yi nyɛ porɔmporɔm.

Literal translation:

We pray for life and pray for grace
Let not death be with us by day or by night;
May we be blessed with children,
And may what we plant bear good fruit.
Let there be peace in the world,
And may there be prosperity
In this land abundantly.

71

71. *SOM ONYANKOPƆN* - WORSHIP GOD

Symbol of DEVOTION and WORSHIP

From the expression: *Som Onyankopɔn.*
Literal translation: Worship God.

72

72. *ASɛM A ONYANKOPƆN ADI ASIE NO* - WHAT GOD HAS ORDAINED

Symbol of GOD'S EVER ENDURING WORD

From the maxim: *Asɛm a Onyankopɔn adi asie no, onipa ntumi nnane no.* Or, *Adeɛ a Onyame ahyehyɛ no, onipa ntumi nsɛe no.*

Literal translation: What God has ordained, no human being can change.

Akan people have a hierarchical view of beings with Nyame (God) at the apex. This view implies that a lower entity cannot subvert a higher entity. While human beings make obeisance to God, human beings cannot worship lower deities that are below human beings.

73

73. *ONYANKOPƆN, W'AHENNIE MMRA* - GOD, THY KINGDOM COME

Symbol of the SUPREMACY of GOD, DIVINE POWER, and ROYALTY
From the expression: *Nyame ne hene*. Or, *Onyankopɔn w'ahennie mmra*.
Literal translation: God is King. Or, God, thy kingdom come.

74

74. *AGYA, ƆBA NE SUNSUM KRƆNKRƆN* - THE FATHER, THE SON AND THE HOLY SPIRIT

Symbol of the HOLY TRINITY and SPIRITUALITY
The Akan concept of TRINITY is constituted of elements from the MOTHER (*mogya* - blood), the FATHER (*ntoro* - spirit, personality), and GOD (ɔkra - soul). These elements combine to form the CHILD.

75

75. *NKRABEA* - DESTINY

Symbol of the UNEQUAL DISTRIBUTION OF TALENTS, INEQUALITY
From the expression: *Ɛsono onipa biara ne ne nkrabea*. Or, *Onyame nkrabea nni kwatibea*.
Literal translation: Everyone and his/her unique destiny or talents.

76

76. *ONYANKOPƆN BƆ YƐN HO BAN* - GOD PROTECT US

Symbol of GOD'S PROTECTION, SECURITY IN GOD, and PEACE
From the expression: *Onyankopɔn bɔ yɛn ho ban*.
Literal translation: God protect us.

77

77. *ONYANKOPƆN ADOM NTI YƐTE ASE* - BY GOD'S GRACE WE LIVE

Symbol of GOD'S GRACE, GOODNESS, BENEVOLENCE, CHARITY, and VIRTUE
From the aphorism: *Onyankopɔn adom nti yɛte ase*.
Literal translation: By God's grace we live.
Without the life-giving force from God, the human being ceases to exist.

78

78. *ONYANKOPƆN HYIRA YƐN ADUANE SO DAA* - GOD, BLESS OUR FOOD ALWAYS

Symbol of SUCCOR, SUSTENANCE, BLESSINGS, STRENGTH, and VITALITY
From the expression: *Onyankopɔn hyira yɛn aduane so daa*.
Literal translation: God, bless our food always.

79

79. *ONYANKOPƆN , MA YƐN ADUANE DAA* - GOD, FEED US ALWAYS

Symbol of SUSTENANCE, VITALITY, ENERGY, and STRENGTH
From the aphorism: *Nyame na ɔgu ahina hunu mu nsuo*. Or, *Onyankopɔn ma yɛn aduane daa*.
Literal translation: God fills the empty pot with water. Or, God, feed us always. In other words, God provides sustenance for the needy.

80

80. *BIRIBIARA BƐTWAM AKƆ* - ALL WILL PASS AWAY

Symbol of the PERMANENCY OF GOD'S WORD, ENDURANCE, STABILITY, and PERSISTENCE
From the maxim: *Biribiara bɛtwam akɔ, nanso Onyankopɔn asɛm bɛtena hɔ daa*.
Literal translation: All will pass away, but not the word of God.

81

81. *ONYANKOPƆN DƆ WO* - GOD LOVES YOU

Symbol of GOD'S LOVE, KINDNESS, and CHARITY
From the expression: *Onyankopɔn dɔ wo*.
Literal translation: God loves you.

82. *ONYANKOPƆN, WO PƐ NYƐ HƆ* - GOD, THY WILL BE DONE
Symbol of GOD'S WILL
From the expression: Onyankopɔn, wo pɛ nyɛ hɔ.
Literal translation: God, thy will be done.

83. *ONYANKOPƆN NE YƐN NTENA* - MAY GOD BE WITH US
Symbol of GOD'S PRESENCE, PROTECTION, and COMPANY
From the expression: *Onyankopɔn ne yɛn ntena.*
Literal translation: May God be with us.

84. *KAE ONYANKOPƆN ASƐM* - REMEMBER GOD'S WORD
Symbol of BELIEF, FAITH IN THE HOLY BOOK
From the expression: *Kae Onyankopɔn asɛm a ɛwɔ Twerɛ Kronkron no mu.*
Literal translation: Remember God's word in the Holy Bible.

85. *ONYANKOPƆN, TENABEA WƆ M'AKOMA MU MA WO* - GOD, THERE IS ROOM IN MY HEART FOR YOU
Symbol of DEDICATION
From the expression: *Onyankopɔn, tenabea wɔ m'akoma mu ma wo.*
Literal translation: God, there is room in my heart for you.

86. *YƐDA ONYANKOPƆN ASE* - WE THANK GOD
Symbol of GRATITUDE, THANKFULNESS, and APPRECIATION
From the expression: *Yɛda Onyankopɔn ase.*
Literal translation: We thank God.

87. *KRISTONI PAPA* - GOOD CHRISTIAN
Symbol of RELIGIOSITY, GOD-FEARING, FAITHFULNESS and DEDICATION
From the expression: Kristoni papa na ɔse: Me ne Nyame nam nti mensuro.
Literal translation: The good christian says: I am not afraid for God is with me

88. *NEA ONYANKOPƆN AKA ABƆ MU NO* - WHAT GOD HAS JOINED TOGETHER
From the expression: *Nea Onyankopɔn aka abɔ mu no, mma obiara mpae mu.*
Literal translation: What God has joined together, let none separate.

89. *ASƆRE DAN* - HOUSE OF WORSHIP
Symbol of PRESENCE OF GOD, HOLY PLACE, and PLACE OF WORSHIP
From the expression: Nyamesom te sɛ asɔredan mu tokuro mu ahwehwɛ; wogyina akyiri hwɛ a, ɛyɛ wo kusuu; sɛ wokɔ mu a, na wohunu ne fɛ.
Literal translation: Religion is like a church building's stained glass window which is dark when one views it from outside; one appreciates its beauty only when one enters the building.

90-93. *OWUO ATWEDEƐ* - DEATH'S LADDER
Symbol of the MORTALITY of human beings
From the expression: *Owuo atwedeɛ, ɔbaakofoɔ mforo.*
Or, *Obiara bɛforo owuo atwedeɛ*
Literal translation: Death is inevitable for every person. Or, death is the ultimate equalizer. Also, death is no respecter of persons.
The Akan belief is that the physical part of the human being is mortal. The SOUL (SUNSUM or OKERA), however, never dies.

94

94. *OWUO KUM NYAME* - DEATH KILLED GOD

Symbol of the INVINCIBILITY OF DEATH

From the expression: *Nyame bɔɔ owuo na owuo kum Nyame.*

Literal translation: God created Death and Death killed God.

The Eternal One created death only to be taken away by death, but God also created the antidote to death (*Ɔte nanka aduro*) and God, therefore, overcame death. God created the antidote to the instrument of death.

Akan believe that:

	Translation:
Ɔdomankoma	The Creator
Ɔbɔɔ adeɛ	created things;
Ɔbɔɔ nkwa;	When He created things,
Ɔbɔɔ nkwa no,	He created Life;
Ɔbɔɔ owuo;	When He created Life,
Ɔbɔɔ owuo no,	He created Death;
Owuo bɛkum no;	When He created Death,
Owuiɛ no,	Death killed Him;
Nkwa bɛnyanee no,	When He died,
Nti ɔte ase daa.	Life came into Him
	and woke Him up;
	Thereafter, He lived forever.

95

95. *OWUO DE DƆM BƐKƆ* - DEATH WILL CLAIM THE MULTITUDE

Symbol of DEATH AS THE EQUALIZER and DEATH AS THE LEVELLER

From the expression: *Owuo ne yɛn reko, ɔpatafoɔ ne hwan?*

Or, *Owuo bɛgya hwan?*

Literal translation: We are in a struggle with death, who is the mediator?

Who will death leave behind?

96

96. *ONYANKOPƆN BƐTUMI AYƐ* - GOD CAN DO IT

Symbol of VERSATILITY OF GOD, DIVINE POWER, GOD'S SUPREMACY

From the expression: *Onyankopɔn bɛtumi ayɛ adeɛ nyinaa.*

Literal translation: God can do all things.

97

97. *ONYANKOPƆN KA YƐN BOM* - GOD, UNITE US

Symbol of FELLOWSHIP and UNITY IN GOD

From the expression: *Ɔdodoɔ so Nyame a, baako nnuru akyakya.*

Or, *Onyankopɔn ka yɛn bom.*

Literal translation: When many serve God, He is not the individual person's burden.

Or, God, unite us.

98

98. *OWUO MPƐ SIKA* - DEATH ACCEPTS NO MONEY

Symbol of the INEVITABILITY OF DEATH for the Rich as well as the Poor.

From the maxim: *Owuo mpɛ sika.*

Literal translation: Death accepts no money.

Some rich people make it seem like they can buy everlasting life with their money. This symbol suggests that no amount of money will save one from the claws of death. Death is inevitable for the poor as it is for the rich.

99

99. *OWUO BƐGYA HWAN?* - WHO WILL BE SPARED BY DEATH?

Symbol of the INEVITABILITY OF DEATH FOR ALL PEOPLE

From the question: *Owuo bɛgya hwan?*

Literal translation: Who will be spared by death?

This symbol suggests that no one will be spared by death; death is inevitable for all people.

100

100. *YESU WUO* - JESUS' DEATH
Symbol of the INVINCIBILITY OF DEATH and REDEMPTION
From the expression: *Nyame bɔɔ owuo na owuo kum Nyame.*
Literal translation: The Eternal One created death only to be taken away by death.

101

101. *ASIEEε* or *BANMU* - MAUSOLEUM
Symbol of SACRED GROUNDS
There are two mausoleum places for the preservation and interment of the Asante royalty: Banpanase where the corpse is embalmed in a place called Asɔnee, and Bantama where the Afenhyiasom takes place every year. After the British ransacked Kumase during the war of 1874, another place was developed at Breman as the royal mausoleum. Asiiε is not only sacred grounds because that is where corpses are buried. Asieeε also marks the place where the physical aspect of the human being is returned to the womb of Mother Earth.

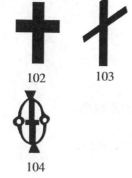
102   103

102-103. *YESU ASεNDUA* - CROSS OF JESUS
Symbol of SUPREME SACRIFICE, REDEMPTION and SELFLESSNESS
From the aphorism: Yesu bεwuu wɔ asεndua so bεgyee adasa nkwa.
Literal translation: Jesus died on the cross to save mankind.

104. *YESU WUSɔRE* - JESUS' RESURRECTION
Symbol of the VICTORY OF JESUS OVER DEATH, ETERNAL LIFE, REINCARNATION, SALVATION, and REJUVENATION
From the expression: Yesu wuiε a, woasɔre.
Literal translation: Jesus has risen from death.
If God has the antidote for the venom of death, and Jesus is the Son of God, then to the Akan that Jesus would arise from death would be possible. This symbol poses the question: O Death, where is thy sting?
The Akans believe that death is not the end of the human spirit, but the moment of its passage from this life to the next.

104

105

105. *MEMA WO HYεDEN* - ACCEPT MY CONDOLENCES
Symbol of CONDOLENCE, SYMPATHY, and CONSOLATION
From the expression: *Mema wo hyεden.*
Literal translation: Accept my condolences.

106. *AKOKɔBEDEε NE KOSUA* - THE HEN AND THE EGG
Symbol of the BEGINNING OF LIFE
From the expression: *Akokɔbedeε ne kosua, hwan ne ɔpanin*?
Literal translation: The hen and the egg, which came first?
Similar expressions about the beginning of life include: *Bosom po bɔtoo abɔɔ; Asase trε na Nyame ne panin.*

106

107. *ABIBIREM BURONYA* - CHRISTMAS IN AFRICA
Symbol of CHRISTMAS, REBIRTH, REJUVENATION, and REJOICING
From the expression: *Afenhyia pa.*
Literal translation: Happy new year

107

108. *ADWERε* - WATERY SHRUB
Symbol of PURITY, SANCTITY, CONSECRATION,
CLEANLINESS, CHASTITY, and GOOD FORTUNE
From the expression: *Adwerε nsuo, wo ne nkwansuo,*
nsu korɔgyenn a wohuru nso wonhye.
Literal translation: Water of life, you are the pure crystal
clean water that boils, but does not burn.
Adwerε is a watery shrub (Trianthema species) the leaves of
which are used in *asubɔ* ceremony.
When one recovers from a long bout of illness one performs an *asubɔ* (purification) ceremony
to sanctify one's soul and appease the spirits for protecting one's life. This ceremony starts with
a bath of water that has been seeped in *adwera* leaves.

108

109   110

Death provokes dualistic "thoughts of darkness and light, weakness and strength, evil and good, sorrow and joy, non-existence and life, war and peace, defeat and victory, vice and virtue, ignorance and knowledge, in short, confusion (Sarpong, 1974, p. 21).

Death is inevitable for all as symbolized by *owuo atwedeε* (death's ladder - # 90-93) and *owuo de dɔm bεkɔ* (death will claim the multitude - # 95). It does not discriminate between the rich and the poor (owuo mpε sika - death accepts no money - # 98); yεbεdane agya (we shall leave everything behind - # 599), or the old and the young. This

109-110   *ANIKUM NNIM AWEREHOƆ* - SLEEP DOES NOT KNOW SADNESS

From the expression: *Anikum nnim awerεhoɔ, anka mesi hɔ redi awerεhoɔ a, na mereda.*
Literal translation: Sleep does not know sadness otherwise I will not fall asleep when I am sad.

111

111.   *WOYε HWAN?* - WHO ARE YOU?
Symbol of HUMAN BEING'S ESSENCE, SOCIAL STATUS and CLASS CONSCIOUSNESS
From the expression: *Nkonsa, woyε hwan? Ahemfo koraa yεwo wɔn.*
Literal translation: Nkonsa (name of a person), who are you? Even kings are born.
This symbol alludes to the essential nothingness of human beings.

112

112.   *ONIPA BεWU NA SIKA TE ASE* - ONE WILL DIE AND LEAVE ONE'S WEALTH BEHIND
Symbol of the RELATIVE INSIGNIFICANCE OF MATERIAL WEALTH
From the aphorism: *Onipa bεwu na sika te ase.*
Literal translation: One will die and leave one's wealth behind.
The rich person cannot be saved from death by his/her wealth.

113   114

113-115.   *OWUO SεE FIE* - DEATH DESTROYS THE HOUSEHOLD
Symbol of the DESTRUCTIVE POWER OF DEATH, TRAGEDY and CALAMITY
From the maxim: *Owuo sεe fie.*
Literal translation: Death destroys the household.

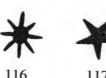

115

116   117

118   119

116-121.   *NSOROMMA - STAR*
Symbol of PATRONAGE, DEPENDENCY ON GOD, HOPE, HIGH EXPECTATION, FAITH, BELIEF, and POWER OF THE PEOPLE
From the aphorisms: *Ɔba nyankonsoromma te Nyame so na ɔnte ne ho so.* Or, *Nyankonsoromma na ɔman wɔ no na nnyε ɔsrane.*
Literal translations: Like the star son of God, I depend on God not on myself. Or, The state belongs to the people and not to the king. The stars represent the people and are contrasted with the moon, representing the king. People are always there though kings may come and go.

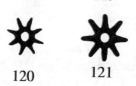

120   121

122   123

122-123. *ANIDASOƆ NSOROMMA* - STAR OF HOPE
Symbol of HOPE, EXPECTATION, DESIRE, and ASPIRATION
From the expression: *Manidasoɔ nsoromma bɛpue anɔpa hemahema*. Or, *Anidasoɔ wɔ wiem*.
Literal translation: My star of hope will rise early in the morning. Or, There is hope in the heavens above.

124

124. *NYAME ADOM NTI (ADOM WƆ WIEM)* - GRACE OF GOD
Symbol of HOPE, TRUST, ASPIRATION, and EXPECTATION
From the aphorism: *Adom dɔɔso wɔ wiemu; ɔman frɛ yie na Nyame yɛ adom a na biribiara wie yie*. Also, *Nyame adom nti, mɛyɛ yie*. Also, *Nyame nti merenwe ahahan*.
Literal translations: Grace is abundant in the heavens, but God only grants it so that all goes well for those who come together in unity to do well. Also, By the Grace of God, I will prosper. Also, By the Grace of God I will not eat leaves.

125

125. *ADE PA BƐBA* - SOMETHING GOOD WILL BE FORTH-COMING
Symbol of HOPE, EXPECTATION, and ANTICIPATION
From the aphorism: *Nyame yɛ adom a, ade pa bɛba da bi*.
Literal translation: God willing, something good will be forthcoming.

126   127

126-128. *BIRIBI WƆ SORO* - THERE IS SOMETHING IN THE HEAVENS
Symbol of HOPE, EXPECTATION, and ASPIRATION
From the aphorism: *Nyame, biribi wɔ soro na ma ɛmmɛka me nsa*.
Literal translation: God, there is something in the heavens, let it reach me.
This symbol was hung above the lintel of a door for the king to touch three times repeating the words of the aphorism for good luck, high hope and good expectations as he went out to carry out his duties each morning (see *KERAPA* also).

128

129. *ONYANKOPƆN BƐKYERƐ* - GOD WILL PROVIDE
Symbol of HOPE and TRUST IN GOD
From the expression: *Onyankopɔn bɛkyerɛ*.
Literal translation: God will provide.

129

130. *ONYANKOPƆN BƐYƐ ME KƐSE* - GOD WILL MAKE ME GREAT
Symbol of EXPECTATION, TRUST and CONFIDENCE IN GOD,
From the expression: Onyankopɔn bɛyɛ me kɛse.
Literal translation: God will make me great.

130

131. *ONYANKOPƆN ADOM NTI BIRIBIARA BƐYƐ YIE* - BY GOD'S GRACE ALL WILL BE WELL
Symbol of HOPE, PROVIDENCE and FATE
From the expression: *Onyankopɔn adom nti biribiara bɛyɛ yie*.
Literal translation: By God's grace all will be well.

131

132. *ABOA A ƆBƐYƐ NNAM NO* - PREDATORY ANIMAL
Symbol of LIMITATION, IMPERFECTION, BALANCE OF FORCES, and EQUAL PROTECTION
From the expression: Aboa a ɔbɛyɛ nnam no, Nyame mma no mmɛn.
Literal translation: The predatory animal usually has no horns.
This suggests the limitation in the individual. If God had not placed limitations on human beings and some wild animals they would have been utterly ruthless.

132

133

133. ONYANKOPƆN MMERɛ NE MMERɛ PA - GOD'S TIME IS THE BEST

From the expression: *Onyankopɔn mmerɛ ne mmerɛ pa.*
Literal translation: God's time is the best.

134

134. ONYANKOPƆN HYIRA YɛN DAA - MAY GOD BLESS US ALWAYS

Symbol of PRAYER and REQUEST
From the expression: *Onyankopɔn hyira yɛn daa .*
Literal translation: May God bless us always.

135

135. NYA GYIDIE - HAVE FAITH

Symbol of FAITH, ASSURANCE, and BELIEF
From the expression: *Nya gyidie wɔ Onyame mu.*
Literal translation: Have faith in God or Believe in God.

136   137

136-137. AKYEMFRA - SWALLOW

Symbol of TALENT, ABILITY, DESTINY, and AGILITY
From the aphorism: *Nyame amma akyemfra hwee no na ɛnyɛ ne ntware ho a.*
Literal translation: If God did not give the swallow anything at all He gae its swiftness and turning ability.

The following *adinkra* symbols depict some of the various aspects of governmental organization among the Akan.

138   139

140   141

138-147. ABAN - CASTLE, FORTRESS, PALACE or STONE HOUSE

Symbol of STRENGTH, SEAT OF POWER, AUTHORITY, LEGITIMACY, RESPECT FOR LAW, INNOVATION, and MAGNIFICENCE

This symbol records a historical event - the building of a magnificent palace for the Asantehene. The building was made of carved stone and was completed in 1822 during the reign of Osei Bonsu. It was roofed with brass laid over an ivory framework, and the windows and doors were cased in gold, and the door posts and pillars were made of ivory. Wealthy merchants of Elmina are believed to have aided in the construction of the king's stone house at Kumasi. The aban has been referred to as the Palace of Culture. This fortress was ransacked and blown up by the British in the 1874 war. An illustration of the Stone Castle appeared in London News, 2 May 1874.

142   143

144   145

146   147

148   149

148-149. *TUMI AFENA* - SWORD OF POWER
Symbol of STATE AUTHORITY, LEGITIMACY, and POWER
At the Pampafie ceremony for the installation of the Asantehene-elect, the Waree Adwumakasehene unsheathes the Bosomuru Sword and passes it on to the King-elect, repeating three times the following:

> Mede wotumi ma wo
> Wo Nana Osei Tutu ne Bosommuru ɔde dii ako no ni
> Mede hyɛ wo nsa

> I pass on to you your authority
> This is the Bosommuru Sword with which your ancestor,
> King Osei Tutu, waged his wars
> I hand it over to you

To this the King-elect replies three times: *Magye* - I accept

150

150. *MPƆMPƆNSUO* - RESPONSIBILITY
Symbol of RESPONSIBILITY, POWER, LOYALTY, BRAVERY, and AUTHORITY
This symbol depicts the state sword used by the king in taking the oath of office. It is also used by the sub-chiefs to swear allegiance to the king. In the Asante society, this sword and the Golden Stool constitute the spiritual embodiment (the soul) of the nation. The mpɔmpɔnsuo was the highest state sword and the Ahwehwebaa was the second highest sword in the Asante state. Other principal state swords were the Bosommuru and Bosompra.

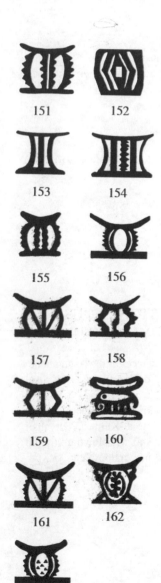

151   152

153   154

155   156

157   158

159   160

161   162

163

151-163. *ƆHENE ADWA* - KING'S STOOL
Symbol of AUTHORITY, STATE POWER, LEGITIMACY, PERMANENCE, CON-TINUITY, PRESTIGE, WELCOME, and HOSPITALITY
From the expression: *Ɔte nananom nkonnwa so.* Or, *Sɛ wobɛka me ho asɛm a, fa akon-nwa na tenase.*
Literal translation: He is sitting on the stool of the ancestors (i.e., He is the King). Or, If you want to talk about me, take a stool and sit down.
The stool is believed to inhabit the soul of the nation. As a symbol of state power it embodies the past, present, and the future of the nation, that is, it marks continuities across generations and groups and close solidarities between the living and the dead. Through the stool, the king serves as a link between the living and the dead as well as the yet-to-be-born members of the society. The king has the responsibility to preserve the stool for posterity. The stool binds all the members of the family (and thus the nation) together. Each king decides on the symbol to be incorporated in his stool. For example, Nana Prempeh II chose the *nyasapɔ* (wisdom knot) to convey the notion that he would solve the nation's problems by sagacity rather than by the power of the sword. In the past the stool was used for gender differentiation in the society. When a successful king dies in office his stool is blackened and added to the ancestral stools in the Temple of Stools (*Nkonnwafieso*).

164   165

166   167

168   169

164-169. *AKOFENA* - STATE SWORDS

Symbol of STATE AUTHORITY, LEGITIMACY, GALLANTRY, and POWER

From the aphorism: *Konim ko a, wɔbɔ afena hyε no safohene.*

Literal translation: The great war hero is given a royal sword and promoted to the rank of a general.

There are various state swords that are used for specific functions. Akofena is also known as *NSUAEFENA* as it is used to swear the oath of office and to swear allegiance to a higher authority. State swords are carried by state traders, royal messengers and ambassadors, and are used in the rituals for purifying the chief's soul and various ancestral stools. Chiefs maintain a group of sword-bearers, each of whom carries one of the various state sword on public occasions. While swords were an important military weapon in the past, their use these days is ceremonial as they have unsharpened blades.

170

170. *ƆHENE KYINIIε* - CHIEF'S UMBRELLA

Symbol of POWER, LEGITIMACY, PROTECTION and SECURITY

From the aphorism: *Dea kyiniiε si no soɔ na ɔyε ɔhene.*

Literal translation: He who has the umbrella over his head is the king.

The Asantehene has no less than 23 different umbrellas each of which is used on a particular occasion. Some of these umbrellas include the *akropɔnkyiniwa, bɔaman kyiniwa* and *akatamanso kyiniwa*. On the top of the umbrella is usually placed a carved symbol (*ntuatire*) with a meaning. When a king dies the women wail out the following:

Nana atu ne kyiniiε;

Awia na εbεku yεn.

Wonim sεdeε wo gyaa me

Εyε a ma nsuo ntɔ na masɔ bi anom.

Sε womane me a, mane me dεnkyεmmoɔ na

Mannya gya a, mawe no mono.

Literal translation:

Nana has removed his umbrella;

We shall be scorched to death by the sun.

You know the condition in which you have left me

See to it that there is rain so that I can collect some of it to drink.

When you are sending me something

Send me parched corn

So that I can eat it raw if I am unable to find fire to cook it on.

171. *ƆHENE KYε* or *ƆHENE ABOTIRE* - THE KING'S CROWN

Symbol of AUTHORITY, POWER, and SUPREMACY

Ɔhene kyε or *abɔtire* comes in various shapes either as a head band, turban, skull cap or a crown. *Dεnkyεmkyε* (which Osei Tutu brought from Akwamu when he was recalled to become Asantehene - is made up of the following symbols: *dwennimmεn* - ram's horns, *sebɔ dua* - tail of a leopard, and *twerεku ti* - the head of a crown bird) is one of the symbolically important crowns in the Asantehene's regalia. The dεnkyεmkyε is worn by the Asantehene-elect when he demonstrates his ability of commander-in-chief to ensure state security and defence during his swearing in ceremony. Other head bands or crowns include the *kabisakyε* and *krɔbɔnkyε.*

172-173. *ABεNTIA* - STATE HORN

Symbol of STATE AUTHORITY, LEGITIMACY, APPELLATION, and PRAISE

From the expression: *Mmεn na εma yεhunu sε ɔhene wɔ hɔ.* Or, *Ntahera se: Asansa a ɔkyini aman, Akorɔma, ɔrekɔ a, ɔde nim bεba.*

Literal translation: It is the horns that make us know who is a king or a chief. Or, The horn says of the King: He is like the hawk that roams all nations, he will come home with victory.

172   173

174

174.   *SUMPIE* - PYRAMID or ROYAL DAIS

Symbol of AUTHORITY and STATE ASSEMBLY

This is the royal dais from which the king makes public addresses. At the Asantehene's Manhyia Palace there are two such daises: Sumpie Kumaa (Bogyawe) and Sumpie Kɛseɛ (Dwaberem).

175

175.   *ƆHENE PAPA* - GOOD KING

Symbol of EXEMPLARY LEADERSHIP

From the expression: Ɔhene dɔ wo a, ɔmma wonto ntam. Or, Ɔhene nya ahotenafo pa a, ne berɛ so dwo.

Literal translation: The good king prevents his subjects from getting into trouble. Or, If a king has good counsellors, his reign is peaceful.

176

176.   *ƆHEMMAA PAPA* - GOOD QUEENMOTHER

Symbol of GOOD LEADERSHIP, HEROIC DEEDS, and BRAVERY

From the expression: Ɔhemmaa pa Yaa Asantewaa, ɔbaabasia a ɔkura tuo ne akofena de di ako.

Literal translation: Yaa Asantewaa the good queenmother, the warrior woman who carries a gun and the sword of state to do battle.

Yaa Asantewaa was the queenmother of Ɛdweso (Ejisu). It was she who rallied the Asante nation to rebel against the British in 1900 after the Asantehene Prempeh I had been captured and exiled to the Seychelles Islands in the Indian Ocean. The war, Yaa Asantewaa War marked the last time a great queenmother led an army to war.

177

177.   *NEA ƆPƐ SƐ ƆBƐDI HENE* - HE WHO WANTS TO BE A KING

Symbol of the QUALITIES OF A LEADER, SERVICE, and LEADERSHIP SKILLS

From the expression: Nea ɔpɛ sɛ ɔbɛdi hene daakye no, firi ase sua som ansa.

Literal translation: He who wants to be a king in the future, should first learn to serve.

178   179

180   181

182   183

184

185

178-185.   *ADINKRAHENE* - KING OF THE ADINKRA SYMBOLS

Symbol of GREATNESS, PRUDENCE, FIRMNESS, MAGNANIMITY, SUPREMACY and OMNIPOTENCE OF GOD

From the expression: Yɛde brɛbrɛ bɛkum Adinkra.

Literal translation: Slowly, but surely we will defeat Adinkra.

The concentric circles signify the universe and its creator. Only the Creator of the universe, like the creator of the circle, knows its beginning and its end. This symbol is believed to have been named in memory of King Adinkra of Gyaman. King Adinkra was defeated in a war against the Asante. The Asante King at that time was Osei Bonsu. The defeat of King Adinkra was a relief for everyone. King Adinkra was authoritarian, a man of his word, and an intransigent king.

186   187

186-187.   *ADINKRAHENE NTOASO* - DOUBLE ADINKRAHENE

Symbol of GREATNESS, PRUDENCE, FIRMNESS, MAGNANIMITY, SUPREMACY and OMNIPOTENCE OF GOD

The concentric circles signify the universe and its creator. Only the Creator of the universe, like the creator of the circle, knows its beginning and its end. This symbol is believed to have been named in memory of King Adinkra of Gyaman

142

188   189

190   191

192

193

194

195

197   198

199   200

201   202

203

188-189. *ADINKRA BA APAU* - THE SON OF ADINKRA
Symbol of ROYALTY, STATUS and AUTHORITY

Oral tradition has it that Nana Adinkra's son, Apau was captured together with other Gyamans and brought to Asokwa near Kumasi. At Asokwa Apau is believed to have introduced technological innovations in the making of *adinkra* cloths.

190-192. *ƆHENE ANIWA* - THE KING'S EYES
Symbol of VIGILANCE, FAR-SIGHTEDNESS, INTELLIGENCE, PROTECTION, SECURITY, DEFENCE, AUTHORITY, and POWER

From the aphorism: *Ɔhene aniwa twa ne ho hyia.*

Literal translation: The king's eyes are placed all around him. Or, The king sees everything.

The king's sense of justice deriving from the norms and mores of the society must be constant, active and fair to all. The people are the eyes and ears of the king. The king is, therefore, said to see and hear all things that happen in the society.

193. *ABAN PA* - GOOD GOVERNMENT
Symbol of DEMOCRATIC RULE, STABLE SOCIETY, DEVELOPMENT, and PROGRESS

From the expression: *Sɛ ɔman mu yɛ dɛ a, yɛn nyinaa te mu bi.* Or, *Ɔman mu yɛ dɛ a, ene wo fie.*

Literal translation: If there is peace and stability in a state, we all live in it. Or, What peace and progress a society knows may be indicated by what prevails in the households in that society.

194. *ƆHENE KƆ HIA* - THE KING IS GONE TO THE HAREM
Symbol of PROTECTION, SECURITY, and WARMTH

From the expression: *Ɔhene kɔ hia.*

Literal translation: The king is gone to the women's quarters (harem).

Hia is where the king's wives live, that is, the female quarters. This is where the hearth is, and therefore, it is associated with warmth and food.

195-203. *NKURUMA KƐSE* - BIG OKRA
Symbol of GREATNESS, SUPREMACY, SECRECY, CARE-GIVER, and BENEVOLENCE

From the aphorisms: *Nkuruma kɛse, ɛbɔ ne ya hyɛ ne yam.*

Also, *Amoawisi, Nkuruma kɛse a ɔwo mma aduasa nso ɔgye abayɛn.* Also, *Amoawisi a ɔwo mma aduasa nso ɔgye abayɛn.*

Literal translation: The okra does not reveal its seeds through its skin; or, There is more in man's mind than shows in his face. Also, Amoawisi, the benevolent who raised thirty children of her own, yet was kind enough to raise other people's children.

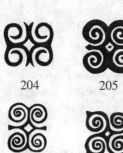

204

205

206

207

208

209

210

211

212

213

214

204-211. *DWENNIMMƐN* - RAM'S HORNS

Symbol of STRENGTH and HUMILITY

From the proverb: *Dwenini ahooden ne n'ammɛn; wo pan n'ammɛn na woayi no awie.* Also, *Dwenini yɛ asisie a ɔde n'akoma nnyɛ ne mmɛn.*

Literal translation: The strength of the ram lies in its horns, once they are plucked off, then it is caught in a trap. Also, The ram may bully only when it is provoked to do so.

212-214. *DWENNIMMƐN NTOASOƆ* - DOUBLE RAM'S HORNS

Symbol of POWER, AUTHORITY, STRENGTH, and HUMILITY

215

216

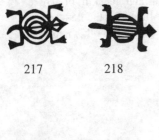

217

218

215-218. *ƆDƐNKYƐM* - CROCODILE

Symbol of GREATNESS, POWER, ADAPTABILITY, SKEPTICISM, SCRUPULOUSNESS, and ADVANCEMENT

From the aphorism: *Ɔdɛnkyɛm da nsuo mu nso ɔhome mframa.* Also, *Dɛnkyɛm ninampa a ɛduru afe a, ɔmene boɔ.*

Literal translations: Though the crocodile lives in water, yet it breathes air directly. Also, The great crocodile that swallows a stone every year.

This symbol is also referred to as *dɛnkyɛmma* (Young Crocodile).

219

220

219-220. *ƐSONO* - ELEPHANT

Symbol of GREATNESS, POWER, PROTECTION, and AUTHORITY

From the expression: *Wodi ɛsono akyi a hasuo nka wo.* Or, *Ɛsono nni wiram a, anka ɛkoɔ yɛ bɛpɔn.* Also, *Ɛsono kokuroko, adowa na ɔman wɔ no.* Also, *Ɛsono akyi nni aboa biara.*

Literal translation: When you follow the elephant you do not get wet from the dew on bushes. Or, But for the presence of the elephant in the bush, the buffalo would be a powerful animal. Also, Despite huge size of the elephant, the nation belongs not to the elephant but to the deer. Also, There is no animal greater than the elephant in size.

221   222

221-222. *ƐSONO ANANTAM* - ELEPHANT'S FOOTPRINT
Symbol of LEADERSHIP, PROTECTION, POWER, and SECURITY
From the aphorism: *Wodi ɛsono akyi a, hasuo nka wo.*
Literal translation: When you follow the elephant you do not get wet from the dew on bushes.

PUBLIC SERVICE SYMBOLS

223   224

225   226

227   228

229

223-229. *MPUA ANUM* - FIVE TUFTS, HAIRSTYLE OF KING'S ATTENDANTS
Symbol of LOYALTY, DISTINGUISHED PUBLIC SERVICE, DIGNITY, ADROITNESS, and PATRIOTISM
Hairstyle of loyal service to the nation worn by the king's male attendants. It is also a hair style of joy and a symbol of priestly office.

230

230. *NKWANTANAN* - FOUR TUFTS, HAIRSTYLE OF THE KING'S KEY BEARERS
Symbol of LOYALTY, SECURITY, and TRUTHFULNESS
From the expression: *Aso mu nni nkwanta.*
Literal translation: There are no crossroads in the ear.
This symbol indicates the need for a public servant to be truthful and non-contradictory. One cannot accept truth and falsehood at the same time, or no statement can be both true and false.

231   232

231-232. *ƆHENE* or *ƆHEMMAA PAPA* - THE KING'S or QUEEN'S FAN
Symbol of PUBLIC SERVICE and LOYALTY

233-234. *NKOTIMSEFOƆ PUA* - HAIRSTYLE OF THE QUEEN'S ATTENDANTS
Symbol of LOYALTY, DEVOTION TO DUTY, DISTINGUISHED PUBLIC SERVICE
Hairstyle of loyal service to the nation worn by the queen's female attendants. It signifies readiness to serve.

233   234

235   236

235-237. *NKOTIMSEFOƆ PUA* - HAIRSTYLE OF THE QUEEN'S ATTENDANTS

Symbol of LOYALTY, DEVOTION TO DUTY, DISTINGUISHED PUBLIC SERVICE

Hairstyle of loyal service to the nation worn by the queen's female attendants. It signifies readiness to serve.

237

238   239

238-239. *MMƆDWEWAFOƆ PUA* - HAIRSTYLE OF THE QUEEN'S ATTENDANTS

Symbol of LOYALTY, DISTINGUISHED PUBLIC SERVICE, and PATRIOTISM

240

240. *NSAFOA* - KEYS

Symbol of LOYALTY, TRUSTWORTHINESS, and DISTINGUISHED PUBLIC SERVICE

Keys served as the insignia of *fotosanfoɔ* or the *kotokuosanfoɔ* (treasury public servants) who carried the King's treasury bag of gold dust and gold weights. *Fotoɔ* was a leather bag made from the skin of a monkey. Another leather bag used in the king's treasury was called sanaa and this was made from the elephant's ear. Some of these treasury staff served as toll collectors in the markets and on the highways. *Nsafoa* (keys) also refer to the historic capturing of European forts by the Akan.

241   242

241-242. *AGYIN DAWURO* - AGYIN'S IRON BELL

Symbol of ALERTNESS, LOYALTY, DUTIFULNESS, and MERITORIOUS PUBLIC SERVICE

From the expression: *Dawuroboni Agyin nsuro mantamu.*

Literal translation: The town crier Agyin is not afraid of the nooks and cronies of any neighborhood.

The iron bell is used to announce the king's decrees and to convey messages and public announcements from the king's palace to the people. This particular symbol is in recognition of the loyal service rendered to the state by a prominent public servant called Agyin. He was affable and ready to serve his country.

243   244

243-245. *DAWURO* - IRON BELL

Symbol of PUBLIC ANNOUNCEMENTS, COMMUNICATION, and POLITICAL DISCOURSE

The iron bell is used to announce the king's decrees and to convey messages and public announcements from the king's palace to the people. It is also used to call people to public meetings that are not of crisis nature. Iron bells are also used by priests for religious ceremonies.

245

MILITARY SYMBOLS

246   247

248   249

250   251

252

246-252.   *GYAWU ATIKƆ* - GYAWU'S HAIRSTYLE OF BRAVERY

Symbol of HEROIC DEEDS, BRAVERY, VALOR, and FEARLESSNESS

From the expression: *Katakyie Gyawu atikɔ pua no, ɔno na ɔnim deɛ ɛkyerɛ.*

Literal translation: Only he Gyawu the general knows the meaning of his hair-cut.

Hairstyle of BRAVERY first worn by the military GENERAL (*KATAKYIE*) GYAWU during a war victory parade. KATAKYIE GYAWU was a Bantamahene.

253   254

255   256

257

253-257. *AKOBƐN* - WAR HORN

Symbol of READINESS, VOLUNTARISM, PATRIOTISM, CALL TO ACTION, and SUMMONS TO ACTION

From the expression: *Kɔsankɔbi, wokasa ɔbaa ano a, Kobiri nku wo.*

Literal translation: Deserter, may Kobiri (a deity) kill you if dare speak as a man to a woman.

The Akans had no standing army, yet in times of war or national disaster (e.g., floods, fire, or missing person) the WAR HORN and ASAFO DRUMS would sound calling every able-bodied person to action. Answering the clarion call was deemed an honorable and patriotic act. One was considered a coward who was able but would not volunteer one's services in times of national disaster. Cowards were highly derided as *kɔsankɔbi*.

258

259

260

258-260. *ƆHENE TUO* - THE KING'S GUN

Symbol of ADAPTATION, AUTHORITY, POWER, STRENGTH, PROTECTION, DEFENCE, and GREATNESS

From the proverb: *Tuo nya otiafoɔ a, na ɔdi abaninsɛm.*

Literal translation: It is only when a gun has a man to cock it, that it performs warlike deeds.

At the Banpanase Installation of the Asantehene-elect the Queenmother, speaking through the Akyeamehene would say:

Wo wɔfa (nua anaasɛ nana) na ɔdi Asantehene yi,

Ɛnnɛ ɔkɔ ne kraa akyi.

Adare bu a, yɛbɔ bi poma mu

Enti wo wɔfa (nua, nana) ne tuo na ɔhemmaa ne Kumasi Mpanimfoɔ yɛde ma wo ahwɛ ɔman yi so sɛnea wo wɔfa hwɛɛ ɔman yi soɔ

Ɔman yɛnto no mmradɛ;

Wose tuntum na tuntum; fufuo na fufuo

Yɛde wo wɔfa (nua, nana) tuo no ma wo

Yɛhyira wo kosɛ, kosɛ, Anɔkye komaa mu.

Your uncle (brother or grand-uncle) who has been Asantehene,
Today his soul has gone whence it came from
When the handle of an axe comes out
A new one is carved to replace it
Thus the Queenmother and Kumasi Elders pass on to you the gun of your uncle (bother or grand-uncle)
You are not to deceive the nation
Your black must be black; your white white
We present to you your uncle's (brother's or grand-uncle's) gun
We wish you well
May Anɔkye from his sanctuary bless you.

* The Asantehene-elect later fires the *ɔhene tuo* to demonstrate that he would be capable of commanding the state's military forces on the battlefield.

261   262

261-262. *AKOO MMƆWERƐ* - PARROT'S TALONS

Symbol of SWIFTNESS, POWER, and INTELLIGENCE

263

263. *ƆKƆDEƐ MMƆWERƐ* - EAGLE'S TALONS

Symbol of AUTHORITY, POWER, STRENGTH, and SWIFTNESS

From the aphorism: *Ɔkɔdeɛ se: Gye tuo, gye ɔwɔ.* Or, *Ɔkɔdeɛ ɔnsuro wiram aboa biara gye ɔwɔ ne tuo nko ara.*

Literal translation: Except for the snake and the gun, the eagle fears nothing.
Emblem of the Oyoko clan and it reflects their idea of unity and strength.

264

265

264-265. *KƆTƆKƆ* - PORCUPINE

Symbol of BRAVERY, PREPAREDNESS, GALLANTRY, and POWER

From the expression: *Asante kɔtɔkɔ, kum apem a, apem bɛba.* Or, *Kɔtɔkɔ renko a, hwɛ n'amiadeɛ.* Or, *Aboa biara ne kɔtɔkɔ nni ntohyia.* Or, *Asante kɔtɔkɔ, monka ntoa.*

Literal translation: Asante porcupine, you kill a thousand, a thousand more will come. Or, You can tell from the armament (quills) of the porcupine whether he is prepared to fight or not. Or, No animal dare meet the porcupine in a struggle. Or, Asante porcupines seize your powder belts.

The Asante military was likened to the porcupine's strategy of shooting its quills in barrages and would quickly it reproduce them for protection against its predators.

266   267

266-267. PAGYA - STRIKES FIRE

Symbol of BRAVERY, POWER, and VALOR

From the proverb: *Twereboɔ nti na tuo di abaninsɛm.* Or, *Etuo yɛnto no brɛɛ.*

Literal translation: Thanks to the flint-stone, the gun performs warlike deeds. Or, The gun does not strike in times of peace.

This was a kind of gun owned by men of valor and dexterity. It is now mostly used on ceremonial and funeral occasions.

268

268. *AKOFENA NE TUO* - SWORD AND GUN

Symbol of POWER, MILITARY MIGHT, NATIONAL SECURITY, PROTECTION and GREATNESS

The sword and the gun are used in swearing a new chief into office and this signifies the responsibility of the new ruler to continue to protect and guard the nation as did his forbearers. After the Asantehene-elect has been sworn into office he holds the *Mpɔmpɔnsuo* sword in his right hand and the *ɔhene tuo* in the left and dances to the *atoprɛtea* rhythm of the *fɔntɔmfrɔm* ensemble.

269

269. *ƐKYƐM* - SHIELD

Symbol of BRAVERY, HEROIC AND GLORIOUS DEEDS, and ACCOMPLISHMENT

From the aphorism: *Ɛkyɛm tete a, ɛka ne meramu.* Also, *Ɔkogyeatuo na ɔse: Ma me ɛkyɛm ma menkɔgye etuo mmra.*

Literal translation: When a shield wears out, the framework still remains. Also, It is the brave warrior that says: Give me a shield so I may go and capture the enemy's guns. This symbolizes bravery as well as the immortality of the glory of a great person.

JUSTICE, LAW AND ORDER SYMBOLS

270

270. *ANKONAM BOAFOɔ NE ONYANKOPƆN* - GOD IS THE HELPER OF THE LONELY

Symbol of IMPARTIALITY, FAIRNESS, JUSTICE, ADVOCACY, and BENEFICENCE

From the expression: *Ankonam boafoɔ ne Onyankopɔn.* Or, *Aboa a ɔnni dua no, Nyame na ɔpra ne ho.*

Literal translation: God is the helper of the lonely. Or, It is God who drives away the fly from the body of the animal which has no tail.

This symbol points out the Akan belief that God ensures that there is justice and fairness for all, irrespective of their social class, status, or condition in life.

271

271. *NEA WOPƐ SƐ NKURƆFOɔ YƐ MA WO NO* - DO UNTO OTHERS

Symbol of FAIR PLAY, SOCIAL JUSTICE, and RECIPROCITY

From the expression: Nea wopɛ sɛ nkurɔfoɔ yɛ ma wo no, yɛ saa ara ma wɔn.

Literal translation: Do unto others the things you want them to do for you.

272

273

274

275

276

277

278

272-278. *OBI NKA OBI* - BITE NOT EACH OTHER

Symbol of JUSTICE, FAIR PLAY, EQUITY, PEACE, UNITY, and HARMONY

From the expression: *Obi nka obi kwa.*

Literal translation: No one should bite the other without justifiable cause.

No one should bite another or outrage or provoke another.

279

280

281

282

283

284

285

279-285. *DWANTIRE* - RAM'S HEAD

Symbol of INNOCENCE, GUILTLESSNESS

From the proverb: *Dwantire se: me tiri mu faa; ɔkwasea bobonya menni fɔ nti na mabɔ hyire.*

Literal translation: The head of the ram says: My conscience is free; the righteous fool who never tastes of guilt should not be dressed in black, hence I am always in white. Or, the guiltless fears no accusation.

286

287

288

289

286-289. *MMARA KRADO* - SEAL OF LAW

Symbol of AUTHORITY, LEGITIMACY, LEGALITY, and POWER OF THE COURT

From the expression: *Etire nte sɛ krado na yɛde safoa abue ahwɛ mu.*

Literal translation: The head is not like a lock to be opened with a key to view the inside.

150

290   291

292   293

294

290-294. *MMARA KRADO* - SEAL OF LAW

Symbol of AUTHORITY, LEGITIMACY, LEGALITY, and POWER OF THE COURT

From the expression: *Etire nte sɛ krado na yɛde safoa abue ahwɛ mu.*

Literal translation: The head is not like a lock to be opened with a key to view the inside.

295   296

297   298

295-298. *ƐPA* - HANDCUFFS

Symbol of JUSTICE, LAW, ORDER, and CONTROL

From the aphorism: *Onii a ne pa da wo no, n'akoa ne wo.* Or, *Wokɔ kurom na sɛ hɔ ɔdekuro mantam dedua mu a, yɛmmusa sɛ kuro mu hɔ yɛ.*

Literal translation: You are the subject of he whose handcuffs you wear. Or, When you go to a town and you see the chief of the town is in handcuffs you do not ask whether everything is alright in that town.

It also signifies that the law is no respecter of persons.

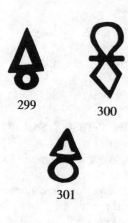

299   300

301

299-301. *SƐPƆ* - DAGGER

Symbol of JUSTICE, CAPITAL PUNISHMENT

Knife used in executions to prevent a curse on the king.

302. *OBI NKYƐ OBI KWAN MU SI* - TO ERR IS HUMAN

Symbol of FALLIBILITY, MORTALITY and IMPERFECTION

From the aphorism: *Obi nkyɛ obi kwan mu si.*

Literal translation: To err is human.

302

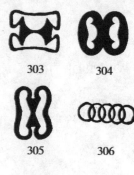

303   304

305   306

307

303-307. *NKƆNSƆNKƆNSƆN* - CHAIN

Symbol of FAMILY RELATIONS, UNITY, BROTHERHOOD, and COOPERATION

From the aphorism: *Yɛtoatoa mu sɛ nkɔnsɔnkɔnsɔn; nkwa mu a, yɛtoa mu, owu mu a, yɛtoa mu; abusua mu nnte da.*

Literal translation: If we are linked together like a chain, in life we are linked, in death we are linked; family ties are never broken. Or, people who share common blood relations never break away from one another.

308   309

310   311

312   313

314   315

308-315. *FUNTUMFUNAFU DƐNKYƐM FUNAFU* - JOINED OR SIAMESE-TWIN CROCODILES

Symbol of UNITY IN DIVERSITY, DEMOCRACY, and UNITY OF PURPOSE

The symbol is also referred to as *ɔdɛnkyɛm mmɛmu* - Siamese twin crocodiles joined at the stomach.

From the proverb: *Funtumfunafu, dɛnkyɛmfunafu, wɔn afuru bɔ mu nso wodidi a na wɔrefom efiri sɛ aduane ne dɛ ye di no menewa mu.*

Literal translation: Two headed crocodiles fight over food that goes to a common stomach because each relishes the food in its throat. This symbol stresses the oneness of humanity in spite of cultural diversity. It also emphasizes the need for unity in the family or state. Members should not quarrel or fight for selfish interests, for what each gains is for the benefit of all. It also emphasizes the reality of individuality in relation to one's membership in a society. Much as the community interests are to be pursued for the common good, individual rights, interests, passions and responsibilities cannot and must not be trampled on.

316

317

316-317. *KOKUROMOTIE* - THUMB

Symbol of COOPERATION, PARTICIPATION, TEAMWORK, INDISPENSABILITY, and HARMONY

From the expression: *Yɛnsiane kokuromotie ho mmɔ pɔ.* Also, *Wode kokuromotie kɔ ayiiɛ a, yɛde sotrɔ gya wo kwan.*

Literal translation: One cannot make a knot without the thumb. Also, When one throws one's weight about at the funeral, one is bound to get slapped in the face.

The symbol depicts the indispensability of the elderly (or chief or king) in the resolution of social problems. The elderly or king is the ultimate repository of wisdom.

318

318. *NKABOM MA YETUMI GYINA HƆ* - UNITED WE STAND

Symbol of UNITY, STRENGTH IN UNITY, and NATIONAL INTEGRATION

From the expression: *Nkabom ma yetumi gyina hɔ, mpaapaemu ma yɛhwe ase.*

Literal translation: United we stand, divided we fall.

Symbol emphasizes the need for united action, unity in diversity, and national unity. The Akan society comprises seven matri-clans, therefore there is need for these subgroups to unite for the good of the greater society. The Asante nation was built on the principle of nkabom that was enunciated by the legendary Ɔkomfo Anɔkye.

152

319

319. *KOROYε* - UNITY

Symbol of UNITY, FRATERNITY, FELLOWSHIP, and ORDER

From the riddle: *Nnomaa miεnsa bi na won su sε: kyee, kaa, ne kasakranka; won ni ne hwan? Won ni ne koryε.*

Literal translation: Three baby birds are crying: kyee, kaa, and kasakranka; who is their mother? Their mother is unity.

This symbol is based on a story of three baby birds that had lost their mother. Their wailing from a tree near a farm attracted the attention of the farmer. The farmer decided to nurse the birds. The farmer became a mother to the birds. Very soon, the birds fought among themselves because each wanted their nest all to itself. Eventually two of them left to be on their own. The next day the farmer came to feed them and found out they had broken up, he urged the remaining to go and look for its siblings before the farmer would feed them together. The Asante nation was built on the principle of *nkabom* (unity).

320

322

321

320-322. *εSE NE TεKRεMA* - TEETH AND TONGUE

Symbol of INTERDEPENDENCE, COOPERATION, UNITY, GROWTH, DEVELOPMENT, and IMPROVEMENT

From the aphorisms: *Wɔnnwo ba a ɔwɔ ne se dada. Or, Tεkrεma wɔ hɔ a, εse mmɔ nkuro. Also, εse ka tεkrεma nso wɔte bɔ mu.*

Literal translations: No child is born with an already developed set of teeth. Or, In the presence of the tongue, the teeth do not litigate. Also, The teeth bite the tongue sometimes, yet they continue to live in harmony. The symbol depicts the complementary nature of human beings as well as nations. Or, the tongue lying between the two rows of teeth, literally staves off tension between the two.

323

324

323-324. *PEMPAMSIE* or *MMɔMUDWAN* - PREPAREDNESS

Symbol of STEADFASTNESS, READINESS TO SERVE, UNITY, COOPERATION, UNITY OF PURPOSE, and STRENGTH

From the aphorism: *Pempamsie se: Bεbirebe ahoɔden ne koroyε. ɔman si mpoma dua dadebo a, εkɔ akɔterenee.*

Literal translation: The strength of the many lies in unity. Once people are resolved in unity, nothing stops them from reaching their goal. Or, in unity lies strength.

The point being stressed by this symbol is that each link in a chain is important, and must, therefore, be strong and ready to serve. Everyone is important in their own right. No one is left over and so everyone should be ready to fill that "space" which he/she alone, but none, can occupy.

325

326

325-326. *TI KORɔ NKɔ AGYINA* - ONE HEAD DOES NOT CONSTITUTE A COUNCIL

Symbol of DEMOCRACY, POWER SHARING, CONSULTATION, and DISCUSSION

From the expression: *Ti korɔ nkɔ agyina. Or, Ti korɔ mpam. Also, Ti korɔ mu nni nyansa.*

Literal translation: One head does not constitute a council. Or, two heads are better than one. The symbol depicts the value of consultation and discussion in arriving at decisions especially at the court of the king. Democratic rule requires consultation, discussion, consensus building, and coalition formation.

327

327. *KONTIRE NE AKWAMU* - COUNCIL OF STATE

Symbol of DEMOCRACY, PARTICIPATORY GOVERNMENT, and PLURALITY OF IDEAS

From the aphorism: *Ti kɔrɔ mpam*. Or, *Ɔbaakofoɔ mmu man.*

Literal translation: One head does not constitute a council. Or, one person does not rule a nation.

The Council of State was first created by the Asante King, Osei Tutu to commemorate his sojourn in Akwamu before the Asante-Denkyira War of 1700-1702. The King is the supreme commander and the Kontirehene is the military general and deputizes as the head of state in the absence of the king. The Akwamuhene is second in command after the Kontirehene.

328

328. *WO NSA DA MU A* - IF YOUR HANDS ARE IN THE DISH

Symbol of PARTICIPATORY GOVERNMENT, DEMOCRACY, and PLURALISM

From the aphorism: *Wo nsa da mu a, wonni nnya wo.*

Literal translation: If your hands are in the dish, people do not eat everything and leave you nothing.

The symbol reflects empowerment of the masses through participatory government.

329

330

329-330. *TUMI TE SƐ KOSUA* - POWER IS LIKE AN EGG

Symbol of the FRAGILITY OF STATE POWER, DEMOCRACY

From the aphorism: *Tumi te sɛ kosua, wosɔ mu den a ɛpae, na sɛ woansɔ mu yie nso a, ɛfiri wo nsa bɔ fam ma ɛpae.*

Literal translation: Power is like an egg, when held tightly it might break and when held loosely it might fall and break.

The symbol points out the fragile nature of state power. As a symbol of democracy it suggests the virtue of sharing political power. Power held in one hand is not safe. Power wielded by chiefs is not absolute, nor is it expected to lead to tyranny. A chief is expected to exercise the power he wields cautiously and judiciously, or else he incurs the wrath of his subjects.

331

331. *BOA ME* - HELP ME

Symbol of COOPERATION

From the aphorism: *Woforo dua pa a, na yɛpia wo.*

Literal translation: When you climb a good tree, you are given a push.

When one undertakes a good cause, one is given all the support one would need.

332

332. *BOA ME NA ME MMOA WO* - HELP ME AND LET ME HELP YOU

Symbol of COOPERATION, INTERDEPENDENCE

From the aphorism: *Benkum dware nifa na nifa so dware benkum.* Or, *Woamma wo yɔnko antwa nkron a, wonnya edu ntwa.*

Literal translation: The left hand washes the right, and the right in turn washes the left. Or, If you do not allow a friend to get a nine, you will not be able to get a ten for yourself.

This suggests that just as one hand cannot wash itself, so it is difficult for an individual to provide for himself/herself all that she/he may need. People and countries depend on one another for much that they require in order to survive.

333

333. *NSA KƆ, NA NSA ABA* - HAND GO, HAND COME

Symbol of COOPERATIVE ACTION and CONCERTED ACTION

From the expression: *Akyekyedeɛ se: nsa kɔ, na nsa aba.*

Literal translation: The tortoise says: hand go, hand come.

334   335

334-335. *BOAFO YƐ NA* - THE RARITY OF A WILLING HELPER
Symbol of SUPPORT, PATRONAGE, COOPERATION, and TEAMWORK
From the expression: *Boafo yɛ na.*
Literal translation: It is hard to come by a good sponsor or patron or a willing helper.

336

336. *BOA W'ABAN* - HELP YOUR GOVERNMENT
Symbol of PATRIOTISM, NATIONALISM, CIVIC RESPONSIBILITY, GOOD CITIZENSHIP, and PARTICIPATORY GOVERNMENT
From the expression: *Ɔmampam se: Me deɛ ne sɛ merepam me man, nyɛ amambɔeɛ.*
Literal translation: The monitor lizard says: Mine is to help to build up, but not to destroy my state.
This symbol reflects the civic responsibility of the citizenry to participate in the democratic process to promote national development, peace and stability in the state.

337

337. *NNAMFO PA BAANU* - TWO GOOD FRIENDS
Symbol of FRIENDSHIP, FELLOWSHIP, and COMRADESHIP
From the aphorism: *Hu m'ani so ma me nti na atwe mmienu nam daa no.* Or, *Adwen yɛdwen no baanu.*
Literal translation: The deer is always seen in pairs so that one will help the other out in case of any emergency. Or, Fruitful ideas are born when two heads come together.

338   339

340   341

338-342. *FAWOHODIE* - INDEPENDENCE
Symbol of FREEDOM, INDEPENDENCE, EMANCIPATION, SELF-DETERMINATION, and SELF-GOVERNMENT
From the expression: *Fawohodie ɛne ɔbrɛ na ɛnam.*
Literal translation: Independence comes with its responsibilities.

343

343. *DUA KORƆ* - ONE TREE
Symbol of INDIVIDUALISM, PARTICULARISM, and ECCENTRICITY
From the maxim: *Dua korɔ gye mframa a, ebu.* Also, *Dua korɔ nyɛ kwaeɛ.*
Literal translation: One tree cannot last a storm. Also, One tree does not constitute a forest.

344

344. *YƐREPERE ADEƐ A* - WHEN WE STRIVE FOR WEALTH
Symbol of NATIONALISM, PATRIOTISM, and SOCIAL ROLE
From the maxim: *Yɛrepere adeɛ a, yɛpere ba fie; na obi a ɔrepere adeɛ akɔ kɔtɔkɔ no, yensi no kwan.*
Literal translation: When we strive for wealth, we bring it home; and we don't stop him, who strives for wealth for the land of the porcupine.

345   346

345-346. *ƆWƆ AFORO ADOBƐ* - THE SNAKE CLIMBS THE RAFFIA PALM TREE
Symbol of NEGOTIATION, TACTICAL MOVE, INGENUITY, and DIPLOMACY
This symbol is based on an observation of the unusual behavior of a snake in climbing a raffia palm (or any other) tree. The snake negotiates each twist and turn by a tactical and deliberate movement. The symbol extols the importance of diplomacy and prudence as the necessary ingredients of real valor.

347.

347. *ANOMA NE ƆWƆ* - BIRD AND SNAKE

Symbol of PATIENCE, STRATEGIC PLANNING, CALCULATION
and TACTICAL MOVE

From the adage: *Nanka bobonya, ɔda asase anya ɔnwam.* Or, *Wosuo ɔwɔ ti a, dea aka nyinaa yɛ ahomaa.*

Literal translation: The puff adder that cannot fly has caught the hornbill that flies. Or, If you get hold of the snake's head, the rest of it is mere thread. If one succeeds in capturing the chief or the military general, then the whole state is doomed to defeat. This depicts the military strategy of destroying first a state's military base to facilitate complete conquest.

348.

348. *NTEASE* - UNDERSTANDING

Symbol of UNDERSTANDING, TOLERANCE, PERCEPTION and DISCERNING

From the expression: *Aso pa nkyɛre asɛm ase te.*

Literal translation: The good ear easily understands an issue.

349.

349. *ADWO* - PEACE OR CALMNESS

Symbol of PEACE, CALMNESS, SPIRITUAL COOLNESS, and CONTINUITY

From the expression: *Ɔhene nya ahotenafo pa a, ne berɛ so dwo.*

Literal translation: When the king has good counselors, then his reign will be peaceful. This symbol is associated with the practice of the planting of trees by newly installed chiefs as a sign of continuity of state authority and proper succession. During the ceremony for planting a new tree, the trees planted by his predecessors are decorated white, and before them the newly installed chiefs would take the oath of office to bring peace and prosperity to his state and people. The trees also represent a state of calmness, and the shady grove provided by the trees is the center for various ceremonies or the village or town common (*NGYEDUASE*).

350.

350. *ETUO NE AKYEKYEDEɛ* - THE GUN AND THE TORTOISE

Symbol PEACE, SKILL and DEXTERITY

From the expression: *Ɛka akyekyedeɛ ne nwaa a nka etuo nnto da wɔ wiram.* Also, *Gye akyekyedeɛ kɔ ma agya, ɛnyɛ ahayɔ.*

Literal translation: Left with the snail and the tortoise, there would not be any gun shots in the forest. Also, Taking a tortoise to one's father is not a mark of good hunting skills.

351.

351. *AKYEKYEDEɛ* - TORTOISE

Symbol of PEACE, STRATEGIC PLANNING, TACTFULNESS, or FUTILE ENDEAVOR

From the aphorism: *Ɛkaa akyekyedeɛ ne nwa a, ɛnka etuo rento da wɔ wiram.* Also, *Akyekyedeɛ se: Ɛhia ma adwen. Or, Hurue si akyekyedeɛ akyi a, osi hɔ kwa.*

Literal translation: Left with the snail and the tortoise, there would not be any gun shots in the forest

352.

352. *TUO ABOBA* - GUN BULLETS

Symbol of BRAVERY, MARKSMANSHIP, RESOURCEFULNESS, AND PREPAREDNESS

From the expression: *Atwerɛboɔ a ɛnyɛ nam no, yɛmfa nhyɛ tuo ano.* Or, *Atwerɛboɔ asa ɛnyɛ Akwawua ntoa mu a.*

Literal translation: One does not load a gun with spent bullet. Or, The cartridge-belt of Akwawua has never been known to lack bullets.

A resourceful and well-prepared person is never found wanting.

353

353. *MPABOA* - SANDALS

Symbol of PROTECTION, VALOR, VIGILANCE, ALERTNESS, and DECLARATION
OF WAR

From the ultimatum: *Wonni atuduru a pɛ bi, wonni mpaboa a pɛ bi na me ne wo wɔ bi ka
wɔ ɛseram. Or, Wosuro atɛkyɛ mpaboa a, wofira ne ntama.*

Literal translation:Prepare for war and meet me on the battlefield. Or, If you are scared to
get your feet wet in a muddy place you fall down and get your whole body wet. In the past
a war parcel comprising a pair of sandals, gun-powder and a small bundle of sticks would
be sent by a king to his enemy as a declaration of war.

This symbol suggests the need for readiness and vigilance to use war to maintain peace
and tranquility in society.There were various types of sandals the Akan people made in the
past and these included *mpaboapa, nkuronnua,* and *kyaw-kyaw.*

354

354. *ASASE ABAN* - EARTH FORTRESS

SYMBOL OF RESILIENCE, VIGILANCE

From the expression: *Asase aban, yɛnte gyae agye nkɔsoɔ.*

Literal translation: Earth fortress, we are unrestrainable until there is progress.

355

355. *ETUO KORAA MENSURO NA ABAA?* - EVEN THE GUN

Symbol of BRAVERY, VALOR, DEFIANCE, CHIVALRY, and HEROISM

From the expression: *Etuo koraa mensuro na abaa?*

Literal translation: Even the gun I fear not, how much more the stick?

356   357

358

356-358. *FIE MOSEA* - HOUSEHOLD PEBBLES

Symbol of WARNING AGAINST THE INTERNAL ENEMY, ALERTNESS, and
VIGILANCE

From the aphorism: *Fie mosea twa wo a sene sekan.*
Or *Ɔhɔhoɔ hunu dea amani aka akyerɛ.*

Literal translation: The smooth pebbles of the household when they cut they cut sharper
than a knife. Or, Societal secrets are learnt by the enemy through the revelations of
unpatriotic citizens.

This symbol serves as warning for the need for vigilance and awareness of the enemy
from within as it is more dangerous than the enemy from without. Warning that internal
feuds and disloyalty can be very destructive.

359

359. *MPATAPɔ* - PEACE KNOT

Symbol of PEACE, PEACEFUL COEXISTENCE, NEGOTIATION, DIPLOMACY, and
RECONCILIATION

360

360. *ASOMDWOEƐ* - PEACE

Symbol of HARMONY, RECONCILIATION, PEACE and SERENITY

From the aphorism: *Wonni asomdweɛ a, woyɛ teasewu.*

Literal translation: If one does not have peace, one is like the living dead.

361

361. *ASOMDWOEƐ FIE* - HOUSE OF PEACE

Symbol of PEACEFUL COEXISTENCE, TRANQUILITY, NON-VIOLENCE, and

From the aphorism: *Nteaseɛ ne aboterɛ tena fie baako mu a, asomdwoeɛ na ɛba.*

Literal translation: When understanding and patience live together in a house, peace prevails.

157

362

362. *NAM PORƆ A* - **WHEN THE FISH ROTS**

Symbol of CORRUPT LEADERSHIP

From the aphorism: *Nam porɔ a, efiri ne ti.*

Literal translation: When the fish rots, it first rots from the head.

Corruption in a society starts from the leaders of the society.

363

363. *NEA ƆRETWA SA* - **THE PATH-MAKER**

Symbol of LEADERSHIP PROBLEMS, NEED FOR A LEADER TO HEED ADVICE

From the aphorism: *Nea ɔretwa sa nnim se n'akyi akyea.*

Literal translation: The path-maker or the trailblazer does not know that the path is curved behind him.

364   365

366

364-366. *NSA KORƆ* - **ONE HAND**

Symbol of CONCERTED ACTION, COOPERATION, and TEAMWORK; also symbol of HUMAN FRAILTY and IMPERFECTION

From the aphorism: *Nsa korɔ ntumi nkata Nyame ani.*

367

367. *APESE YE KESE A* - **WHEN THE HEDGEHOG GROWS FAT**

Symbol of MUTUAL BENEFIT

From the aphorism: *Apese ye kese a, ɔye ma dufookyee.*

Literal translation: When the hedgehog grows fat, it benefits the wet log.

368

368. *ƆMAN ASENKYEREDEE* - **NATIONAL COAT OF ARMS** (GHANA)

Symbol of NATIONAL IDENTITY, FREEDOM AND JUSTICE, NATION-STATE-HOOD, and SOVEREIGNTY

This symbol depicts the coat of arms of Ghana. This symbol incorporates other adinkra symbols such as the castle, state swords, and cocoa tree.

369. *ƆMAN ASENKYEREDEE* - **NATIONAL COAT OF ARMS** (HOLLAND)

Symbol of NATIONAL IDENTITY, FREEDOM AND JUSTICE, NATION-STATE-HOOD, and SOVEREIGNTY

A sample of cloth in the Leiden Rijksmuseum voor Volkenkunde has the semblance of the Dutch coat-of-arms in the center. This cloth, together with other gift items, is believed to have been shipped from Fort St. George d'Elmina on the Gold Coast on September 23, 1825 on board the Dutch brig Amalia Elisabeth to be presented to King Willem I.

369

The following are examples of adinkra symbols that encode some of the Akan people's ideas about family relations.

370

370. ƆDƆ ANIWA - LOVE EYE

Symbol of AFFECTION, LOVE AT FIRST SIGHT, SMILING EYES, and LUSTFUL LOOKS

From the expression: *Ɔdɔ foforɔ yɛ anifuraeɛ ne adammɔ*. Or, *Ɔdɔ mehu wo a, mebɔ m'ani asu; mefa wo a, mefa siadeɛ*.

Literal translation: First love is both blinding and illogical. Or, My love, when I look at you, my eyes are sanctified; I abound in good luck when I touch you.

371   372

373

371-373. *AFAFANTƆ - BUTTERFLY*

Symbol of BEAUTY, GRACEFULNESS, DEVOTION, CHANGE, and DEVELOPMENT

From the expression: *Afafantɔ se: nsa ni o, na sika a yɛde tɔ.*

Literal translation: The butterfly says: Here is wine, where is the money to buy with?

374   375

376

374-376. *ASAMBO* - THE CHEST FEATHERS OF THE GUINEA FOWL

Symbol of ELEGANCE, BEAUTY, and GRACEFULNESS

From the expression: *Fɛfɛ na ɛyɛ fɛ na ɔdaammani tu mmirika a, ɔsɔ ne nufu mu, na ɛnyɛ te a ɛbɛte atɔ ntira.*

Literal translation: It is to dignify her beauty that makes a young woman hold her breast as she runs, not because they would fall off.

377

377. *MAMPAM SE* - THE MONITOR LIZARD'S TEETH

Symbol of BEAUTY, GOOD PERSONAL HYGIENE, RADIANCE, and ATTRACTION

From the expression: *Ne se nwɔtwe a ɛsisi nyaaanyaa sɛ mampam se; ɔbaa ahoɔfɛ, amampamma, mepɛ wo nkonse.*

Literal translation: Her teeth have gaps between them like the aligator lizard's; beautiful woman with spirals around your neck, I love you.

The Akan's concept of a beautiful person is expressed by one with a round, broad face, a smile, and white, clean set of teeth, and well groomed or coiffured hair.

378   379

380   381

378-381. *DUA AFE* - WOODEN COMB

Symbol of PATIENCE, PRUDENCE, FONDNESS, LOVE, BEAUTY, GOOD FEMINIE QUALITIES, and CARE

From the expression: *Ɔdɔ yɛ wu.*

Literal translation: Love survives till death or Love is everlasting.

Young men in love would present wooden combs to their women friends. On the handle of the comb would be carved symbols with such names as *Kae me* (Remember me), *Megye wo awodɔm* (I wish you to be a mother of several children), and *ɔdɔ yɛ wu* (Love survives till death or Love is everlasting).

382-384.   *DUA AFE* - WOODEN COMB

Symbol of PATIENCE, PRUDENCE, FONDNESS, LOVE, BEAUTY, GOOD FEMINIE QUALITIES, and CARE

From the expression: Ɔdɔ yɛ wu.

Literal translation: Love survives till death or Love is everlating.

Young men in love would present wooden combs to their women friends. On the handle of the comb would be carved symbols with such names as *Kae me* (Remember me), *Megye wo awodɔm* (I wish you to be a mother of several children), and *ɔdɔ yɛ wu* (Love survives till death or Love is everlasting).

385-389. *AKOMA* - HEART

Symbol of GOODWILL, LOVE, FAITHFULNESS, CARE, PATIENCE, and ENDURANCE

From the expression: *Nya akoma*. Also, *Ɔdɔ firi akoma mu, nyɛ tirim*.

Literal translation: Be patient. Also, Love is from the heart, not the the head.

Love is an exercise in patience and faithfulness.

390-392.   *ƆDƆ FIRI AKOMA MU* - LOVE IS FROM THE HEART

Symbol of DEVOTION, COMMITMENT

From the expression: *Ɔdɔ firi akoma mu, nyɛ tirim*.

Literal translation: Love is from the heart, not the head.

393.   *ƆDƆFO NYERA FIE KWAN* - THE LOVER WILL FIND HIS/HER WAY HOME

Symbol of DEVOTION, PERSISTENCE, and COMMITMENT

From the expression: *Ɔdɔfo nyera ɔdɔ fie kwan*.

394.   *ƆDƆ NISUO* - LOVE TEARS

Symbol of LOVE, JOY, SORROW, DEVOTION, and SUFFERING

Love tears may be tears of joy or that of sorrow. Love is full of happiness and joy, or may be long suffering and full of agony.

395.   *ƆDƆ BATA AKOMA HO* - LOVE IS IN THE HEART

Symbol of FAITHFULNESS, LOVE, and AFFECTION

From the expression: *Ɔdɔ bata akoma ho*.

Literal translation: Love is in the heart.

Love emanates from the heart.

160

396

396. *FA W'AKOMA MA ME* - GIVE ME YOUR HEART
Symbol of DEVOTION, LOVE, and COMMITMENT
From the expression: *Fa w'akoma ma me.*
Literal translation: Give me your heart..

397

397. *KAE ME* - REMEMBER ME
Symbol of FAITHFULNESS, DEVOTION, and COMMITMENT
From the expression: *Kae me.*
Literal translation: Remember me.

398

398. *NNAADAA ME* - DO NOT DECEIVE ME
Symbol of SINCERITY, TRUTHFULNESS, FAITHFULNESS, and COMMITMENT
From the expression: *Aware yɛdi no ɔdɔ, ɛnyɛ anoasɛm hunu; ɔdɔfo, nnaadaa me.*
Literal translation: Marriage springs out of love, not empty boasts; do not deceive me my love.

399

399. *MƐWARE WO* - I SHALL MARRY YOU
Symbol of COMMITMENT, PESEVERANCE, DETERMINATION, and STEADFASTNESS
From the expression: *Obi ntutu mmirika nkɔdɔn aware-dan dɔteɛ.*
Literal translation: No one rushes into the job of mixing the concrete for building the house of marriage.
Marriage depends on proper and deliberate planning.
The promise to marry someone carries such responsibility that one is urged not to rush into marriage as marriage is a commitment for life.

400

400. *DƐNKYƐM DUA* - CROCODILE'S TAIL
Symbol of LOVE, MARRIAGE, CONUBIALITY, MATRIMONY
From the expression: *Aware ɛyɛ ayɔnkofa, ɛnyɛ abusuabɔ.*
Literal translation: The contract of marriage is a contract of friendship; it is not like the bond of blood in family relationships.
This symbolizes the original Mother Goddess, the Creator in whom was embodied the union of male and female; the biological union of the two opposite sex - a God who was a manifestation of the dual sexual parts present in living creatures before being separated.

401

401. *AKOMA NTOASOɔ* - JOINED HEARTS
Symbol of PEACE, GOODWILL, TOGETHERNESS, LOVE, and UNITY
From the expression: *Obi dɔ wo a, dɔ no bi.*
Literal translation: When someone loves you, show your love in return.
This symbol signifies the joining together of the families of the couple in marriage. Marriage is a union not only of two people, but also of two families. It also stresses the need for concerted action or united front.

402   403

404

402-404. *ɔSRANE NE NSOROMMA* - THE CRESCENT MOON AND THE STAR
Symbol of DEVOTION, PATIENCE, LOVE, FAITHFULNESS, FONDNESS, HARMONY, CONSISTENCY, and AFFECTION
From the proverb: *Kyɛkyɛ pɛ aware, ɔsrane ara na ɔbɛware no.*
Literal translation: *Kyɛkyɛ* (the North Star) is in love; she is always waiting the return of her husband, the moon.
This symbols stresses the importance of cooperation between two people in a marriage relationship.

405. *AWARE MU NSƐM* or *AWARE YƐ YA* - MARITAL PROBLEMS

Symbol of MARITAL PROBLEMS, COMPROMISE, GIVE-AND-TAKE,

From the aphorism: *Aware yε ya*. Or, *Barima mfa n'ahooden nware*. Or, *Obaa ko nsuo anopa a, odom ne ho anwummerε*. Also, *Aware nyε nsafufuo na yεaso ahwε*.

Literal translation: Marriage is a difficult undertaking. Or, A man should treat his wife as an equal not a subservient dependent. Or, A woman who fetches water in the morning saves herself the trouble of fetching water in the evening. Also, Marriage is not like the palm-wine to be tasted before it is drunk.

Marriage is always a trial for the partners. In order to have a successful marriage, each partner must be willing to make sacrifices and compromises.

406. *DONNO* - BELL DRUM

Symbol of ADORATION, CAJOLERY, PRAISE and RHYTHM

Donno is an hour glass-shaped drum. In outline the drum shows two triangles that meet at the apex, the symbol of the bisexual Mother God as the ruler of the sky, earth, and the underworld. The Donno is one the very few drums females are allowed to play in the Akan society. Young women use the *donno* to sing the praises and appellations of a young woman when celebrating her puberty rites (*bragoro*)

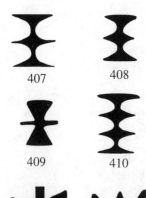

407-415. *DONNO NTOASO* - JOINED BELL DRUM

Symbol of PRAISE, ADULATION, UNITED ACTION, UNITY, and JUBILATION

From the expression: *Obaawarefoo ahoofε gyam ne kunu te n'anim*.

Literal translation: The good appearance or beauty of the married woman is a credit to her husband to whom it sings praises.

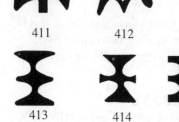

416. *AWARE PAPA* - GOOD MARRIAGE

Symbol of SUCCESSFUL MARRIAGE, MARITAL BLISS

From the expression: *Obaa nya aware pa a, εyε animuonyam ma ono ne n'abusuafoo*. Or, *Aware pa gyina aboterε afuo mu*.

Literal translation: Good or a very successful marriage is beneficial for the woman as well as her family. Or, Marriage prospers only in the farm of patience.

417. *AWARE BONE* - BAD MARRIAGE

Symbol of BAD MARRIAGE, DIFFICULTIES IN MARRIAGE, and UNSUCCESSFUL MARRIAGE

From the expression: *Aware bone tete obaa pa*. Or, *Me ne m'aware bone; meso kεntεn hunu na worehwehwε mu*. Also, *Ko aware te adwerε, na mereyε no dεn ni o?*

Literal translation: Bad treatment in marriage destroys or corrupts a good woman. Or, Me and my disastrous marriage; I am carrying an empty basket and you are searching through it. Also, What am I to do with an ill-fated marriage that always requires propitiatory rituals?

418

418. *KƐTƐ PA* - GOOD BED

Symbol of GOOD MARRIAGE, SUCCESSFUL MARRIAGE, GOOD CARE

From the expression: *Ɔbaa kɔ aware pa a, na yɛde no to kɛtɛ pa so.*

Literal translation: A successful or good marriage begins with the good bed on which the wife sleeps in her marital home.

419   420

419-420. *ƆBAATAN* - MOTHERLINESS

Symbol of DOUBLE LIFE, PREGNANCY, REPRODUCTIVE POWERS, and MOTHERLINESS

From the aphorism: *Ɔbaatan na ɔnim deɛ ne ba bɛdie. Also, Eno baatan pa, nkuruma kɛse a ne yam abaduasa na ɔmmoa. Also, Eno, woyɛ sɛn kɛseɛ a wogye adididodoɔ. Or, Wo nuabaa aserɛ so a, wonna so.*

Literal translation: The mother knows what her child will eat. Also, Good mother, the okra full of the seeds of many issues and proven. Also, Mo``ther, you are the big cooking pot that feeds many people. Or, If your sister has big and beautiful thighs, that is not where you sleep.

A pregnant woman is said to have a DOUBLE LIFE: her's and the baby's.

421

421. *MMƆFRA BƐNYINI* - THE YOUNG SHALL GROW

Symbol of GROWTH, MATURATION, DEVELOPMENT, RESPONSIBILITY, and PARENTAL CARE

From the aphorism: *Obi hwɛ wo ma wo se fifiri a, wo nso wohwɛ no ma ne deɛ tutu.*

Literal translation: When one takes care of you as you grow your teeth, you return one's favor by taking care of one during one's old age when one's teeth begin to fall out.

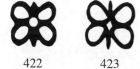

422   423

422-423. *ƆBAATAN AWAAMU* - THE WARM EMBRACE OF A MOTHER

Symbol of MOTHERHOOD, PARENTAL CARE, WARM EMBRACE, and LOVE

From the aphorism: *Ɔaatan pa na ɔnim deɛ ne mma bɛdi. Or, Wo nuabaa aserɛ so a, wonna so.*

Literal translation: The good mother knows what her children will eat. Or, If your sister has big and beautiful thighs, that is not where you sleep.

424   425

426   427

424-427. *AKOKƆ NAN or AKOKƆ NANTAM* - HEN'S FEET

Symbol of PARENTAL DISCIPLINE, PROTECTION, PARENTHOOD, CARE, and TENDERNESS

From the proverb: *Akokɔ nan tia ne ba so a, ɛnku no.*

Literal translation: When the hen treads on its chicken, she does not mean to kill them. Or, Parental admonition is not intended to harm the child.

428

428. ƐBAN - FENCE
Symbol of SAFETY, SECURITY, and LOVE
Fenced homes are regarded as safe and secure.

429   430

431   432

433   434

429-434. *FIHANKRA* - COMPOUND HOUSE
Symbol of SAFETY, SECURITY, SOLIDARITY, and BROTHERHOOD
From the expression: *Yɛbisa sɛ kyerɛ me osimasi ne fie, nyɛ ne sika dodoo a ɔwɔ.*
Literal translation: We ask to be shown one's house, not how much money one has.
The symbol reflects the Akan's organic conception of a family. This symbol depicts a kind of architecture which is highly regarded by the Akans. It is a kind of house in which there is a central quadrangle with rooms on each of the four sides.

435   436

435-436. *MFRAMADAN* - WINDY or WELL VENTILATED HOUSE
Symbol of PROTECTION, SOCIAL SECURITY, FORTITUDE, PREPARED-NESS, ELEGANCE, and EXCELLENCE
The symbol depicts a reinforced or well-built, and well-ventilated house.

437   438

439   440

437-440. *BLƆK DAN* - BLOCK HOUSE
Symbol of SECURITY, PROTECTION, WEALTH, and PROPERTY
From the expression: *Wonni sika a,wonsi blɔk dan.*
Literal translation: One builds a cement or cinder block house when one has the money.

441   442

443

441-443. *BLƆK DAN* - BLOCK HOUSE
Symbol of SECURITY, PROTECTION, WEALTH, and PROPERTY
From the expression: *Wonni sika a,wonsi blɔk dan.*
Literal translation: One builds a cement or cinder block house when one has the money.

444

444. *ABIREKYI MMƐN NE ƆDƆ* - RAM'S HORNS AND LOVE
Symbol of LOVE, HAPPINESS, MARITAL BLISS
From the expression: *Mmaa pɛ dɛ, kyiri ka.* Or, *Sokoo na mmaa pɛ.* Or, *Kwakye adeɛ yɛ fɛ, nso yɛde sika na ɛtɔ.*
Litral translation: Women tend to enjoy the assets, but not the liabilities that flow from a relationship with a man.

445

446

447

448

449

445. *ABUSUAFOƆ HO TE SƐN?* - HOW IS THE FAMILY?

Symbol of FRATERNAL GREETINGS
From the expression: *Abusuafoɔ ho te sɛn?*
Literal translation: How is the family?
This greeting is exchanged between family members when they meet away from home.

446. *TENA FIE* - STAY AT HOME

Symbol of FAMILY RESPONSIBILITY
From the expression: *Tena fie.* Or, *Wonam nam a, hyia na wohyia; aboa antena fie a, ɔgye abaa.*
Literal translation: Stay at home. Or, When one does not stay at home one gets into trouble, the animal that roams is often beaten as it is always falling into troubles

447. *ABUSUA PA* - GOOD FAMILY

Symbol of FAMILY UNITY, KINSHIP TIES, FAMILY SUPPORT

448. *ABUSUA BƆNE* - MALEVOLENT FAMILY

Symbol of FAMILY DISUNITY, BLAMING ONE'S FAMILY
From the expression: *Wontumi wo ho a, na wose abusuafoɔ anhwɛ me.*
Literal translation: The lazy person always blames it on his/her family.

449. *ABUSUA HWEDEƐ* - FAMILY DISPUTE

Symbol of DISUNITY WITHIN A FAMILY, FAMILY DISPUTE, and FAMILY IN CRISIS
From the expression: *Abusua hwedeɛ gu nkuruwa, me nko me deɛ na egya da mu.*
Literal translation: Every family has its internal crisis or dispute that may be simmering, mine is ablaze.
Hwedeɛ is a species of grass that grows scattered in little tufts. In this symbol the abusua is seen like this grass, and like grass it burns in the typical wildfire manner when set ablaze by family disputes. The abusua is made up of clusters of sisters and their children. Sibling rivalry, family disputes, and petty jealousies can set sisters apart as if they are enemies not family members.

450   451

452

453

450-452. *ABUSUA TE SƐ KWAEƐ* - THE FAMILY IS LIKE FOREST

Symbol of UNITY IN DIVERSITY, FRATERNITY, VARIATION, and HETEROGENEITY
From the aphorism: *Abusua te sɛ kwaeɛ, wokɔ mu a, na wobɛhu deɛ ɛwɔm.* Or, *Abusua te sɛ kwaeɛ, wokɔ mu a, na wohu sɛ nnua a ɛwɔm no sisi mmaako mmaako.*
Literal translation: The family is like forest, it is when you have entered it that you will see what is inside. Or, The family is like forest, if you view it from far away, the trees appear to be together, but when one gets closer to it one sees that each tree has a specific location or that each tree stands alone as individuals.

453. *ABUSUA PANIN KYERƐ WO DƆ* - FAMILY HEAD, ASSERT YOUR AFFECTION

Symbol of KINDNESS, BENEVOLENCE, HOSPITALITY, SYMPATHY, GENEROSITY, and PARENTAL LOVE
From the expression: *Agya a woyɛ mmɔfra ni.* Or, *Woyɛ damprane a ase yɛ nwunu; abusua panin kyerɛ wo dɔ.*
Literal translation: A father who is a mother to children. Or, You are like the giant shade tree in the desert; family head assert your affection.

454

455

456

457

458

454-458. *ABUSUA DƆ FUNU* - THE FAMILY LOVES THE DEAD

Symbol FAMILY UNITY, SOLIDARITY, and FAMILY RESPONSIBILITY
From the expression: *Abusua dɔ funu.*
Literal translation: The family loves the corpse.
Funeral is an occasion on which the unity and solidarity of the lineage receive public expression as funeral expenses are shared among adult members of the lineage.

459

459. *BOA W'AWOFO* - HELP YOUR PARENTS

Symbol of FAMILY SUPPORT, INTERDEPENDENCE OF FAMILY MEMBERS, RECIPROCAL FAMILY OBLIGATIONS, and FAMILY BONDS
From the expression: *Boa w'awofo.*
Literal translation: Help your parents.

460

460. *BOA MPANIMFOƆ* - HELP THE ELDERLY

Symbol of SUPPORT FOR THE ELDERLY, RESPECT FOR OLD AGE, and SECURITY AND WELFARE OF THE ELDERLY
From the expression: *Boa mpanimfoɔ.*
Literal translation: Help the elderly.

461

461. *WOYƐ ABƆFRA A* - WHILE YOU ARE YOUNG

Symbol of RESPECT, TOLERANCE OF DIVERSITY, and VENERATION
From the expression: *Woyɛ abɔfra a, nsere akwatia.*
Literal translation: While you are young, do not laugh at a short person for you never can tell how you will look in your old age.

462

462. *MOMMA YƐNNODƆ YƐN HO* - LET US LOVE ONE ANOTHER

Symbol of UNITY, LOVE, FRATERNITY, and FELLOWSHIP
From the expression: *Obi dɔ wo a, dɔ no bi.* Also, *Momma yɛnnodɔ yɛn ho na nipa nkyɛre na wamia.*
Literal translation: When someone loves you, show your love in return. Also, Let us love one another for the individual is insufficient unto himself/herself.

The following *adinkra* symbols capture some aspects of the Akan social value system.

463

463. *YƐ PAPA* - DO GOOD
Symbol of VIRTUE, GOODNESS, and SELFLESSNESS
From the aphorism: *Woyɛ papa a woyɛ ma wo ho, woyɛ bɔne nso a, woyɛ ma wo ho.*
Literal translation: When you do good you do it unto yourself.

464

464. *BU WO HO* - RESPECT YOURSELF
Symbol of SELF RESPECT
From the expression: *Bu wo ho.*
Literal translation: Respect yourself.

465

465. *MA W'ANI NSƆ NEA WOWƆ* - BE CONTENT WITH YOUR LOT
Symbol of CONTENTMENT, GRATIFICATION, and SATISFACTION
From the aphorism: *Nsuo anso adwareɛ a, ɛso nom.* Or, *Wo tiri sua na wotete dɔteɛ tetare ho sɛ wo rema no ayɛ kɛse a, nsuo tɔ a, ɛtete gu.* Also, *Ma w'ani nsɔ nea wowɔ.*
Literal translation: If a quantity of water does not suffice for a bath, it will at least be sufficient for drinking. Or, If you have a small head and you try to increase the size by adding layers of mud onto your head, when it rains such layers will be washed off. Also, Be content with your lot.

466

467

466-475. *ANI BERE A ƐNSƆ GYA* - FIRE IS NOT SPARKED IN EYES RED WITH ANGER
Symbol of PATIENCE, SELF-CONTROL, SELF-DISCIPLINE, and SELF-CONTAINMENT
From the proverb: *Ani bere a, ɛnsɔ gya.* Or, *Ɛnye obiara a ne bo afu na ɔmuna.*
Literal translation: No matter how flaming red one's eyes may be, flames are not sparked in one's eyes. Or, Every frowned face does not necessarily depict an angry person.
In angry situations one should not succumb to one's emotions. This symbol signifies the need for one to defy odds and the exercise of restraint in difficult times.

468

469

470

471

472

473

474

475

476

476. *NYA ABOTERƐ* - BE PATIENT
Symbol of PATIENCE, DILIGENCE, SELF-CONTROL, TOLERANCE, and FOREBEARANCE
From the aphorism: *Aboterɛ tutu mmepɔ.* Or, *Nya aboterɛ.* Or, *Wofa nwansena ho abufuo a, wobere wo kuro.*
Literal translation: Patience moves mountains. Or, Have patience. Or, If you get annoyed with the housefly, you bruise your sore.

477

477. *NYƐ AHANTAN* - DO NOT BE ARROGANT
Symbol of WARNING AGAINST ARROGANCE
From the expression: *Nyɛ ahantan.*
Literal translation: Do not be arrogant.

478

479

480

481

482

483

484

485

486

487

488

EKAA
OBI
NKOA
489

490

EKA NSEE
NKOA
491

EKAA
NSEE
NKOA
492

493

478. *NNI AWU* - DO NOT KILL

Symbol of RESPECT FOR HUMAN LIFE, WARNING AGAINST MURDER
From the expression: *Nni awu na nkwa yɛntɔn.*
Literal translation: Do not kill for life cannot be purchased.
This symbol depicts the high value Akans place on human life. Human life is too precious to be wasted by senseless killing.

479. *DI MMARA SO* - OBSERVE RULES

Symbol of BEING LAW ABIDING, CONFORMITY,
RESPECT FOR THE LAW
From the expression: *Nipa ho antɔ no a, na ɛfiri n'asɛm.*
Literal translation: If one is not happy, one's conduct is the cause.

480. *MMƆ ADWAMAN* - DO NOT FORNICATE

Symbol of CHASTITY, DECENCY, CONTINENCE, SELF CONTROL, and ABSTINENCE
From the expression: *Wo nuabaa asrɛ so a, wonna so.*
Literal translation: If your sister has beautiful thighs, that is not where you sleep.

481-484. *MFOFOO ABA* - SEED OF THE *MFOFOO* PLANT

Symbol of WARNING AGAINST JEALOUSY, INTOLERANCE, and ENVY
From the proverb: *Deɛ mfofoo pɛ ne sɛ gyinantwi abɔ bidie.*
Literal translation: What the fofoo plant always wishes is that the gyinatwi seeds should turn black.
The symbol reminds one that jealousy and covetousness are unbecoming of a good citizen.

485-486. *KATA WO DEƐ SO* - COVER YOUR OWN

Symbol of JEALOUSY, BICKERING, GOSSIP, and SLANDER
From the expression: *Kata wo deɛ so na bue me deɛ so.* Also *Gyae me ho nkontabuo na pɛ wo deɛ.*
Literal translation: Cover your own shortcomings and expose mine. Also, Stop all this slanderous accounts about me and put your time to productive work.

487-488. *ATAMFOƆ REBRƐ* - ADVERSARIES ARE SUFFERING

Symbol of ENVY, ENEMITY, and JEALOUSY
From the expression: *Wotiatia obi deɛ so hwehwɛ wo deɛ a, wonhu.*
Literal translation: If you trample upon what belongs to someone in the hope of finding what belongs to you, you never find it.

489. *ƐKAA OBI NKO A* - SOMEONE WISHES

Symbol of PETTY JEALOUSY, ENVY, MALICE, and RESENTMENT
From the expression: *Ɛkaa obi nko a, nka mawu.*
Literal translation: Someone wishes I was dead.

490-492. *ƐKAA NSEE NKO A* - THE WEAVER BIRD WISHES

Symbol of PETTY JEALOUSY, ENVY, MALICE, and RESENTMENT
From the expresion: *Ɛkaa nsee nko a, anka onyina dua awu.*
Literal translation: The woodpecker wishes the *onyina* (silk cotton) tree were

493. *ƐNNI NSEKURO* - DO NOT GOSSIP

Symbol of WARNING AGAINST SLANDER, GOSSIP, IDLE TALK
From the expression: *Ɛnni nsekuro.*
Literal translation: Do not gossip.

494

494. *WOAYε AFεRE* - YOU HAVE PERSISTED AND ENDED IN DISGRACE

Symbol of DISHONOR, DISGRACE, SHAME, and HUMILIATION

From the expression: *Fεdeε ne owuo, fanyinam owuo. Or, Woayε afere. Or, Ne tiboa abu no fɔ.*

Literal translation: Death and dishonor, death is preferable. Or, You have persisted and ended in disgrace. Or, One's conscience has judged one guilty.

495

496

495-497. *SESA WO SUBAN* - CHANGE YOUR BEHAVIOR

Symbol of WARNING AGAINST ARROGANCE, BAD MANNERS, and DISHONORABLE BEHAVIOR

From the expression: *Sesa wo suban na ti bɔne wɔfa no fam, wɔmfa nwo. Or, Sesa wo suban na wo nneyεeε nkyerε suban pa.*

Literal translation: Change your character for one is not born with bad character but one learns it on earth. Or, Change your character for your deeds do not indicate good character.

One's character is determined by one's deeds or actions. Since one can desist from certain actions, then one can certainly change one's character.

497

498. *ɔBRA TE Sε AHWEHWε* - LIFE IS LIKE A MIRROR

Symbol of LIFE AS A REFLECTION, SELF-PICTURE, SELF-CONCEPT, and SELF-ESTEEM

From the maxim: *ɔbra te sε ahwehwε wohwε mu a, wohunu wo ho.*

Literal translation: Life is like a mirror in which you see a reflection of yourself. The Akan regard self-concept as the attitudes and feelings one has about one's self.

498

499-501. *NKYINKYIMIIε* - TWISTINGS or ZIGZAGS

Symbol of TOUGHNESS, ADAPTABILITY, DEVOTION TO SERVICE, and RESOLUTENESS

From the expression: *ɔbra kwan yε nkyinkyimiiε.*

Literal translation: The course of life is full of twistings, ups and downs, and zigzags.

This symbol emphasizes the need for critical appraisal and reappraisal of one's situation in life.

499

500

501

502

503

502-506. *WAWA ABA* - SEED OF THE WAWA TREE

Symbol of PERSEVERANCE, TOUGHNESS, HARDWORK, and RESILIENCE

From the expression: *ɔyε den sε wawa aba.*

Literal translation: One is as tough as the seed of the wawa tree.

The inference is that a keen sense of purpose is not easily overcome or put off by difficulties and adversities.

504

505

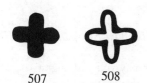

506

507

508

507-508. *TABONO* - PADDLE

Symbol of STRENGTH, PERSISTENCE, PERSEVERANCE, UNITY OF PURPOSE, and HARD WORK

From the aphorism: *εhyεn wɔka no afanu a, na εkɔ tee.*

Literal translation: The canoe must be paddled on both sides to make it go straight.

Steady paddling inspires confidence and industry. Or, Unity is strength. Tabono is also used as a bait in fishing, or it is the spatula that gold weight-casters use.

169

509

509. ƆSRANE or ƆSRANEFA - CRESCENT MOON
Symbol of FAITH, PATIENCE, DETERMINATION, PERSEVERANCE
From the aphorism: *Ɔsrane mfiti prɛko pɛ ntware ɔman.*
Literal translation: The moon does not go round the nation at one go. Or the moon does not form a circle hastily.

510   511

512   513

514   515

516   517

518   519

510-519. AYA - FERN
Symbol of INDEPENDENCE, PERSEVERANCE, AUTONOMY, ENDURANCE, DEFIANCE AGAINST OPPRESSION, and RESOURCEFULNESS
From the expression: *Mensuro wo.*
Literal translation: I am not afraid of you. I am independent of you.
Persistence is invariably rewarded with success. The *aya* plant grows in very hardy conditions and the symbol reflects endurance and defiance of difficulties.

520

520. MO NO YƆ - CONGRATULATIONS
Symbol of PRAISE, REWARD, HONOR and RECOGNITION
From the expression: *Mema mo mo-no-yɔ, me man.* Also, *Ɔbrane twa apɔ yɛma no mo.*
Literal translation: I congratulate you my people. Also, When one performs a good deed, one is recognized and praised.

521

521. PAGYA WO TI NA GYE ASEDA - RAISE YOUR HEAD AND ACCEPT THANKSGIVING
Symbol of GRATITUDE, BENEFICENCE, and THANKFULNESS
From the expression: *Ɔkanni kyɛ adeɛ a, ɔgye aseda.*
Literal translation: If an Akan makes a present he accepts thanks.

522-523. WOYƐ ƆHƆHO PAPA A - WHEN YOU DO GOOD TO A STRANGER
Symbol of INGRATITUDE and UNGRATEFULNESS
From the expression: *Woyɛ ɔhɔhoɔ papa a, ɔde wo ti bɔ dua.* Also, *Ɔhɔhoɔ annya wo adeɛ a, ɔgya wo ka.*
Literal translation: If you do good to a stranger, he may repay you with ingratitude. Also, If your visitor does not leave you in wealth, he leaves in debt.

522   523

170

524

524. *W'ANO PƐ ASƐM* - YOU'RE NOSY

Symbol of BEING NOSY, INQUISITIVE, and MEDDLESOME

From the expression: *Asɛm mpɛ nipa, nipa na ɔpɛ asɛm.* Also, *Onipa ho antɔ no a, na ɛfiri n'asɛm.*

Literal translation: Trouble does not seek out a trouble-maker, the trouble-maker courts trouble. Also, If one is unhappy, one's conduct is the cause.

525

525. *NTWITWA WO HO NKYERƐ ME* - DO NOT BE BOAST-FUL TO ME

Symbol of WARNING AGAINST ARROGANCE, HAUGHTINESS and POMPOSITY

From the expression: *Ntwitwa wo ho nkyerɛ me.*

Literal translation: Do not be boastful to me.

526   527

528   529

526-529. *ANI HUNU YEYA A* - THE EYES SEE SUFFERING

Symbol of PAIN, FORTITUDE, FOREBEARANCE, and LONG-SUFFERING

From the expression: *Ani hunu yeya a, ɛtim deɛ ɛtim.*

Literal translation: The eyes see all pain and suffering, yet they remain in their place.

530

530. *AKA M'ANI* - ONLY MY EYES

Symbol of PATIENCE

From the expression: *Aka m'ani na mede hwɛ woɔ.*

Literal translation: I have nothing but my eyes to look at you.

531

531. *MEKYIA WO* - I SALUTE YOU

Symbol of GREETINGS, RECOGNITION, and RESPECT

From the expression of greetings: *Mekyia wo.*

Literal translation: I salute you.

When Akans meet, they exchange greetings first before they carry out any converstion. Greetings are not just exchange of handshake or words, but recognition of a fellow human being.

532

532. *MAHU WO DADA* - I HAVE ALREADY SEEN YOU

Symbol of SURPRISE, EXCITEMENT, and WELCOME

From the expression: *Mahu wo dada.*

Literal translation: I have already seen you.

533

533. *AKWAABA* - WELCOME

Symbol of HOSPITALITY, GREETING, and RECEPTION

From the expression of welcome greetings: *Akwaaba.*

Literal translation: Welcome.

534

534. *WO HO TE SƐN?* - HOW ARE YOU?

Symbol of GREETINGS, RECOGNITION, and FRIENDLINESS

From the expression of greetings: *Wo ho te sɛn?*

Literal translation: How are you?

535

535. *WOASESA* - YOU HAVE CHANGED

Symbol of ADMIRATION, SURPRISE, and WONDER

From the expression of greetings: *Woasesa!*

Literal translation: You have changed!

536

536. SAA? - IS THAT SO?
Symbol of DOUBT, ENQUIRY, and SKEPTICISM
From the question: *Saa?*
Literal translation: Is that so?

537

537. GYE W'ANI - ENJOY YOURSELF
Symbol of THE JOY OF LIVING, REJOICING, MERRY-MAKING, HAPPI-NESS, and the WORTH OF LIVING
From the maxim: *Onua gye w'ani na nipa nkwa yɛ tia.*
Literal translation: Enjoy life for one has a short stay in this world.
This means more than having fun. This urges one to make the best out of life.

538

538. FIRI HA KƆ - GO AWAY
Symbol of BEING UNWELCOME
From the expression: *Firi ha kɔ.* Or, *Menyɛ nanabene na woaka akyerɛ me sɛ firi ha kɔ.*
Literal translation: Go away. Or, I am not a stranger for you to ask me to leave.

539   540

539-540. YƐBƐHYIA BIO - WE'LL MEET AGAIN
Symbol of FAREWELL
From the expression of parting greetings: *Yɛbɛhyia bio.*
Literal translation: We'll meet again.

541

541. ƆKWAN NNI HƆ - NO WAY
Symbol of PESSMISM, LACK OF OPPORTUNITY, and CLOSURE
From the expression: *Ɔkwan nni hɔ.*
Literal translation: There is no way.

542

542. NANTE YIE - GOODBYE
Symbol of FAREWELL, GODSPEED, and SAFE JOURNEY
From the expression of farewell or parting greetings: *Nante yie.*
Literal translation: Goodbye or farewell.

543

543. AHOƆFƐ NTUA KA - BEAUTY DOES NOT PAY
Symbol of GOOD MANNERS, MODESTY and BEAUTIFUL CHARACTER
From the maxim: *Ahoɔfɛ ntua ka, suban pa na ɛhia.*
Literal translation: Beauty does not pay; it is good character that counts.

544

544. ƐHURU A, ƐBƐDWO - IT WILL COOL DOWN AFTER BOILING
Symbol of HUMILITY, MODESTY, and WARNING AGAINST ARROGANCE
From the maxim: *Kuta wo bɔdɔm na ɛhuru a, ɛbɛdwo.*
Literal translation: Slow down for it will cool down after boiling.

545

545. APONKYERƐNE WU A - WHEN THE FROG DIES
Symbol of SIGNIFICANCE, VALUE, and IMPORTANCE
From the maxim: *Aponkyerɛne wu a, na yɛhunu ne tenten.*
Literal translation: It is when the frog dies that we see its full measure.
One is often valued when one is no more.

546

546. ATAMFOƆ ANI AWU - ADVERSARIES ARE ASHAMED
Symbol of SHAME, REMORSE and GUILT
From the expression: *Atamfoɔ ani awu.* Or, *Wotan me a, kata w'ani.*
Literal translation: Adversaries are ashamed. Or, If you hate me, cover your eyes.

547

547. ƆBRA YƐ BƆNA - LIFE IS A STRUGGLE

Symbol of the VICISSITUDES OF LIFE, PERSISTENCE, and DETERMINATION

From the expression: Ɔbra yɛ bɔna. Also, Ɔbra ne deɛ wo ara woabɔ.
Literal translation: Life is a struggle. Also, Life is what you make of it.

548

548. ADASA PƐ MMƆBORƆ - SOME PEOPLE DELIGHT IN THE FALL OF OTHERS

Symbol of JEALOUSY, ENVY and SELFISHNESS

From the expression: Adasa pɛ mmɔborɔ.
Literal translation: Some people delight in the fall of others.

549

549. NNYEGYEƐ - FESTER or DOOR BELL

Symbol of ANNOYANCE, IRRITATION, PESTERING, BOTHER or SYMBOL OF KNOCKING

From the expression: Nipa gyegyefoɔ sen ɔbonsam. Or, Ɔbosom ankɔda a, na ɛfiri nnyegyesoɔ.
Literal translation: The pester is worse than the devil.
Door-bell of the rattling or mobile type was hung in front of the main door of a house or the bedroom to announce the entry of a person.

550

550. ANI NE ANI HYIA - WHEN EYES MEET

Symbol of AGREEMENT, HARMONY, ACCORD, CONFLICT RESOLUTION, and COMPROMISE

From the aphorism: Ani ne ani hyia a, ntoto mma.
Literal translation: When two people see eye to eye, there is bound to be no discord.

551

551. ATAMFOƆ ATWA ME HO AHYIA - ADVERSARIES ARE ALL AROUND ME

Symbol of JEALOUSY, ENVY, ENMITY, and MALICE

From the expression: Yɛkyiri me, yɛnnɔ me, ɛfiri tete. Also, Atamfoɔ atwa me ho ahyia.
Literal translation: They hate me, they don't love me, dates from time immemorial. Also, Adversaries are all around me.

552

552. WO NSA AKYI - THE BACK OF YOUR HAND

Symbol of SELF-DETERMINATION, PERSEVERANCE and TENACITY

From the aphorism: Wo nsa akyi bɛyɛ wo dɛ a, ɛnte sɛ wo nsa yam.
Literal translation: The back of your hand does not taste as good as the palm does.

553

553. NYA AKOKOƆDURO - HAVE COURAGE

Symbol of COURAGE, FORTITUDE, DETERMINATION and VALOR

From the expression: Nya akokoɔduro.
Literal translation: Have courage.

554

554. HWƐ YIE - BE CAUTIOUS

Symbol of CAUTION, CAREFULNESS, VIGILANCE, and ALERTNESS

From the aphorism: Nipa bɛhwɛ yie na ɛfiri deɛ wahunu.
Literal translation:

555

555. BƆ WO HO BAN - PROTECT YOURSELF

Symbol of PROTECTION, SAFEGUARD, and PRECAUTION

From the adage: Bɔ wo ho ban.
Literal translation: Protect yourself; be on your guard.

556

556. HWƐ W'AKWAN MU YIE - BE CIRCUMSPECT

Symbol of CIRCUMSPECTION, PRUDENCE, and ALERTNESS

From the expression: Hwɛ w'akwan mu yie.
Literal translation: Be circumspect.

557

557. *BRƐ WO HO ASE* - BE HUMBLE

Symbol of HUMILITY, MODESTY, and SIMPLICITY

From the adage: *Brɛ wo ho ase.*

Literal translation: Be humble.

558

558. *GYE ME DI* - TRUST ME

Symbol of TRUST, FAITH, ASSURANCE, and BELIEF

From the expression: *Gye me di.*

Literal translation: Trust me.

559

559. *MENSURO WO* - I AM NOT AFRAID OF YOU

Symbol of BRAVERY, COURAGE, and VALOR

From the expression: *Mensuro wo.*

Literal translation: I am not afraid of you.

560

560. *ƆBRA TWA WO A* - LIFE'S AGONIES

Symbol of DETERMINATION, PERSEVERANCE, and RESILIENCE

From the aphorism: *Ɔbra twa wo a, ɛsene sradaa.*

Literal translation: The agonies of life are more painful than the pain one might feel when being cut with a saw.

561   362

561-563. *DWEN WO HO* - THINK ABOUT YOURSELF

Symbol of SELF EXAMINATION

From the aphorism: *Dwen wo ho.*

Literal translation: Think about yourself.

563

564. *ANYI ME AYƐ A* - IF YOU WILL NOT PRAISE ME

Symbol of WARNING AGAINST INGRATITUDE and DEVALUATION OF ONE'S NAME

From the expression: *Anyi me ayɛ a, ɛnsɛe me din.*

Literal translation: If you will not praise me, do not devalue my good name.

564

565. *DADEƐ BI TWA DADEƐ BI MU* - ONE PIECE OF IRON MAY BE STRONGER THAN ANOTHER

Symbol of HUMILITY, POWER, IMPOTENCE and VULNERABILITY

From the adage: *Ɛyɛ a ɛnnka sɛ biribiara rentumi wo na dadeɛ bi twa dadeɛ bi mu.*

Literal translation: Do not boast that there is no power beyond you for one piece of iron may be stronger than another. Some iron can break others. For example, the thin hacksaw can be used to cut through thick iron bar. There is no one that is unconquerable in this world.

565

174

The following are some of the symbols that relate to economics and accounting that are printed in the *adinkra* cloth.

566

566.   *ASƆ NE AFENA* - THE HOE AND THE MATCHET
Symbol of HARDWORK, ENTRERPRENEURSHIP, INDUSTRY, and PRODUCTIVITY

From the expression: *Mmirikisie a yɛantumi annɔ no na yɛfrɛ no nsamampɔ. Or, Woansɔ w'afena ne w'asɔtia mu annyɛ adwuma a, ɔkɔm bɛde wo.*

Literal translation: The farm that is not tended is referred to as a sacred burial ground. Or, One must work to live.

In the past in farming communities, as part of the naming ceremony for a child, the male child was given a matchet in accordance with the gender division of labor to signify to the child that he should grow up to assume the responsibility of the man to clear the land to make a farm to raise food for his family.

567

567.   *AKUMA* - AXE
Symbol of POWER, HARDWORK

From the expression: *Odupɔn biara nni hɔ a akuma ntumi ntwa mu. Also, Adare bu a, yɛbɔ bi poma mu. And, Sɛ aderɛ tumi kwaeɛ a, anka yɛankɔbɔ akuma. Or, Dua biara nni hɔ a ɛyɛ den sɛ akuma ntumi ntwa, nanso asɛm biara yɛ den a, yɛmfa akuma na ɛtwa, na yɛde yɛn ano na ɛka ma no twa.*

Literal translation: There is no tree which cannot be felled by an axe. Also, When the handle of an axe breaks, a new one is carved to replace it. And, If the knife could clear the forest, the axe would not have been manufactured. Or, There is no tree that is so hard that it cannot be felled with an axe; however, no matter how difficult a case may be, it must be settled by counseling and negotiations, not with an axe.

The symbol is used to connote the view that there is no issue or problem so difficult that it cannot be resolved by peaceful means. The lumberer tackles all trees, small and big, by tact and diplomacy so that the tree does not fall on him to kill him. The axe is one of the essential farming tools. It is used to fell trees in the preparation of land for farming.

568

568.   *OKUAFOƆ PA* - GOOD FARMER
Symbol of HARDWORK, ENTRERPRENEURSHIP, INDUSTRY, and PRODUCTIVITY

From the expression: *Okuafoɔ pa ne obi a ɔyɛ nsiyɛfoɔ, ɔno na ɔse: W'afuo so a, woyɛ ne nyinaa.*

Literal translation: The good and industrious farmer says: No matter how big your farm is, you cultivate it all.

569-572.   *AFA* - BELLOWS
Symbol of BEING INDUSTRIOUS, ASSIDUOUS, HARDWORKING, TENACIOUS, and EFFICIENT

From the expression: *Afa na ɔboa odwumfoɔ ma ne tono, anka odwumfoɔ nni ahoɔden.*

Literal translation: It is the bellows that help the blacksmith (or goldsmith) to forge, without them he would be helpless.

569   570

571   572

573.   *KOOKOO DUA* - COCOA TREE
Symbol of WEALTH and OSTENTACIOUS LIVING

From the expression: *Kookoo dua yɛ sika dua. Also, Kookoo sɛɛ abusua, paepae mogya mu.*

Literal translation: Cocoa tree is money tree. Also, Cocoa ruins the family, divided blood relations.

573

Cocoa was introduced in the late nineteenth century as a cash crop. Within a decade or so it became Ghana's number one foreign exchange earner. As a new source of wealth, it has brought in its wake changes in land ownership and tenureship, and social stratification. It has been the source of political upheavals in the country.

574

574. *ABƐ DUA* - PALM TREE

Symbol of SELF-SUFFICIENCY, RESILIENCE, VITALITY, WEALTH and CAUSATION

From the expression: *Nipa nyɛ abɛ dua na ne ho ahyia ne ho.* Or, *Sɛ mmerɛnkɛnsono si ne ti ase a, na ɛwɔ deɛ asase reka kyerɛ no.* Also, *Nnua nyinaa bɛwu agya abɛ.*

Literal translation: The human being is not a palm tree that s/he should be self-sufficient. Or, Whenever the palm tree bends it is because of what the earth has told it. Also, All trees will wither but the palm tree.

The first analogy is based on the unique qualities of the palm tree as a source of various products like oil, wine, yeast, broom, soap, mat, and roofing material. Metaphorically speaking, the power of the king is evergreen and does not diminish with time and circumstances.

575   576

577   578

579   580

581

575-581. *BESE SAKA* - BUNCH OF KOLA NUTS

Symbol of WEALTH, AFFLUENCE, POWER, PLENTIFULNESS, HOSPITALITY, and LIFE SUSTAINER

The kola nuts were once used as currency. Kola is an important crop that is valued as a stimulant. It was highly valued in the old trans-Saharan trade as eating it sustained one for long periods of time before the next meal. It is used in some communities in place of drinks to welcome visitors.

Also, as symbol of WISDOM and KNOWLEDGE

From the aphorism: *Bese pa ne konini ahahan yɛtase no ɔbanyansafoɔ.* Also, *Nhɔhoɔa tare bese ho; ɔno a ɔnte nwe nso ɔnte ntɔn.*

Literal translation: The leaves of the two kinds of kola are gathered with wisdom. The leaves of the white and red kola plants are very similar and it takes skill and experience to separate them. One has to take care in dealing with problems, and separate them carefully. Also, the red ant on the pod of kola nuts does not pluck the kola nuts to eat or sell. The meaning of the symbol alludes to the dog in the manger attitude that some people have towards economic resources.

582

582. *NKATEHONO* - GROUNDNUT (PEANUT) SHELL

Symbol of RESOURCEFULNESS, CONTINUOUS GROWTH

From the aphorism: *Wobɛdua biribi ama me a, dua nkateɛ nnua aburoo.* Or, *Aware te sɛ nkateɛ, wommɔeɛ a, wonhunu deɛ ɛwɔ mu.*

Literal translation: If you want to grow something for me, plant groundnuts (peanuts) not corn. Or, You can't tell what marriage is like until you have tried it.

Peanuts reproduce themselves without being planted and thus symbolize continuous growth or permanent relationship. This symbol depicts the idea of bequeathing a legacy that is self-perpetuating and self-generating rather than a one-shot gift of temporary use. Or it signifies that marriage must be entered into on permanent basis.

583. *APA or APATA* - DRYING MAT

Symbol of PRESERVATION and SECURITY

From the maxim: *Putuo hye a, yɛdi dwo.*

Literal translation: When the yam barn catches fire, that may be the occasion to enjoy a yam meal.

A bad situation may be a blessing in disguise.

This drying mat is used in food preservation through drying in the sun. The mat is spread either on the ground or on an elevated platform or skid in the sun to dry fruits (e.g. cocoa and coffee beans) and food items such as pepper, fish plantain and cassava. The mat is also used to store food or to partition rooms, ceiling, and as a fence. A special kind of apata for storing and preserving yams is called *putuo* (yam barn).

583

584   585

586

584-586. *SITIA BƐKUM DOROBA* - THE DRIVER MAY DIE AT THE STEERING-WHEEL
Symbol of OCCUPATIONAL HAZARDS, INDUSTRY, and HARDWORK
From the expression : *Sitia na ɛbɛkum doroba.*
Literal translation: The driver may die at the steering-wheel of his vehicle.

587

587. *ƆBOHEMMAA* - DIAMOND
Symbol of PECIOUSNESS, GEM, and TREASURE
From the maxim: *Wode wo sika to aboo a, wowe.*
Literal translation: When you waste your money in buying non-precious stone, you eat it.

588

589

590

588-590. *ƆKƆTƆ* - CRAB
Symbol of INDUSTRIOUSNESS, HARDWORK, WEALTH, and SOCIAL CLASS
From the expression: *Nwaanwaa koto, wo na wonim mpo daberɛ.* Also, *Sika te sɛ hwene mu nwii, wotu a, na woresu.* Or, *Koto nwo anomaa.* Or, *Ayonkogoro dodoo nti na okoto annya tire.*
Literal translation: The skilled and crafty crab, you know the hiding place of alluvial gold nuggets. Also, Digging for gold is like pulling hair from the nose; it makes one cry. Or, The crab does not give birth to a bird. Or, Playing around too much with friends cost the crab its head.

591   592

593

594

595

596

591-596. *SEREWA* or *SEDEƐ* - COWRIES
Symbol of AFFLUFNCE, WEALTH, FINANCIAL RESOURCES, ENTREPRENEURSHIP, INFLUENCE, and POWER
From the expression: *Wonhyɛ sika pɛtea a, wokasa a, wommu wo.*
Literal translation:The words of one wearing no gold finger ring are not respected.
To the Akan, money makes for influence and power in a society. Coweries were once used as currency for trade. When used by priests it signifies sanctity.

597

597. *SIKA TU SƐ ANOMAA* - MONEY FLIES LIKE A BIRD
Symbol of FRUGALITY, ENTERPRENEURSHIP, or EXTRAVAGANCE
From the expression : *Sika tu sɛ anomaa, na sɛ woanhwɛ no yie a, ɛfiri wo nsa.*
Literal translation: Money flies like a bird; if you do not handle your money properly, you lose it.

598

598. *TOA* or *BRONTOA* - BOTTLE
Symbol of STORAGE, MEASUREMENT, and DIMENSIONALITY
From the expression: *Mpanimfoo se mobae a, mo nsa ntoa mmienu.* Or, *Toa na ɛpɛ na ahoma hyɛ ne kon.*
Literal translation: The elders present you with two bottles of drinks as their indication of welcoming you. Or, The bottle must like it that there is rope tied around its neck.

177

597

598

599

600

601

602

603

604

605

606

607

608

609

610

611

612

599. *YƐBƐDAN AGYA* - WE SHALL LEAVE EVERYTHING BEHIND

Symbol of the RELATIVE INSIGNIFICANCE OF MATERIAL WEALTH

From the expression: *Yɛbɛdan agya.* Or, *Onipa ne asɛm; wofrɛ sika a, sika nnye so, wofrɛ ntama a, ntama nnye so, onipa ne asɛm.*

Literal translation: We shall leave everything behind. Or, It is human being that counts; you call upon gold, it answers not; you call upon clothing, it answers not; it is human being that counts. Material things are not as important as the human being. Material wealth will be left behind when one dies. At the point of death it is only human being that will answer one's cry of desperation.

600-602. EBI TE YIE - SOME PEOPLE ARE BETTER SEATED

Symbol of SOCIAL CLASS, WEALTH, SOCIAL INEQUALITY, and EXPLOITATION

From the expression: *Ebi te yie ma ebi so nte yie koraa.* Or, *Nipa na ɔma nipa yɛ yie.* Also, *Obi akabɔ yɛ obi ahonya, obi amiadie yɛ obi nso nkwa, na obi ahohia ne obi ahotɔ.*

Literal translation: Some people are better seated, yet others are not. Or, The prosperity of one person depends on another person's poverty.

603. *GYE KƆDIDI* - TAKE THIS FOR SUBSISTENCE

Symbol of POVERTY, UNDERPRIVILEGED, and INDIGENCE

From the expression: *Ohia na ɛmaa adoee wee mako.* Or, *Gye kɔdidi ma ohia yɛ animguase.* Or, *Srɛsrɛ bi di nyɛ akorɔnobɔ.*

Literal translation: Poverty forces the monkey to eat pepper. Or, Take this for subsistence makes it a disgrace to be poor. Or, To beg here and there for something to eat does not constitute stealing.

604. ASETENA PA - GOOD LIVING

Symbol of CONSPICUOUS SPENDING, WEALTH, UPPER SOCIAL CLASS

From the expression: *Asetena pa yɛ awerɛfiri.* Or, *Ateyie yɛ awerɛfiri.*

Literal translation: Good living makes one forget one's humble beginnings. Good living makes one forget the inevitability of death for the poor as well as the rich.

605. VW - VW

Symbol of SOCIAL CLASS, STATUS, WEALTH, and PRESTIGE

606-607. BENZ - MERCEDES BENZ

Symbol of SOCIAL CLASS, STATUS, WEALTH, and PRESTIGE

From the expression: *Mehunuu wo na "woabenze."*

Literal translation: When I saw you, you were riding in a Mercedes Benz.

608-612. TV - TELEVISION

Symbol of TECHNOLOGICAL DEVELOPMENT, SOCIAL CLASS, and MASS COMMUNICATION

178

613

614

615

616

617

618

619

620

621

613-615. *MAKO NYINAA* - ALL THE PEPPERS

Symbol of UNEQUAL OPPORTUNITY, UNEVEN DEVELOPMENT

From the expression: *Mako nyinaa mpatu mmere.*

Literal translation: All the peppers on the same tree do not ripe simultaneously.

616. *MEDE ME SE ABƆ ADWE* - I HAVE CRACKED OPEN THE PALM NUT WITH MY TEETH

Symbol of EXPLOITATION, INJUSTICE,

From the expression: *Mede me se abɔ adwe ma obi abɛfa.* Or, *Mede me se na abɔ me ara m'adwe.*

Literal translation: I have cracked open the palm-nut with my bare teeth only for someone else to enjoy it. Or, I have cracked open my own palm nut.

This depicts the exploitative relationship in society where some people appropriate the fruits of the labor of others.

617. *AFIDIE* - HUNTING TRAP

Symbol of COOPERATION, STRATEGIC PLANNING, and DECOY

From the maxim: *Sɛ yɛnam baanu sum afidie a, yɛnam baanu na yɛhwɛ.* Or, *Anomaa nitefoɔ, afidie yi no a, ɛyi no ntɛntɛnoa.*

Literal translation: If two people set a hunting trap, it takes the two people to check it. Or, A cunning bird is always caught in the trap at the edge of a branch.

618. *MESO NANKA MENTUMI* - I CANNOT EVEN CARRY THE PUFF ADDER

Symbol of EXPLOITATION, BEING OVER-BURDENED WITH WORK

From the expression: *Meso nanka mentumi a, wose menkɔfa enini mmɔ kahyire.*

Literal translation: I cannot even carry the puff adder, yet you want me to use the python as the carrying pad.

The puff adder and the python are big and poisonous snakes. The python is heavier than the puff adder. Ordinarily, when the Akan carries a load on his head he uses a carrying pad a support. The carrying pad is much lighter than the load. This symbol depicts the exploitive nature the work one is being asked to undertake: not only is one to carry a very heavy and risky load, but one is to use a much heavier and riskier support system.

619-620. *ABETEƐ NTEMA* - PORTIONING ABETEƐ MEAL

Symbol of DISTRIBUTION OF RESOURCE, EQUITABLE DISTRIBUTION, and ECONOMIC JUSTICE

From the expression: *Yɛretete abeteɛ na ne kyɛ ara ne no.*

Literal translation: As we portion out the abeteɛ meal, that is its distribution.

621. *UAC NKANEA* - UAC LIGHTS (CHANDELIERS)

Symbol of PROSPERITY, ECONOMIC DOMINATION, and ECONOMIC (UNDER)DEVELOPMENT

From the expression: *UAC nkanea dwann mma yɛnhunu awam adwadifoɔ.* Or, *Bata bɔne yɛ animguase.*

Literal translation: The bright UAC lights make it difficult to expose the colluding merchants. Or, Bad trade is a disgrace.

The first street electric light in Kumasi was placed in front of the UAC store in the Adum section of the city. This made the store a very important landmark in the city. This ideograph depicts the ubiquituous presence and the dominant influence of the United Africa Group of Companies, (a subsidiary of the giant Unilever) in Ghana. The UAC presence in Ghana dates back to when Lever Brothers entered the West African market to buy slaves and palm oil. In the 1930s and 1940s UAC spearheaded a ring of European trading companies, Association of West African Merchants (AWAM), that controlled the market for imported items and farm produce, especially cocoa. The machinations of these companies gave rise to the word AWAM which has come to mean shady dealings and corruption in many Ghanaian languages.

622

623

624

625

626

627

628

629

630

631

632

622. *NNOMAA NE DUA* - BIRDS ON ATREE

Symbol of SOCIAL CLASS, CLASS CONSCIOUSNESS

From the maxim: *Nnomaa goro tipɛn tipɛn*. Also, *Dua pa so aba bere a, nnomaa nyinaa di bi.*

Literal translation: Only birds of the same species or class play together on the same tree.

623. WOBU KƆTƆ KWASEA A - WHEN YOU FOOL THE CRAB

Symbol of EXPLOITATION and UNFAIRNESS

From the proverb: *Wobu kɔtɔ kwasea a, Nyame hunu w'akyi.*

Literal translation: When you fool the crab, God sees your rear end.

624. *ASAAWA* - SWEET BERRY

Symbol of SWEETNESS, SWEET TASTE, PLEASURE, and HEDONISM

From the aphorism: *Ɛdɛ nka anomu.*

Literal translation: Sweetness does not last forever. That is, a thing of joy does not last forever.

625. *MENSO WO KƐNTƐN* - I DO NOT CARRY YOUR BASKET

Symbol of INDUSTRY, SELF-RELIANCE and ECONOMIC SELF-DETER-MINATION

From the expression: *Menso wo kɛntɛn.*

Literal translation: I do not carry your basket.

The symbol implies the economic self-determination of one, especially a woman.

Baskets are used to carry food items from the farm to the house, to store things and to decorate rooms. In the past, as part of the naming ceremony, the female child was momentarily covered with a basket to signal to her that she should grow up into an industrious woman whose responsibility would be to collect foodstuff from the farm, carry it home to prepare food for the husband and children.

626-627. *KOFORIDUA NHWIREN* - KOFORIDUA FLOW-ERS

Symbol of URBANIZATION, ECONOMIC PROSPERITY, and CONSPICU-OUS CONSUMPTION

From the expression: *Koforidua nhwiren, deɛ mede wo reyɔ!*

Literal translation: Koforidua flowers, what use do I have of you!

The ideograph stems from the conspicuous consumption by some rich people during the rapid urbanization of Koforidua following the success of the cocoa industry, and later the diamond mining industry in the Eastern Region of Ghana at the turn of the nineteeth century.

628-632. SENCHI BRIDGE - SENCHI BRIDGE

Symbol of ECONOMIC DEVELOPMENT

From the expression: *Ghana abue; onua tu kwan kɔhwɛ Senchi bridge.*

Literal translation: Ghana has progressed; brother, travel and see the Senchi bridge.

180

The following are some of the *adinkra* symbols that reflect various aspects of the Akan's views on knowledge and education:

633-648. *SANKƆFA* - GO BACK AND RETRIEVE

Symbol of WISDOM, KNOWLEDGE, and the PEOPLE'S HERITAGE

From the aphorism: *Sɛ wo werɛ fi na wosan kɔfa a, yɛnkyi.*

Literal translation: There is nothing wrong with learning from hindsight. The word *SANKƆFA* is derived from the words *SAN* (return), *KƆ* (go), *FA* (look, seek and take). This symbolizes the Akan's quest for knowledge with the implication that the quest is based on critical examination, and intelligent and patient investigation. The symbol is based on a mythical bird that flies forwards with its head turned backwards. This reflects the Akan belief that the past serves as a guide for planning the future, or the wisdom in learning from the past in building the future. The Akans believe that there must be movement with times but as the forward match proceeds, the gems must be picked from behind and carried forward on the match. In the Akan military system, this symbol signified the rearguard, the section on which the survival of the society and the defence of its heritage depended.

649

649. *NYANSA PƆ* - WISDOM KNOT

Symbol of CULTUAL HRITAGE, WISDOM, INTELLIGENCE, KNOWL-EDGE, and CRITICAL REASONING

From the proverb: *Nananom nyansa pɔ yɛsiane no ɔbanyansafoɔ.*

Literal translation: It takes the wise to untie the knot of knowledge bequeathed by one's heritage.

650   651

650-651. *HWEHWE MU DUA* or *ƆFAMFA* - MEASURING OR SEARCHING ROD

Symbol of CRITICAL EXAMINATION, EXCELLENCE, QUALITY, PERFECTION, KNOWLEDGE, and RATIONALITY

This is the ideogram for the quest for and love of knowledge. It depicts the Akan's abhorrence of imperfection. It implies that the outcome of research depends on an intelligent, patient and critical examination of evidence. Knowledge must be subjected to CRITICAL EXAMINATION.

From the aphorism: *Wɔse fa na woamfa a, worenhu mu. Wohwehwɛ mu a, na wohu mu; wopusu no a, na wote ne pampan.*

Literal translation: You miss the opportunity of knowing when you refuse to take it upon request. You know what it entails when you examine it critically. You know the smell only when you shake it. Knowledge must be subjected to critical enquiry.

652   653

654

652-654. *MATE MASIE* or *NTESIE* - I HAVE HEARD AND KEPT IT

Symbol of WISDOM, PRUDENCE, KNOWLEDGE, and LEARNING

From the aphorism: *Nyansa bunu mu ne mate masie.* Or, *Tete ka asom na ɛfiri kakyerɛ.*

Literal translation: In the depth of wisdom abounds knowledge and thoughtfulness. I consider and keep what I learn. Or, Preservation of a people's culture has its basis in oral tradition.

Knowledge is divine. To have a good ear and to retain everything heard from the master is a mark of excelence in learning. The symbol reflects the Akan's love of and quest for knowledge, and also respect for the wise person. It originates from the Akan belief that a people without knowledge of their history is like a tree without roots.

655   656

657   658

659

655-659. *NSAA* - HAND-WOVEN BLANKET

Symbol of EXCELLENCE, GENUINENESS, and AUTHENTICITY

From the aphorism: *Nea ɔnnim nsaa na ɔtɔ n'ago.*

Literal translation: He who cannot recognize the genuine *NSAA* (hand-woven blanket made from camel or horse hair), buys its fake. Or, the untutored accepts sophistry as science.

This symbol extols excellence and eschews satisfaction with mediocrity.

660   661

662

660-662. *KRAMO BƆNE* - QUACKERY (FAKE MUSLIM)

Symbol stressing the need for CRITICAL ENQUIRY, and WARNING AGAINST QUACKERY, SOPHISTRY, DECEPTION, and HYPOCRISY

From the expression: *Kramo bɔne amma yɛanhu kramo pa.*

Literal translation: The fake Muslim makes it difficult for the genuine one to be identified. The fake and the genuine look alike because of hypocrisy. Or, to the uneducated sophistry is science.

663   664

663-664. *KRAMO BƆNE* - QUACKERY (FAKE MUSLIM)

Symbol stressing the need for CRITICAL ENQUIRY, and WARNING AGAINST QUACKERY, SOPHISTRY, DECEPTION, and HYPOCRISY

From the expression: *Kramo bɔne amma yɛanhu kramo pa.*

Literal translation: The fake Muslim makes it difficult for the genuine one to be identified. The fake and the genuine look alike because of hypocrisy. Or, to the uneducated sophistry is science.

665   666

665-666. *KUNTANKANTAN* - INFLATED PRIDE or EGO-CENTRICISM

Symbol of WARNING AGAINST INFLATED PRIDE, EGOCENTRICISM, ETHNOCENTRICISM, and ARROGANCE

From the aphorism: *Nea ɔye no ho sɛ menim menim, nnim hwee.*

Literal translation: He who knows all, knows nothing.

The view encoded by this symbol is similar to the view of a specialist as one who knows more and more about less and less, until he knows everything about nothing. This symbol serves as warning against inflated pride, narrow mindedness and arrogance. It urges people to be humble and open-minded.

667

667. *NEA ƆNNIM NO SUA A, OHU* - HE WHO DOES NOT KNOW CAN KNOW FROM LEARNING

Symbol of KNOWLEDGE, LIFE-LONG EDUCATION, and CONTINUED QUEST FOR KNOWLEDGE

From the expression: *Nea ɔnnim no sua a, ɔhu; nea ɔdwen sɛ ɔnim dodo no, sɛ ɔgyae sua a, ketewa no a ɔnim no koraa firi ne nsa.*

Literal translation: He who does not know can know from learning; he who thinks he knows and ceases to continue to learn will stagnate.

To grow is to live, to stagnate is to die. Only as one continues to to search for wisdom will one grow wiser. Education is a life-long process.

668   669

668-669. *DAME DAME* - CHECKERS

Symbol of STRATEGIC PLANNING, ADROITNESS, DEXTERITY, INTELLIGENCE, CRITICAL THINKING, and GAMESMANSHIP

From the aphorism: *Kwasea ani te a, na agorɔ agu.* Or, *Mepɛ kwasea bi ne no ato dame.*

Literal translation: When the fool learns to understand the game, the game ends. Or, I will like to play a game of checkers with some fool.

From the board game of checkers. The stool of the Gyaman King, Kofi Adinkra is believed to be signified by this symbol. This symbolizes that knowledge is accessible even to the fool.

670

670. *NƆKORɛ* - TRUTH

Symbol of VALIDITY, AUTHENTICITY, and VERACITY

From the aphorism: *Nɔkorɛ nsuma.* Or, *Nkontompo ama nokorɛ boɔ ayɛ den.* Or, *Nokorɛ mu nni abra.*

Literal translation: Truth does not hide. Or, Hypocrisy makes truth have a high price. Or, There is no contradiction in truth.

671

responsible for keeping the state accounts. The Gyaasehene also had a functionary detailed to check off the months by dropping a cowrie shell (*serewa* or *sedeɛ* - # 547-551) into a bag each new moon. The calendar kept by this functionary (timekeeper) was based on *adaduanan* (forty days) or six weeks. The month was

672

672. *GYINA PINTINN* - STAND FIRM

Symbol of BEING PRINCIPLED, DISCIPLINE, RESOLUTENESS, and UNDAUNTEDNESS

From the expression: *Gyina pintinn.*

Literal translation: Stand firm; be principled.

673

673. *DWENE HWɛ KAN* - AIM HIGH

Symbol of FORETHOUGHT, PLANNING AHEAD,

From the aphorism: *Dwene hwɛ kan.*

Literal translation: Aim high or think ahead.

674

675

674-675. *NKYƐMU* - DIVISIONS

Symbol of FRACTIONAL PARTS, PRECISION, SKILL, DEXTERITY, INTELLIGENCE, and ADROITNESS

This represents the rectangular divisions made with a wooden comb or a long ruler on the cloth before printing with the other stamps of adinkra symbols.

676

676. *NSƐNEƐ* - SCALES

Symbol of MEASUREMENT, BALANCE, PRECISION, and QUANTIFICATION, WEALTH, FRUGALITY, COMMERCE and TRADE

From the expression: *Wodi wo sika a, wose wo nsɛnea mu nyɛ den.*

Literal translation: When one is being wasteful of one's money one tends to blame it on some imagined defect in one's scale.

The scale was used to weigh gold dust which served as money. Special weights (*mmramoɔ*) were designed and used as counterweights in measuring the gold dust. One who tended to spend one's gold dust on frivolities was considered a spendthrift, but such a person usually tended to blame his/her extravagance on some perceived defect in the scales.

677

677. *NIPA MFƆN KWA* - ONE DOES NOT GROW LEAN WITHOUT A CAUSE

Symbol of CAUSE AND EFFECT, CAUSALITY, and PRINCIPLE OF DETERMINISM

From the expression: *Nipa mfɔn kwa. Also, Sɛ anantuo kɔsene srɛ a, na yadeɛ wɔmu.*

Literal translation: One does not grow lean without a cause. Also, If the calf grows bigger than the thigh, then that must be the sign of illness.

678

known as bosome, and *adaduanan mmienu* (two forty days) was the same as abosome mmiɛnsa (three months). The first new moon after the Odwira festival marked the beginning of the new year (*afe foforɔ*).

The *dapɛn* or *nnawɔtwe* system of counting days reflects the inclusive counting in some aspects of Akan numbering system which includes integers, fractions and operations like addition, subtraction, multiplication and division. Fractional ideas are expressed by words such as *fa* or *abunu* (half), *abusa* (third), *abunum* (fifth), and *nkotuku ano* (percentage). An example of symbols used to indicate Akan people's views about number concepts include nnamfo pa baanu (two good friends - # 337), ti korɔ nkɔ agyina (one head does not constitute a council - # 325-326), and *nkrɔn* (nine - # 702-

679

680

680. *ƆBONSAM A WONIM NO* - THE DEVIL YOU KNOW

Symbol of AWARENESS

From the expression: *Bonsam a wonim no yie sene soro bɔfoɔ a wonni no.*

Literal translation: The devil you know is better than the angel you do not know.

681

681. DABAN - A MEASURE or SURETY or IRON BAR

Symbol of MEASUREMENT, GUARANTEE, IRON SMELTING TECHNOLOGY

From the expression: *Daban da hɔ a, ɛda asɛm so. Or, Daban da aburokyire a, ɔtomfoɔ dea.*

Literal translation: A promisory note or surety has to be honored. Or, The blacksmith owns the iron ore that is discovered abroad.

682

683

682-683. *WODU NKWANTA A* - WHEN YOU REACH THE INTERSECTION

Symbol of SIGNAL, MARK, BEACON, INDICATION, and WARNING

From the expression: *Wodu nkwanta a, gu me ahahan.*

Literal translation: When you reach the intersection (or crossroads) leave me an indication or sign.

684

684. *FRANKAA* - FLAG

Symbol of WARNING, SIGN, IDENTIFICATION

From the expression: *Asɛm kɛseɛ reba a, frankaa nsi so.*

Literal translation: Crises occur without prior warnings.

685

685. *MMERƐ DANE* - TIME CHANGES

Symbol of CHANGE, DYNAMICS OF LIFE, DIRECTION, and MOTION

From the expression: *Mmerɛ dane.*

Literal translation: Time changes.

686

686. *MMERƐ TU SƐ ANOMAA* - TIME FLIES LIKE A BIRD

Symbol of MOTION, and WARNING AGAINST PROCRASTINATION

From the maxim: *Mmerɛ tu sɛ anomaa na wobɛyɛ biribi a, yɛ no prɛko.*

Literal translation: Time flies like a bird; do what you have to do now.

687   688

689   690

687-691. *AFE BI YƐ ASIANE* - A YEAR OF BAD LUCK

Symbol of MISFORTUNE, BAD LUCK, INAUSPICIOUS YEAR

From the expression: *Afe bi yɛ asiane.*

Literal translation: Some years are inauspicious or unlucky.

691

692

693. *DA BI ME NSOROMMA BƐPUE* - MY STAR WILL SHINE ONE DAY

Symbol of HOPE, TRUST, EXPECTATION,

From the expression: *Da bi me nsoromma bɛpue.*

Literal translation: My star will shine one day.

693

694-696. *AKOKƆ* - FOWL (ROOSTER)

Symbol of TIME, and GENDER DIVISION OF LABOR

From the expression: *Akokɔbedeɛ nim adekyeeɛ nso ɔtie onini ano.* Also, *Adekyeeɛ nnyina akokɔbɔneeɛ so; sɛ akokɔ bɛbɔn o, sɛ ɔremmɔn o, adeɛ bɛkye.*

Literal translation: A hen could herself discern the break of the day yet she relies on the cock to announce it. Also, Night and day are determined by nature; it is not cockcrow that changes night to day; whether the cock crows or not night will turn into day.

694   695

696

697. *NNA NYINAA NSƐ* - ALL DAYS ARE NOT EQUAL

Symbol of INEQUALITY, UNEQUAL OPPORTUNITY

From the expression: *Nna nyinaa nsɛ.*

Literal translation: All days are not equal.

697

185

698   699

698-699.   KYƐMFERƐ - POTSHERD (BROKEN POT)

Symbol of TIME, SERVICE, KEEPSAKE, ANTIQUITY, RARITY, and HEIR-LOOM. Also EXPLOITATION

From the expression: *Kyɛmferɛ se ɔdaa hɔ akyɛ, na onipa a ɔnwenee no nso nyɛ dɛn? Or, Obi afa me kyɛmferɛ na ɔkye mu nkateɛ.*

Literal translation: The potsherd claims it is old, what about the potter who moulded it? Or, Someone is using my potsherd to roast his/her groundnuts (peanuts).

Kyɛmferɛ is usually used for oil lamp or for roasting peanuts and corn.

700

700.   ABCD - THE ALPHABETS

Symbol of BEING LETTERED or BEING KNOWLEDGEABLE

From the aphorism: *Sukuu nko na nyansa so nko.*

Literal translation: Knowledge can be independently gained outside the schooling process.

701

701.   AHAHAN - LEAVES

Symbol of KNOWLEDGE, MARK OF DISTINCTION

From the expression: *Yɛnkɔte aduro a, ene ahahan. Or, Wodu nkwanta a gu me ahahan.*

Literal translation: One does not go and pluck any leaf and call it medicinal. No ordinary leaf is medicinal. Or, When you reach the intersection (or crossroads) leave me an indication or sign.

It takes skill and knowledge to determine the medicinal qualities of plants.

702

both numerical and geometrical, was perfected by weavers, carvers, goldsmiths and crafts people. The use of patterns was developed in housing construction and architecture, and for use in games like

703

703). *Dame dame* (# 668-669), *ɔware, ampe* and other games and quizzes provided opportunities for children to learn to count and to portray their mathematical abilities.

The ability to observe and reproduce and utilize patterns,

704   705

704-706.   *NSƐNSAN - LINES*

Symbol of NUMBERING and ACCOUNTING

Lines are drawn with *dua afe* or *nsɛnsan nnua* on the cloth before it is printed with various symbols.The *dua afe* (wooden combs) or nsɛnsan nnua have two, four, six, eight, or ten "teeth." The numbers of lines made by the *dua afe* and *nsɛnsan nnua* have symbolic meanings themselves. San dan ho (mark on the wall), a system of credit in which lines of various colors are utilized is used by entrepreneurs to extend credit to customers.

706

707

707.   *ASANTUROFIE ANOMAA* - THE BIRD OF DILEMMA (THE LONG-TAILED NIGHTJAR)

Symbol of DILEMMA, BEING IN A QUANDARY, IMPASSE, and PREDICAMENT

From the aphorism: *Asantrofie anomaa, wofa no a, woafa mmusuo, wogyae no nso a, woagyae siadeɛ.*

Literal translation: The bird of dilemma, when you take it you incur jeopardy, when you leave you will miss a golden opportunity.

708

708.   *ETIRE* - HUMAN HEAD (MIND)

Symbol of INDETERMINISM, FREE WILL and UNPREDICTABILITY

From the maxim: *Etire nyɛ borɔferɛ na yɛapae mu ahwɛ dea wɔ mu.*

Literal translation: The human head (mind) is not like the papaya fruit to be split open to determine its content.

709. *MEWƆ HA* - I AM HERE
Symbol of PRESENCE, DEPORTMENT, and ALERTNESS
From the expression: *Mewɔ ha.*
Literal translation: I am here.

710. ABURUBURO KOSUA - DOVE'S EGG
Symbol of DESTINY, FATE, and DETERMINISM
From the aphorism: *Aburuburo kosua, adeɛ a ɛbɛyɛ yie nsɛe da.*
Literal translation: Dove's egg, what has been destined to prosper can never be destroyed.

711. *KWADU HONO* - BANANA PEEL
Symbol of PROOF, TESTIMONY and EVIDENCE
From the maxim: *Da bi asɛm nti na yɛdi kwadu a yɛgya ne hono.*
Literal translation: When we eat banana we leave its peel to be used as evidence.

712. *WOFORO DUA PA A* - WHEN YOU CLIMB A GOOD TREE
Symbol of SUPPORT, COOPERATION, and ENCOURAGEMENT
From the maxim: *Woforo dua pa a, na yɛpia wo.*
Literal translation: When you climb a good tree, you are given a push.
When you undertake a good cause, you are given support and encouragement.

713. *SƐ NANTUO KƆSENE SERƐ A* - IF THE CALF IS BIGGER THAN THE THIGH
Symbol of CAUSALITY, SKEPTICISM
From the proverb: *Sɛ nantuo kɔsene serɛ a, na yadeɛ wɔ mu.*
Literal translation: If the calf is bigger than the thigh, then it is diseased.

714. *SƐ ANTIE YƐ MMUSUO* - DISOBEDIENCE CAN BE DISASTROUS
Symbol of WARNING AGAINST DISOBEDIENCE, RESPECT , OBEDIENCE and DISASTER
From the proverb: *Se antie yɛ mmusuo.*
Literal translation: Disobedience can have disastrous results.

715. *ANANSE ANTƆN KASA* - THE SPIDER DID NOT SELL SPEECH
Symbol of FREEDOM OF EXPRESSION, FREEDOM OF SPEECH and HUMAN RIGHT
From the adage: *Ananse antɔn kasa.*
Literal translation: The spider did not sell speech.
Ananse (spider) in Akan folktales realized that speech and wisdom are accessible to all people. Speech cannot be appropriated as the property of one person as Ananse sought to do with wisdom.

716. *OSOHOR* - OSTRICH
Symbol of SEARCHING, INQUIRY and DISCOVERY

717-718. *AHINANSA* - TRIANGLE
Symbol of the PRIDE OF STATE and UNIVERSE
The triangle represents God as the ruler of the universe which is a continuum of the sky *(ewimu)*, the earth *(asase)* and the underworld of spiritual beings *(asamando)*. The symbol also represents *adaeboɔ* - the pendant worn by the king.

719. *NKABOM* - UNITY
Symbol of UNITY, UNITED ACTION and COOPERATION
From the aphorism: *Nkabom te sɛ praeɛ a yɛaka abɔ mu; wo bu mu a ɛmmu.*
Literal translation: Unity is like that has been bound togethr; it cannot be broken easily.

187

BIBLIOGRAPHY

Abraham, W. E. (1962). *The mind of Africa.* Chicago: University of Chicago Press.

Ackah, C. A. (1988). *Akan ethics.* Accra: Ghana Universities Press.

Adjaye, Joseph K. (1994). Editor. *Time in the black experience.* Westport, CT: Greenwood Press.

_____. (1984). *Diplomacy and diplomats in nineteenth century Asante.* Lanham, MD: University Press of America.

Agbenaza, E. (n.d.). *The Ewe Adanudo.* Unpublished B.A. Thesis, Arts Faculty Library, University of Science and Technology, Kumasi, Ghana.

Aggrey, J. E. K. (1992). *ebɔbɔ bra dɛn 1.* Accra: Bureau of Ghana Languages.

_____. (1978). *Asafo.* Tema: Ghana Publishing Corporation.

_____. (1977). *Ebisaa na abrɪme.* Accra: Bureau of Ghana Languages.

Agyeman-Duah, J. (n.d.). *Ashanti stool histories.* Accra: Institute of African Studies, University of Ghana.

_____. 1962. *Ceremonies of enstoolment of Otumfuo Asantehene. Ashanti Stool Histories, Volume 2, Series No. 33.* Accra: Institute of African Studies, University of Ghana.

Aidoo, Agnes. A. (1981). Asante queen mothers in government and politics in the nineteenth century. In Filomena Steady (Editor). *The black woman cross_culturally.* Cambridge, Mass.: Schenckman.

_____. (1977). Order and conflict in the Asante Empire: A study in interest group relations. *African Studies Review,* 20(1): 1-36.

Aidoo, Thomas Akwasi (1983). Ghana: Social class, the December coup, and the prospects for socialism. *Contemporary Marxism,* 6: 142-159.

Akoto, Nana Baafuor Osei. (1992). *Struggle against dictatorship.* Kumasi: Payless Printing Press.

Akuffo, B. S. (1976). *Ahenfie adesua.* Accra: Ghana Publishing Corporation.

Allman, Jean Marie (1990). The youngmen and the porcupine: Class, nationalism and Asante's struggle for self_determination, 1954-57. *Journal of African History,* 31: 263-279.

Alpern, Stanley B. (1995). What Africans got for their slaves: A master list of European trade goods. *History in Africa,* 22: 5-43.

Aning, B. A. (1975). *Nnwonkoro.* Accra: Ghana Publishing Corporation.

Antiri, Janet Adwoa (1974). Akan combs. *African Arts,* 8(1): 32-35

Antubam, Kofi (1963). *Ghana's heritage of culture.* Leipzig: Kehler and Amelang.

_____. (1961). *Ghana art and crafts.* Accra: Ghana Publishing Corporation.

Appiah, Peggy (1979). Akan symbolism. *African Arts,* 13(1): 64-67.

Arhin, Kwame (1990). Trade, accumulation, and the state in Asante in the nineteenth century. *Africa,* 60(4): 524-537.

_____. (1987). Savanna contributions to the Asante political economy. In Enid Schildkrout (Editor). *The Golden Stool: Studies of the Asante center and periphery.* New York: American Museum of Natural History.

_____. (1986). A note on the Asante akonkofo: A non-literate sub-elite, 1900-1930. *Africa,* 56(1): 25-31.

_____. (1983a). Rank and class among the Asante and Fante in the nineteenth century. Africa, 53(1): 2-22.

_____. (1983b). The political and military roles of Akan women. In C. Oppong (editor). *Female and male in West Africa.* London: George Unwin and Allen.

_____. (1968). Status differentiation in Ashanti in the niniteenth century: A preliminary study. *Research Review,* 4: 34_52.

_____. (1967a). The financing of Ashanti expansion, 1700-1820. *Africa,* 37: 283-291.

_____. (1967b). The structure of Greater Ashanti (1700-1824). *Journal of African History,* 8: 65-86.

Aronson, Lisa (1992). The language of West African textiles. *African Arts,* 25 (3): 36-40, 100.

Arthur, G. F. Kojo. (1994). Cloth as metaphor: Some aspects of the Akan philosophy as encoded in the adinkra cloth. Paper presented at the Annual Meeting of the African Studies Association, Toronto, Canada.

Asante, M. K. (1992). *Kemet, Afrocentricity and knowledge.* Trenton, N.J.: Africa World Press.

Astley, P. (1745). *A new general collection of voyages and travels, Volumes II & III.* London: Oxford University Press cited in Fynn (1971).

Balmer, W. T. (1969). *A history of the Akan peoples of the G__ Coast.* New York: Negro University Press.

Bannerman, J. Yedu (1974). *Mfantse-Akan mbɛbusɛm nkyerɛkyerɛmu.* Tema: Hacquason Press.

Bellis, J. O. (1972). *Archaeology and the culture history of the Akan of Ghana, a case study.* Doctoral dissertation, Indiana University, Bloomington, Indiana.

Bledsoe, C. and K. Robey. (1986). Arabic literacy and secrecy among the Mende of Sierra Leone. *Man,* 21: 202-226.

Boahen, A. Adu (1977). Ghana before the coming of Europeans. *Ghana Social Science Journal,* 4(2): 93-106.

_____. (1972). Prempeh I in exile. *Institute of African Studies Research Review*, 8(3): 3_20.

_____. (1966). The origins of the Akan. *Ghana Notes and Queries*, 9: 3_10.

Borgatti, Jean. (1983). *Cloth as metaphor: Nigerian textiles from the Museum of Cultural History*. Los Angeles: Museum of Cultural History.

Bosman, W. (1705). *A new and accurate description of the coast of Guinea*. London cited in T. Garrard (1980). *Akan weights and the gold trade*. London: Longman.

Bowdich, T. E. (1819). *Mission from Cape Coast to Ashantee*. London: John Murray.

Bravmann, R. (1974). *Islam and tribal art in West Africa*. London: Cambridge University Press.

_____. (1968). The state sword _ A pre_Ashanti tradition. *Ghana Notes and Queries*, 10: 1_4.

Brempong, Owusu (1984). *Akan highlife in Ghana: Songs of cultural transition*. Doctoral dissertation, Indiana University, Bloomington, IN.

Britwum, K. A. (1974). Kwadwo Adinkra of Gyaman: A study of the relations between the Brong Kingdom of Gyaaman and Asante from c.1800-1818. *Transactions of the Historical Society of Ghana*, 15(2): 229_239.

Busia, K. A. (1954). The Ashanti of the Gold Coast. In Daryll Forde (Editor). *African worlds: Studies in the cosmological ideas and social values of African people*. London: Oxford University Press.

_____. (1951). *The position of the chief in the modern political system of Ashanti*. London: Oxford University Press.

Charon, Joel (1985). *Symbolic interaction: An introduction, and interpretation, an integration*. 2nd Edition. Englewood Cliffs, NJ: Prentice Hall.

Christian, Angela (1976). *Adinkra oration*. Accra: Catholic Press.

Chukwukere, I. (1982). Agnatic and uterine relations among the Fante: Male/female dualism. *Africa*, 52(1): 61_68.

_____. 1978. Akan theory of conception _ are the Fante really aberrabt? *Africa*, 48(2): 135_147.

Cohen, Abner (1979). Political symbolism. *Annual Review of Anthropology*, 8: 87_113.

Cole, H. M. and D. Ross (1977). *The arts of Ghana*. Los Angeles: UCLA.

Coulmas, Florian (1996). *The Blackwell encyclopedia of writing systems*. Oxford: Blackwell Publishers.

Cruickshank, B. (1853). *Eighteen years on the Gold Coast of Africa*. 2 Volumes. (Reprinted 1966, London: Frank Cass and Co.

Daaku, K. Y. (1970). *Denkyira*. UNESCO Research Project on Oral Traditions, No. 2. Niamey, Niger: OAU.

Danquah, J. B. (1944). *The Akan doctrine of God*. London: Lutterworth Press.

Dantzig, Albert van (1980). *Forts and castles of Ghana*. Accra: Sedco Publishing.

Datta, Ansu (1972). The Fante asafo: A re-examination. *Africa*, 42(4): 305-315.

Davis, Fred (1992). *Fashion, culture, and identity*. Chicago: University of Chicago Press.

de Saussure, Ferdinand (1966). *Course in general linguistics*. New York: McGraw_Hill.

Dickson, K. B. (1971). *A historical geography of Ghana*. Cambridge: Cambridge University Press.

Dolphyne, Florence Abena and Kropp-Dakubu, M. E. (1988). The Volta-Comoe languages. In M. E. Kropp_Dakubu, editor. *The Languages of Ghana*. London: KPI, Ltd.

Domowitz, Susan (1992). Wearing proverbs: Anyi names for printed factory cloth. *African Arts*, 25(3): 82_87, 104.

Dseagu, S. A. (1976). Proverbs and folktales of Ghana: Their form and uses. In J. M. Asimeng (Editor). *Traditional life, culture and literature in Ghana*. New York: Conch Magazine Limited.

Dunn, J. S. (1960). Fante star lore. *Nigerian Field*, 25(2): 52-64.

Dupuis, J. (1824). *Journal of a residence in Ashantee*. London

Dzobo, N. K. (1992a). African symbols and proverbs as source of knowledge and truth. In Kwasi Wiredu and Kwame Gyekye (editors). *Person and community: Ghanaian philosophical studies, I*. Washington, D.C.: Council for Research in Values and Philosophy.

_____. (1992b). Values in a changing society, man, ancestors and God. In Kwasi Wiredu and Kwame Gyekye (editors). *Person and community: Ghanaian philosophical studies, I*. Washington, D.C.: Council for Research in Values and Philosophy.

Edelman, Murray (1988). *Constructing the political spectacle*. Chicago: University of Chicago Press.

_____. (1971). *Politics as symbolic action*. Chicago: Markham Publishing.

_____. (1964). *Symbolic uses of politics*. Urbana, Illinois: University of Illinois Press.

Efa, Edwin (1968, 1944). *Forosie*. 11th Edition. Cape Coast: Methodist Book Depot.

Elder, Charles and Roger Cobb (1983). *The political uses of symbols*. New York: Longman.

Ellis, A. B. (1964). *The Tshi_speaking peoples of the Gold Coast of West Africa: Their religion, manners, customs, laws, language, etc*. Chicago: Benin Press.

_____. (1969). *A history of the Gold Coast of West Africa*. New York: Negro University Press.

Ephrim-Donkor, Anthony S. (1994). *African personality and spirituality: The Akanfo quest for perfection and immortality.* Doctoral dissertation, Emory University, Atlanta, GA.

Erlich, Martha J. (1981). *A catalogue of Ashanti art taken from Kumasi in the Anglo-Ashanti War of 1874.* Doctoral dissertation, Indiana University, Bloomington, Indiana.

Folomkina, S. And H. Weiser (1963). *The learner's English-Russian dictionary.* Cambridge, Mass.: MIT Press.

Fromkin, V. and R. Rodman (1978). *An introduction to language,* 2nd Edition. New York: Holt, Rinehart and Winston.

Fortes, Meyer (1950). Kinship and marriage among the Ashanti. In A. R. Radcliffe-Brown and D. Forde (Editors). *African systems of kinship and marriage.* London: Oxford University Press.

Fortes, M. and E. E. Evans_Pritchard. (1967). Eds. *African political systems.* New York: KPI.

Fraenkel, Gerd (1965). *Writing Systems.* Boston: Ginn and Company.

Fraser, Douglas (1972). The symbols of Ashanti kingship. In D. Fraser and H. Cole (Editors). *African art and leadership.* Madison: University of Wisconsin Press.

_____. and H. Cole (1972). Editors. *African art and leadership.* Madison: University of Wisconsin Press.

Frutiger, Adrian (1991). *Signs and symbols: Their design and meaning.* London: Studio Editions.

Fynn, J. K. (1971). *Asante and its neighbours, 1700-1807.* London: Longman.

Gallant, Thomas W. (1994). Turning the horns: Cultural metaphors, material conditions, and the peasant language of resistance in Ionian Islands (Greece) during the nineteenth century. *Society for Comparative Study of Society and History,* 36(4): 702-719.

Garrard, T. F. (1980). *Akan weights and the gold trade.* London: Longman.

Gerrard, A. (1981). African language literatures: An introduction to the literary history of sub-Saharan Africa. Harlow, Essex, England: Longman.

Gilfoy, Peggy S. (1987). *Patterns of life: West African strip_weaving traditions.* Washington, D. C.: National Museum of African Art.

Glover, Ablade (1971). *Adinkra symbolism* (a chart). Accra: Liberty Press.

Goody, J. (1986). *The logic of writing and the organization of society.* Cambridge: Cambridge University Press

_____. (1977). *The domestication of the savage mind.* Cambridge: Cambridge University Press.

Gott, Edith S. (1994). *In celebration of the female: Dress, aesthetics, and identity in contemporary Asante.* Doctoral dissertation, Indiana University, Bloomington, IN.

Gyekye, Kwame (1992). The Akan concept of a person. *International Philosophical Quarterly,* 18(3): 277_287.

_____. (1987). *An essay on African philosophical thought: The Akan conceptual scheme.* New York: Cambridge University Press.

Hagan, George P. (1970). A note on Akan colour symbolism. *Research Review,* 7(1): 8_13.

_____. (1971). Ashanti bureaucracy: A study of the growth of centralized administration in Ashanti from the time of Osei Tutu to the time of Osei Tutu Kwamina Esibe Bonsu. *Transactions of the Historical Society of Ghana,* 12: 43_62.

Hau, Kathleen (1973). Pre_Islamic writing in West,. *Bulletin del'IFAN,* 35(Series b, 1): 1_45.

_____. (1967). The ancient writing of Southern Nigeria. *Bulletin del'IFAN,* 29(Series b, 1_2): 150_190.

_____. (1964). A royal title on a palace tusk from Benin (Southern Nigeria). *Bulletin del'IFAN,* 26(Seriesb, 1_2): 21_39.

_____. (1961). Obɛri Okaimɛ script, texts, and counting system. *Bulletin del'IFAN,* 23(1_2): 291_308.

_____. (1959). Evidence of the use of pre_Portuguese written characters by the Bini? *Bulletin del'IFAN,* 21: 109_154.

Hayward, Fred M. And Ahmed R. Dumbuya (1984). Political legitimacy, political symbols, and national leadership in West Africa. *Journal of Modern African Studies,* 21(4): 645_671.

Henige, David (1975). Akan stool succession under colonial rule _ continuity or change? *Journal of African History,* 16(2): 285-301.

Hopkins, A. G. (1973). *An economic history of West Africa.* New York: Columbia University Press.

Howard, Rhonda (1978). *Colonialism and underdevelopment in Ghana.* New York: African Publishing Company.

Hunter, David E. And Philip Whitten (1976). Editors. *Encyclopedia of Anthropology.* New York: Harper & Row.

Kay, G. B. (1972). *The political economy of colonialism in Ghana: A collection of documents and statistics, 1900–1960.* Cambridge: Cambridge University Press.

Kayper-Mensah, A. W. (1976). *Sankofa: Adinkra poems.* Accra: Ghana Publishing Corporation.

Kent, Kate (1971). *Introducing West African cloth.* Denver: Denver Museum of Natural History.

Kiyaga_Mulindwa, D. (1980). The "Akan" Problem. *Current Anthropology,* 21(4): 503506.

Kyerematen, A. A. Y. (1964). *Panoply of Ghana: Ornamental art in Ghanaian tradition and culture.* New York: Praeger.

_____. (n.d.). *Kingship and ceremony in Ashanti.* Kumasi: UST Press.

_____. (1971). Interstate boundary litigation in Ashanti. In *African Social Research Documents,* Volume 14.

La Torre, Joseph R. (1978). *Wealth surpasses everything*. Doctoral dissertation, University of California, Berkeley, CA.

Laluah, Aquah (1960). The serving girl. In Langston Hughes (editor). *An African treasury*. New York: Pyramid Books.

Lamb, Venice (1975). *West African weaving*. London: Duckworth.

Lewin, Thomas J. (1978). *Asante before the British: The Prempean years, 1875_1900*. Lawrence, KS: The Regents Press of Kansas.

Liberman, I. Y. and A. M. Liberman (1992). Whole language vs code emphasis. In P. B. Gough, L. C, Ehri and R. Treiman (Editors). *Reading acquisition*. Hillsdale, NJ: Erlbaum.

Lystad, Robert A. (1958). *The Ashanti: A proud people*. New York: Greenwood Press.

Manuh, Takyiwaa. (1988). The Asantehemaa's court and its jurisdiction over women: A study in legal pluralism. *Research Review* (NS), 4(2): 150-166.

Mason, William A. (1928). *A history of the art of writing*. New York: McMillan Company.

Mato, Daniel (1986). *Clothed in symbols – the art of Adinkra among the Akan of Ghana*. Doctoral dissertation, Department of Fine Arts, Indiana University, Bloomington, IN.

McCaskie, T. C. (1989). Death and the Asantehene: A historical meditation. *Journal of African History*, 30: 417-444.

_____. (1986). Komfo Anokye of Asante: The meaning, history and philosophy in an African society. *Journal of African History*, 27: 315-339.

_____. (1984). Ahyiamu – "a place of meeting": An essay on process and event in the history of the Asante state. *Journal of African History*, 25(2): 169-188.

_____. (1983). Accumulation, wealth and belief in Asante history, I: To the close of the nineteenth century. *Africa*, 53(1): 23-43.

_____. (1981). State and society, marriage and adultery: Some considerations towards a social history of pre_colonial Asante. *Journal of African History*, 22: 477-494.

McGuire, Harriet C. (1980). Woyo pot lids, *African Arts*, 13(2): 54-56.

McLeod, M. D. (1981). *The Asante*. London: British Museum.

_____. (1976). Verbal elements in West African art. *Quaderni Poro*, 1: 85-102.

McWilliam, H. O. A. and M. A. Kwamena-Poh (1978). *The development of education in Ghana*. London: Longman.

Mensah, J. E. (1992). *Asantesεm ne mmεbusεm bi*. Kumasi, Ghana: Catholic Press.

Menzel, B. (1972). *Textile aus Westafrika*, Vols. I, II, III. Berlin: Museum fur Volkerkunde.

Meyerowitz, Eva L. R. (1962). *At the court of an African king*. London: Faber and Faber.

_____. (1952). *The Akan traditions of origin*. London: Faber and Faber.

_____. (1951). *The sacred state of the Akan*. London: Faber & Faber.

Minkus, Helaine K. (1980). The concept of spirit in Akwapim Akan philosophy. *Africa*, 50(2): 182–192.

Morgan, G., Frost, P. J. and Pondy, L. R. (1983). Organizational symbolism. In L. R. Pondy, P. J. Frost, G. Morgan, and C. T. Dandridge (Editors). *Organizational symbolism*. Greenwich, CT: JAI Press.

Morris, Van Cleve and Young Pai (1993). *Philosophy and the American school: An introduction to the philosophy of education*, 2nd Edition. Lanham, MD.: University Press of America.

National Museum of African Art. (1997). *Adinkra: The cloth that speaks*. Washington, D.C.: National Museum of African Art.

Niangoran-Bouah, G. (1984). *L'univers Akan des poids a peser l'or*, Volumes I, II, & III. Abidjan, Cote d'Ivoire: Les Nouvelles Editions Africaines.

Nketia, J. H. (1974). *Ayan*. Accra: Ghana Publishing Corporation.

_____. (1969). *Funeral dirges of the Akan people*. New York: Negro Universities Press.

Obeng, Ernest E. (1988). *Ancient Ashanti chieftancy*. Tema: Ghana Publishing Corporation.

Obeng, J. Pashington (1995). *Asante women dancers: Architects of power realignment in Corpus Christi*. Boston: African Studies Center, Boston University.

_____. (1991). *Asante Catholicism: Ritual communicatio of the Catholic faith among the Akan of Ghana*. Doctoral dissertation, Boston University.

Ofori-Ansah, Kwaku (1978). *Symbols of adinkra cloth* (a chart). Washington, D.C.: Department of Art, Howard University.

_____. (1993). *Symbols of adinkra cloth* (a chart).

Opoku, Kofi Asare (1976). The destiny of man in Akan traditional religious thought. In J. M. Asimeng (Editor). *Traditional life, culture and literature in Ghana*. New York: Conch Magazine Limited.

_____. (1978). *West African traditional religion*. Accra: FEP International.

Oppong, Christine (1973). *Growing up in Dagbon*. Accra: Ghana Publishing Corporation.

Oroge, E. A. A. (1974). The rise and fall of the Asante. *Tarikh* 5(1): 31-45.

Ott, Albert (1968). Akan gold weights. *Transactions of the Historical Society of Ghana*, 9: 17-42.

Ott, J. Steven (1989). *The organizational culture perspective*. Chicago: Dorsey Press.

Owusu-Ansah, Nana J. V. (1992). *New versions of the traditional motifs*. Kumasi: deGraft Graphics and Publications.

Patton, Sharon (1984). The Asante umbrella. *African Arts*, 7(4): 64-73, 93-94.

_____. (1980). *The Asante stool*. Doctoral dissertation, Northwestern University, Evanston, Illinois.

_____. (1979). The stool and Asante chieftancy. *African Arts*, 13(1): 74-77, 98.

Picton, John M. (1979). *African textiles*. London: British Museum.

_____. (1992). Tradition, technology, and lurex: Some comments on textile history and design in West Africa. In National Museum of African Art. *History, design, and craft in West African strip-woven cloth*. Washington, D. C.: National Museum of African Art.

Plass, Margaret W. (1967). *African miniatures: Goldweights of the Ashanti*. New York: Praeger.

Platvoet, J. G. (1985). Cool shade, peace and power: The gyedua (tree of reception) as an ideological instrument of identity among the Akan peoples of Southern Ghana. *Journal of Religion in Africa*, 15(3): 174-200.

Polakoff, Claire (1982). *African textiles and dyeing techniques*. London: Routledge and Kegan Paul.

Posnansky, M. (1987). Prelude to Akan civilization. In Enid Schildkrout (Editor). *The Golden Stool: Studies of the Asante center and periphery*. New York: American Museum of Natural History.

Preston, George Nelson (1973). *Twifo-Heman and the Akan art-leadership complex of Ghana*. Doctoral dissertation, Columbia University, New York.

Quarcoo, A. K. (1994). *The language of adinkra patterns*, 2nd edition. Legon, Ghana: Sebewie Ventures.

_____. (1972). *The language of adinkra patterns*. Legon, Ghana: Institute of African Studies.

_____. (1968). A debut of Ghanaian traditional visual art into liturgical art of the Christian church of Ghana. *Research Review*, 4: 53-64.

Ramseyer, F. A. And J. Kuhne. (1875). *Four years in Ashantee*. New York: R. Carter & Bros.

Rattray, R. S. (1969a). *Ashanti law and constitution*. New York: Negro Universities Press.

_____. (1969b). *Ashanti Proverbs*. Oxford: Clarendon Press.

_____. (1927). *Religion and art in Ashanti*. London: Oxford University Press.

_____. (1923). *Ashanti*. London: Oxford University Press.

Reynolds, Edward (1973). Agricultural adjustments on the Gold Coast after the end of the slave trade, 1807-1874. *Agricultural History*, 47(4): 308-318.

Ritzer, George (1992). *Contemporary sociological theory*, 3rd Edition. New York: McGraw Hill.

Robertson, A. F. (1982). Abusa: The structural history of an economic contract. *Journal of Developing Studies*, 18(4): 447-478.

Rosenstein, D. and H. Oster (1988). Differential facial responses to four basic tastes in newborns. *Child Development*, 59: 1555-1568.

Ross, Doran H. (1977). The iconography of Asante sword ornaments. *African Arts*, 11(1): 16-25, 90.

Sarpong, Peter (1990). *The ceremonial horns of the Ashanti*. Accra: Sedco Publishing.

_____. (1977). *Girls' nubility rites in Ashanti*. Tema: Ghana Publishing Corporation.

_____. (1974). *Ghana in retrospect: Some aspects of Ghanaian culture*. Tema: Ghana Publishing Corporation.

_____. (1972). Aspects of Akan ethics. *Ghana Bulletin of Theology*, 4(3): 40-44.

_____. (1971). The sacred stools of the Akan. Tema, Ghana: Ghana Publishing Corporation.

Schildkrout, Enid. (1987). Editor. *The Golden Stool: Studies of the Asante center and periphery*. New York: American Museum of Natural History.

Schneider, Jane (1987). The anthropology of cloth. *Annual Review of Anthropology*, 16: 409-448.

Schneider, Jane and Annette B. Weiner (1989). Introduction. In Schneider, Jane and Annette B. Weiner (Editors). *Cloth and human experience*. Washington, D. C.: Smithsonian Institution Press.

Scribner, S. and Cole, M. (1981). *The psychology of literacy*. Cambridge, MA.: Harvard University Press.

Smolkin, Laura B. And David B. Yaden, Jr. (1992). O is for mouse: First encounters with the alphabet book. *Language Arts*, 69: 432-441.

Szereszewski, Robert (1966). Regional aspects of the structure of the economy. In W. B. Birmingham, I. Neustadt and E. N. Omaboe (Editors). *A study of contemporary Ghana, I: The economy of Ghana*. London: Allen and Unwin.

Thompson, Robert F. (1974). *African art in motion*. Los Angeles: University of California Press.

Tordoff, William. (1965). *Ashanti under the Prempehs, 1888-1935*. London: Oxford University Press.

Tsien, Tsuen-Hsuin (1962). *Written on bamboo and silk: The beginnings of Chinese books and inscriptions*. Chicago: University of Chicago Press.

Tufuo, J. W. and Donkor, C. E. (1989). *Ashantis of Ghana: People with a soul*. Accra: Anowuo Educational Publications.

Ward, W. E. F. (1991). *My Africa*. Accra: Ghana Universities Press.

_____. (1958). *A history of Ghana*. London: George Allen & Unwin.

Webster, J. B. and A. A. Boahen (1970). *History of West Africa*. New York: Praeger.

Wilks, Ivor (1993). *Forests of gold: Essays on the Akan and the Kingdom of Asante*. Athens, OH: Ohio University Press.

_____. (1992). On mentally mapping Greater Asante: A study of time and motion. *Journal of African History*, 33: 175-190.

_____. (1982). Wangara, Akan 'and Portuguese in the fifteenth and sixteenth centuries, I. The matter of Bitu. *Journal of African History*, 23(3): 333-349.

_____. (1975). *Asante in the nineteenth century: The structure and evolution of a political order*. New York: Cambridge University Press.

_____. (1962). The Mande loan element in Twi. *Ghana Notes and Queries*, 4: 26-28.

Willis, Elizabeth A. (1987). A lexicon of Igbo Uli motifs. *Nsukka Journal of the Humanities*, 1: 91-120.

Wolfson, Freda (1953). A price agreement on the Gold Coast – The Krobo oil boycott, 1858-1866. *Economic History Review*, 2nd Series, 6(1): 68-77.

Yankah, Kwesi (1995). *Speaking for the chief: Okyeame and the politics of Akan royal oratory*. Bloomington: Indiana University Press.

_____. (1989). *The proverb in the context of Akan rhetoric: A theory of proverb praxis*. Bern, Germany: Peter Lang.

Yarak, Larry W. (1986). Elmina and Greater Asante in the nineteenth century. *Africa*, 56(1): 33-52.

ISBN 9988 - 0 - 0791 - 4